Arms Control and Cooperative Security

Arms Control and Cooperative Security

edited by

Jeffrey A. Larsen
and James J. Wirtz

Viva Books

New Delhi | Mumbai | Chennai | Kolkata | Bangalore | Hyderabad | Kochi | Guwahati

First Indian Edition 2011

VIVA BOOKS PRIVATE LIMITED

- 4737/23 Ansari Road, Daryaganj, New Delhi 110 002
  E-mail: vivadelhi@vivagroupindia.net, Tel. 42242200
- 76, Service Industries, Shirvane, Sector 1, Nerul, Navi Mumbai 400 706
  E-mail: vivamumbai@vivagroupindia.net, Tel. 27721273, 27721274
- Jamals Fazal Chambers, 26 Greams Road, Chennai 600 006
  E-mail: vivachennai@vivagroupindia.net, Tel. 28290304, 28294241
- B-103, Jindal Towers, 21/1A/3 Darga Road, Kolkata 700 017
  E-mail: vivakolkata@vivagroupindia.net, Tel. 22836381, 22816713
- 7, Sovereign Park Apartments, 56-58, K. R. Road, Basavanagudi, Bengaluru 560 004
  E-mail: vivabangalore@vivagroupindia.net, Tel. 26607409, 26607410
- 101-102 Mughal Marc Apartments, 3-4-637 to 641, Narayanguda, Hyderabad 500 029
  E-mail: vivahyderabad@vivagroupindia.net, Tel. 27564481, 27564482
- Beevi Towers, First Floor, SRM Road, Kaloor, Kochi 682 018, Kerala
  E-mail: vivakochi@vivagroupindia.net, Tel: 0484-2403055, 2403056
- 232, GNB Road, Beside UCO Bank, Silpukhuri, Guwahati 781 003
  E-mail: vivaguwahati@vivagroupindia.net, Tel: 0361-2666386

www.vivagroupindia.com

Published by arrangement with

Lynne Rienner Publishers, Inc.
1800 30th Street, Suite 314
Boulder, Colorado 80301
USA

ISBN : 978-81-309-1530-2

Published by Vinod Vasishtha for Viva Books Private Limited, 4737/23, Ansari Road, Daryaganj, New Delhi - 110 002. Printed and bound by Raj Press, R-3, Inderpuri, New Delhi - 110 012.

S0000 / S0800 / S0810 / S0640

Contents

Foreword

Ronald F. Lehman II
Director, Center for Global Security Research
Lawrence Livermore National Laboratory

After two decades of dramatic change, an updated introduction to arms control and cooperative security is long overdue. Political, economic, demographic, and technological transformations around the globe require us to stay on a steep learning curve. In parallel, an equally steep "forgetting curve" grows deeper as the lessons of the past recede with declining memories of the substance and context of the arms control agreements that peaked in the early 1990s.

These challenges—learning what is different and remembering what is important—make solving contemporary arms control problems daunting. Fortunately, the experienced contributors to this volume have illuminated fundamental issues, both new and old. This forward-looking introduction will help a younger generation develop the more advanced, multidisciplinary skills required to reduce the risks inherent in today's volatile, globalized insecurity. These risk reduction skills, however, can only be honed with a deeper understanding of history, trends, and the backlash against those trends.

Arms control and cooperative security measures are not new. Nor has their substance and purpose been as narrowly focused as the renewed debate over final nuclear disarmament might suggest. Grand arms control negotiations of the Cold War, such as the Strategic Arms Reduction Treaty (START), had their precedents in the Washington and London Naval Treaties of the 1920s and 1930s. Contemporary cooperative security measures have their antecedents in the 1958 Antarctic Treaty, but also in the "just war" restraints that shaped international law and diplomatic practice over many centuries. Efforts to prevent war or to restrain its destructiveness extend even further back in time. Even today, the roots of some customs and taboos within traditional societies can be traced back to the desire to restrain violence. From such simple practices emerged—concurrent with the evolution of nation-states, international organizations, and transnational networks—extensive laws of warfare, diverse measures of cooperative restraint, numerous treaties, and several international arms control bodies.

By the end of the twentieth century, the study and practice of arms control and cooperative security had morphed into distinct subspecialties within a discipline, often called simply "arms control." Arms control was considered distinguishable from careers in the military, law, or diplomacy. Still, arms control and cooperative security cannot be isolated from these broader approaches and a wider context, nor can they reflect only arms control objectives. Their value is always measured by reference to broader security, economic, and political goals. Nation-states and nonstate actors shape and apply arms control and cooperative security measures to serve many different goals, both cooperative and competitive.

This ongoing manipulation of arms control concepts to serve multiple purposes extends to the very names that we employ for arms control and cooperative security. The contributors here offer a number of alternative nomenclatures and highlight the external political dynamics that are inevitably linked to arms control. Some prefer to use "arms control" as the all-encompassing term for both partial and comprehensive arms restraint. Others define arms control narrowly as applying only to limited, often pragmatic arrangements short of the total elimination of weapons. Frequently, the term is used even more narrowly, referring only to the negotiation of formal treaties, in contrast to more informal agreements and unilateral actions commonly labeled "cooperative" or "confidence-building." "Disarmament" was once the most widely used all-inclusive term, incorporating the elimination of weapons but also any partial measures toward that goal. This term fell out of favor as ideas such as general and complete disarmament (GCD) were seen as beyond the actionable time horizon of governments and were replaced by step-by-step processes driven more by immediate security needs, even when described as on the path toward distant goals.

Selecting nomenclature does send political signals. One sees this in the polarized distinctions between "nonproliferation" and "counterproliferation." Both are often used as comprehensive terms; but to the degree that nonproliferation is focused on prevention and counterproliferation on responses after proliferation, they quickly become competing priorities—polarizing rather than synergistic. A new all-encompassing term such as "antiproliferation" might suggest a more optimal balance among the multitude of options, but the debate has not yet moved in that direction.

The entire field of arms control, disarmament, cooperative security, confidence building, peer engagement, and the like could be given a different umbrella moniker such as "international arms restraint," whether by treaty, law, or policy. A new descriptor might permit a richer taxonomy of options, for example, mapping different measures by the degree to which they are cooperative (from unilateral through negotiated to imposed sanctions) or the degree to which they are detailed (from abstract norms through operational guidelines to embedded peer-to-peer collaboration).[1] What one calls these measures and how one maps them, however, are less important than that we recognize the variety of measures and the diverse purposes for which they are used, a point well illustrated by the contributors here.

Fitting arms control and cooperative security into a broader international security strategy can also be politically contentious. Defined narrowly, arms control or disarmament are often seen as alternatives to defense or deterrence, which themselves are often contrasted. Defined more broadly, concepts like diplomacy, disarmament, defense, deterrence, or even development (the "D's") can be analyzed as complementary parts of a single strategy employing both readiness and restraint to balance threats or reduce them. Integrating these strategies of readiness and restraint, however, is complicated not only by the external and competing goals of policymakers, but also by the self-identification of analysts into camps such as functionalists versus regionalists, or idealists versus realists. Throughout this volume, one sees the frustration that is created by the lack of a common framework for problem solving or of commensurate measures to determine merit.

At times, the arms control and cooperative security debate echoes the battle over gun control. Do guns kill people or do people kill people? Must we deal with the instruments or with the motivations? Supply or demand? Capability or intent? Historically, arms control has focused on the weapons, but progress was often dependent on political change. Indeed, the rise of cooperative security measures has illustrated the growing need to deal with the underlying insecurities and their international and domestic political manifestations. As highly destructive weapons technology spreads, an age of weapons latency is emerging in which the priority will shift from constraining capabilities to shaping intent. Again, this is not a new development. And again we will look to arms control and cooperative measures to influence and gauge intent as well as capability.

The traditional critique of arms control and disarmament is that if you can't trust other nations then such agreements do you no good. If you can trust other nations, then why do you need such agreements? These two antagonistic views may anchor the opposite ends of a continuum of possibilities based upon levels of trust, but the real world is found in the many possibilities in between. One sees this in discussions of treaty monitoring and verification. One is often asked whether a particular treaty is verifiable or not, without reference to a definition of verifiability or a stipulation of the standard by which we should judge. In all cases, however, these are actually questions driven by how much we trust those with whom we negotiate.

Verification evaluations must address a number of questions. How precisely are the terms defined? How likely can a detected activity be identified as a violation and attributed to a perpetrator in public with confidence?

What is the military significance? What is the political significance? What are the prospects for enforcement or remedy? What are the consequences of no compensating remedy?

Questions like these suggest that no treaty will be perfectly verifiable or completely unverifiable. The 1974 US-Soviet Threshold Test Ban Treaty (prohibiting nuclear weapons tests over 150 kilotons) with its 1988 on-site Verification Protocol is not perfectly verifiable, but it is precisely verifiable under most circumstances. The Biological Weapons Convention (BWC), with its ban on research based upon the intent of that research, gives little confidence that much beyond fortuitous disclosure might identify noncompliant research. Thus, few consider the research constraints of the BWC to be verifiable to any demanding standard. Nevertheless, nearly all nations are parties to the BWC because the costs have been kept low, burdensome regulation or inspection has been avoided, and nuclear deterrence against the use of biological weapons exists for many.

The verifiability of most treaties falls somewhere between these two treaties, one precisely verifiable and one with key provisions verifiable only by remote chance. Verification debates are often couched in terms of whether a particular treaty can at least meet a basic standard of being "adequately" verifiable, meaning that undiscovered cheating could not radically alter the military balance, or whether it must reach the higher standard of "effective verification," meaning in part that no undetected cheating would have military or geopolitical significance at a level far lower than fundamentally altering the strategic balance. Any arms control agreement will be vulnerable to some cheating, and the standard to be applied is based on some risk-benefit calculation fundamentally linked to confidence in the other parties and also to confidence that the political climate created by the treaty would not inhibit a timely response to adverse developments. In short, verification concerns confidence in both capability and intent for both sides.

The contemporary debate over nuclear disarmament highlights the need for a more precise understanding of the relationship of capability and intent to international security. So long as the nuclear arsenals of the United States and Russia were large, the goal of the elimination of nuclear weapons seemed very distant from the time horizons that most influenced governments. "Nuclear zero" was more an inspirational vision than an operational goal. For the United States and the Soviet Union, the nuclear restraint negotiated in the Cold War emphasized crisis stability and verification confidence as the substantive preconditions for the political goal of reductions.

As relations between the United States and Russia improved after the Cold War and Russia entered a period of domestic turmoil, however, concern about crisis stability in many public policy communities was supplanted by a preoccupation with accident or miscalculation and even weapons theft. Interest in verification waned, especially after the negotiation of the extremely intrusive measures associated with the Chemical Weapons Convention. Open societies complained of the burdens, and closed societies complained of the insinuations they believed underlay calls for transparency. The desire for universal membership in treaty regimes further complicated development of verification because intrusive and expensive measures that are required in some cases may be totally inappropriate in others. Verification fatigue remains widespread and the desire to substitute normative declarations for detailed compliance monitoring remains strong for both "hawks" and "doves." That may be about to change.

Even without new arms control agreements, US and Russian nuclear arsenals have declined numerically at a rate such that, if the same rate of reductions from their peak until today were to continue, both nations would reach zero by 2020. But few even among the most ardent advocates of rapid nuclear disarmament believe that the world can be ready to eliminate nuclear weapons so soon. As the arsenals of nuclear powers descend into the range in which the unthinkable could become thinkable, we see a renewed interest in understanding crisis stability at low numbers. The extensive (and spreading) latent potential to acquire nuclear weapons has also revived concerns about geostrategic stability.

Renewed interest in stability and the concern about incentives to proliferate have increased interest in verification. This includes the most difficult verification challenges to nuclear disarmament; namely, how do you confirm that no weapons could exist outside an agreed database, or that no weapons-exploitable material could be outside of airtight control? Once again, we return to the fundamental question of evaluating potential capability and intent. These two questions involve a risk-benefit analysis whose validity will ultimately be based upon an assessment of trust that could be placed in other parties under challenging conditions.

Some believe that the elimination of nuclear weapons can be achieved only under the most draconian monitoring and enforcement of compliance with limits on capability and scientific potential. Others believe that it can be achieved only by a radical transformation of political regimes or of the nature and behavior of mankind. Still others believe that some balance of arms control and political change will be good enough. Experts are beginning to realize that zero is currently a realm of uncertainty and danger being approached by the nuclear powers from above, but also by potential proliferators from below; nuclear zero would involve the major leveling of the nuclear weapons table, a situation desired by some and feared by others.

In this realm of widespread nuclear weapons latency, it may be that the fundamentals of both disarmament and deterrence will have to be revisited. If the analogy for deterrence and disarmament in the Cold War was Newtonian physics (with its concepts of equilibrium, inertia, and satellites), then perhaps the better analogies for the world of small numbers will come from quantum mechanics in such ideas as the uncertainty principle, nonlocality, or entanglement. Perhaps zero will be best understood by reference to cosmology and its fascination with parallel universes, dark energy, and the Big Bang. On the other hand, perhaps the best analogies for solutions to the nuclear danger will come from some other field such as medicine, or even hybrid disciplines such as quantum biology or neuroeconomics in which we look at our potential for health and at how we manage disease, physical and psychological. The contributors to this volume provide key insights into these fundamental questions just as a new generation of experts empowered by advances in many different fields can be recruited to help.

Note

1. Ronald F. Lehman, "International Arms Restraint by Treaty, Law, and Policy," in John Norton Moore and Robert F. Turner, eds., *National Security Law*, 2nd ed. (Durham, NC: Carolina Academic Press, 2005), pp. 523–660.

Preface

For the past fifteen years, the editors and most of the contributors to this volume have been involved in an ongoing study of the issues and trends that shape the contemporary arms control and cooperative security agenda. This book reflects our continued analysis of arms control and cooperative security and our considered judgment about the contributions they can make to national security. None of us believe that arms control or cooperative security initiatives are a panacea; they are best considered in conjunction with diplomacy, economic measures, and military power. Nevertheless, there is a renewed interest in devising ways to meet the challenges posed by globalization, the horizontal and vertical proliferation of dual-use technologies, and the threat posed by nonstate actors. There is a growing realization that arms control, cooperative security, and more ad hoc efforts to increase international transparency might constitute an appropriate response to the threats generated by informal networks and even individuals engaged in various illegal or nefarious activities.

The chapters in this book assess the role, value, and purpose of arms control and cooperative security. They explore arms control theory, arms control's successes and failures, changes to the international security environment in recent years, and the likelihood of future cooperative security arrangements or arms control agreements in various issue areas and geographic regions. The underlying principles and objectives of arms control remain relevant. Opportunities exist to devise new formal and informal international cooperative mechanisms to minimize and contain emerging security threats. Arms control may not be as paramount a diplomatic concern as it was during the last half of the twentieth century, but it still has a role to play in a globalizing world that has ongoing security concerns.

In addition to our authors, several other individuals played an important part in our project. We would first like to thank the commentators who participated in our authors' workshop held in Washington, DC, in April 2007:

Reb Benson; Cdr. Chris Bidwell, United States Navy; Beverly Dale; David Hamon; Peter Hays; Jo Husbands; David Jonas; Daryl Kimball; Kurt Klingenberger; Tim Miller; Lt. Col. Nancy Rower, United States Air Force; and Capt. Bob Vince, United States Navy. All of these discussants provided valuable feedback to our authors about their draft chapters, thereby immensely improving our volume. We also would like to thank David Saylor and the Navy Treaty Implementation Program not only for supporting our workshop on arms control, but for their continued support of our research programs on the future of arms control and cooperative security. And we are grateful to Lynne Rienner and her staff in Boulder for their continued belief in the importance of this topic.

We dedicate this volume to our colleague James M. Smith, who is also one of our authors. As the director of the Air Force Institute for National Security Studies for the past eleven years, he has done much to keep alive the concepts of arms control and cooperative security. Jim has hosted conferences and supported research on arms control, cooperative security, and nonproliferation topics. He also has ensured that there has been at least one panel on arms control at annual meetings of the International Studies Association and the American Political Science Association to provide a venue for young scholars to explore the past, present, and future of cooperative security.

—*Jeffrey A. Larsen and James J. Wirtz*

Arms Control and Cooperative Security

1

An Introduction to Arms Control and Cooperative Security

Jeffrey A. Larsen

In this book, we assess the role, value, and purpose of arms control and cooperative security in the new millennium. We explore arms control theory, arms control's successes and failures during the Cold War, changes to the international security environment in recent years, and the likelihood of future cooperative security arrangements or arms control agreements in various issue areas and geographic regions.

What Is Arms Control and Why Is It Important?

Arms control can be defined as any agreement among states to regulate some aspect of their military capability or potential. The agreement may apply to the location, amount, readiness, or types of military forces, weapons, or facilities. Whatever their scope or terms, however, all plans for arms control have one common factor: they presuppose some form of cooperation or joint action among the participants regarding their military programs.

Although the negotiating methods, regions of concern, and weapons involved may have changed, the underlying principles and objectives of arms control remain relevant today. Arms control may not be as centrally important as it was during the second half of the twentieth century, but in its broadest definition—one that encompasses not only traditional negotiations and agreements but also nonproliferation, counterproliferation, and disarmament—it still has a role to play in a globalizing world that has ongoing security concerns.[1] Arms control and cooperative security initiatives should be seen as part of a nation-state's foreign policy toolbox, available when necessary to enhance that state's security. Seldom are they the only tools available; they complement, rather than substitute for, diplomatic, economic, and coercive military actions.

Arms control is but one of a series of alternative approaches to achieving international security through military strategies. As an early writer on the topic explained, arms control belongs to a group of closely related views whose common theme is "peace through the manipulation of force."[2] One conceivably could achieve such an end state in multiple ways: by placing force in the hands of a central authority, by creating a system of collective security, by accepting a balance of power between the key actors in the system, by establishing a system of mutual deterrence, by abolishing or reducing force, or by imposing restraints and limits on forces. The latter choice reflects what we generally call arms control.

In a system of sovereign states with the capability to build and maintain sizable armed forces, states cannot always ensure that rival states will not attempt to achieve influence by pursuing military superiority. Trust often does not exist. States therefore interpret incoming information about the military capabilities of rival states in the worst light. Evidence of a new military program or spending by one state requires other states to respond in a similar fashion to prevent an adversary from achieving superiority. This security dilemma can produce an arms race, thereby increasing political tension between states, raising the probability and severity of crises, and possibly causing war. Arms control tries to address the negative effects of this security dilemma.[3]

Early theorists defined arms control in the broadest sense to refer to all forms of military cooperation between potential enemies in the interest of ensuring international stability. As Hedley Bull put it, arms control is "cooperation between antagonistic pairs of states in the military field, whether this cooperation is founded upon interests that are exclusively those of the cooperating states themselves or on interests that are more widely shared."[4]

Arms control analysts of the early 1960s were in agreement that the objectives of arms control were threefold. For Thomas C. Schelling and Morton Halperin, these were reducing the likelihood of war, reducing the political and economic costs of preparing for war, and minimizing the scope and violence of war if it occurred.[5] Bull visualized similar objectives for arms control: to contribute to international security and stop the drift to war; to release economic resources otherwise squandered in armaments; and to preclude preparing for war, which is morally wrong.[6] Students and practitioners have debated which of these objectives should take priority, but most national security analysts have agreed that the prevention of war should be the foremost goal of arms control.

Until recently, political leaders and the media seemed to have a more limited definition of arms control. They generally believed that it was a set of activities dealing with specific steps to control related weapon systems as codified in formal agreements or treaties. During the Cold War, many analysts and much of the general public focused on the bilateral arms control negotiations between the United States and the Soviet Union. They came to expect that arms control required a formal treaty, a system of inspections to ensure compliance, and an enforcement mechanism to compel compliance. But those three elements are not always necessary for arms control. Arms control is a process involving specific, declared steps by a state to enhance security through cooperation with other states. These steps can be unilateral, bilateral, or multilateral. Cooperation can be implicit as well as explicit.

Cooperative Security

This book places arms control under the rubric of cooperative security, a concept that has grown in popularity in recent years. The term has been used to outline a more peaceful and idealistic approach to security. One commonly accepted definition of *cooperative security* is "a commitment to regulate the size, technical composition, investment patterns, and operational practices of all military forces by mutual consent for mutual benefit."[7] Cooperative security is slightly different in meaning than collective security or collective defense. *Collective security* is "a political and legal obligation of member states to defend the integrity of individual states within a group of treaty signatories."[8] *Collective defense* is more narrowly defined as "the commitment of all states to defend each other from outside aggression." By contrast, cooperative security can include the introduction of measures that reduce the risk of war; that is, measures not necessarily directed against any specific state or coalition. International institutions such as the Organization for Security and Cooperation in Europe and the European Union (EU) certainly fall under the definition of collective security, but groups such as the North Atlantic Treaty Organization (NATO) just as easily fall within collective defense. Such cooperation can take place among states that have little in common but, as the cases of NATO and the EU show, cooperative security can advance much further when the states are like-minded, liberal democratic market economies. In those cases, the parties can use their shared liberal values to move beyond simple defense pacts, perhaps even achieving proactive efforts in the field of collective diplomacy, economics, and military action outside their common space.

Arms Control Versus Disarmament

There is a difference between conceiving of arms control as a means to achieving a larger goal and seeing arms control as an end unto itself.[9] The arms control process is intended to serve as a means of enhancing a state's national security. Arms control is but one approach toward achieving this goal. Arms control could even lead states to agree to increases in certain categories of armaments if such increases would contribute to crisis stability and thereby reduce the chance of war. This conception of arms control should be distinguished from general and complete disarmament. Proponents of disarmament see its goal as simply reducing the size of military forces, budgets, explosive power, and other aggregate measures. Their rationale is that armaments have been the major cause of international instability and conflict, and only through reductions in the weaponry of all nations can the world achieve peace.

Advocacy of disarmament as part of a state's arms control policy can also be part of a "means to an end" approach. For example, the United States and other countries have negotiated two global conventions that endeavor to rid the world of chemical and biological weapons (CBW). The United States decided in both cases that maintaining such weapons would not enhance its security, even if they were still possessed by other states. Efforts to rid the world of CBW were perceived to enhance the security of all states. Similarly, the United States and Russia have agreed to eliminate certain classes of strategic arms.

Disarmament has a longer legacy than arms control and was a common theme in international relations literature of the 1950s. In the early 1960s, international security specialists began using the term *arms control* in place of *disarmament,* which they believed lacked precision and smacked of utopianism. The seminal books on arms control published during that era all referred to this semantic problem and preferred arms control as a more comprehensive term.[10]

Bull suggested that, although disarmament and arms control are not the same, they nevertheless intersect with one another. Disarmament is the reduction or abolition of armaments while arms control is restraint internationally exercised on armaments policy, which not only addresses the number of weapons, but also their character, development, and use.[11] Yet in the early 1960s, many members of the pro-disarmament crowd viewed Schelling and Halperin as traitors to the cause when they published *Strategy and Arms Control* because their book abandoned the utopian goals of many disarmers. These two authors believed that they were merely extending the breadth and reach of disarmament studies to make them more operationally relevant to military studies.[12]

Disarmament is not a dead concept. Indeed, several recent high-profile op-ed pieces in the *Wall Street Journal* called for the United States to pursue global nuclear zero as a primary national security and foreign policy goal. The authors included a former secretary of state, secretary of defense, national security advisor, and senator. They argued that

> reassertion of the vision of a world free of nuclear weapons and practical measures toward achieving that goal would be, and would be perceived as, a bold initiative consistent with America's moral heritage. The effort could have a profoundly positive impact on the security of future generations.

> Without the bold vision, the actions will not be perceived as fair or urgent. Without the actions, the vision will not be perceived as realistic or possible. We endorse setting the goal of a world free of nuclear weapons and working energetically on the actions required to achieve that goal.[13]

These types of sentiments suggest that both policymakers and academics might again champion nuclear disarmament as the ultimate motivation for contemporary diplomatic initiatives. The level of interest in disarmament concepts is seen in the fact that, since the first of those op-eds was published in January 2007, the principles and vision they espouse have been endorsed by two-thirds of all living former US national security advisors, secretaries of state, and secretaries of defense as well as President Barack Obama.[14]

Arms Control: History, Theory, and Policy

Arms control held a preeminent position during the second half of the Cold War, as shown in the United States by the creation of a separate Arms Control and Disarmament Agency, years of effort spent negotiating strategic arms limitation and reduction treaties with the Soviet Union, and the widespread confluence of policy requirements and academic interest in the field. Despite all its successes, however, arms control was never of decisive importance. As the authors of an acclaimed text on security have stated, arms control "has rarely been seen as decisively important or a solution in its own right. On the contrary it is a fundamentally conservative policy, aimed solely at introducing some measure of predictability into an adversarial relationship. It cannot by itself create stability, much less peace, and to hope otherwise is to saddle it with unreasonable expectations that are bound to go unfulfilled."[15] Arms control alone could not resolve the world's security problems or the confrontational nature of US-Soviet relations.

After forty years as the centerpiece of US national security policy, however, arms control lost its luster after the Cold War ended, especially after 2001. Some policymakers and analysts claimed that arms control was not living up to its promises despite considerable optimism immediately following the end of the Cold War. To survive as a viable international security policy, they argued, arms control needed to adapt itself to new arenas and new approaches. Suggestions abounded at the turn of the millennium for enhancing the role of cooperative security measures as a supplement or complement to more traditional attempts to control arms. Yet official Washington lost interest in thinking about new arms control issues or dealing with the operational and funding aspects of existing treaties and agreements. These feelings emerged during the administration of President Bill Clinton, but they grew stronger when George W. Bush took office in 2001. As one expert wrote, "The traditional arms control process of negotiating legally binding treaties that both codify numerical parity and contain extensive verification measures has reached an impasse and outlived its utility."[16]

The Development of Arms Control Theory

National security objectives of the United States include protecting and preserving its fundamental freedoms and institutions by deterring or preventing attack on US national interests at home and abroad.[17] New threats have necessitated reordering the priorities among traditional US national security objectives. Deterring nuclear attack is now less urgent than, for example, preventing or countering proliferation of weapons of mass destruction (WMD) and terrorism, or securing fissile materials. Yet the grand strategic objectives of arms control as an instrument of national security remain virtually unchanged, at least in general terms.

Nevertheless, the conceptual problems facing defense planners and arms control policymakers at the operational level are fundamentally different today from those that confronted the founders of traditional arms control theory in the late 1950s and early 1960s.

Arms control and national security. The founding premise of traditional arms control theory—that arms control can be an important adjunct to national security strategy—has, in practice, not always been obvious or consistently observed because arms control is inherently a counterintuitive approach to enhancing security. Arms control makes national security dependent to some degree on the cooperation of prospective adversaries. It often involves setting lower levels of arms than would otherwise appear prudent based on a strict threat assessment. It mandates establishing a more or less interactive relationship with potential opponents and, in the case of mutual intrusive verification and data exchanges, exposes sensitive national security information and facilities to scrutiny by foreign powers. It requires seeking and institutionalizing cooperation where the potential for conflicts of interest seemingly far outweigh common objectives. It is fundamentally a high-stakes gamble, mortgaging national survival against little more than the collateral of trust and anticipated reciprocal restraint, often in a geopolitical context fraught with political hostility and tension. It is, in fact, a voluntary (and not always reversible) delimitation of national sovereignty. Viewed from this perspective, arms control is not obviously better than its alternative—unilaterally providing for one's own security.[18]

What then has compelled the United States and other nations to structure so much of their national security posture on an approach that seemingly contradicts a country's natural instincts toward self-sufficiency and self-preservation? An answer to this apparent paradox is that arms control allows security to be established by negotiation at levels of weapons lower than would be the case if these levels were determined unilaterally. The mere act of negotiating arms control also may lead to better communication, deepened understanding, and reduced hostility among adversaries.

Arms control theory. Arms control theory refers to the assumptions and premises of strategic analysts who first developed arms control as an adjunct to national security in the 1958–1962 time frame. Traditional arms control theory was the product of a unique confluence of factors, and it reflected the assumptions, analyses, and policy priorities of defense analysts and policymakers of that era.[19] The rethinking of arms control in this period was part of a general reevaluation of US defense and foreign policy that was precipitated by dissatisfaction with the postwar diplomatic and arms control stalemate. Negotiations over armaments policy with one's potential adversary was not a novel concept. Since 1945, the United States had sought to establish through diplomatic means a variety of disarmament arrangements (e.g., the Baruch Plan, Open Skies, and the Atoms for Peace proposal). Nevertheless, long negotiations and multiple proposals had yielded no tangible results, primarily because of Soviet objections to those verification regimes deemed essential by the West. In the mid-1950s, policymakers began rethinking an approach that had emphasized general and complete disarmament, and to consider instead limited, partial measures that would gradually enhance confidence in cooperative security arrangements. Thus, more modest goals under the rubric of arms control came to replace the propaganda-laden disarmament efforts of the late 1940s and early 1950s.

Basic tenets of traditional arms control. The period that began with the 1958 Surprise Attack Conference and lasted through the 1962 publication of the proceedings of a Woods Hole Summer Study and the parallel studies going on at Oxford University produced the canons of modern arms control theory.[20] Out of the literature of this golden era of arms control emerged a virtual consensus on several key assumptions, which may be considered the basic tenets of traditional arms control theory.

First, arms control was conceived as a way to enhance national security. As Bull explained, "arms control or disarmament was not an end in itself but a means to an end and that end was first and foremost the enhancement of security, especially security against nuclear war."[21] Or, as Schelling and Halperin stated near the end of their book, "the aims of arms control and the aims of a national military strategy should be substantially the same."[22] This principle established national security as the dominant goal of arms control, not the reduction of arms per se. In fact, it was understood that not all reductions were necessarily useful. There was an explicit recognition that arms control could be harmful if not properly guided by overall national security strategy. According to Schelling,

> many of the ideas that came to be identified as the arms control point of view were pertinent to the unilateral shaping of military forces. Most of the academics associated with arms control probably did not consider themselves arms controllers but rather analysts of foreign policy or national security policy. Most believed that there was no contradiction between an interest in military strategy and an interest in the possibility of collaborating with potential enemies to reduce the likelihood of a war that neither side wanted.[23]

Second, the superpowers shared a common interest in avoiding nuclear war; this common interest could and should be the basis for effective arms control agreements. According to Bull, "The fact that the United States and the Soviet Union were locked in a political and ideological conflict, one moreover that sometimes took a military form, did not mean that they could not recognize common interests in avoiding a ruinous nuclear war, or cooperate to advance these common interests."[24] This assumption was one of the most important (and controversial) conceptual departures from past thinking promulgated by the new arms control theory. Previously, it was assumed that relaxation of political tensions had to precede achieving substantive arms control agreements. The founders of traditional arms control theory, on the other hand, believed that the threat of global nuclear annihilation was so paramount that it transcended political or ideological differences. It was not necessary to fully resolve political conflicts before proceeding to negotiate arms control agreements; solutions to both could be advanced simultaneously.

Third, arms control and military strategy should work together to promote national security. The unity of strategy and arms control was a central tenet of traditional arms control theory. Such unity was essential if arms control and defense policy were to avoid working at cross purposes. For example, if the implementation of US defense strategy required deploying certain types of weapons that were restricted by arms control agreements, this could defeat the overall purpose of the United States' national security posture and erode the legitimacy of both the arms control process and US defense policy.

Finally, it was understood from the beginning that arms control regimes need not be limited to formal agreements, but also could include informal, unilateral, or verbal agreements. The US-Soviet Presidential Nuclear Initiatives (PNI) of 1991–1992 are among the best known examples of these efforts.

The authors of a book published by the Brookings Institution proposed that modern arms control should focus on two overarching dangers, and they postulated three new tenets for the field. As its central organizing principle, they recommended that arms control attempt to prevent the spread of nuclear materials and biological pathogens.[25] In this proposal, they were following in the footsteps of the early pioneers in the field of arms control while changing the focus from nuclear deterrence to WMD proliferation—focusing especially on the two types of WMD deemed most dangerous. They then identified three critical needs, or organizing principles: (1) to provide early warning of the proliferation of these weapons' components to dangerous regimes, (2) to integrate coercive enforcement aspects into the body of arms control capabilities, and (3) to harmonize arms control and nonproliferation efforts into larger US foreign policy goals. They suggested that arms control can simultaneously assuage concerns by allies and other states, encourage cooperative actions on a narrow set of issues, reduce the inclination of potential adversaries to acquire or use such weapons, and deter or deny the use of such weapons against the advanced countries.[26] This approach widened arms control's purpose into the realm of cooperative security.

Objectives of Arms Control Theory

For arms control to be an effective instrument of national security, its objectives must be determined by, and be in close harmony with, the broader objectives of overall national security strategy.[27] At the most basic level of abstraction, three grand conceptual dilemmas dominated strategic thinking and the formulation of US national security objectives during the Cold War: (1) What deters? (2) How much is enough? (3) What if deterrence fails? Arms control was developed in an attempt to deal with these three questions.[28]

Traditional arms control theory was based on the premise that the superpowers inherently shared an area of common ground (avoiding nuclear war), and that this element of mutual interest could serve as the basis for limited, cooperative arrangements involving reciprocal restraint in the acquisition of weapons of mass destruction. In defining the scope and application of arms control, Schelling and Halperin set forth three general objectives for arms control:

> We believe that arms control is a promising, but still only dimly perceived, enlargement of the scope of our military strategy. It rests essentially on the recognition that our military relation with potential enemies is not one of pure conflict and opposition, but involves strong elements of mutual interest in the avoidance of a war that neither side wants, in minimizing the costs and risks of the arms competition, and in curtailing the scope and violence of war in the event it occurs.[29]

Clearly, establishing the requirements of deterrence must precede and form the basis for creating policies for reducing the risk of nuclear war while the goal of reducing defense spending must be informed by some notion of what constitutes sufficient levels of weapons. And any scheme for limiting damage should war occur presupposes at least some thought as to the nature of warfare and how forces are to be employed in combat. Thus, the primary objectives of traditional arms control theory—reducing the risk of war, reducing the costs of preparing for war, and reducing the damage should war occur—are necessarily determined by the three great dilemmas of military policy.

Reducing the risk of war. Arms control was seen as a prime means of setting limits on and restraining strategic arms race behavior. For early arms control theorists, restraining certain types of technology was practically synonymous with reducing the risk of war. The underlying premise was that war was most likely to begin with a surprise nuclear attack made possible by unrestrained competition in ballistic missiles, guidance and control technology, and nuclear weapons. Therefore, those weapon systems employing technologies that in theory most contributed to the ability to execute a surprise nuclear attack against the nuclear retaliatory forces of the other side, or that undermined the ability of either side to hold deterrent targets at risk, became principal candidates for arms limitation agreements.

Reducing the cost of preparing for war. Arms control theorists believed that controls would release economic resources otherwise squandered on military spending. They believed that armaments races were economically ruinous and that disarmament or arms control would make possible the diversion of resources toward worthier objectives.[30] If arms control succeeded in providing the same degree of security at lower levels of weapons than would otherwise be the case, it could lead to fielding fewer weapons and thus lower overall defense spending. Further, if certain types of technology were mutually outlawed, there would be fewer costs associated with defense research and development, weapon production, and force deployment, operations, and maintenance.

Reducing the damage should war occur. If fewer weapons were fielded as a result of arms limitation agreements, and nevertheless war should occur, overall damage would be less than it otherwise would have been. But fielding fewer weapons is not the only way to reduce damage in the event of war. Damage also could be limited by developing certain types of active defense strategies and technologies such as ballistic missile defense.

* * *

In practice, the first of the three main objectives proposed by traditional arms control theory—reducing the risk of war or, more specifically, reducing the risk of surprise nuclear attack—came to eclipse and overshadow the other two. Achieving the first objective would also indirectly satisfy the second and third objectives. The process grew in complexity over the next four decades. It usually involved negotiations, but sometimes was accomplished through unilateral decisions or reciprocated arrangements.

Arms control during the Cold War assumed a high priority on the national security agenda as a way of managing the superpower nuclear rivalry. The new importance of arms control was a reaction to the bipolar structure of the international system and the revolutionary nature of nuclear weapons. Generally, these negotiations were limited in scope and focused on increased strategic nuclear stability between the superpowers. The conduct of bilateral negotiations became very formal; agreements took years to reach. Every possible implication for the strategic balance was scrutinized while increasingly complex provisions for verification became part of the process to guard against cheating. Even after a treaty was concluded, the benefits and pitfalls of arms control continued to be hotly debated.

Arms Control in the Post–Cold War Era

As the Cold War ended, the conception and execution of what was referred to as arms control began to change. The changes began with an increase in the number and types of bilateral arrangements between the superpowers. As rapprochement between the superpowers deepened, the fora and scope for other negotiations began to broaden. Regions beyond Europe began to turn to arms control as a means to build security.

In the immediate aftermath of the Cold War, the West experienced a flush of optimism and activity regarding arms control. The early 1990s were truly a high-water mark for arms control as formal agreements and cooperative measures were signed and entered into force with astounding speed. Many of these, in fact, were agreements reached years before, but finally were being ratified. Arms control found a place in dealing with the new concerns of advanced weapon proliferation, regional instability, and economic and environmental security. The value of arms control appeared to be growing in the new world as states attempted to implement treaties already in place, stem the illegal proliferation of WMD to rogue nations or groups, and meet their security needs in a multipolar, more interdependent world. The early post–Cold War years now appear to have been an era of excessive optimism about new opportunities for arms control. In fact, there has been considerable debate over the past decade regarding the future value of arms control—even with respect to existing treaties and agreements.

The traditional role for arms control in the Cold War—to enhance stability and forgo potentially devastating misunderstandings between the two superpowers—may no longer be of central concern within the international community nor achievable in some new fields. The United States must seriously consider what role arms control can play in enhancing its future national security considerations. These new roles might be considerably different than the way we have thought about arms control in the past. The George W. Bush administration came into office with a particular mindset that disliked arms control agreements because treaties appeared to hobble the United States from adopting a unilateral approach to enhancing its national security. As a result, the Bush presidency represented a series of setbacks for arms control advocates: abandoning negotiations on a third Strategic Arms Reduction Treaty, withdrawal from the Anti-Ballistic Missile Treaty (ABM Treaty), signing a bare-bones Strategic Offensive Reductions Treaty (Moscow Treaty) with no verification or compliance provisions, rejecting the Ottawa Convention on Landmines, rejecting further consideration of the Comprehensive Test Ban Treaty, rejecting negotiations on a verification provision for the Biological Weapons Convention, and refusing to sign the UN Arms Trade Treaty. At the same time, the United States began to pursue more unilateral approaches to guaranteeing its security such as preventive war, preemption, and counterproliferation.

The Bush administration's early decision to abandon the ABM Treaty and to deemphasize the role of arms control in US foreign policy was welcomed by some observers as a realistic response to the end of the Cold War. The traditional role of arms control for the preceding generation—to enhance stability and forgo potentially devastating misunderstandings between the two superpowers—was no longer a central concern within the international community. By contrast, less formal international collaboration that organized collective action to stem the threat posed by clandestine terrorist networks and entrepreneurial groups that traffic in weapons of mass destruction, dual-use items, and associated delivery systems increased in importance. Cooperative security, which even included extensive collaboration in domestic policy, seemed to offer a new and promising policy instrument in the fight against terrorism and the threat posed by WMD. For example, the Proliferation Security Initiative, a relatively informal effort that enables an international consortium to coordinate existing national capabilities and policy to combat trafficking in illicit materials, is often identified as the prototype for future cooperative security efforts. The problem, as some authors have pointed out, is that the Bush administration's plan to deemphasize arms control, which may have seemed reasonable or at least workable in early 2001, was never adjusted to the post-9/11 security environment or the global war on terror. All of these challenges required international cooperation rather than a unilateral, go-it-alone approach. Yet the latter was the attitude of the Bush administration during its eight years in office.

Does Arms Control Have a Future?

Today, there is considerable debate over the future value of traditional arms control. We are at a crossroads, with the future direction of arms control uncertain but its past value indisputable. As one recent article put it, "The practice of formal arms control is not dead, but it is definitely ill."[31] The United States must seriously consider what role arms control can play in enhancing future national security considerations. These new roles might be different than the way policymakers and scholars have thought about arms control in the past. In fact, as I have written elsewhere, one could make the counterintuitive case that, despite its unwillingness to admit the value of arms control for national security, the Bush administration actually pursued a form of "neo–arms control" with its approaches to international security concerns.[32] The goals were basically the same as those of traditional arms control; only the means and the terminology were changed. The Bush administration's emphasis on preemption, preventive war, enhanced national military capabilities, and a willingness to undertake unilateral actions were simply a different, and sometimes more effective, means of handling security challenges formerly dealt with by arms control.

So is arms control dead? Does it still have a role to play in enhancing a state's security? Can it make a comeback as a US policy option in the Obama administration? These questions call out to the national security community. As one analyst has written, "The place of arms control in US national security strategy and its continued relevance to the evolving global strategic landscape cannot be taken for granted. Times are changing, and it is right and necessary to ask what arms control strategies best suit US interests."[33] President Obama announced during his campaign that arms control would be returned to its rightful place in the panoply of national security tools, but what its purpose will be in dealing with modern threats from proliferation, rogue states, and nonstate actors is not completely clear. Indeed, one hopes that the Obama administration does not abandon the more innovative and constructive cooperative security initiatives launched by its Republican predecessors, especially if it chooses to champion a return to a more traditional arms control agenda. The whole concept of how one achieves national security must be reconsidered—in much the same way that the global security environment must have appeared to the founders of the theory of arms control in the early 1960s.

Concern about the future of arms control, however, may be misplaced; there still remains a vital role for this process to play. Many Americans no longer view Russia as much of a strategic threat, but it is still a spoiler in terms of arms control and cooperative security. This raises multiple questions: Should arms control be geared toward different problems? Should Russia now take a backseat to new concerns, such as an emerging China, troublesome relationships in South Asia, or the threat posed by global terrorism? Can Cold War arms control institutions work in terms of the new strategic relationship between the United States, Russia, China, and other nations? Are existing arms control institutions and treaties obsolete? Perhaps a new combination of unilateral approaches, nontraditional incentives, joint activities, and other imaginative collective security measures can supplant the reliance on classic, treaty-based negotiations.

At the same time, the threat of WMD proliferation continues, particularly given the heightened threat from emboldened terrorist organizations (as has been shown by major terrorist attacks since 2001 on the United States, Great Britain, Spain, Russia, Indonesia, Malaysia, and elsewhere), the emergence of spontaneous cells that harbor a grudge against local authorities, and the emergence of new proliferation challenges. In the face of these threats, how can arms control address emerging security relationships and regional arms races?

As bipolarity fades, what new multilateral institutions are needed for arms control? What new kinds of arms control are necessary or possible? In recent years, attention has focused on several new topics of interest in the security realm that call out for means of control, including information warfare, landmines, space, cyberspace, and biological weapons. Will agreements to manage these areas call for new types of provisions such as requiring states to criminalize certain activities or requiring cooperation in the face of nonstate threats? UN Security Council Resolution 1540, approved in 2005, was a major step in this direction.

Efforts to reach agreement in many of these areas face great challenges if the traditional arms control focus on force structure levels and strict verification is used as criteria for evaluation. Nonstate actors have also become players by raising issues to the international agenda and creating momentum for agreements such as the 1997 Ottawa Treaty. We need to broaden the definition of arms control to encompass nonstate as well as state actors.

One might consider arms control in broader terms as encompassing all nonproliferation and counterproliferation efforts. These can be broken into two major categories: *preemption,* which is a state's military response to the consequences of proliferation that focuses on the weapons and their delivery systems; and *prevention,* the response to a failure of nonproliferation processes.[34]

Overview of the Book

This book has assembled chapters by a dozen experts on arms control, national defense, proliferation, and regional studies to explore arms control theory, arms control's successes and failures during the Cold War, changes to the international security environment in recent years, cooperative security, and the likelihood of future arms control agreements in various issue areas and geographic regions. These analysts explore the contemporary role of arms control and assess the future prospects for US arms control policy and national security strategy. The book's objective is to offer a fundamental assessment of the future of arms control and cooperative security, especially as some crucial Cold War arms control agreements near expiration dates codified in their treaties.

The chapters address issues that are larger than simple overviews of past approaches and current policy—they incorporate themes, directions, vectors, and future possibilities for the concepts of arms control and cooperative security. Each chapter assesses the role, value, and purpose of arms control and cooperative security in the new millennium. The book deals with the conceptual and historical background of arms control, weapon-specific concerns and issues, regional considerations, and new topical areas in which arms control may have a role to play.

The first four chapters relate arms control to national security objectives and the national security–making process. They also examine efforts by the superpowers and their allies to use arms control during the Cold War to enhance their security as well as the legacy of these efforts on the post–Cold War environment. These chapters establish the underlying concepts and principles that guide the conduct of arms control by reviewing the history of arms control efforts, the international and domestic contexts in which the process takes place, and the fundamental requirement for effective transparency, verification, and compliance measures.

James M. Smith begins, in Chapter 2, with a review of historical themes across the arms control era from disarmament to Cold War arms control to today's return of nonproliferation as the central organizing theme. In Chapter 3, Kerry M. Kartchner gives us an overview of the international system, and provides us with a new arms control paradigm for dealing with the most dangerous threat we face today: WMD proliferation. The world has changed since 2000, Kartchner argues, and the old Cold War–style arms control must also change in order to prove useful in today's security environment. In Chapter 4, Jennifer E. Sims provides an overview of the politics and strategic culture of the arms control policymaking process, using the United States as a case study.

In the second half of the book, the authors discuss specific types of weapons and efforts to control their proliferation and use. These include strategic nuclear systems, chemical and biological weapons, conventional forces, and the fissile components of nuclear weapons. They also look at global regions of particular interest to the United States and examine their perspectives on arms control—past and future. The authors consider how arms control might prove useful in improving security in new, nontraditional areas of particular importance to the United States. They consider the asymmetries and vulnerabilities that face the international system and, in particular, the United States in the years ahead, as well as the argument for the international acceptance of the normative aspects of cooperative security. They also project the long-term future for arms control.

In Chapter 5, Forrest E. Waller Jr. reviews the core arena for Cold War arms control: strategic nuclear systems. He lays out four potential directions for future arms control efforts, which all point to the logical conclusion of such a movement: zero nuclear weapons. In Chapter 6, Leonard S. Spector looks at the nonproliferation regime in all of its aspects, seeing it as composed of four major components that fall under the larger constellation of international efforts to stem the spread of WMD and advanced delivery systems. And in Chapter 7, Michael Moodie examines specific regions of the world that are of greatest concern as well as new threats and opportunities for arms control that seem most important in those regions. He also asks whether regions actually matter in an increasingly interdependent and interconnected world.

The next two chapters each address new approaches to dealing with the global security environment. In Chapter 8, Lewis A. Dunn focuses on the large toolkit of actions that a state can undertake to improve its security in the context of cooperative security, a means and process for enhancing the mutual security of partnering countries. In Chapter 9, Guy B. Roberts focuses on some of those new initiatives for multilateral and unilateral approaches, including counterproliferation, preemption, compliance, and the use of international law. He takes a skeptical view of traditional arms control treaties and argues for alternative means of providing for enhanced national security, including cooperative international security initiatives that create a web of proliferation denial.

In Chapter 10, Rebecca E. Johnson provides a thoughtful discussion of the potential development of international norms through universal arms control agreements and regimes. She reminds us that human security needs are broader and unlikely to be resolved by means of hard power. Johnson also echoes most of the previous chapters by pointing out that traditional arms control has been failing to deliver on its promises in recent years, which calls out for a new approach to dealing with tomorrow's security challenges. She advocates universal normative regimes and a return to disarmament as preferable to traditional arms control. Finally, in Chapter 11, James J. Wirtz captures the themes and key points of the book and points us toward arms control's future.

Conclusion

The arms control momentum from the Cold War, which infused books on the subject in the 1990s, has waned. Nevertheless, with new arenas for arms control consideration, a better appreciation for arms control's place in the larger pantheon of cooperative security efforts, and new partners to deal with, the whole concept of arms control must be reconsidered.

The future direction and roles for arms control and cooperative security initiatives are uncertain. But the authors in this book believe that they can continue to play an important part in helping to mitigate contemporary security challenges. As Schelling and Halperin wrote in 1961, "Adjustments in military postures and doctrines that induce reciprocal adjustments by a potential opponent can be of mutual benefit if they reduce the danger of a war that neither side wants, or contain its violence, or otherwise serve the security of the nation. That is what we mean by arms control."[35] Nearly fifty years later, those perspectives on the role and value of arms control as a tool of national security remain valid. As the authors show in the chapters that follow, these can be extrapolated to new fields of interest in international relations.

Notes

1. In their attempt to update the definition of arms control, for example, Michael Levi and Michael O'Hanlon wrote that "properly defined, [arms control] is any coordinated international action to constrain the development, production, and use of dangerous technologies," including weapons and their delivery systems. Michael A. Levi and Michael E. O'Hanlon, *The Future of Arms Control* (Washington, DC: Brookings Institution Press, 2005), pp. 128–129.

2. Hedley Bull, *The Control of the Arms Race: Disarmament and Arms Control in the Missile Age* (New York: Praeger, 1961), pp. 4–5.

3. Two classic works dealing with arms races are Samuel P. Huntington, "Arms Races Prerequisites and Results," in C. J. Friedrich and S. E. Harris, eds., *Public Policy: Yearbook of the Graduate School of Public Administration,* vol. 8 (Cambridge: Harvard, 1958), pp. 41–86; Colin Gray, "The Arms Race Phenomenon," *World Politics* 24, no. 1 (1971): 39–79.

4. Bull, *The Control of the Arms Race,* p. xxxv.

5. Thomas C. Schelling and Morton H. Halperin, *Strategy and Arms Control* (Washington, DC: Pergamon-Brassey's, 1985), p. 3. (Orig. pub. 1961.)

6. Bull, *The Control of the Arms Race,* pp. 3–4.

7. Ashton B. Carter, William J. Perry, and John D. Steinbruner, *A New Concept of Cooperative Security* (Washington, DC: Brookings Institution Press, 1992), p. 6. Other good works on this subject include Janne Nolan, ed., *Global Engagement: Cooperation and Security in the 21st Century* (Washington, DC: Brookings Institution Press, 1994); Ashton B. Carter and William J. Perry, *Preventive Defense: A New Security Strategy for America* (Washington, DC: Brookings Institution Press, 1999); John D. Steinbruner, *Principles of Global Security* (Washington, DC: Brookings Institution Press, 2000); and Dan Caldwell, "Cooperative Security and Terrorism," paper presented at the annual meeting of the International Security Studies Section of the International Studies Association, Whittier, CA, October 2001.

8. One can envision four rings of security that make up collective security writ large: individual security, collective security, collective defense, and promoting

stability. For more on this argument, see Richard Cohen and Michael Mihalka, *Cooperative Security: New Horizons for International Order,* The Marshall Center Papers No. 3 (Garmisch, Germany: George C. Marshall European Center for Security Studies, April 2001).

9. Some of the concepts in the following sections are expansions of ideas from the introduction to the first edition of this book. See Gregory J. Rattray, "Introduction," in Jeffrey A. Larsen and Gregory J. Rattray, eds., *Arms Control Toward the 21st Century* (Boulder: Lynne Rienner, 1996), pp. 1–15.

10. For more on the background of these terms, see Richard Dean Burns, *Encyclopedia of Arms Control and Disarmament* (New York: Charles Scribner's Sons, 1993), pp. 2–3.

11. Bull, *The Control of the Arms Race,* p. vii.

12. Thomas Schelling, comments at the authors' conference for the second edition of this book, McLean, VA, 12 July 2001; also remarks made by Professor Schelling at a Roundtable in Honor of Thomas Schelling at the annual meeting of the American Political Science Association, San Francisco, August 2001.

13. George P. Shultz, William J. Perry, Henry A. Kissinger, and Sam Nunn, "A World Free of Nuclear Weapons," *Wall Street Journal,* 4 January 2007, p. A15. See the same authors in a follow-up editorial, "Toward a Nuclear-Free World," *Wall Street Journal,* 15 January 2008.

14. As reported by Ivo Daalder and Jan Lodal, "The Logic of Zero: Toward a World Without Nuclear Weapons," *Foreign Affairs* 87, no. 6 (2008): 81. See also President Barack Obama's arms control and nonproliferation goals on the White House website at www.whitehouse.gov/agenda/foreign_policy.

15. John Baylis, James Wirtz, Colin S. Gray, and Eliot Cohen, *Strategy in the Contemporary World,* 2nd ed. (Oxford: Oxford University Press, 2007), p. 249.

16. Richard D. Sokolsky, "Renovating US Strategic Arms Control Policy," *Strategic Forum* no. 178 (Washington, DC: National Defense University, Institute for National Strategic Studies, February 2001), p. 1.

17. My thanks to Kerry Kartchner for providing much of the material in this section from his chapter in the first edition of this book. See Kartchner, "The Objectives of Arms Control," in Jeffrey A. Larsen and Gregory J. Rattray, eds., *Arms Control Toward the 21st Century* (Boulder: Lynne Rienner, 1996), pp. 19–34.

18. Ibid.

19. The term *traditional* is used here to denote something of historical origin that retains its vitality and relevance, and captures the connotation that the objectives of traditional arms control theory remain cogent and compelling in the present era. See Hedley Bull, "The Traditional Approach to Arms Control Twenty Years After," in Uwe Nerlich, ed., *Soviet Power and Western Negotiating Policies,* vol. 2 (Cambridge, MA: Ballinger, 1983), pp. 21–30.

20. The three basic works on traditional arms control theory were all published in 1961: Schelling and Halperin, *Strategy and Arms Control;* Bull, *The Control of the Arms Race;* and Donald G. Brennan, ed., *Arms Control, Disarmament, and National Security* (New York: George Braziller, 1961), earlier published as a special issue devoted to arms control in *Daedalus: Proceedings of the American Academy of Arts and Sciences* (1960).

21. Bull, "The Traditional Approach to Arms Control Twenty Years After," p. 21.

22. Schelling and Halperin, *Strategy and Arms Control,* p. 142.

23. Thomas Schelling, "Foreword," in Jeffrey A. Larsen, ed., *Arms Control: Cooperative Security in a Changing Environment* (Boulder: Lynne Rienner, 2002), pp. xii–xiii.

24. Bull, "The Traditional Approach to Arms Control Twenty Years After," p. 22.

25. Levi and O'Hanlon, *The Future of Arms Control,* p. 9.

26. Ibid., pp. 9–16.

27. In the introduction to their seminal book, *Strategy and Arms Control,* Schelling and Halperin stated: "There is hardly an objective of arms control to be described in this study that is not equally a continuing urgent objective of national military strategy—of our unilateral military plans and policies," p. 3.

28. Throughout much of the Cold War, these three dilemmas were elaborated mostly in nuclear terms: What deters nuclear war? How many nuclear weapons are enough? What if nuclear deterrence fails? But they are equally applicable to the full range of defense scenarios, including policies and threats involving conventional, chemical, biological, and other weapons.

29. Schelling and Halperin, *Strategy and Arms Control,* p. 1.

30. Bull, *The Control of the Arms Race,* p. 3.

31. "US Nuclear Weapons Policy and Arms Control," *Policy Dialogue Brief* (Muscatine, IA: The Stanley Foundation, 13 November 2007).

32. See Jeffrey A. Larsen, "Neo Arms Control and the Bush Administration," *Disarmament Diplomacy* 80 (2005): 49–54.

33. Brad Roberts, "The Road Ahead for Arms Control," *Washington Quarterly,* 80 (2005): 49–54.

34. Baylis et al., *Strategy in the Contemporary World,* p. 247.

35. Schelling and Halperin, *Strategy and Arms Control,* p. 143.

Suggested Readings

Arms Control and National Security: An Introduction (Washington, DC: The Arms Control Association, 1989).

"Arms Control: Thirty Years On," special issue, *Daedalus: Journal of the American Academy of Arts and Sciences* 120, no. 1 (1991).

Brennan, Donald G., ed., *Arms Control, Disarmament, and National Security* (New York: George Braziller, 1961).

Bull, Hedley, *The Control of the Arms Race: Disarmament and Arms Control in the Missile Age* (New York: Praeger, 1961).

Burns, Richard Dean, ed., *Encyclopedia of Arms Control and Disarmament,* 3 vols. (New York: Charles Scribner's Sons, 1993).

Carter, Ashton B., William J. Perry, and John D. Steinbruner, *A New Concept of Cooperative Security* (Washington, DC: Brookings Institution Press, 1992).

"Is Arms Control Dead?" special issue, *Washington Quarterly* 23, no. 2 (2000): 171–232.

Larsen, Jeffrey A., *Arms Control: Cooperative Security in a Changing Environment* (Boulder: Lynne Rienner, 2002).

Larsen, Jeffrey A., and Gregory J. Rattray, eds., *Arms Control Toward the 21st Century* (Boulder: Lynne Rienner, 1996).

Larsen, Jeffrey A., and James M. Smith, *Historical Dictionary of Arms Control and Disarmament* (Lanham, MD: Scarecrow Press, 2005).

Levi, Michael, and Michael O'Hanlon, *The Future of Arms Control* (Washington, DC: Brookings Institution Press, 2005).

Schelling, Thomas C., and Morton H. Halperin, *Strategy and Arms Control* (Washington, DC: Pergamon-Brassey's, 1985). (Orig. pub. 1961.)

Woolf, Amy F., Paul K. Kerr, and Mary Beth Nikitin, *Arms Control and Nonproliferation: A Catalog of Treaties and Agreements,* CRS Report for Congress (Washington, DC: Congressional Research Service, 9 April 2008). (Updated regularly.)

2

A Brief History of Arms Control

James M. Smith

A watchword within the US government policy community across the past several years has been "arms control is dead." This obituary typically would be accompanied by explanations that reflected the notion that "arms control is for enemies, and Russia is no longer our enemy." Initiatives such as Cooperative Threat Reduction (CTR) and other cooperative security programs were intended to replace the confrontational Cold War process of arms control. More recently, however, the obituary has been followed by the acclamation "long live arms control" to acknowledge the continuing relevance of cooperative efforts to control or eliminate dangerous weapons.

The policy debate about the continued relevance of arms control is in essence a semantic exercise. As long as there have been arms, and as long as the actions of one state or group have been seen as threatening by another state or group, there have been efforts to avoid or limit the costs and consequences of conflict. As long as there have been arms, there has been arms control. And as long as arms remain an instrument of policy, arms control will remain a potential foreign policy option.

The focus, character, and prominence of the cooperative side of arms have indeed changed in the past decade, and they will change again. The title under which these efforts reside and their organizational home within the various policy communities have shifted, and they will shift in the future. Since the dawn of recorded history, people have sought to develop better means of attack and defense while concurrently seeking ways to control the effects of those weapons. That trend will not end with the current era of great power cooperation. The urge to control violence will adapt and adjust to the contemporary and future systems, find new forms, and engender new debates, but it will endure.

This chapter briefly traces the place and practice of the cooperative side of security to gain some insight into what the near-term future might hold. It briefly summarizes traditional disarmament efforts and the arms control undertaken during the Cold War. It also explores the transition from Cold War arms control into today's nonproliferation and disarmament efforts. It then discusses the legacies, short-term vectors, and longer-term themes that must be considered in projecting either the "end of history" for arms control or its continuing relevance in the twenty-first century.

Traditions of Disarmament

Examples of efforts toward disarmament can be found almost as far back as the beginnings of recorded Western history. A classical tradition emerged as political organizations matured toward the establishment of states and as the technologies of war became ever more threatening and destructive. Warring parties imposed postconflict disarmament on the vanquished from well before the creation of the Westphalian system. Belligerents also sought to demilitarize possible areas or regions of contact and conflict, and to restrict the use of new and destructive technologies.

Since the advent of the state system in Europe, more formalized disarmament efforts can be organized into three broad categories. The first was a continuation of earlier efforts to impose postconflict disarmament and to ban the use of new—and therefore potentially destabilizing—weapons. Weapons that were deemed to be horrific for some reason also were singled out for special attention. Historians have cited efforts by the Philistines to ban the Israelites from ironworking, and thus producing iron weapons, in the eleventh century BC. They also have noted the 201 BC Rome-Carthage treaty to ban the use of war elephants. Later efforts sought to ban the use of new technologies (crossbows, for example, in 1139) and weapons considered to be inhumane (including poison gases and toxins from at least 1675). These early efforts generally failed unless imposed by force of arms, which remains the principal regulatory mechanism of interstate relations in the modern era. But even though many of these efforts saw only limited or temporary effect, as technologies advanced so too did attempts to control those technologies, providing a legacy to the modern attempts to rein in weapon technologies in the twentieth century.

The second area of early disarmament focus also was a continuation of early practice, extending efforts at conflict avoidance by creating buffers and even demilitarizing colonial flash points. The 448 BC Athens-Persia Accord, for example, demilitarized the Aegean Sea. The 1814 Treaty between Great Britain and Spain sought to end British merchants' provision of arms and munitions to rebels in Spain's American colonies. Perhaps the "poster child" of this thread of traditional disarmament would be the 1817 Rush-Bagot Agreement to demilitarize North America's Great Lakes by limiting naval vessels to a number below militarily significant levels. This agreement effectively demilitarized the US-Canada border, a situation that still pertains today.

A third focus of early disarmament was the formulation of legal standards and norms of acceptable practices and just war. These efforts were begun in the Roman Catholic Church to impose limits on combat practices, and they date from at least the 989 Synod of Charroux, which produced the so-called Peace of God that defined the status of combatants and provided for protection of noncombatants. This thread matured across the Middle Ages as people of goodwill recognized the short-term futility of eliminating conflict and therefore sought to establish norms of just war and regulate belligerent practice. The best known legacies of this third disarmament tradition are the Hague Conventions of the late nineteenth and early twentieth centuries that codified the rules of war at that time.

Thus, the traditional practices in these three areas form the foundation for twentieth-century efforts to curb technologies of war. These practices involved banning some weapons and limiting others, establishing buffers through geographic limits on arms deployment, and establishing standards and norms on which to build legal and regulatory regimes to control the use of weapons and other conflict behaviors. By the twentieth century, however, technologies of war were developing at rates and in directions that would challenge these traditional practices and norms.

Controlling Mass Industrial Warfare

The practices and weapons of World War I brought about a postwar flurry of activity aimed at banning poison gases and limiting the number of naval combatants. The 1925 Geneva Protocol on Poisonous Gases codified the ban on combat use of such weapons into international law. On the other hand, the Washington (1922) and London (1930 and 1936) Naval Treaties that sought to limit the number and tonnage of major surface combatants for the world powers fell well short of universal law. The legacy of this post–World War I activity was the establishment of an international process and practice of negotiation on issues related to the elimination or control of certain types of weapons.

The horrors of modern conflict as witnessed in "the war to end all wars" also led to the ultimate expression of the tradition of disarmament in proposals such as the 1928 Soviet Draft Convention to the League of Nations for "Immediate, Complete, and General Disarmament" and the 1928 Kellogg-Briand Pact, which condemned and renounced war as an instrument of policy. These treaties formalized a division of theory and practice between those seeking the elimination of weapons and their use—those who advocated disarmament—and those seeking the less complete step of somehow reducing or controlling weapons and their use.

The Arms Control–Disarmament Divide

The umbrella term *disarmament* traditionally represented the full range of cooperative and imposed efforts to reduce or restrict military weapons and practices. Disarmament included efforts to eliminate arms and efforts to limit arms in number or employment. It applied before, across, and after actual conflict, and it applied to military activities both at home and throughout the world. Increasingly, disarmament efforts focused on controlling new technologies and weapon types, and on bounding practices toward establishing behavioral norms and standards. The traditional concept of disarmament provided a single umbrella under which all of these efforts and means of implementation could reside. However, with the narrowed focus of some in the disarmament community on literal disarmament, as represented in the Kellogg-Briand Pact, and with the failure of efforts to eliminate or at least internationalize atomic weapons following World War II, the era of simultaneous disarmament and arms control initiatives was launched.

Cold War Nonproliferation and Arms Control

The end game of World War II and the advent of the Cold War brought revolutionary new technologies and modes of military application. These new technologies and emerging battle spaces also became part of an ideological competition that shaped every aspect of interstate relations. This conceptual and technological complexity led to the development of a new, multifaceted approach to controlling weapons and changed the language of disarmament. Nuclear weapons were seen by policymakers and influential observers as a fixture of the strategic landscape, and much of what had traditionally resided under the unitary disarmament umbrella became "arms control" and "nonproliferation."[1] The purpose of arms control centered on mitigating some of the most dangerous aspects of nuclear weapons in order to bound an existential national security problem to manageable dimensions.

This perspective was perhaps best captured by Thomas Schelling and Morton Halperin in their seminal 1961 book *Strategy and Arms Control*. Schelling and Halperin provided an enduring definition of arms control:

> We believe that arms control is a promising . . . enlargement of the scope of our military strategy. It rests essentially on the recognition that our military relation with potential enemies is not one of pure conflict and opposition, but involves strong elements of mutual interest in the avoidance of a war that neither side wants, in minimizing the costs and risks of the arms competition, and in curtailing the scope and violence of war in the event it occurs.[2]

Arms control in a world of nuclear weapons was an integral component of overall national security policy and military strategy. Its goals revolved around the employment of diplomacy to enhance security. Arms control sought to foster and exploit a more cooperative side of the US-Soviet relationship, with significant preconditions and constraints facing any agreement at this strategic level. This arms control diplomacy, however, was not intended to replace the threat of force or the further development of nuclear arsenals; it was used as one instrument in a larger national security policy.

A complementary set of cooperative efforts on the multilateral front sought to bound the nuclear problem to a small number of players; this effort was termed *nuclear nonproliferation*. Alongside these efforts was pursued a more punitive unilateral policy track to be implemented to reverse nonproliferation failures; this initiative was termed *counterproliferation*. Military forces also provided a credible nuclear deterrent in the event of cooperative failure. All three tracks sought the same goals of war avoidance, cost containment, and damage and casualty limitation if war should erupt. This set of activities constituted multilateral and bilateral arms control during the Cold War.

Multilateral Practice: Nonproliferation

Multilateral nonproliferation efforts reached their zenith in the Nuclear Nonproliferation Treaty (NPT) in 1968. This treaty sought to freeze the number of nuclear weapon states (NWS) while simultaneously sharing peaceful nuclear technology for electric power generation, preventing the spread of military nuclear capability, and eventually reversing the further development of nuclear weapons and denuclearizing the world. It was at once a treaty to cooperate, to control, and to disarm, and it represents a valiant effort to create linkages behind these somewhat artificial distinctions. It represents the grand compromise of the Cold War: states could develop peaceful nuclear power for energy generation and prestige while safely forgoing a nuclear weapon program. Disarmament advocates received the promise of eventual nuclear weapon elimination. NWS benefited from the bounded, balanceable nuclear weapon landscape and from broad, if often reluctant, acceptance of the concept of controls that promised to safeguard nuclear materials.

In this emerging arms control regime, treaty compliance and verification became concepts of central importance. Compliance is the implementation phase of arms control. Arms control agreements imply some significant degree of real or potential conflict, and if that conflict is truly going to be reduced, the controls, reductions, and elimination must be real. Because it is so central to security, compliance must be subject to some acceptable means and level of verification. National security issues, programs, and forces are not normally open to absolute visibility so verification is most often based on an acceptable level of transparency, allowing "comfort" to a party that others are complying with limits and controls. The NPT includes provisions for verification of peaceful nuclear program compliance through declarations to and inspection by the International Atomic Energy Agency (IAEA), an arm of the United Nations. In addition, the United States and the Soviet Union also developed independent means of detecting nuclear tests as national verification of their bilateral arms control agreements. The unilateral verification efforts of the superpowers were undertaken in parallel with multilateral verification activities of international organizations.

Following India's nuclear weapon test in 1974, several states took it upon themselves to expand the enforcement mechanisms of the NPT. They also launched formal and informal efforts to restrict the trade in the materials, equipment, and technologies needed to develop nuclear weapons. Two simultaneous efforts created export control lists, so-called trigger lists, to strengthen the nonproliferation enforcement toolbox. One of these efforts was by the NPT Exporters Committee, which also is referred to as the Zangger Committee after its first chairman, and it expanded compliance provisions under the NPT. The other effort, known as the Nuclear Suppliers Group, including both NPT signatory states and non-NPT states, broadened the reach and effectiveness of the treaty.

This attention to compliance and verification within the framework of the NPT suggests that the treaty has expanded into a larger system of explicit and implicit standards and norms. It now makes sense to talk about the existence of a nonproliferation "regime" in world politics. This nonproliferation regime continues today, bringing much of the world's disarmament efforts under its banner.

One significant nonproliferation achievement is the family of agreements that have created nuclear-weapon-free zones (NWFZs) in Antarctica, outer space, and the earth's seabed, as well as in Latin America, the South Pacific, Africa, Central Asia, and Southeast Asia. Negotiations also are underway toward the creation of other NWFZs. These NWFZs are disarmament agreements that demonstrate the hope of effectively eliminating nuclear weapons from international relations.

Other developments point to continued expansion of multilateral disarmament. One example is the expansion of export controls for nuclear weapon materials and technology. Another is arms control efforts directed at the means of weapon delivery. The Missile Technology Control Regime, for example, contributes to the nonproliferation regime by controlling trade in ballistic missiles. Other approaches to disarmament outlaw weapons such as antipersonnel land mines, or focus on regulating and controlling development and transfer of other conventional weapons.

Chemical and Biological Weapons Bans

Highly significant Cold War–era disarmament efforts resulted in bans on chemical and biological weapons (CBW). The Geneva Protocol of 1925 had banned the use of CBW in war. However, some states, including the United States, had never ratified that agreement. In an effort to expand multilateral disarmament beyond the nuclear arena, a Biological Weapons Convention (BWC) was agreed to in 1972 (and was ratified by the United States in 1975). It bans the development, production, possession, and acquisition of biological and toxin weapons. National concerns about safeguarding proprietary industrial information and intellectual property have to date stymied efforts to reach agreement on effective verification provisions to implement the BWC. The United States had destroyed its biological weapons (BW) by the end of 1975, but the Soviet Union, for example, maintained a BW capability well beyond the date of their declaration to the contrary. Effective verification of compliance with the pact remains an open item on the international arms control agenda.

By contrast, the 1993 Chemical Weapons Convention (CWC), which bans the production, possession, transfer, and use of chemical weapons (CW), includes extensive provisions for compliance verification. The CWC requires full declaration of weapons and facilities, and full destruction of existing CW within ten years of signing the convention. There are provisions for routine and intrusive on-site inspections, and for short-notice challenge inspections, which can be set into motion when parties to the treaty have compliance concerns. The CWC also established an organization to carry out challenge inspections and oversee compliance and verification. But even with that infrastructure and such far-reaching verification provisions, the dual-use nature of chemical precursors and processes—for weapons and for industrial purposes—poses compliance challenges even for this pact. As a result, states have placed significant emphasis on unilateral counterproliferation and war-fighting measures to ensure national capabilities to defend forces and conduct military operations in a chemical warfare environment.

So while absolute certainty of compliance verification perhaps remains a utopian goal, multilateral efforts across the nuclear age have continued the historical threads of disarmament aimed at banning particularly dangerous weapons and technologies, of creating weapon-free zones and buffers, and of establishing international norms and standards.

Bilateral Practice: Nuclear Arms Control

The arms control track took a distinct focus on the US and Soviet nuclear arsenals and threat, an effort that ran parallel to the efforts in the nonproliferation track. Here, the dangers of nuclear weapons were anything but abstract: nuclear weapons were seen as posing direct and existential threats by both sides in the conflict. Distrust had to be overcome slowly, with confidence reinforced by technical advances that allowed independent verification of compliance before meaningful controls could be contemplated. Following a decision by President Harry S. Truman in 1951 (National Security Council 112), the United States noted that limited transparency would be necessary for verification of compliance and so embarked on a staged, deliberate strategy of incremental arms control. An agreement on a relatively inconsequential restraint would be used to build confidence in the next, more ambitious step in the arms control process. Only an independent verification capability could allow larger steps forward. For example, the early series of agreements limiting nuclear weapon testing was made possible by over-the-horizon detection of nuclear explosions by Vela Hotel satellites and other verification technologies, and more significant limits on future force development and deployment were later enabled by the fielding of "national technical means" of independent surveillance such as reconnaissance satellites in earth orbit. US-Soviet arms control then became a highly technical, formal process involving detailed negotiations and technical sessions to build agreements that centered on independent compliance verification regimens. To advance beyond limiting nuclear capabilities toward actual reductions in nuclear weapon numbers and capabilities would require on-site inspection for verification. It took until the very end of the Cold War to achieve the level of trust and confidence to allow such intrusive inspection. Only with those late–Cold War active reductions (and even the elimination of one class of weapons in the Intermediate-Range Nuclear Forces Treaty), could arms control again merge conceptually into nonproliferation and disarmament.

One way to view Cold War arms control is to describe it as a two-phase process. First came the effort to bound nuclear arsenals using specific bilateral agreements that limited technical advances and managed the course and scope of the arms race. Second came a set of efforts to reduce strategic inventories and delivery systems, shrinking the existing threat and managing the Cold War endgame. The first phase began in the multilateral arena and then shifted to bilateral US-Soviet negotiations, and the second saw a continuing bilateral focus alongside a reemerging multilateral track. And both phases were characterized by psychological and political drivers that were both enabled and limited by technical capabilities of independent verification.

Phase I: Bounds and limits. The first phase of Cold War arms control started as an effort to bound the international problem posed by nuclear weapons. By the early 1960s, the great power nuclear club was complete (the United States, the Soviet Union, Great Britain, France, and China), international and national organizational structures to address the management of nuclear matters were in place, and the stage was set for complementary formal approaches to freeze the number of NWS and limit nuclear weapon testing and deployment. The year 1962 was particularly important in this effort because the Cuban missile crisis provided the political motivation to act and the Vela Hotel satellite provided a means of final verification of test ban compliance—the key ingredient in these early bounding efforts. The results of this multilateral focus were, most notably, the NPT and the first set of agreements establishing nuclear-weapon-free zones (Antarctica, outer space, and Latin America). The major nuclear arms control effort then shifted to the bilateral arena between the United States and the Soviet Union. For the Soviets and the United States, the purpose of arms control was to bound the scope and pace of growth in strategic weapon systems, thereby keeping the nuclear arms race in check and stabilizing two-way deterrence between the superpowers.

The pivotal year in these efforts was 1968, which saw the creation of the NPT, a shift of emphasis to bilateral superpower arms control, and the emergence of a full array of US "national technical means" to help in the verification of potential agreements. Serious negotiations thus could go forth on creating force limits that could be verified by the technical capabilities that these systems represented. Formal Strategic Arms Limitations Talks were pursued along with confidence-building agreements toward bilateral strategic forces and nuclear test limits, for example, the Strategic Arms Limitation Treaties (SALT I and II); the Threshold Test Ban Treaty, and the Peaceful Nuclear Explosions Treaty.

The negotiations process during the Cold War was extremely formal, slow, and detailed. Both sides flooded the talks with technical experts, and the compliance and verification provisions of these early bilateral nuclear treaties literally filled volumes. The talks had multiple committees, and delegates spent weeks arguing over single words and minute details. When the talks reached the point where only a few contentious issues remained, summitry was used to force the final agreements through. The limits of arms control during this period were largely governed by the capabilities of national technical means to verify compliance with the proposals. Higher levels of trust and transparency were at least a generation in the future.

Progress in arms control during the Cold War can be seen graphically in Figure 2.1. The progress of various initiatives flows from the upper left descending across the columns to the bottom right: from influencing events dating from the onset of the nuclear age; through multilateral efforts, to bound the nuclear problem to a two-sided game; down the series of step-by-step confidence-building measures and technical verification-enabling developments; and, finally, to meaningful negotiations and agreements to limit future growth in strategic systems. As progress was made in US-Soviet

Figure 2.1 The Arms Control Process Phase I: Bounds and Limits

Year	Influencing Event	Multilateral Disarmament	US-Soviet Confidence and Security Building	US-Soviet Arms Control	East-West Confidence and Security Building
1945	US atomic bomb				
1946		US Baruch Plan			
1949	Soviet Union atomic bomb				
1952	Britain atomic bomb				
1953		US Atoms for Peace proposal			
1955			US Open Skies proposal		
1956		International Atomic Energy Agency			
1957	*Sputnik*				
1958	US intercontinental ballistic missile test		US-Soviet test moratorium		
1959		Antarctica Treaty			
1960	France atomic bomb		US proposes test ban		
1961			US Arms Control and Disarmament Agency formed		
1962	Cuban missile crisis	UN Conference on Disarmament formed	US Vela Hotel satellite		
1963		Limited Test Ban Treaty	US-Soviet Hotline Agreements		
1964	China atomic bomb				

Figure 2.1 continued

Year	Influencing Event	Multilateral Disarmament	US-Soviet Confidence and Security Building	US-Soviet Arms Control	East-West Confidence and Security Building
1967	US multiple independently targetable reentry vehicle	Outer Space Treaty; Treaty of Tlatelolco	Glassboro summit		
1968		Nuclear Nonproliferation Treaty	US national technical means		
1969			Strategic Arms Limitation Talks		
1971		Seabed Treaty	Nuclear War Risk Reduction Agreement		
1972		Biological and Toxin Weapons Convention	Incidents at Sea Agreement	Strategic Arms Limitation Treaty (SALT I)	Conference on Security and Cooperation in Europe talks
1973			Prevention of Nuclear War Agreement	Anti-Ballistic Missile Treaty	Mutual and Balanced Force Reduction talks
1974	India atomic test	Zangger Committee; Nuclear Suppliers Group	Vladivostok summit	Threshold Test Ban Treaty	
1975					Helsinki Final Act
1976				Peaceful Nuclear Explosions Treaty	
1977		Environmental Modification Treaty			
1979	NATO dual-track; Soviet Union invades Afghanistan			Strategic Arms Limitation Treaty (SALT II)	

negotiations, it also facilitated progress in broader East-West bilateral measures involving the European allies of both sides.

So the first phase of Cold War arms control began with multilateral efforts to transform the strategic nuclear problem to a bilateral game, and then shifted to bilateral efforts to slow the numerical growth of the superpowers' arsenals. The impetus behind these efforts was the combination of weapon capabilities and political imperatives, and the parameters within which they took place were dictated by the technical abilities to verify compliance with the major provisions of various agreements.

Phase II: Reductions and elimination. The second phase of Cold War arms control saw the transition to a very different post–Cold War strategic environment. This second phase began slowly in terms of the production of formal treaties. The end of the Cold War, however, highlights the importance of how established bilateral processes can facilitate the adjustment to significant shifts in the strategic environment. With SALT I and II limiting future developments in strategic systems, the next logical step in US-Soviet arms control was to reduce the vast number of weapons deployed by both sides. But this step would require on-site inspections and monitoring measures that would place national technical capabilities of independent compliance verification closer to the opponent's deployed forces. Thus, the phase began with a series of sidebar agreements and other confidence-building measures, which culminated in the acceptance of an on-site verification regime. Figure 2.2 depicts this flurry of confidence-building and transparency-enhancing activity as an essential foundation for the step to on-site inspection. With the signing and implementation of the Intermediate-Range Nuclear Forces Treaty (INF Treaty) that provided for on-site inspection and direct verification of the destruction of various systems, the path was paved for strategic nuclear force reductions that were codified in the Strategic Arms Reduction Treaties (START I and II).

The negotiations process matured as the Cold War came to an end. The process leading to a new treaty in this phase often started with a summit or other high-level talk, and the "final numbers" and broad outlines of the agreement were usually agreed on at the opening meeting. The talks then focused on key issues of implementation and verification. The technologies available to each side for independent verification were improved, and a generation of experience and trust also streamlined the process. Agreements at the end of the Cold War were considerably shorter than earlier agreements that filled volumes but, at their heart, they still consisted of counting rules and compliance and verification standards.

The fall of the Soviet system did not pose major disruptions to the arms control process. The non-Russian former Soviet republics that held strategic nuclear weapons agreed to consolidate those assets under Russian control, and the US CTR program was initiated to jointly account for, move, and control these former Soviet weapons. In this environment, and after a series of unilateral and reciprocated Presidential Nuclear Initiatives (PNI) by presidents George H. W. Bush, Mikhail Gorbachev, and Boris Yeltsin, the START process resumed, leading to the completion of START II and eventually the Strategic Offensive Reductions Treaty (SORT, also known as the Moscow Treaty).

This reductions-oriented phase of Cold War arms control also saw significant weapon limitations and mutual verification advances among the European states involved in the North Atlantic Treaty Organization (NATO) and the Warsaw Pact. Agreements limited deployment areas and numbers of conventional forces, provided for verification by direct overflight monitoring, and established the spirit of cooperation that has eased the transition from adversarial confrontation to European integration.

Moscow Treaty as Phase II endgame. The Moscow Treaty of 2002 was founded in the "new strategic framework" of cooperation and competition between the United States and Russia. This treaty changed the context of arms control from a cooperative initiative in an otherwise adversarial relationship to an integral component of a cooperative security relationship. The US-Russia relationship that was formerly driven by maintaining a stable nuclear balance is now a reflection of a more "normal" relationship. Even though "friends don't need arms control," the depth of this particular friendship is still an open concern and the sheer sizes of the nuclear inventories held by the United States and Russia mandate continued caution. Mutual reduction agreements such as the broadly defined Moscow Treaty, which is only a few pages long, can continue to play a constructive role. On the other hand, the possibility that third-party nuclear challenges might emerge gives added weight to the call for continued caution. A significant shift in the nuclear balance at or near a critical sector of the Russian border, for example, could in turn possibly destabilize the US-Russia relationship. The reality of global proliferation—especially the actual employment of weapons of mass destruction (WMD) anywhere—also could pose severe challenges to ongoing drawdowns in the size of US and Russian nuclear forces. Thus, the Moscow Treaty, a formalized, yet not overly burdensome agreement, forms a sensible hedge against the possibility that nuclear weapons could increase in salience in US-Russia relations. The cooperation, stability, and predictability—leading to strategic transparency—fostered by formal agreements are important vehicles for continuing on the path toward a normal bilateral relationship. Whether or not further formal arms control agreements between the United States and Russia are ever concluded, the process of strategic engagement and cooperation has been established and it provides the vehicle to extend the bilateral security benefits of arms control into the future.

Figure 2.2 The Arms Control Process Phase II: Reductions and Eliminations

Year	Influencing Event	Multilateral Disarmament	US-Soviet Confidence and Security Building	US-Soviet Arms Control	East-West Confidence and Security Building
1981		Convention on Certain Conventional Weapons	Intermediate-Range Nuclear Forces (INF) negotiations		
1982			Strategic Arms Reduction Talks		
1983	US Strategic Defense Initiative program; US INF deployment		Strategic Arms Reduction Talks/INF talks/Mutual and Balanced Force Reductions talks suspended		
1985		Treaty of Rarotongo	Nuclear and space talks resumption/expansion		
1986			Soviet Union accepts on-site inspection in principle; Early Notification of a Nuclear Accident agreement; Reykjavik summit		Brussels Declaration (Conventional Forces in Europe [CFE]); Stockholm Agreement (confidence- and security-building measure [CSBM])
1987			Nuclear Risk Reduction Centers; Ballistic Missile Launch Notification Agreement	INF Treaty (on-site inspections)	
1989	Berlin Wall falls		Dangerous Military Activities Prevention Agreement; Notification of Strategic Exercises Agreement; Chemical Weapons Convention Data/Inspections Agreement		CFE talks begin
1990					Charter of Paris
1991	Gulf War; Soviet Union dissolved	Big Five Nonproliferation Initiative	US-Russia Cooperative Threat Reduction program; Presidential Nuclear Initiatives I	Strategic Arms Reduction Treaty (START I)	CFE Treaty; Vienna Document (CSBM)

1992		Agreed Framework (US-North Korea)	Presidential Nuclear Initiatives II		Open Skies Treaty; CFE 1A Treaty
1993		Chemical Weapons Convention		Strategic Arms Reduction Treaty (START II)	
1994		Fissile Material Cutoff Treaty talks			Conference on Security and Cooperation in Europe (CSCE)/Organisation for Security and Cooperation in Europe (OSCE)
1996		Treaty of Pelindaba; Wassenaar Agreement; Comprehensive Test Ban Treaty			
1997	India atomic bomb; Pakistan atomic bomb	Ottawa Convention on Landmines; Treaty of Bangkok	Helsinki summit		
1998	North Korea missile test		US Defense Threat Reduction Agency formed		
1999	Kosovo conflict				OSCE Vienna Document
2000		US rejects Comprehensive Test Ban Treaty	US Arms Control and Disarmament Agency disbanded		
2001	9/11 attacks; US in Afghanistan		US withdraws from Anti-Ballistic Missile Treaty		
2002	Iran nuclear program			Moscow Treaty	
2003	US in Iraq, no weapons of mass destruction; North Korea withdraws from Nuclear Nonproliferation Treaty	Six-Party Talks on North Korea			
2004	Libya nuclear program rollback				
2006	North Korea nuclear test				
2007			Russia withdraws from CFE Treaty; Russia questions INF Treaty		
2008	Russia invades Georgia				

Although the history of arms control suggests that a maturation and stabilization of the US-Russia strategic relationship has occurred, the bilateral agenda between the United States and Russia is still open in several areas. Despite the strategic stability provided by START and the Moscow Treaty, and the strategic engagement surrounding them, START I expires in 2009 and the Moscow Treaty expires in 2012. Concerted efforts will be required to ensure a continued and substantive strategic engagement beyond those dates. Additionally, nonstrategic nuclear weapons are not on the bilateral table, nor have they ever been. Russia's concerns about its extensive borders that now lack the protective buffers provided by the former Soviet republics, combined with its current conventional force weakness, drive its reluctance to limit nonstrategic nuclear weapons. Russia's recent withdrawal from the Conventional Forces in Europe Treaty (CFE Treaty) regime and its open discussion of the wisdom and utility of remaining a party to the INF Treaty are also related to Moscow's concerns about long-range security trends.

Proliferation Points the Way Ahead

In terms of process, the Moscow Treaty represents the endgame of Cold War arms control, the logical conclusion of the superpower confrontation that defined international relations for forty years. It extends the limits of combined off-site and on-site independent verification, and it transitions the two sides from confrontation toward cooperation. The Moscow Treaty also is based on the notion that arms control, as defined in Cold War practice, is not a policy tool for cooperative relationships. The Moscow Treaty caps the requirement to control strategic nuclear weapons and security challenges resulting from them, at least in terms of Russia and the current strategic balance, and it makes significant reductions in the number of deployed warheads. Although few would recognize this fact, the Moscow Treaty constitutes an important step toward eventual nuclear disarmament pledged in Article VI of the NPT. But even as the Moscow Treaty continues as one face of arms control today, the established process, cooperative framework, and technical assurances of this bilateral treaty process also underscore the absence of these "luxuries" when it comes to the current and growing threat of global proliferation. This threat—manifested in the early twenty-first century by a defiant nuclear challenge from North Korea and Iran—represents another current and future face of arms control. The cluster of proliferation activities in the lower left corner of Figure 2.2 graphically depicts the return of nuclear proliferation to center stage. Today, arms control and disarmament return to a focus on those proliferation challenges and multilateral venues.

The success of the US-Russia nuclear process centered on growing two generations of trust under independent national compliance verification assurances ("trust but verify" was the byword of the day). There is little international or independent compliance verification capability, however, in terms of monitoring compliance with nuclear nonproliferation agreements, and there is even less for dual-use chemical and biological technologies or associated weapon delivery capabilities. The treaties aiming to prevent proliferation focus on transparency largely through declarations of holdings from the signatories and, although inspection and verification structures and processes exist along with enforcement provisions under UN auspices, these treaties and regimes are limited. The difficulties of discovery of violation in dual-use environments, the near universality of technical knowledge of these weapons and systems, along with the need for broad international agreement on penalties for violation, make it difficult to verify compliance with existing and potential agreements. The limited ability of current intelligence systems to pinpoint the existence, let alone the details, of proliferation programs has prompted states to resort to self-help and extra-treaty cooperative efforts to address proliferation concerns.

Controversial steps such as preventive war and preemption complicate efforts toward building international consensus to extend and strengthen arms control and cooperative security regimes. Yet ongoing progress and process is essential to preserve and extend the stability and security that those regimes promise. More widely accepted cooperation through programs such as the Proliferation Security Initiative, which tracks and intercepts international shipments of banned materials, helps make existing regimes more relevant to meeting the challenges of emerging threats. In addition to these types of initiatives, resources have been devoted toward US and coalition capabilities to continue to mount military operations despite chemical and biological attack. WMD forensics and consequence management are being developed to respond to attacks that cannot be deterred or physically stopped.

Contradictory imperatives of today's complex security challenges create an even more complicated proliferation challenge. For example, global trends dictate expanded US-India nuclear cooperation, and immediate security requirements dictate US-Pakistan cooperation. The other edge of this sword is that both the NPT and US domestic law require sanctions on these two nuclear proliferants. If arms control focuses on the cooperative side of security challenges, events could drive realpolitik to reemerge.

So where do these threads of history and practice point? What lessons, legacies, and unfinished business do they present to us in the foreseeable future? The full range of activities and policies under the inclusive umbrella of arms control remain vital and relevant. Human history is a chronicle of efforts to prevent war and to mitigate death and destruction should war occur. Today, as modern technologies threaten massive suffering and even catastrophic destruction, nations, groups, and individuals will continue to strive for security-enhancing limitations and restrictions on military capabilities. As long as weapons remain tools of international relations, international actors will be involved in cooperative efforts to enhance state security by addressing horrific and destabilizing weapons, creating and maintaining buffers and demilitarized zones, and formulating and institutionalizing legal standards and norms related to weapons and conflict. This dimension of security policy will remain viable and vital. US national security can only be enhanced by giving deliberate and thoughtful attention to arms control and cooperative security.

Notes

1. An early distinction between the disarmament tradition and Cold War arms control was drawn by Hedley Bull, *The Control of the Arms Race: Disarmament and Arms Control in the Missile Age* (New York: Praeger, 1961).
2. Thomas Schelling and Morton Halperin, *Strategy and Arms Control* (New York: Twentieth Century Fund, 1961), p. 1.

Suggested Readings

Burns, Richard Dean, ed., *Encyclopedia of Arms Control and Disarmament* (New York: Charles Scribner's Sons, 1993).

Larsen, Jeffrey A., and James M. Smith, *Historical Dictionary of Arms Control and Disarmament* (Lanham, MD: Scarecrow Press, 2005).

Schelling, Thomas C., and Morton H. Halperin, *Strategy and Arms Control* (New York: Twentieth Century Fund, 1961).

Wheeler, Michael O., "International Security Negotiations: Lessons Learned from Negotiating with the Russians on Nuclear Arms," Institute for National Security Studies Occasional Paper No. 62 (USAF Academy, CO: February 2006).

3

The Evolving International Context

Kerry M. Kartchner

The international context for arms control has changed dramatically over the past five years with the emergence of nonstate actors and the vertical and horizontal proliferation of weapons of mass destruction (WMD) and associated delivery systems.[1] These trends have been accelerated by globalization.[2] However, despite the increasing pace of these trends and the challenges they pose, arms control—in one form or another—can and should remain a key pillar of international security and stability.

Arms control is an instrument of national security policy. Its purpose is to contribute to a nation's security by reducing the likelihood of war, reducing the costs of preparing for war, and reducing the damage should war occur, through negotiated or implicit agreements with partners and prospective adversaries.[3] It is not an end in itself. Achieving an arms control agreement is not, by itself, a measure of success. Arms control also is a means of underwriting international stability. In theory, arms control can moderate otherwise hostile interstate dynamics and help reduce political tensions, although in practice arms control agreements usually follow rather than precede the relaxation of tensions. The problems that must be addressed by arms control mechanisms, and the forms those mechanisms have taken, are so fundamentally different from the original or classical conception of arms control that it is best to now refer to an emerging "new paradigm" of arms control. That is, the classical approach to arms control can no longer describe arms control's new meanings, applications, or objectives. And the traditional criteria for evaluating the success or failure of arms control are no longer adequate to measure the effectiveness of the new approaches to arms control that have arisen in the past five years.

This chapter focuses on the role of arms control in combating the use and proliferation of WMD. This is only one issue encompassed by arms control, which can address the full range of weapons and arms from trafficking in handguns and rifles to international efforts to demilitarize space.

The use of arms control to control and mitigate the consequences of the dispersal and use of these weapons makes an important contribution to regional peace. WMD proliferation, however, is widely recognized as posing the most serious threat to the international community, especially in terms of potential consequences. States and international organizations have devoted their greatest efforts to institutionalize arms control regimes aimed at WMD. It also is within the domain of mitigating WMD proliferation that we have seen the most radical changes in arms control.

The chapter begins by describing the major aspects of the international context in which arms control operates, including the principal actors, components, and regimes that shape and help implement the international arms control agenda. It then reviews global factors that are radically altering how arms control is formulated, executed, and perceived as an instrument of national security and global stability. It identifies recent revolutionary changes in the international security landscape with regard to their impact on the efficacy, legitimacy, and sustainability of arms control. It describes a new arms control paradigm, one that has become an established aspect of current international relations and the practice of arms control. The chapter concludes by describing the importance of this new approach to arms control and how scholars can contribute to improving international security by revitalizing the theory of arms control.

The International Context for Arms Control: Actors and Regimes

International context involves those circumstances, perspectives, attitudes, institutions, initiatives, and proposals on the part of the international community that favor or undermine the formation, implementation, and enforcement of arms control mechanisms for addressing current and emerging global security challenges. If the international context is favorable, nations and international organizations will be more inclined to use, support, and contribute to arms control initiatives. If the international context is not favorable, members of international society will be disinclined to turn to arms control solutions to solve international security challenges. This section describes the major actors and principal regimes that comprise the international context for arms control.

International Actors

The United Nations. The international context for arms control is shaped by states and governmental and nongovernmental collective actors. The most important collective actor is the United Nations. The UN is an international organization whose stated aims are to facilitate cooperation in international law, international security, economic development, social progress, and human rights issues. The UN was founded in 1945 to replace the League of Nations in the hope that it would intervene in conflicts between nations and thereby avoid war. The organization began with fifty countries signing the UN Charter. The organization's structure still reflects in some ways the circumstances of its founding. The five permanent members of the UN Security Council are the victors of World War II or their successor states: the People's Republic of China (which replaced the Republic of China in 1971), France, Russia (which replaced the Soviet Union in 1991), the United Kingdom, and the United States.

There are currently 192 member states in the United Nations, encompassing almost every recognized independent state. From its headquarters in New York City, the UN and its specialized agencies decide on substantive and administrative issues in regular meetings held throughout the year. The organization is divided into administrative bodies, including the General Assembly, Security Council, Economic and Social Council, Secretariat, and the International Court of Justice. Additional bodies deal with the governance of all other UN-system agencies, such as the World Health Organization and the UN Children's Fund. The UN's most visible public figure is the Secretary-General. The current Secretary-General is Ban Ki-moon of South Korea, who assumed the post on 1 January 2007.

The Security Council is the UN's most important and powerful decisionmaking body. The UN Charter gives the Security Council "primary responsibility for the maintenance of international peace and security." The Security Council can authorize the deployment of troops drawn from UN member countries, mandate cease-fires during conflict, and can impose economic penalties on countries for violating their UN or other international security obligations. It dispatches military operations, imposes economic sanctions, mandates arms inspections, deploys human rights and election monitors, and more. Five powerful countries (China, France, Russia, the United Kingdom, and the United States) sit as permanent members along with ten other member states that are elected for two-year terms. The five permanent members of the Security Council enjoy the privilege of veto power. The Security Council was largely paralyzed by the US-Soviet standoff during the Cold War through the exercise of this veto power, and it was convened only periodically then.[4] Since 1990, however, the Council has dramatically increased its activity and it now meets in nearly continuous session. The Security Council has passed more than 1,700 resolutions since its founding in 1946.[5]

The five permanent members of the Security Council are the only nations recognized as possessing nuclear weapons under the 1968 Nuclear Nonproliferation Treaty (NPT) (although not all nuclear nations have signed the treaty, specifically, India, Pakistan, and Israel), and are the only members of the Council with veto power. The effectiveness of the Council essentially requires a consensus among these states. Whether such consensus can be established on any matter of creating or enforcing arms control obligations is another key indicator of the status of the international context for arms control. If such a consensus is difficult to form, then the international context will not be conducive to arms control. If such a consensus coalesces, then the international context becomes more favorable to arms control.

The International Atomic Energy Agency. Another important collective actor in the field of arms control is the International Atomic Energy Agency (IAEA), a subordinate organization of the UN. The IAEA was established by President Dwight D. Eisenhower in 1957 to promote the peaceful uses of nuclear energy while guarding against the diversion of nuclear material and equipment to military purposes.[6] The subsequent negotiation of the NPT led to a large expansion of the IAEA's role in "safeguarding" nuclear material. Today, the IAEA has 134 members and assists developing countries in a wide range of peaceful nuclear applications, advises its members on critical nuclear safety matters, and implements safeguards agreements with more than 140 countries. These agreements play an important role in international security because they allow the IAEA to serve as a watchdog, alerting the international community to nuclear weapon proliferation activities. The IAEA also is well placed to help countries to expand their national programs to protect against nuclear terrorism.

The IAEA is the main authority responsible for verifying and assuring, in accordance with the statute of the agency and the agency's safeguards system, compliance with safeguards agreements with states parties undertaken in fulfillment of their obligations under Article III, paragraph 1, of the NPT Treaty, with a view to preventing diversion of nuclear energy from peaceful uses to nuclear weapon production. States parties that have concerns regarding noncompliance with the safeguards agreements of the NPT by the states parties can direct such concerns, along with supporting evidence and information, to the agency to consider, investigate, and draw conclusions and decide on necessary actions in accordance with its mandate.

Three areas of work underpin the IAEA's mission: Safety and Security, Science and Technology, and Safeguards and Verification. As an independent international organization related to the UN system, the IAEA's relationship with the UN is regulated by special agreement. In terms of its statute, the IAEA reports annually to the UN General Assembly and, when appropriate, to the Security Council regarding noncompliance by states and on matters relating to international peace and security.[7]

Over the past ten years, the IAEA has taken several steps to improve its safeguards systems. It has an important role to play in monitoring the nuclear programs of Iraq and North Korea, but these countries have continued to impose obstacles in the way of IAEA efforts to fulfill its responsibilities. The IAEA has served as an important source of assistance to developing countries, which might otherwise not obtain the benefits of peaceful nuclear applications as envisaged for NPT parties in good standing. In the aftermath of the 1986 Chernobyl accident, the IAEA also expanded its programs to advise and train some states in the safe operation of nuclear power reactors. Adoption by member states of the Model Additional Protocol to existing safeguards agreements, approved by the IAEA in 1997, would strengthen the effectiveness and improve the efficiency of the safeguards system. After the 9/11 terror attacks, the IAEA moved promptly to expand its programs to combat nuclear terrorism, although it is premature to judge the effectiveness of this effort. A strong, effective, and efficient IAEA serves important US interests.

The effectiveness of the IAEA has been subject to considerable debate, and judgments about its effectiveness are critical to a favorable assessment of the international context for arms control regimes. Member states must have confidence that the IAEA can do its job well, and potential proliferants must be deterred by the conviction that the IAEA will be able to ferret out any diversion of fissile material. A recent report by the Nonproliferation Policy Education Center found a number of shortcomings in the IAEA. These are representative of the criticisms often directed at the IAEA.[8] This report found, for example, that serious flaws exist in the IAEA's methods of monitoring and verification efforts to certify that no nuclear materials or activities are being diverted to weapons as banned by the NPT. In addition, the quantity of potential bomb-grade nuclear material (highly enriched uranium [HEU] or plutonium) that is being produced is growing much faster than funds at hand for safeguarding it, undermining the IAEA's ability to provide timely warning of diversions from nuclear fuel-making plants. Moreover, the IAEA's original estimate for how much nuclear material is needed to make one bomb, and how long it takes to convert HEU or plutonium into a weapon, were established in the 1970s and are, according to this report, anywhere from 25 percent to 800 percent too high. This means that smaller quantities can be incorporated into weapons at a rate faster than assumed, and faster than can be monitored and detected by periodic or intermittent inspections. Finally, chronic funding shortages have handicapped the IAEA with insufficient equipment and antiquated laboratories to test environmental samples taken from sites of concern. According to the report, "Only about a third of the nuclear facilities where the IAEA has remote sensors have near real-time connectivity with Vienna (IAEA headquarters), and almost all these facilities are in countries of minimal proliferation risk."[9]

Nevertheless, under pressure from the United States and other countries, the IAEA has been responsive to many of these criticisms and significant reforms have been accomplished over the past few years.

Treaty Regimes

Several regimes and treaties have made important contributions in slowing WMD and missile proliferation worldwide. By enforcing comprehensive export controls, cooperating in halting shipments of proliferation concern, and reaching out to key nonmembers to increase their awareness of proliferation threats, regime members have made it more difficult, more costly, and more time-consuming for programs of proliferation concern to obtain the necessary expertise and material. The treaties have established a global norm against the proliferation of WMD and provided a basis for the international community to enforce that norm. In the case of the Chemical Weapons Convention (CWC) and the NPT, there are international verification organizations to enforce the global norm against WMD proliferation. In the case of the CWC and the NPT, there are international verification organizations that have a legal right to inspect and require other measures from states parties to promote compliance with these treaties. Several important treaties and their associated regimes shape the international context for arms control, as shown in Figure 3.1.

The Nuclear Nonproliferation Treaty. The NPT is the principal arms control mechanism underwriting international security and stability, and serves as the umbrella treaty for several other actors and arms control agreements. It was signed in 1968, and entered into force in 1970. Its objectives are to prevent the spread of nuclear weapons and weapon technology, to promote cooperation in the peaceful uses of nuclear energy, and to promote general and complete disarmament. According to the UN, more countries have ratified the NPT than any other arms limitation or disarmament agreement. Nearly every nation in the world has signed the NPT. Currently, there are 188 member states. Only Pakistan, Israel, and India are not signatories. North Korea gave notice of withdrawal on January 10, 2003, but in September 2005, and again in February 2007, agreed to resume honoring its obligations under the treaty.

The NPT represents a kind of "grand bargain" between the five acknowledged nuclear weapon states ([NWS]; China, France, Great Britain, Russia, and the United States) and the non–nuclear weapon states (NNWS). It commits nuclear weapon states to aid NNWS in the development of peaceful uses of nuclear energy, and "to pursue negotiations in good faith on effective measures relating to cessation of the nuclear arms race at an early date and to nuclear disarmament."[10] It commits NNWS not to acquire nuclear weapons, and to accept measures known as safeguards to detect and

Figure 3.1 International Arms Control Treaties and Regimes

Nuclear-Weapon-Free Zones (NWFZs)	Constraints on Weapon Systems	Confidence-building Measures	Nuclear Testing Constraints	Suppliers Clubs and Export Control Regimes
• Outer Space Treaty • Seabed Treaty • African NWFZ • Latin American NWFZ • South Pacific NWFZ • Southeast Asian NWFZ • Central Asian NWFZ	• Intermediate-Range Nuclear Forces Treaty • Conventional Forces in Europe Treaty (CFE Treaty) and CFE 1A Treaty • Strategic Arms Reduction Treaty (START I) • Moscow Treaty • Biological Weapons Convention • Chemical Weapons Convention	• Hot Line Agreements • Open Skies • ICBM and SLBM launch notifications • Detargeting agreements (US-Russia; US-China)	• Limited Test Ban Treaty • Threshold Test Ban Treaty • Peaceful Nuclear Explosions Treaty • Comprehensive Test Ban Treaty	• Nuclear Nonproliferation Treaty • Zangger Committee • Australia Group • Missile Technology Control Regime • Fissile Material Cutoff Treaty

deter diversions of nuclear materials from peaceful activities, such as power generation, to the production of nuclear weapons or other nuclear explosive devices. Safeguards agreements are concluded between each NNWS party and the IAEA. Under these agreements, all nuclear materials in peaceful civil facilities under the jurisdiction of the state must be declared to the IAEA, whose inspectors have routine access to the facilities for periodic monitoring and inspections.

The NPT is the model on which most other international arms control agreements are based. The health and status of the NPT is considered a touchstone for assessing the health and status of the international context for arms control. Confidence in the NPT, or lack thereof, is a principal indicator of the well being of the international arms control environment and the prospects for progress in further reducing or controlling armaments.

Nuclear Nonproliferation Treaty Exporters Committee (Zangger Committee). The purpose of the Zangger Committee, a group of thirty-five nations, is to harmonize implementation of the NPT's requirement to apply IAEA safeguards to nuclear exports.[11] It was established between 1971 and 1974 in Vienna by a group of fifteen nuclear supplier states chaired by Professor Claude Zangger of Switzerland. Article III.2 of the treaty requires parties to ensure that IAEA safeguards are applied to exports to NNWS of source or special fissionable material, or equipment or material especially designed or prepared for the processing, use, or production of special fissionable material. The committee maintains and updates a list of equipment and materials that may be exported only if safeguards are applied to the recipient facility. The group operates on an informal basis and its decisions are not legally binding on its members. The relative informality of the committee has enabled it to take the lead on certain nonproliferation issues that would be more difficult to resolve in the Nuclear Suppliers Group (NSG). All of the NPT NWS, including China, are members of the Zangger Committee. China is the only member of the Zangger Committee that is not a member of the NSG. China has not been willing to accept the NSG's policy of requiring full-scope safeguards as a condition of nuclear supply to non-nuclear states.

Since the Zangger Committee agreed to admit China in 1997, Beijing has played a constructive role in the committee's work. The committee also agreed on a strong statement of concern following India's and Pakistan's respective nuclear tests in May 1998. The committee took the lead in developing supplier consensus to add enrichment, reprocessing, and heavy water production equipment to the NSG's trigger list of items to be controlled.

The Australia Group. The Australia Group develops coordinated export controls on goods related to chemical and biological weapons (CBW).[12] It was established in 1984, in the wake of chemical weapons (CW) use during the Iran-Iraq war. Both Iran and Iraq had produced CW using supplies and materials acquired from foreign companies. The Australia Group was formed to ensure that companies and persons in participating countries did not intentionally or inadvertently assist states and other actors seeking to acquire a CW or biological weapons (BW) capability. The Australia Group provides a venue for discussion of CW or BW threats and trends, including those related to terrorism. It also serves as a forum for exchanging participants' experiences in implementing and enforcing CBW export controls. In addition, it works toward harmonizing participants' export controls. The Australia Group control list covers fifty-four precursor chemicals used for CW production, many biological toxins and microorganisms with high potential for BW use, as well as dual-use production equipment, technology, and facilities.

By the 1990s, the Australia Group had largely succeeded in removing its members as inadvertent sources of supply for illicit CBW programs under state auspices. Since 9/11, the group has been focusing on revamping its control lists to better address the terrorist threat. In 2002, the Australia Group adopted licensing guidelines and became the first regime to require participants to have catchall controls (covering items not listed by the Australia Group) to control intangible transfers of technology that are directed toward countries that possess a CW or BW program. The Australia Group also agreed to control technology for the development and production of listed biological agents and equipment. In recent years, Australia Group members have begun to consider measures to address the challenges posed by nonmember countries. Although the Australia Group has been criticized by some members of the Non-Aligned Movement seeking to abolish export controls on controlled goods and technologies, participating states agree on the continued necessity and viability of the Australia Group and the need to educate nonmembers about the regime.

The Missile Technology Control Regime. The Missile Technology Control Regime (MTCR) was created in 1987.[13] Its member states (known as partners) seek to limit the proliferation of missiles capable of delivering WMD and related equipment and technology. Like other informal regimes, the MTCR is not a treaty or a legally binding arrangement. The centerpiece of the regime is a common export policy known as the MTCR Guidelines, applied to a common list of controlled items known as the MTCR Annex, which each partner country implements according to its own laws. The MTCR restricts transfers of missiles—and equipment and technology related to such missiles—capable of delivering at least a 500-kilogram payload to a distance of 300 kilometers. These are referred to as MTCR Category I or MTCR-class missiles, and are considered inherently capable of WMD delivery. Examples include the Scud and the North Korean No Dong. The MTCR Annex controls the key equipment and technology needed for missile development, production, and operation. The MTCR export controls are not licensing bans, but rather regulatory efforts by individual regime partners to prevent the transfer of goods and technology that could contribute to the development, production, and operation of missiles for proscribed purposes.

Over the course of the MTCR's twenty-two-year history, the regime has slowed missile proliferation worldwide. For example, the MTCR partners have persuaded most major suppliers (including Brazil, the European Union countries, Japan, South Korea, Ukraine, and South Africa) to control responsibly their missile-related exports. They have reduced the number of countries with MTCR-class programs, eliminating Argentina's Condor missile program and missile programs in the Czech Republic, Hungary, Poland, and the Slovak Republic. The regime is currently attempting to eliminate Bulgaria's missile program. In addition, MTCR partner countries have cooperated to halt numerous shipments of proliferation concern. The MTCR has established a broad outreach program to increase awareness of the global missile threat among transshipment centers and other MTCR nonpartners. The MTCR Guidelines and Annex have become the international standard for responsible missile-related export behavior.

The Nuclear Suppliers Group. The NSG was formed in 1974 following the Indian nuclear explosion, which demonstrated how nuclear technology and materials transferred for peaceful purposes could be misused.[14] The NSG Guidelines for Nuclear Transfers, first published in 1978, required the following for exports of nuclear materials and equipment: (1) formal recipient government assurances confirming the application of IAEA safeguards and pledges not to use the materials transferred for the manufacture of nuclear explosives, (2) adequate physical protection, and (3) particular caution in the transfer of sensitive materials. In 1992, the NSG added the requirement for full-scope IAEA safeguards as a condition of supply to NNWS of nuclear trigger-list items (the list is called the "trigger list" because such exports trigger the requirement for safeguards). Nuclear technology was added to the trigger list in 1995. Part 2 of the 1992 NSG Guidelines governs exports of nuclear-related dual-use equipment, materials, and technology.

The NSG's greatest successes include reaching agreement in 1992 to require full-scope safeguards as a condition of nuclear supply to nonnuclear states; and to control nuclear dual-use equipment, material, and technology that could be of significant use in nuclear explosive programs. In the late 1990s, the majority of NSG members adopted dual-use catchall controls. These controls cover items that could be of nuclear weapon significance, but are not included on the control list.

The Biological Weapons Convention. The Biological Weapons Convention (BWC) entered into force in 1975. By that time, the United States had already implemented President Richard M. Nixon's 1969 order to dismantle the US BW program. Under the terms of the convention, the parties undertake not to develop, produce, stockpile, or acquire biological agents or toxins "of types and in quantities that have no justification for prophylactic, protective, and other peaceful purposes" as well as weapons and associated delivery systems. There are currently 146 states parties and 17 additional signatories to the BWC.

The BWC has served for nearly thirty years as an important international prohibition on nearly all activities associated with BW. The BWC does not include a mechanism for checking compliance because the convention is inherently unverifiable. From 1995 until 2001, an Ad Hoc Group of States Parties worked toward completion of a legally binding protocol to enhance transparency and promote compliance. The draft protocol was based on traditional arms control measures, which have not proven effective when it comes to detecting violations involving biological technology or agents. In early 2001, the United States reviewed its policy toward the BWC protocol and concluded that the United States could not support the approach embodied in the draft protocol and that the protocol's flaws could not be fixed. It determined that the draft protocol would not improve the US ability to verify BWC compliance nor deter countries seeking to develop BW, and that the draft protocol would have put US national security and confidential business information at risk. In July 2001, the United States informed BWC states parties of its decision. In response to its rejection of the BWC verification protocol, the United States has proposed several important alternative measures to combat the BW threat.

The Chemical Weapons Convention. The CWC, which entered into force in 1997, bans CW. It prohibits the development, production, stockpiling, and use of CW and requires destruction of such weapons and the facilities used to produce them. The convention also establishes a detailed verification regime. Currently, 145 countries are parties to the convention. Nonmembers of concern include North Korea, Iraq, Libya, Syria, Egypt, and Israel.

The CWC has resulted in international disclosure of CW programs in a number of countries, including India, China, and Iran. Stockpiles of CW, and CW production facilities, are being destroyed in the United States, Russia, and other countries. Around the world, facilities that could be used for CW-related purposes are subject to international inspection. The CWC demonstrates the value of multilateral agreements for placing constraints on potential proliferators. Experience with the CWC demonstrates the need for supplementary mechanisms, such as the Australia Group, to assist like-minded states in coordinating national efforts to prevent the export of materials to those who would use them to produce CW. Challenges facing the CWC include implementation of its provisions and verification that all parties are in compliance with its terms. This requires a strong secretariat for managing the treaty's obligations. The United States has recently spearheaded an ongoing effort to restore the health of the international organization responsible for monitoring compliance—the Organisation for the Prohibition of Chemical Weapons (OPCW), which is headquartered in The Hague, the Netherlands.

These actors and regimes form the main components of the international context for arms control. The next section assesses changes that have been occurring in the relationships among these actors and regimes over the past several years, and the impact of these changes and the rise of new threats on traditional approaches to arms control.

The Demise of the Cold War Arms Control Paradigm

Over the course of the past eight years, the traditional approach to arms control has suffered a series of setbacks that have radically transformed the international context for arms control. These include the skepticism of the George W. Bush administration toward traditional arms control, the defiance of rogue regimes determined to violate or circumvent their international arms control obligations, and the rise of nonstate actors and other threats not covered by traditional arms control agreements or methods.

When the Bush administration entered office in January 2001, it brought to policymaking a critical view of traditional arms control and a determination to change it. This attitude, more than any other factor, has been responsible for radically altering the international arms control context. Based on official statements and policy initiatives, the Bush administration's views toward traditional arms control can be summarized as follows:

- Traditional arms control has a poor track record, with either modest or even harmful outcomes.
- Arms control is only possible where it is least needed, and cannot be successful where it is most needed.
- Arms control has generally failed to deliver on its promise to reduce the risk of war, reduce the cost of preparing for war, and reduce damage should war occur.
- Some existing treaties are no longer relevant; some are even counterproductive to US national security.

Moreover, many in the administration also believed that the inflexibility of some traditional arms control agreements had made it difficult to revise or alter those agreements whose provisions had been overtaken by events. There was also a view that enforcement of compliance had been nearly nonexistent and that it had often been taken for granted that nations do not enter agreements unless it is in their interest to assume that agreement's obligations, thus yielding the assumption that treaties are essentially "self-enforcing." They also believed that some agreements, such as the BWC, were inherently unverifiable.

Based on these convictions, the Bush administration undertook a systematic process of reviewing the relevance of existing agreements to see which ones needed revising, which ones needed strengthening, and which ones needed to be discarded. In connection with this review, early Bush administration analyses concluded that the international context for US defense policy was too dynamic to allow the United States to get locked into narrowly defined arms control limitations. Most importantly, the administration decided that traditional approaches to arms control were not necessarily relevant to the new threats faced by the international community.

In connection with this review, the Bush administration wasted no time in reversing long-standing US policies on two important arms control issues pending before the international community: the Comprehensive Test Ban Treaty (CTBT), and the proposed protocol to the BWC. The CTBT was signed in 1996 and bans all nuclear testing. It has been signed by 177 nations, of which 138 have ratified it. This is a measure of its widespread support throughout the international community. To enter into force, however, the CTBT must be ratified by forty-four countries that possessed nuclear research or power reactors in 1996. At present, forty-one of these forty-four countries have signed the treaty, but only thirty-one have ratified it. Nonsignatories include India, North Korea, and Pakistan. The United States, which led the effort to conclude a CTBT and was the first to sign the treaty, is (along with China) among those who have signed but not ratified. Pending its entry into force, most nuclear powers have agreed to observe a voluntary moratorium on testing. On 13 October 1999, the US Senate, whose advice and consent is required for international treaties to become valid and binding, voted not to consent to ratification. Beside partisan considerations, this was prompted by concerns with the ability of the United States to maintain the safety, security, and reliability of the US nuclear weapon stockpile, and with the adequacy of the treaty's verification provisions to detect low-yield tests. After reviewing the matter, the Bush administration concluded that it would not seek Senate reconsideration of the treaty. Nevertheless, it supported the continuation of the voluntary testing moratorium as well as completing the associated International Monitoring System (IMS), which is seen as a supplement to US national technical means of verification.

The US rejection of the proposed BWC protocol is another signal of the demise of the old arms control paradigm and the rise of a new one. It has frequently been used as an example of the Bush administration's abandonment of arms control, but should be seen as representative of a new, more realistic and demanding approach to verification against which the draft protocol fell short. The draft protocol to the BWC relied on a traditional approach to arms control verification; that is, it proposed imposing inspection requirements only where such measures would be convenient and possible, taking into account states parties' sensitivities, industry opposition to possible exposure of trade secrets, and other constraints. Its focus was primarily on the dual-use biological technologies of the major powers. It would have penalized large industrialized states, whose pharmaceutical infrastructures are easily monitored, while ignoring small, dual-use operations more likely to be exploited by terrorists, but which are more difficult to find and monitor.

In the view of the Bush administration, the draft protocol represented a classic fault of the traditional arms control paradigm—the illusion of security and verification masquerading as "real arms control." As John Bolton, then undersecretary of state for arms control and international security, said in a statement to the Fifth Review Conference of the Biological Weapons Convention on 22 September 2004:

> The United States has repeatedly made clear why the arms control approaches of the past will not resolve our current problems. This is why we rejected the flawed mechanisms of the draft Protocol previously under consideration by the Ad Hoc Group. . . . We will continue to reject flawed texts like the draft BWC Protocol, recommended to us simply because they are the product of lengthy negotiations or arbitrary deadlines, if such texts are not in the best interests of the United States and many other countries represented here today.[15]

The Rogue Threat

The ruling governments in North Korea and Iran currently pose the greatest threats to the international arms control regime and constitute the second set of factors precipitating a decline in the legitimacy of traditional arms control. Their defiance of the international arms control regime demonstrated the impotence and fallibility of the old arms control paradigm and has substantially contributed to its demise. Both have been found guilty by the Security Council of violating their international nonproliferation obligations.[16] Both have engaged in the covert pursuit of nuclear weapon programs while receiving the privileges and benefits of membership in the NPT, including financial and technical assistance in the peaceful applications of nuclear energy. Both have exposed a number of serious flaws in the international nonproliferation regime, thus undermining its credibility and support. For example, North Korea proclaimed that it was withdrawing from the NPT in 2003, and suffered practically no adverse repercussions from the international community, signaling that noncompliant states could withdraw from the regime with impunity or could even use withdrawal to escape punishment under regime procedures. Only when North Korea tested a nuclear device three years later did it become subject to significant international sanctions and condemnation. This has caused consternation within international nonproliferation circles, which are now debating how to deter states from withdrawing from the NPT, after having exploited their privileges and rights under the treaty to put in place the infrastructure for a clandestine nuclear weapon program. Ultimately, these states will withdraw from the treaty at the point when their programs either mature and can no longer be kept secret from the international community, or when they conduct a nuclear test that is detected by the regime's verification measures or by other nations' intelligence services.[17]

Iran pursued a covert nuclear program for nearly twenty years before a dissident group exposed this program. These actions directly erode the international climate for confidence in existing arms control mechanisms, and support for pursuing new arms control arrangements. After all, why negotiate further arms control agreements if rogue states are going to exploit them to build clandestine nuclear weapons or pursue other WMD programs?

Because Iran remains a state party to the NPT while defying its obligations under that treaty, in some respects it presents an even greater challenge to the nonproliferation regime than North Korea.[18] Many members of the international community have concluded that Iran has violated its Article III safeguards obligations for two decades by pursuing a secret program involving the undeclared procurement and use of nuclear materials while aiming to acquire the most sensitive elements of the nuclear fuel cycle. Such activities have included unsafeguarded enrichment programs, unsafeguarded plutonium separation activities, the import of undeclared uranium compounds, and diversion of nuclear material from safeguarded to unsafeguarded locations and uses.

Nonstate Actors

The rise of nonstate actors represents the third factor invalidating the traditional approach to arms control. The old arms control paradigm never envisioned this development. Until recently, no arms control agreement pertained to nonstate actors. Arms control was strictly a state-to-state project. It was negotiated among states, was signed and ratified by state legislatures, was implemented and verified by instruments of state power, involved obligations undertaken only by states, and used enforcement mechanisms that applied only to states.

Two recent developments with respect to nonstate actors have shaken the foundations of traditional arms control theory and forced the international community to reckon with the rise of nonstate actors. The first was the horrific attacks of 9/11 orchestrated by the Al-Qaida terrorist group. The second was the discovery of an active proliferation network operated by nonstate actors that was trading in nuclear materials, production capacities, and expertise.

The attacks of 9/11 brought into sharp focus the dangers of terrorists armed with WMD. International arms control experts were skeptical about this threat, and many believed that deterrence threats to potential state sponsors of terrorism diminished the likelihood that WMD terrorism would become a reality. After 9/11, few doubted that, if terrorists had access to WMD, they would not hesitate to use them. Subsequent investigation found substantial terrorist interest in obtaining WMD materials and expertise. The threat of terrorism had not previously been altogether ignored by the international community, but had been addressed primarily through threat reduction assistance to Russia to prevent "loose nukes" from being sold or pilfered from the Russian stockpile.

The events of 9/11 created consternation and uncertainty in the defense community because it was not clear how to identify groups that posed WMD threats or how to respond to, deter, or prevent such groups from carrying out further attacks. These events especially struck home with the international arms control community, which had not assigned much credibility to this threat. They shattered the assumption that the existing arms control regime would deter state sponsors of terrorism from providing the necessary materials and expertise to nonstate actors, and revealed a gap in the fabric of the international nonproliferation regime highlighting that the existing approach to arms control did not address the threat of nonstate actors.

Another development was the discovery, and subsequent efforts to dismantle, the so-called A. Q. Khan network. Abdul Qadeer Khan is a Pakistani scientist and metallurgical engineer widely regarded as the founder of Pakistan's nuclear program. In January 2004, Khan confessed to having been involved in a clandestine international nuclear technology supply network that stretched from Pakistan to Libya, Iran, and North Korea. On 5 February 2004, the president of Pakistan, General Pervez Musharraf, announced that he had pardoned Khan, who was widely regarded as a national hero. In a 23 August 2005 interview with Kyodo News, Musharraf confirmed that Khan had supplied gas centrifuges, gas centrifuge parts, and possibly an amount of uranium hexafluoride gas to North Korea.

The Bush administration, in concert with the international community, responded to the challenge posed by nonstate actors with new tools to fight the proliferation threat. The Security Council passed Resolution 1540. The

United States and other nations assembled and formed the Proliferation Security Initiative (PSI). The United States and Russia, later joined by dozens of other countries, launched the Global Initiative to Combat Nuclear Terrorism. Together, these constitute significant components of the new arms control paradigm.

The Emergence of a New International Arms Control Paradigm

On 13 December 2001, President Bush announced that the United States had given Russia formal notice of its decision to withdraw from the Anti-Ballistic Missile Treaty (ABM Treaty), stating that "the ABM Treaty hinders our government's ability to develop ways to protect our people from future terrorist or rogue state missile attacks."[19] Within just a few hours of this announcement, the Russian government released a statement by President Vladimir Putin characterizing the US decision as "a mistake" but stating that it was not a security threat to Russia (thus, there would be no arms race response), that Russia was determined to sustain improvements in US-Russian relations (thus, there would be no return to the Cold War), and urging the United States to enter into a legally binding agreement on further reductions in strategic offensive arms (thus, there would be prospects for further arms control arrangements between the United States and Russia).[20] This remarkable series of events demarcates the demise of the old arms control paradigm and the nascence of a new one. (See Figure 3.2.)

The US withdrawal from the ABM Treaty in June 2002 is emblematic of this paradigm shift. The ABM Treaty was a classic example of the old paradigm. It was a formal agreement that was the culmination of a protracted negotiating process that institutionalized (at least from the US perspective) mutual assured destruction as the basis for security and stability. It was no longer relevant to the new security relationship between the United States and Russia. It actually blocked responding to new threats by prohibiting the exploration of new active defense technologies and international cooperation on missile defenses. It also emblemized several criticisms of the old paradigm of arms control. It was inflexible and impervious to revision. It did not keep pace with the altered security environment. It prevented adapting to new security requirements.

The US withdrawal from the ABM Treaty had an important impact on the global context for arms control. The US withdrawal did not cause the much anticipated collapse of the international arms control regime, start a new arms race, or precipitate a new cold war. Instead, it was replaced by new unilateral, bilateral, and multilateral agreements to confront missile proliferation threats, reflecting the establishment of the new arms control

Figure 3.2 Comparing the Old and New Arms Control Agendas

Old Objectives	New Objectives
First Strike Stability: Mitigate the danger of surprise nuclear attack between the two superpowers.	*Surprise Attack Stability:* Address the threat of nuclear terrorism (or other WMD terrorism) posed by an unknown number of nonstate actors, with unknown capabilities and intentions.
Arms Race Stability: Halt, slow, or stabilize the bipolar nuclear arms race.	*Nonproliferation Stability:* Halt, slow, or stabilize the proliferation of WMD in multiple regions around the globe, including securing "loose nukes."
Alliance Stability: Promote or underwrite extended deterrence between the two major alliance systems.	*Regional Escalation Stability:* Enhance regional stability around the globe and strengthen dozens of regional security alliances.
Escalation Stability: Codify conventional stability in Central Europe; seek to deter or control the escalation of a conventional conflict to nuclear exchanges.	

paradigm. It was a remarkable diplomatic success for the Bush administration, for which it has received little credit. It proved that an arms control agreement can become obsolete and can be discarded without disrupting the remaining international arms control regime.

Although the old arms control paradigm focused on controlling and stopping arms races and surprise attacks, the new paradigm focuses on combating the proliferation of WMD, a kind of arms race in itself. The new paradigm seeks to close gaps in the international nonproliferation regime by creating, for example, coalitions of states to intercept and interdict air, ground, and sea transportation of WMD. The old paradigm was state-centric while the new paradigm addresses the new threat from nonstate actors. The old paradigm had few mechanisms other than formal agreements or unilateral declarations. The new paradigm includes bilateral and multilateral initiatives, "coalitions of the willing," public-private partnerships, and, where necessary, legally binding treaties. The new international arms control paradigm has developed its own criteria for evaluating its success. First, it seeks to deter and respond to treaty withdrawal by states in violation of the NPT's obligations. Second, it seeks to achieve universal adherence to the IAEA Model Additional Protocol, giving international inspectors the authority they need to detect undeclared nuclear activity and making the protocol part of the safeguards standard. Third, it seeks to ensure compliance with the nonproliferation obligations that form the core of the NPT and prevent the emergence of more states armed with nuclear weapons. Fourth, it seeks to foster recognition of the need for all states to live up to the strictest standards of safety and security in their peaceful nuclear activities. Fifth, it supports the fullest possible cooperation in the peaceful uses of nuclear energy consistent with nonproliferation norms.

The new paradigm recognizes that the main threat to national and international security is the intersection of WMD and the rise of extremist groups. Arms control is but one instrument among a full complement of tools for promoting international security and responding to new threats. Nuclear disarmament must be pursued within the context of appropriate conditions within the international global environment, including concrete steps toward general and complete disarmament by all states. Strengthening the international nuclear nonproliferation regime will require multilateral efforts outside the regime as well as steps to close gaps in existing mechanisms.

The New Paradigm in Practice

There are several examples of the consolidation of this new arms control paradigm, including the signing and ratification of the Strategic Offensive Reductions Treaty (SORT, also called the Moscow Treaty), which further reduced US and Russian strategic nuclear arms; Libya's decision to divest itself of its WMD programs; several recent initiatives to combat the proliferation and transshipment of WMD; and the US-Indian agreement to pursue bilateral cooperation on civil nuclear energy.

The Strategic Offensive Reductions Treaty. The Moscow Treaty, signed on 24 May 2002, calls for reductions to 1,700 to 2,200 strategic nuclear warheads by 31 December 2012. It establishes a Bilateral Implementation Commission that meets twice a year. According to the terms of the treaty, each side may determine its own force structure and composition.[21]

The Moscow Treaty has been criticized precisely for its deviation from the traditional arms control paradigm. It has been criticized for lacking its own verification provisions; instead, it explicitly relies on the verification and inspection provisions of the Strategic Arms Reduction Treaty (START) to monitor compliance. The Moscow Treaty's proponents have countered that standard national technical means of verification (consisting of overhead surveillance satellites and other intelligence-gathering means) can monitor its terms. Some have noted that the reductions are not permanent, and that warheads are not required to be destroyed and may therefore be placed in storage and later redeployed; yet no treaty has ever required the actual destruction of warheads. Most treaties focus on limiting observable delivery systems such as bombers, missiles, and submarines.

The date that the Moscow Treaty reductions are required to be completed, 31 December 2012, is also the date on which the treaty itself expires, unless extended or superseded by both parties. Because there exists a clause in the treaty that provides that withdrawal can occur on three months' notice and no benchmarks are required in the treaty, either side could feasibly perform no actions in furtherance of the treaty and then simply withdraw in December 2012. This sort of outcome is extremely unlikely, however, given the momentum of radical drawdowns occurring in both sides' strategic nuclear arsenals and the likelihood that such actions would be met with considerable international and domestic criticism.

There are several notable features of the Moscow Treaty that reflect the new arms control paradigm. For instance, the treaty codifies a range of limitations, rather than a specific numerical limit on all covered systems, to allow either side greater flexibility in setting its own force structure. Specifying a range also disassociates the treaty from the traditional requirement for absolute parity in force levels because both sides could have different levels, yet remain in compliance with the treaty. The Moscow Treaty is unusually short for a strategic arms reduction agreement (only one and one-half pages, compared to more than 400 pages for START I). It also was negotiated quickly through consultations among senior officials. It was not produced in a formal process involving respective negotiating delegations. These features, rather than being considered weaknesses by the standards of the old arms control paradigm, actually reflect the strengths and advantages of a new strategic relationship between Russia and the United States, one based on a greater degree of trust and a shared common interest in abandoning their previous adversarial relationships.

Libya. Libya's decision in December 2003 to disclose and eliminate its WMD program is a validation of the new arms control paradigm. Following nine months of secret and delicate negotiations with a small circle of officials from the United States and the United Kingdom, the government of Libya announced on 19 December 2003, that it had committed to reveal and eliminate its WMD programs, including its accumulated infrastructure for building nuclear weapons. Subsequently, Libya accepted the IAEA Model Additional Protocol inspections. The United States and the United Kingdom have assisted Libya by removing proliferation-sensitive items and material from Libya, helping to convert remaining facilities to peaceful uses, and assisting Libya in meeting its IAEA safeguards obligations. In January 2004, the IAEA began inspections inside Libya pursuant to this commitment. In April 2004, the Security Council took note of an IAEA resolution conveying certification of Libya's compliance, welcomed Libya's decision to abandon its programs for developing WMD and their means of delivery, and encouraged Libya to ensure the verified elimination of all of its WMD programs.

There are two important implications for arms control from this recent experience with Libya. First, it confirmed the ineffectiveness of the old arms control paradigm. Libya's covert violations of the NPT went undetected and undeterred by the NPT regime. This underscores the inability of the old approach to arms control to thwart noncompliance and ensure the viability of existing arms control obligations through inaction on the part of the international community, even when the United States brought its suspicions regarding Libya's violations to the attention of that community. Furthermore, Libya's violations were assisted by the A. Q. Khan network of nonstate actors, which operated under the state-centric radar screen of international awareness and was unaffected by state-centric arms and export control arrangements. Moreover, together with the North Korean and Iranian episodes, this experience further invalidated the assumption that states do not join arms control regimes that they ultimately intend to violate.

Second, the Libyan experience simultaneously confirmed and validated the ascendance of the new arms control paradigm. Libya's about-face was motivated by many factors, but among these were the Bush administration's strong emphasis on counterproliferation, with new tools aimed at interdicting and blocking transshipments of WMD materials and expertise. The highly visible effectiveness of theater missile defense in the Iraq war may also have contributed to convincing Libyan officials that ballistic missile threats and attacks could be countered by active defenses, and that it was counterproductive to invest substantial national resources in their pursuit. Measures intended to block access to international financial markets on the part of the would-be proliferants also may have played a part in the decision to abandon WMD programs.

Finally, the exposure of the A. Q. Khan network in connection with the interception of a ship headed for Libya carrying centrifuge parts—upon which Libya depended for access to critical materials, production capabilities, and ballistic missile delivery assets—certainly played a role in Libya's decision to roll back its WMD programs.

New international partnerships. Recent international security initiatives also demonstrate the growth of the new arms control paradigm, although they do not necessarily take the form of traditional arms control agreements.

The G8 Global Partnership Against the Spread of Weapons and Materials of Mass Destruction (Global Partnership) is a good example of these new types of initiatives. Launched by leaders of the G8 (an international forum comprised of the governments of Canada, France, Germany, Italy, Japan, Russia, the United Kingdom, and the United States) at their June 2002 summit in Kananaskis, Canada, the Global Partnership is aimed at preventing terrorists or states that support them from acquiring or developing WMD. The Global Partnership addresses nonproliferation, disarmament, counterterrorism, and nuclear safety issues through cooperative projects in such areas as destruction of CW, the dismantlement of decommissioned nuclear submarines, the security and disposition of fissile materials, and helping former weapon scientists gain other employment. This initiative supplements the global nonproliferation regime by supporting compliance with the NPT and by building "partnership capacity" through contributions by wealthier or more technologically advanced states to improve the ability of states with limited resources to confront the challenges of WMD proliferation.

The Proliferation Security Initiative is another global initiative aimed at stopping shipments of WMD, their delivery systems, and related materials worldwide. Announced by President Bush on 31 May 2003, the goal of the PSI is to create a dynamic approach to preventing proliferation to or from nation-states and nonstate actors. It calls for actions to be taken consistent with national legal authorities and relevant international law and frameworks. In September 2003, eleven core countries agreed to the PSI Statement of Interdiction Principles listing specific steps for interdicting WMD shipments and preventing proliferation facilitators from transferring WMD. Participation in the PSI is voluntary. Participants commit to enact legal statutes to facilitate interdiction and seizure of WMD-related items. Participants also are to take measures to ensure that their national facilities are not utilized to transfer illicit weapon cargoes. Support for the PSI is an acknowledgement of the need for stronger measures to defeat proliferators through international cooperation. Currently, about ninety nations have agreed to participate on an ad hoc basis in supporting PSI activities. Since April 2005, there have been more than two dozen successful interdictions of WMD-related shipments under the auspices of the PSI.

The Global Initiative to Combat Nuclear Terrorism was announced jointly by presidents Bush and Putin in July 2006. This initiative is a partnership of nations committed to developing their individual and collective capabilities to detect, deter, and defeat nuclear weapons in the hands of terrorists. Sixty nations have agreed to its Statement of Principals, including Russia, Japan, France, Germany, and the United Kingdom. This initiative brings the world's leading experts together to share best practices, train, and develop relationships to better combat the threat of nuclear terrorism.[22]

The Global Nuclear Energy Partnership is an international partnership aimed at reducing the risk of nuclear weapon proliferation that might result from an expansion of the civilian use of nuclear power by developing new technologies to recycle nuclear fuel without separating plutonium and establishing a reliable supply of nuclear fuel. Japan has been a strong supporter of the Global Nuclear Energy Partnership since it was announced in early 2006. South Korea and Egypt both participated in a ministerial-level Global Nuclear Energy Partnership meeting in Vienna on 16 September 2007.

On 3 July 2007, presidents Bush and Putin launched the US-Russian

Declaration on Nuclear Energy and Nonproliferation. It offers a new format for enhanced cooperation to promote the expansion of peaceful nuclear energy in a way that supports nuclear nonproliferation. Russia and the United States will enter into discussions jointly and bilaterally with other states to assist them to acquire the benefits of peaceful nuclear energy while creating a viable alternative to the acquisition of enrichment and reprocessing technologies.

Some see the joint US-India partnership, announced by President Bush and India's prime minister Manmohan Singh in July 2005, as a threat to the NPT in particular and the international context for arms control in general because it creates an exception to a series of international nonproliferation regimes. Yet under the July 2005 accord, India committed to a series of actions that it previously had avoided. In particular, India agreed to implement strong and effective export control legislation, and to exercise export restraint on enrichment and reprocessing technologies. It also agreed unilaterally to adhere to the NSG and MTCR Guidelines on nuclear and ballistic missile transactions; to separate its civil and military facilities and programs, placing all its civil facilities and activities under IAEA safeguards; to sign and adhere to the Model Additional Protocol covering its civil facilities; and to maintain its nuclear testing moratorium. India also has promised to work toward a Fissile Material Cutoff Treaty. Each of these activities is significant. Together they constitute a substantial change of course in India's nuclear policies, allowing it to move into closer conformity with international nonproliferation standards and practices.[23] This agreement reflects another component in the new international arms control paradigm.

Conclusion

The 2000 NPT Review Conference represented the high-water mark of the old arms control paradigm. At the 2000 Review Conference, all 187 member governments—including the Permanent Five of the Security Council (P-5)—agreed to a 13-point action plan for arms control.[24] In nearly every respect, these "13 steps" represented the culmination of the old arms control paradigm. Virtually every measure related exclusively to the disarmament obligations of the P-5. There was no mention of enforcement of Article I, II, III, or IV obligations on the part of NNWS, nor any mention of the danger posed by the potential for rogue states to withdraw from the treaty after having exploited its benefits and privileges. There was no mention of the need to verify compliance with the NPT by states pursuing clandestine nuclear weapon programs, nor any mention of the potential for nonstate actors to exploit lax export control laws and other loopholes in the nonproliferation regime to create a network of private proliferation partners willing to supply nuclear materials, weapon designs, and production expertise to the highest bidder. Instead, it called for retaining outdated arms control treaties such as the ABM Treaty (in effect endorsing a perpetuation of mutual assured destruction between the United States and Russia as the foundation of international security), and a continuation of other traditional arms control policies.

By the time of the next NPT Review Conference, in May 2005, the fatal flaws in that old paradigm could no longer be ignored. In many respects, the 2005 Review Conference reflected a turning point in the emergence of the new arms control paradigm. Between the 2000 and 2005 Review Conferences, the world had experienced the terrorist attacks of 9/11, the discovery of the A. Q. Khan network, the defiance of Iran and North Korea, and the descent into a war in Iraq.

Many delegates to the 2005 NPT Review Conference came away from the four weeks of meetings frustrated that consensus had not been reached on a final document and that no new arms control initiatives had been supported.[25] That is, they were disappointed that the traditional agenda of complaining about the lack of progress in nuclear disarmament had not prevailed. In particular, reference was frequently made to the 13-point action plan for arms control and the fact that the United States, under the Bush administration, had explicitly repudiated several of these steps.

The US delegates presented a different perspective. They argued that, although the Review Conference had not reached consensus, it had broken new ground and had substantively altered the terms of the debate over nonproliferation, shifting the focus from disarmament on the part of the P-5 to enforcement of the nonproliferation regime. They underscored the general recognition that had emerged from the Review Conference that recent challenges to the nonproliferation regime, including evidence of noncompliance on the part of some members, a first-ever treaty withdrawal (by North Korea), the discovery of a clandestine nuclear weapon supply network (orchestrated by Pakistani scientist Khan), and the failure to complete the implementation of a host of agreed nuclear disarmament steps, had demonstrated that the old paradigm with its emphasis on P-5 disarmament was not addressing these new challenges. They noted that the 2005 Review Conference had been the first to examine in detail indicators of noncompliance with Article II, which concerned the obligation of NNWS not to acquire nuclear weapons or other nuclear explosive devices. It had explored the relationship of Article IV, which concerned the right of NPT parties to use nuclear energy for peaceful purposes, to the obligations contained in Articles I, II, and III of the treaty.[26] They also pointed out that constructive ideas had been explored on the steps that states parties, the IAEA, and the Security Council should take to hold accountable those in noncompliance with their NPT obligations. Also, for the first time, the Review Conference discussed seriously how states parties, the IAEA, the NSG, and the Security Council should address notifications of withdrawal. There had also been an important discussion of the grave challenges to security and to the nonproliferation regime posed by Iran's and North Korea's noncompliance with their nonproliferation and safeguards obligations as well as by the proliferation network operated by nonstate actors.

Dramatic developments in the international context for arms control have led to the emergence and consolidation of a new arms control paradigm with new objectives, new forms or modalities, and new criteria for assessing success or failure. The international community is facing a phalanx of security challenges that the classical arms control paradigm cannot solve. Replacing the Cold War arms control paradigm is essential to preserving the relevance, salience, and effectiveness of arms control as a critical component of international security and stability. Arms control is an instrument of policy. If the policy changes, arms control also must change.

Arms control during the Cold War had become the explicit instrument of a prevailing theory of strategic stability. That theory no longer pertains. Over the course of the past five years, a new international arms control paradigm has emerged which, although not yet fully mature, has established the basis for becoming a revitalized instrument responsive to new threats and new kinds of stability.

Notes

1. This chapter represents the personal views of the author. Nothing in it should be construed as necessarily representing the official positions of the US Department of State or any other US government agency.

2. This chapter focuses on developments in international arms control occurring during the past five years. For an excellent discussion of post–Cold War changes in the international context for arms control leading up to the period beginning about five years ago. see Schuyler Foerster, "The Emerging International Context," in Jeffrey A. Larsen, ed., *Arms Control: Cooperative Security in a Changing Environment* (Boulder: Lynne Rienner, 2002), pp. 41–54.

3. Kerry M. Kartchner, "The Objectives of Arms Control," in Jeffrey A. Larsen and Gregory J. Rattray, eds., *Arms Control on the Eve of the Twenty First Century* (Boulder: Lynne Rienner, 1996), pp. 19–34.

4. Dan Sarooshi, "The Security Council," available at http://www.globalpolicy.org/security/gensc.htm (accessed 8 October 2007).

5. Matt Rosenberg, "The United Nations Security Council," 20 September 2007, available at http://geography.about.com/od/politicalgeography/a/security council.htm (accessed 15 October 2007).

6. More information on the IAEA can be found at www.iaea.org (accessed 25 September 2007).

7. For further information, see www.iaea.org/About/index.html (accessed 30 September 2007).

8. "Falling Behind: International Scrutiny of the Peaceful Atom," a report by the Nonproliferation Policy Education Center, available at www.strategicstudiesinstitute.army.mil/pubs/display.cfm?pubID=841 (accessed 16 March 2009). This report is summarized and cited in "Nuclear Safeguards: In Pursuit of the Undoable," *The Economist*, 24 August 2007, available at www.economist.com/world/international/displaystory.cfm?story_id=9687869 (accessed 25 September 2007).

9. Ibid., p. 44, note 18.

10. NPT, Art. VI.

11. Members of the Zangger Committee include Argentina, Australia, Austria, Belgium, Bulgaria, Canada, China, the Czech Republic, Denmark, Finland, France, Germany, Greece, Hungary, Ireland, Italy, Japan, Luxembourg, the Netherlands, Norway, Poland, Portugal, the Republic of Korea, Romania, the Russian Federation, the Slovak Republic, Slovenia, South Africa, Spain, Sweden, Switzerland, Turkey, Ukraine, the United Kingdom, and the United States. More information on the Zangger Committee can be found at www.zanggercommittee.org/Zangger/default.htm (accessed 25 September 2007).

12. The thirty-three members of the Australia Group are Argentina, Australia, Austria, Belgium, Bulgaria, Canada, the Czech Republic, Cyprus, Denmark, Finland, France, Germany, Greece, Hungary, Iceland, Ireland, Italy, Japan, the Republic of Korea, Luxembourg, the Netherlands, New Zealand, Norway, Poland, Portugal, Romania, the Slovak Republic, Spain, Sweden, Switzerland, Turkey, the United Kingdom, and the United States. See the Australia Group website at www.australiagroup.net/index_en.htm (accessed 25 September 2007).

13. The thirty-three MTCR partners are Argentina, Australia, Austria, Belgium, Brazil, Canada, the Czech Republic, Denmark, Finland, France, Germany, Greece, Hungary, Iceland, Ireland, Italy, Japan, Luxembourg, the Netherlands, New Zealand, Norway, Poland, Portugal, Russia, South Africa, South Korea, Spain, Sweden, Switzerland, Turkey, Ukraine, the United Kingdom, and the United States. See the MTCR website at www.mtcr.info/english/ (accessed 25 September 2007).

14. The NSG now includes forty countries: Argentina, Australia, Austria, Belarus, Belgium, Brazil, Bulgaria, Canada, Cyprus, the Czech Republic, Denmark, Finland, France, Germany, Greece, Hungary, Ireland, Italy, Japan, Kazakhstan, Latvia, Luxembourg, the Netherlands, New Zealand, Norway, Poland, Portugal, the Republic of Korea, Romania, the Russian Federation, the Slovak Republic, Slovenia, South Africa, Spain, Sweden, Switzerland, Turkey, Ukraine, the United Kingdom, and the United States. More information on the NSG can be found at www.nuclearsuppliersgroup.org/ (accessed 25 September 2007).

15. "Statement of the Honorable John R. Bolton, Under Secretary of State for Arms Control and International Security to the Fifth Review Conference of the Biological Weapons Convention, 22 September 2004" (US Department of State), available at www.us-mission.ch/press2001/1911bolton.htm (accessed 16 September 2007).

16. See *Challenges of Nonproliferation Noncompliance* (Washington, DC: US Department of State, Bureau of International Security and Nonproliferation 18 April 2007), available at www.state.gov/t/isn/rls/other/83398.htm (accessed 29 September 2007).

17. For a more thorough discussion of the implications of the threat of states withdrawing from the NPT, see *Article X of the Nuclear Nonproliferation Treaty: Deterring and Responding to Withdrawal by Treaty Violators* (Washington, DC: US Department of State, Bureau of International Security and Nonproliferation, 2 February 2007), available at www.state.gov/t/isn/rls/other/80518.htm (accessed 29 September 2007).

18. The following material is drawn from *Challenges of Nonproliferation Noncompliance* (Washington, DC: US Department of State, Bureau of International Security and Nonproliferation, 18 April 2007), available at www.state.gov/t/isn/rls/other/83398.htm (accessed 16 September 2007).

19. "Remarks by the President on National Missile Defense," 12 December 2001, available at www.whitehouse.gov/news/releases/2001/12/20011213-4.html.

20. This material is drawn from Kerry M. Kartchner and Jeffrey A. Larsen, *Emerging Missile Challenges and Improving Active Defense*, Counterproliferation Papers, Future Warfare Studies No. 25 (Montgomery, AL: USAF Counterproliferation Center, Air University, Maxwell Air Force Base, August 2004).

21. The treaty text and associated documents can be found at www.state.gov/t/ac/trt/18016.htm (accessed 16 September 2007).

22. *Fact Sheet: The Global Initiative to Combat Nuclear Terrorism* (Washington, DC: White House, Office of the Press Secretary, 15 July 2006), available at www.whitehouse.gov/news/releases/2006/07/20060715-3.html (accessed 15 October 2007).

23. Andrew K. Semmel, "Is the Non-Proliferation of Nuclear Weapons Still Attainable?" remarks at the United Nations Foundation, Washington, DC, 1 June 2006, available at www.state.gov/t/isn/rls/rm/67707.htm (accessed 30 September 2007).

24. The 13-step action plan is buried deep inside the final document of the 2000 NPT RevCon, but is extracted at www.reachingcriticalwill.org/legal/npt/13point.html (accessed 29 September 2007).

25. "Review Conference for Nuclear Non-Proliferation Treaty Concludes, with Many States Expressing Deep Disappointment at Outcome," UN press release DC/2969, 27 May 2005, available at www.un.org/News/Press/docs/2005/dc2969.doc.htm (accessed 29 September 2007).

26. Those articles concern the obligation of NNWS not to transfer or receive nuclear weapons and to accept IAEA safeguards for the exclusive purpose of verifying fulfillment of those obligations, with a view to preventing diversion of nuclear energy from peaceful uses to nuclear weapons or other nuclear explosive devices.

Suggested Readings

Bailes, Alyson J. K., director, Stockholm International Peace Research Institute, Remarks at the China Arms Control and Disarmament Association, Beijing, 8 May 2007, available at www.sipri.org/archive/ab/Bejing20070508/.

Campbell, Kurt M., Robert J. Einhorn, and Mitchell B. Reiss, eds., *The Nuclear Tipping Point: Why States Reconsider Their Nuclear Choices* (Washington, DC: Brookings Institution Press, 2004).

Challenges of Nonproliferation Noncompliance (Washington, DC: US Department of State, Bureau of International Security and Nonproliferation, 18 April 2007), available at www.state.gov/t/isn/rls/other/83398.htm.

Cheema, Pervaiz Iqbal, "Nuclear World Order and Nonproliferation, II," *Strategic Insights* 6, no. 4 (2007), available at www.ccc.nps.navy.mil/si/2007/Jun/cheemaJun07.asp.

Fact Sheet: The Global Initiative to Combat Nuclear Terrorism (Washington, DC: White House, Office of the Press Secretary, 15 July 2006), available at www.whitehouse.gov/news/releases/2006/07/20060715-3.html.

Flanagan, Stephen J., and James A. Schear, eds., *Strategic Challenges: America's*

Global Security Agenda (Washington, DC: National Defense University, Institute for National Strategic Studies, 2008).

Flynn, Dan, "Mapping the Global Future: Report of the National Intelligence Council's 2020 Project," *Strategic Insights* 6, no. 4 (2007), available at www.ccc.nps.navy.mil/si/2007/Jun/flynnJun07.asp.

Kartchner, Kerry M., and Jeffrey A. Larsen, *Emerging Missile Challenges and Improving Active Defense,* Counterproliferation Papers, Future Warfare Studies No. 25 (USAF Counterproliferation Center, Air University, Maxwell Air Force Base, August 2004).

Larsen, Jeffrey A., "National Security and Neo-arms Control in the Bush Administration," *Disarmament Diplomacy,* no. 80 (2005), available at www.acronym.org.uk/dd/dd80/80jal.htm.

Sokolski, Henry, and James M. Ludes, eds., *Twenty-First Century Weapons Proliferation* (London: Frank Cass, 2001).

4

The Changing Domestic Politics of the Arms Control Process

Jennifer E. Sims

In September 2005, President George W. Bush announced his intent to pursue full civil nuclear cooperation with India, a state that had, for almost forty years, refused to join the Nuclear Nonproliferation Treaty (NPT) and had surprised Washington by testing a nuclear weapon in 1998. Critics assumed that the US Congress would not go along with this agreement. After all, it threatened to undermine relations with Pakistan, a key ally in the war on terror, and damage a nonproliferation regime that had been the linchpin of US arms control policy for over thirty years. The critics were wrong. In short order, Congress approved the agreement, citing India's need for safe nuclear power and hinting at the need to counterbalance the growing power of China in the region. Despite the new accord, the US State Department was quick to announce its continuing disapproval of India's nuclear weapons policy. Yet within days of the announcement in Washington, Indian prime minister Manmohan Singh reassured the Indian parliament that "there is nothing in the Joint Statement that amounts to limiting or inhibiting our strategic nuclear weapons program."[1] Although India's draft nuclear doctrine of 1999 had stated that "India shall continue its efforts to achieve the goal of a nuclear weapon-free world at an early date," it also had suggested that nuclear weapons were in India to stay: "Arms control measures shall be sought . . . to reduce potential threats and *to protect our own capability and its effectiveness.*"[2]

The events summarized above remind us that arms control is infused with politics at every level—international, national, and bureaucratic. This fundamental truth was perhaps less obvious during the Cold War when the need to preserve the strategic stability of the bipolar balance turned US-Soviet arms control discussions into highly technical exchanges on matters of throw weight and warhead numbers. But with the return of a more fluid international system, the enhanced effects of globalization, and the rise of nonstate actors in international relations, politics has returned to center stage in the conduct of arms control policy. It is politics of a transnational kind.

Political drivers and related institutional processes influence arms control policy. Without an understanding of these drivers, policymakers will lack an ability to anticipate the moves of others and cooperative security will suffer. As shocking as the Indian nuclear test was in 1998, those steeped in India's domestic politics and the dynamics of South Asia could have—and did—anticipate it. The same might be said of the George W. Bush administration's announcement in 2005. It would seem that one antidote for diplomatic surprise might be, as the saying goes, "keeping an ear to the ground."

This chapter uses the US case to illustrate how politics shapes arms control. The United States has a relatively open policy process and, because it has sustained a heavy national security burden since the early 1950s, it also offers a rich record of arms control negotiations. Although governments have practiced regulated war and weapons restraint for centuries, arms control may never have had as bold, vigorous, and enduring a champion as the post–World War II United States. After the defeat of Japan and Germany, the United States persistently advocated negotiated restraints in bilateral and multilateral diplomacy. American intellectuals developed new approaches to arms control theory and played a role in urging their application by policymakers. Since the early 1960s, arms control not only has permeated the postwar literature on national security, but has been tested repeatedly in practice. The US case also poses some of the most interesting questions when considering the politics of arms control. For example, why was Washington's intense commitment to arms control during the Cold War accompanied by the exponential growth, diversification, and proliferation of weapons arsenals? How did domestic forces contribute to a process at once both morally compelling and yet arcane and seemingly inconsequential in its outcomes during this period, at least at the strategic level? Sustained so unflinchingly during the bipolar contest with the Soviet Union, why is arms control now, during a period of increased international turbulence, of seemingly minimal interest to most Americans?

This chapter explores how domestic politics, especially strategic culture, institutions, prevailing economic and technological conditions, and public opinion influence the use of arms control as an instrument of foreign and defense policy. Although the international system shapes national leaders' perceptions of jeopardy, providing incentives for controlling the likelihood and destructiveness of war, domestic conditions affect how state officials use arms control as an instrument of foreign and defense policy.

The Domestic Context: Culture, Law, and Process

The fact that internal politics affects external behavior is an observation that Thucydides made about Greek city-states centuries ago; yet this insight is probably even more apt today as the cross-border flows of international finance, information, and technology have greased the mechanisms that cause local politics to reverberate internationally. For example, poor domestic management increases local crime rates within a state, and in today's connected world it presents vulnerabilities that put other states at risk. Thus, ineffective border security in Europe, poorly monitored chemical facilities in Africa, or lax accounting for nuclear materials in Asia can increase the risks of, and damage from, terrorist attacks against the United States. Modern arms control recognizes that these risks invite retaliatory or collaborative policies among states and seeks to manage them. Indeed, as ease of manufacture expands the definition of "arms" to include commercial or civil-scientific precursors—such as chemicals, biological organisms, enriched uranium, and the like—arms control increases in domestic importance and impact. The number of stakeholders for arms control policy increases correspondingly. The domestic politics of twenty-first-century arms control are therefore likely to be messy, making the negotiation of international treaties all the more problematic.

As a government considers an arms control initiative, it assesses each party's interest in reaching compromises and its abilities to abide by agreements, to implement them in a timely way, and to monitor the compliance of the other parties. Understanding such domestic factors helps negotiators find a marketable middle ground for all. A minor concession by one party might, in the domestic context of another, be seen as a huge win leading to unexpected agreement and enhanced security for both. Finding non–zero-sum solutions to national security dilemmas thus requires attentiveness to wide-ranging elements of the domestic context.[3] In this domain, four factors are of particular importance for arms control policy: (1) strategic culture; (2) the political and legal institutions for negotiating, concluding, and sustaining arms control agreements; (3) prevailing economic and technological conditions; and (4) the role of public opinion, particularly as it is expressed through key interest groups.[4]

Strategic Culture

A nation's strategic culture is composed of the ideals, interests, and propensities that influence decisionmakers as professionals and as citizens. Strategic culture, a subset of political culture, embodies those national paradigms of greatest relevance to national security. Strategic culture helps to explain why, in any given country, particular arms control solutions win; why they sometimes fail to be accepted abroad; and why, even when discredited, they may nevertheless regularly reappear. The keys to unlocking any country's strategic culture are the ideas, myths, and national beliefs that are regularly recorded in academic literature, the speeches of politicians, and the press releases of policy advocates.

Assessing a nation's strategic culture requires sensitivity to its historical, psychological, and religious components, including the impact of transcendent leaders and traumatic events. Strategic cultures are often shaped by geographic circumstance and the experience of repeated wars. Arguably, Israel's approach to security—what some have called its "security anxiety"—is derived from lessons of the Holocaust.[5] Despite winning conventional wars in 1949, 1967, and 1973, Israel has concluded that it needs nuclear weapons. Tel Aviv may now have as many as 100 to 170 of them, with the first obtained as early as 1966.[6] Clearly, Israel's strategic culture is infused with fear. In contrast, Pakistan's strategic culture has been shaped less by a unifying fear than by ethnic division. The need for national cohesion has led to a melding of militarism and Islam, especially after the 1971 war that led to an independent Bangladesh. For this reason, Pakistani prime minister Pervez Musharraf's 2002 speech rejecting terrorism and Pakistan's long-standing "Kalashnikov culture" was widely regarded as revolutionary. Until his resignation in 2008, the distinction he drew between foreign terrorists and violence related to Kashmir revealed the persistent cultural attitude that makes this notional "revolution" not nearly so certain.[7] Approaches to weapons restraint in states with strategic cultures as diverse as those of Israel and Pakistan are likely to be quite different.

The US case. In the United States, strategic culture has shaped attitudes toward weapons and war. Its impact was evident in the widespread acceptance of mutual assured destruction (MAD) as a force-sizing doctrine and formula for stability during the Cold War. Acceptance of MAD became almost a prerequisite for credibility in arms control circles during the 1960s and 1970s, culminating in the conclusion of the Anti-Ballistic Missile Treaty (ABM Treaty). This treaty institutionalized strategic vulnerability for both sides during the Cold War. Although arms control critics railed against negotiated restraint based on mutual vulnerability—calling it the United States' new civil religion—they constituted a minority for decades.[8] In fact, arms control advocates seemed to embrace the almost theological underpinning of the ABM Treaty, arguing that such belief systems were stabilizing if shared. According to this view, one of the purposes of negotiation should be to influence the strategic cultures of adversaries. The conclusion of the ABM Treaty seemed to signal success in this regard because it registered Moscow's willingness to deny itself nuclear superiority in the interest of stability. For arms controllers, the decision to abolish the ABM Treaty during the George W. Bush administration meant more than the loss of a particular accord; it meant the loss of the entire philosophical basis for agreed limits.

Yet in a larger sense, MAD was a transitory manifestation of deeper cultural proclivities that doomed agreements such as the ABM Treaty. These include a tradition of unilateralism, a belief in US exceptionalism based on scientific rationalism, and a decidedly "realist" orientation toward the exercise of power.

Unilateralism. Of these four aspects of strategic culture, the unilateralist impulse is perhaps best understood by Americans. Interest in preserving the country's freedom of action, articulated since George Washington's Farewell Address, has biased the American public against binding agreements with foreign powers. As President Woodrow Wilson discovered when he sought popular support for US entry into the League of Nations after World War I, even liberals and progressives of an internationalist bent could blanch at the prospect of tying the United States' fortunes to those of other nations.[9] It therefore should not be surprising that, to the extent that arms control has involved binding US defense policies to agreed and verifiable limits, limiting arms has often been a hard sell in the United States. The American public has easily endorsed morally symbolic agreements, such as the 1925 Geneva Protocol against the use of chemical weapons, but has not easily ratified treaties. Indeed, the first golden age of arms control, from the late 1950s to early 1960s, was built on an approach that denigrated formal agreements. Tacit agreements and signaling of defensive intentions became the tools of arms control policy; its objective—stability—required the maintenance of a bipolar equilibrium of power. Arms controllers became absorbed with maintaining each side's ability to obliterate the other with nuclear weapons and with preserving sufficient conventional capabilities so that lesser interests could be litigated without resort to nuclear war.[10]

Those formal agreements that were ratified during the Cold War were advocated as much for the military options they preserved as for those they foreclosed. The Limited Test Ban Treaty, for example, reduced environmental contamination but, in simply driving testing underground, hardly decelerated US efforts to develop new nuclear warheads. The 1968 NPT slowed nuclear proliferation without significant enforceable constraints on the United States and other nuclear weapon states (NWS). The Strategic Arms Limitation Treaties (SALT) contained the bipolar strategic competition within certain stabilizing parameters, but permitted both sides to expand their strategic nuclear weapons inventory and, significantly, to retain the technological option of pursuing multiple independently targetable reentry vehicles—the technology Washington believed would redress the strategic balance, which was then perceived as tilting dangerously in the Soviets' favor.

Until the Strategic Arms Reduction Treaty (START) negotiations of the late 1980s, few agreements had eliminated any options for the United States.

Exceptionalism. Closely tied to the American public's penchant for unilateralism has been an abiding faith in US exceptionalism, which is grounded in the values of liberty, freedom, and individualism enshrined in the US Constitution. This belief in exceptionalism is also based on confidence in the advantages of free enterprise and the American work ethic. A fusion of entrepreneurial spirit with moral purpose has led Americans to believe they are uniquely adept at solving complex problems—an opinion that accentuates the impulse to unilateralist solutions. Moreover, Americans expect that US technological development will tend to guide the choices of others and, left unconstrained, will naturally bring about results superior to those of their competitors. Such beliefs help explain the notion in the United States that the Soviets could be taught what a stabilizing force structure might look like and could be made to accept it by force of example as well as reason.

American confidence in US technological superiority, however, was repeatedly challenged throughout the Cold War. The first Soviet nuclear test in 1949, Soviet acquisition of thermonuclear weapons in 1953, and the *Sputnik* launch of 1957 fed a national paranoia that the Soviets must be stealing US secrets (which history has demonstrated they often did). Later, the Soviet challenge to US scientific prowess inspired not only US technological competitiveness, but also a certain respect for the adversary. The American public went from regarding the Soviet system as crude and unsophisticated in the late 1940s to viewing it as almost invulnerable as it teetered on the verge of collapse in the 1980s.

National leaders who have framed security programs compatible with the major elements of US strategic culture—particularly the notion of exceptionalism—have found the public to be a powerful ally. For example, few modern arms control and defense proposals have more quickly captured the American public's imagination than did President Ronald Reagan's 1983 Strategic Defense Initiative (SDI). The can-do spirit in Reagan's pursuit of space-related technologies is again evident in the debate today over national missile defense. As with the declared mission of sending a man to the moon, conceiving a technology can seem, in the American psyche, tantamount to acquiring it. This kind of technological confidence is awe inspiring among allies; for the American public, it is simply motivational. In fact, arms control has always fared best domestically when it has not prohibited the development of exciting technologies or adventures toward new frontiers. The United States likes to be first; it does not like to be told the finish line is unreachable.

Scientific rationalism versus realism. The American public has historically held reason and science in high regard. World War II accentuated this trend as the results of the Manhattan Project brought heightened stature to engineers and physicists. In the immediate postwar period, the American scientific ethic, which incorporates principles of universalism and openness, became infused with a potent internationalism. Émigré scientists who had fled excessively authoritarian regimes in Europe held deep suspicions of the state system. After the first atom bomb was dropped on Hiroshima, some of these scientists, articulating an ever-deepening distrust of the government's use of science for augmenting national power, warned that the United States ought not trust that its political or technological ingenuity could preserve nuclear peace. To these scientists, the nuclear age meant the end of exceptional states and the arrival of the imperative of world government and global disarmament.

Yet for others, the postwar stature of science brought new faith in scientific and social engineering. Respected physical scientists joined an increasing number of their behavioralist colleagues in the social sciences in applying scientific principles to the art of changing international society and managing—not abolishing—the nuclear weapons establishment. These scientists believed that the state system should not be ignored or abolished, but rather reorganized. In their view, arms control should be the instrument of such reform. David Lilienthal, chairman of the Tennessee Valley Authority in the 1940s and a chief architect of the first US effort to control the atom, advocated a scientific methodology and functionalist approach to controls. His disarmament plan, based on rigorous study of the scientific facts, was later endorsed by Bernard Baruch when the latter pressed his adaptation—the Baruch Plan—on the international community. By the mid-1960s, social and physical scientists had coalesced in arms control advocacy and study groups under the auspices of organizations such as the American Academy of Arts and Sciences (AAAS) and Pugwash. These scientists' influence on arms control literature throughout the postwar period was profound.

Although the special stature accorded scientific expertise was temporarily lost during the period of virulent anticommunism known as the McCarthy era, it reemerged during the later years of the Dwight D. Eisenhower administration with the establishment of the President's Science Advisory Committee. Such deference to experts was so strong and longlived that it may have contributed to public complacency as arms control became increasingly formulaic, expensive, and opaque to the American public during the 1970s and 1980s. By the time that SALT II was negotiated and Reagan was elected president, the arcane business of planning stabilizing strategic limitations had become politically rootless. The public's rapid endorsement of the Reagan administration's simpler proposals for strategic arms reductions and its extraordinary plan for strategic defense was arguably a reflection of the nation's faith in scientific expertise under a new guise.

Yet as strong as the scientific and rationalist themes have been in US strategic culture, their effects on national security and arms control policies have been neither monolithic nor uniform. Indeed, the influence of science on politics following World War II triggered an intellectual revolt by the realist school in the United States that has been regularly reflected in postwar arms control debates. Realist theorists objected to scientific rationalism's permeation of Western political culture as well as to the notion of exceptionalism so deeply ingrained in the US strategic psyche. For example, Hans J. Morgenthau, a political scientist at the University of Chicago, cautioned against US visions of sustainable superiority at the start of the Cold War. Morgenthau criticized excessive faith "in the power of science to solve all problems and, more particularly, all political problems which confront man in the modern age."[11] Morgenthau believed that the scientific community's universalistic, liberal bias had caused the decline of Western political thought since the eighteenth century. Indicative of this trend had been the rise of legalistic, ahistorically optimistic solutions to world order problems as epitomized by President Wilson's League of Nations and evolving notions of "scientific disarmament."[12]

As postwar efforts to achieve internationalist solutions to the arms race collapsed in the late 1950s, it was the joining of realist balance-of-power principles with rationalist methodologies that created the most powerful and cohesive arms control school of modern times. This theoretical approach dominated arms control and general strategic thought in the United States for more than two decades. The approach, designed for a bipolar contest between superpowers, treated strategic nuclear stability, not disarmament, as the primary objective of arms control and based weapons management and controls on the principles of MAD. With the collapse of Soviet power in the late 1980s, this approach gave way to new paradigms that, not surprisingly, were influenced by impulses both unilateralist and technological in nature.

Political and Legal Institutions

Knowledge of the intellectual backdrop to US arms control policy helps explain the texture of its defense and other weapons-related policies. Texture alone, however, cannot describe or predict outcomes for this state or any other. Ideas are the tools wielded by advocates; political processes determine who will have the opportunities to influence arms control outcomes. The internal institutional framework of a state affects the way that arms control is negotiated and the reliability of its implementation. Governments with strong executives tend toward greater flexibility and decisiveness in negotiations; those with effective legislatures offer enhanced confidence in the durability of agreements even as they may bring delays in their ratification and implementation. Similarly, states with civil societies shaped by strong traditions of legal process, including contract law, will tend to take international legal commitments more seriously than states with less well-grounded legal institutions. For example, the American public took the efforts to outlaw war between the two world wars quite seriously, an approach that aggressor nations arguably exploited.

When assessing the impact of political institutions on arms control processes, several cautionary points are in order. First, one must distinguish between real and what might be termed "Potemkin" structures such as legislatures without power or presidents who function more as symbols of the state than as its executive.[13] What matters is not the constitutional or formal structure of governance so much as the informal one—the way things really work. For example, though Pakistan has democratic traditions and both a president and parliament, its governing belief in an existential threat from India has led to the overwhelming influence of the armed forces, especially the army, in Pakistan's policy and governance.[14] Assessing policymaking in Pakistan without appreciating the role played by the military would be as misleading as considering institutional factors without the cultural underpinning of Islam that animates much of the country's politics.

Second, when assessing the impact of political institutions on arms control, cultural and normative predilections—say against the exercise of secret power in democracies—must be abandoned in favor of a clear-eyed assessment of roles and responsibilities of the players. The intelligence institutions of an adversary may be a measure not only of threat, but of that state's capacity to be a responsible arms control partner. One of the greatest dangers for leaders using the arms control instrument is the possibility of being duped (or of being perceived as being duped) by the other side. Arms control agreements can incorporate agreed procedures for data exchange while enhancing the capabilities and legitimacy of intelligence institutions among the parties concerned. In such circumstances, secrecy within domestic institutions may actually, if ironically, enhance transparency among states. During the Cold War, arms control agreements acknowledged "national technical means" for monitoring their terms. Stability was arguably enhanced by the confidence each side had in the other's intelligence capabilities. Strong intelligence institutions can thus arguably protect governments against irrational decisionmaking. Of course, weak or rampant intelligence systems can make democratic decisionmaking worse than it would otherwise be or cause political processes to be hijacked through the secret exercise of independent power. Similarly, stable and effective military institutions tend to enhance the viability of any accord, provided that they participate as a legitimate part of the government's decisionmaking processes.

The US case. The United States is governed by a system of checks and balances that often seems designed for stalemate, particularly in the field of arms control. During the period between the twentieth century's two world wars, US presidents successfully negotiated agreements with foreign governments, only to be foiled in getting them ratified at home. Even initially popular treaties foundered in the absence of conscious efforts to rally domestic interest groups and the support of key members of Congress. Thus, President Wilson lost in his effort to secure US participation in the League of Nations and President Calvin Coolidge failed to win ratification of the 1925 Geneva Protocol against chemical and bacteriological warfare, a US initiative that thirty nations had already signed. In contrast, as arms control became an institutionalized element of national security policy during the Cold War, intragovernmental negotiations over the formulation and ratification of arms control agreements became routine. These bureaucratic interactions, insofar as they forged compromises along the way, had a decisive impact on the shape of treaties and agreements as well as the evolution of the defense establishment.

The Office of the President. The US Constitution provides several instruments for concluding international arms control agreements: treaties, congressional-executive agreements, and presidential agreements. The first and second of these instruments are of greatest weight because they are legally interchangeable and, once concluded, constitute the law of the land.[15] In Article II, Section 2, the Constitution reads that the president "shall have the power, by and with the advice and consent of the Senate, to make treaties, provided two-thirds of the Senators present concur."[16]

With the power to make treaties, the president sets the overall pace and tone of an administration's arms control policy. If committed to an arms control agenda, the president can direct the national security advisor and the staff of the National Security Council to work aggressively to resolve differences among members of the cabinet; alternatively, this staff, despite having no line authority over executive branch departments, can hinder the process of reaching consensus. Because negotiators must have leverage to win favorable terms in any draft accord, arms control policymakers rely heavily on good access to the president and strong bureaucratic staff work. And it is the president's Office of Management and Budget that ensures that funding is available for programs essential to the monitoring and verification of any future agreement. The president can also counter political pressure to conclude an accord he does not favor by quietly withholding crucial support to a negotiation.

The president generally has delegated authority to negotiate treaties to the secretary of state who, in turn, has delegated these powers to specially appointed ambassadors, undersecretaries, and assistant secretaries. The president also has exercised the option to appoint special negotiators. The ability of the president to look outside government for expertise has, at times, caused tensions in the arms control community.

The State Department. Bureaucratic stature and access alone do not guarantee success for an arms control negotiator. Because national security policy involves a broad range of departments, successful policymaking requires consensus building. Presidential guidance and bureaucratic power also matter. In the later years of the Eisenhower administration, a cabinet-level committee advised the president on arms control policy. President Eisenhower's insistence on consensus decisions, however, meant that policymaking became paralyzed whenever disagreements ran deep.

By the end of the Eisenhower administration, the weakness of arms control policymaking was widely acknowledged. Congress created the Arms Control and Disarmament Agency (ACDA) in 1961 to mend perceived flaws in the institutional infrastructure. ACDA was to be a quasi-independent agency attached to the State Department, but with direct access to the president. The purpose behind ACDA was to lend bureaucratic weight to arms control interests within the executive branch and to provide Congress better access to information on policy developments.[17] Although other departments, including the State Department, originally concurred with this development, official opinion was deeply divided. Former secretary of defense Robert Lovett announced that the agency would be a "Mecca for a wide variety of screwballs." The Joint Chiefs of Staff (JCS) worried that the director's direct access to the president might undermine defense interests and national security policy. Senator Barry Goldwater opined that the United States was "developing a new mother-love type of agency."[18]

Not surprisingly, the bureaucratic influence of ACDA and its director waxed and waned over subsequent decades. ACDA's awkward position—being both within and outside the State Department—created tensions with Foggy Bottom that persisted through the SALT, START, and post–Cold War period. Its substantive bureaus overlapped with those of the State Department. Without an authoritative voice on relevant foreign policy issues or comprehensive intelligence support, ACDA tended to be eclipsed by the larger department on matters outside the confines of highly structured negotiations. ACDA's direct access to the president never consistently compensated for the handicap of having to operate on a day-to-day basis at the subcabinet level. Neither did it compensate for the exclusion from the deliberations of the National Security Council. Indeed, ACDA's longevity may have reflected the ease with which any president could effectively include or exclude it from inner policy circles. In 1993, Congress blocked the State Department from responsibility for arms control policy in a new bureau. But by 1999, the impulse to cut costs led to a merger that dismantled ACDA, but kept most of its functions intact within the department. The undersecretary for arms control and international security affairs now oversees three bureaus with arms control mandates: International Security and Non-Proliferation; Political-Military Affairs; and Verification Compliance and Implementation. High-profile regional negotiations are often conducted by the appropriate regional bureau with the support of the functional bureaus.[19]

The intelligence community. The US intelligence community plays a critical role at all stages of the arms control process. Apart from testifying before congressional committees on the government's ability to monitor compliance with a given accord, intelligence officials also must maintain adequate capabilities to support existing agreements, laws, and negotiations. The community funds research, technological development, and deployment of collection capabilities for existing and anticipated arms control measures to maximize the prospects for maintenance, negotiation, and ratification of agreements.

The critical support role that the intelligence community plays, however, can cause considerable friction with arms control policymakers. First, the intelligence community's assessments of monitoring capabilities with regard to a proposed treaty can undermine prospects for ratification. US intelligence, which has traditionally embodied such core American values as objectivity and balanced consideration of facts, wields a powerful voice in a rationalistic US strategic culture. To guard against the rise of unforeseen monitoring issues at the treaty ratification stage, modern presidents usually have required intelligence officers to work closely with delegations that are negotiating accords. But conflicts can develop as policymakers, eager to build a policy consensus on negotiating strategy, discover contrary intelligence community views. Charges of politicization have thus arisen from both supporters and opponents of arms control.[20]

Second, particularly in eras of budget downsizing, the intelligence community can make financial and budgetary decisions that affect prospects for an accord by underfunding research, development, and procurement of intelligence collection capabilities critical to monitoring it. Neither ACDA nor the State Department has ever had significant influence over intelligence-related budgets and programs, 80 percent of which are funded through the Department of Defense (DoD). Moreover, cuts by separate working-level program managers may make independent sense, yet collectively destroy a crucial monitoring capability. When negotiations begin, diplomats can be blindsided, on the one hand, or accused by Congress of being disingenuous on the other. State Department officials also may suspect that an accord opposed by DoD is being deliberately, if quietly, sabotaged in this budgetary manner. For these reasons, in 1996 the State Department created an Intelligence Resources Board, chaired by the Bureau of Intelligence and Research, designed to coordinate intelligence-related budgets and programs across bureaus and with other departments. The functional arms control bureaus were among the most vigorous users of this new coordination mechanism. In 1999, the department went further, creating the Office of Intelligence Resources Planning, reporting directly to the undersecretary of state for management.[21]

Third, the intelligence community, in its efforts to fulfill its statutory obligations to protect sources and methods, can object to or delay the use of intelligence to démarche a foreign government suspected of being in violation of a law or treaty. It also can object to sharing intelligence with international organizations dedicated to implementing safeguards and monitoring a control regime.

Fourth, since the establishment of the congressional intelligence oversight committees, the intelligence community has tended to regard Congress as a legitimate consumer of its products. Policymakers have often chafed at the willingness of intelligence officials to provide products and tailored briefings to individual members of Congress intent on building cases against an administration's arms control policies and appointments. Broad intelligence sharing on contentious topics risks disclosures from Capitol Hill; opponents of policy may reveal intelligence judgments out of context to disrupt negotiations.

Despite these sources of friction, the policy community has generally developed a close, complex, and healthy relationship with the US intelligence establishment. After the intelligence community's failure to accurately assess Iraq's stockpile of weapons of mass destruction (WMD) prior to the start of the Iraq war in 2003, a commission was established to investigate the problem. The commission concluded that, in many ways, US intelligence capabilities were strong. However, a tendency toward groupthink, a failure to test long-held assumptions, and the rising threat from terrorists intent on acquiring access to WMD demanded a new, more imaginative approach to assessing proliferation threats. The commission recommended the creation of a nonproliferation center in the new Office of the Director of National Intelligence to fuse all-source intelligence on WMD and to coordinate with the newly created National Counterterrorism Center. These new centers, which have broad mandates and community-wide participation, were established by statute in 2004 as part of the Intelligence Reform Act.

The military. DoD has been a major player in the US arms control process ever since arms control was distinguished from disarmament and accepted as an integral aspect of national security policy. Although this new approach to arms control began in the early 1950s with Undersecretary of State Dean

Acheson, it did not become institutionalized until the administration of President John F. Kennedy. By that time, arms control thought had progressed to the point where substantial weapons restraint was believed possible through manipulation of force deployment and doctrine alone. Under the leadership of Secretary of Defense Robert McNamara, DoD began using its annual statements on doctrine and budgets to signal to its adversary the US government's interest in stabilizing deployments and force-sizing concepts. Even though that approach to self-restraint was later largely abandoned, the Office of the Secretary of Defense has remained heavily involved in arms control policy.

Apart from the obvious stake military services have in weapons restraints, DoD's involvement in arms control derives from several interests. First, arms control strategy and policy can significantly affect force sizing, deployment, and doctrine. Negotiating strategies can drive defense policies and spending priorities by accelerating or decelerating weapons-building programs in order to create or deny "bargaining chips."[22] Members of the JCS testify separately on the military impact of treaties and are expected to give an unvarnished view. The JCS has, on occasion, opposed administration policies, almost always severely damaging the administration position by doing so.

Second, arms control's impact on regulatory, export, and security assistance policies can jeopardize the health of key industries in defense and high-tech commercial sectors. DoD has often weighed in strongly on Capitol Hill and in the executive branch to ensure that policymakers are aware when arms control policies may jeopardize technological capabilities in civilian and defense-related areas. To the extent that arms control infuses budgetary life into systems and technologies that DoD considers unnecessary, obsolete, or too costly, such congressional-industrial relationships work against DoD's interests.

Third, DoD also manages a substantial part of the monitoring infrastructure for arms control, including the On-Site Inspection Agency and its associated overseas gateways as well as the logistical infrastructure for providing access to foreign inspectors coming to the United States.[23] Therefore, any increase in monitoring activities has a direct impact on DoD budgets and personnel allocations.

Congress. Congress participates in the arms control process by shaping public opinion; ratifying treaties; regulating commerce (via export controls and sanctions); appropriating funds; and overseeing executive branch departments, including legislating changes in their organization, operations, and statutory authorities.[24] Congress's greatest arms control powers lie in its role in amending and ratifying treaties and passing executive agreements. Treaty ratification involves the Senate Foreign Relations Committee, Senate

Armed Services Committee, and Senate Select Committee on Intelligence. The Senate can add unilateral statements, such as reservations and declarations, that modify the legal effect of a treaty for the United States. Such steps can threaten to destroy the agreement, however, if other parties to the treaty object to the changes. Unilateral declarations may clarify an understanding or interpretation that is shared among the parties. Once treaties are concluded, however, most legal opinion holds that they can be terminated only by the president or by the president and Senate acting together.

Although the Constitution specifies no particular role for the House of Representatives in the treaty-making process, the implementation of treaties often requires the passage of domestic laws or appropriations of funds that require the involvement of the House.[25] In practice, the Senate and House work closely together as the relevant committees consider the terms of treaties and the implementing legislation they require. The Chemical Weapons Convention (CWC), signed in 1993 and ratified by the Senate in 1995, is an excellent example of a treaty demanding coordinated consideration. Although the convention itself technically required only the concurrence of the Senate, implementing legislation necessarily involved multiple committees in both chambers. Senators and representatives considered the impact of the convention's arrangements for on-site inspections of suspect facilities (which included private firms and households) on constitutionally protected privacy rights. Moreover, appropriations for funding the large bureaucracy necessary for handling the convention's national reporting requirements and for creating the international secretariat to administer the convention required House approval.

Both houses of Congress also are involved in the regulation of commerce and the provision of military assistance and foreign aid. Congressionally authorized and funded security assistance programs and annual authorization and appropriations acts have proven to be particularly attractive tools for sanctioning states that fail to abide by arms control norms.[26] The Arms Export Control Act, which authorizes the president to control the export of defense-related equipment and services, prohibits firms from marketing destabilizing and dangerous technologies and provides for punishment of those who do.

When Congress acts on any of its authorities, it almost always uses formal hearings or briefings to establish a historical and legal record. Given the opportunities that hearings provide for shaping subsequent votes on the floors of the House and Senate, presidents have been wise to co-opt key senators, representatives, and even congressional staff members in positions to influence the hearing process. The executive may offer concessions on political appointments, give in on legislative matters, and, perhaps most effectively, offer senators participation on delegations to the arms control talks. In return, senators may make public speeches of support and exert quiet influence through the process of selecting witnesses, timing hearings to the administration's advantage, and meeting with fence-sitting colleagues to trade favors and votes. Of course, a president who ignores Congress may have all these subtle efforts turned against him, resulting in a congressional momentum powerful enough to sink treaties once considered publicly popular. Such was the case with the Comprehensive Test Ban Treaty which, though publicly popular, suffered a quick defeat in Congress.

Industry exercises considerable power in Congress through its extensive lobbying efforts. Most major private sector firms have Washington-area offices that focus on courting congressional members and staff. They also keep in close contact with representatives from the districts and states that host their facilities. Industrial lobbying efforts equip politicians to shape decisions early and quietly. Lobbying techniques are often successful when used to shape the terms and timing of arms transfers. Arms control efforts are politically difficult for firms to oppose or alter once they come before Congress as matters of national security policy.

Of course, arms control has its industrial lobbyists too. Many of the firms that gain from weapons sales also gain from an expanded need for monitoring equipment; the platforms on which weapons ride such as unmanned aerial vehicles (UAVs), aircraft, or ships; and the new technological requirements these sensors and platforms generate for hiding weapons such as stealth and camouflage. This powerful connection between technological development and the politics of arms control suggests the need to consider economic issues in greater depth.

Economic and Technological Factors

Despite generating advances in surveillance capabilities, rapid technological change is not generally conducive to arms control. Today, for example, advances in biogenetics, artificial intelligence, robotics, and nanotechnology are revolutionizing strategy and warfare.[27] Although such advances, bleeding into weapon systems, may foster fears of an arms race and thus heighten public interest in controls, negotiated restraint is often frustrated by governments' uneven hold over these industries and the belief that a decisive technological advantage may lie just around the corner for one or both parties. The greater both sides' confidence in their ability to keep pace with the technological changes under way, the greater the likelihood that arms control proposals will be a cover for seeking unilateral advantage. This was arguably the case in the 1950s, for example, when Washington's formal disarmament initiatives satisfied a strong impulse to claim the moral high ground while allowing US industrialists to lead the way in explosive technologies, warhead miniaturization, and ballistic missiles.

Capitalist economies are particularly sensitive to limitations on industrial production that affect military strength and mobilization capacities in time of war. In the United States, for example, a comprehensive nuclear test ban has long been opposed by those who fear that, without tests to perform, the domestic infrastructure for weapons research and development would wither, scientists would look elsewhere for jobs, and inequalities in capabilities would result. Such economic fallout would seem to be less problematic for command economies, which can ensure that industries keep producing despite controls placed on them. In fact, as long as the controls hold, these economies pay indirectly by retaining talented labor resources where they are not needed. The only immediate benefit for affected firms, at least in democracies, may be the public relations gains of having aligned themselves with the national interest and popular norms at the apparent expense of near-term profits. In any event, arms control can have the indirect effect of sustaining inefficient foreign military-industrial sectors in command economies while degrading the domestic industries of the democratic parties involved in an agreement.

Economic conditions may also mitigate the effects of technological change on arms control incentives. In prosperous times, commercial industries may exercise their lobbying powers to dissuade political leaders from starting conflicts or raising tensions among trading partners.[28] The process of globalization has tied the health of local industries more tightly than ever to the welfare of foreign firms. An economic downturn at home or among trading partners can make new military capabilities prohibitively costly, increasing the attractiveness of negotiated restraint.

These economic effects are not particularly new. Indeed, some critics of arms control have argued that the negotiations pursuant to the SALT and START talks prolonged the economic viability of the Soviet regime by lowering the cost of competition while providing the prestige of so-called summit diplomacy. Arms control advocates have responded that strategic nuclear stability—not economic destabilization—was the principal purpose of these negotiations. From this perspective, arms control objectives may actually be served by an adversary's improved economic condition if that would lower the risk of preemptive attack, internal instabilities, or the forced export of destabilizing technologies. A key ingredient in multilateral efforts to dissuade North Korea from its pursuit of nuclear weapons, for example, was the offer of economic incentives such as oil shipments. Critics have called this bribery; negotiators call it bargaining.

The US case. In the United States, industry exhibits all the entrepreneurialism, lobbying capacity, and incentive-driven research and development that one might expect in a liberal, capitalist setting. Yet in recent years, the division between defense-related and strictly commercial firms seems heightened. The former, wedded to large-scale government contracting, invests considerable resources in influencing defense-related procurements and policy. The latter produce dual-use technologies whose success in the commercial market matters more to the firms' long-term profitability than prospects of government acquisitions. Unfortunately, these dual-use technologies are emerging as the most destabilizing and dangerous—from chemical and biological products to robotics and artificial intelligence. Controlling weapons, as traditionally defined, is one thing. Controlling the technologies that underpin teenagers' Xbox systems or farmers' disease-resistant crops is another. The industrial infrastructure for defense, and thus arms control, is shifting in ways that liberal democracies and the United States, in particular, will find difficult to manage.

The impact of this change on arms control strategies is only beginning to be recognized. When Cold War competition led the US government to finance large-scale weapons and intelligence projects in the mode of the Manhattan Project, industry responded by developing a capacity for working in secret for a limited client set: federal contracting departments, such as DoD, and their program managers. The military services were joined by the Atomic Energy Commission (later the Department of Energy), the Central Intelligence Agency, and the National Reconnaissance Office. The last two developed particularly close relationships with trusted firms through the use of sole source contracts that permitted sensitive capabilities to be procured with minimal competition. The result was a tightly bound relationship between industry and government that, as early as the 1950s, President Eisenhower famously referred to as "the military-industrial complex."

By the end of the Cold War and with the acceleration of digital information processing, however, the commercial sector was becoming an important engine of defense-related technological advances. Government agencies sponsoring ballistic missile defense (BMD) networks and orbiting spy satellites seemed of decreasing importance relative to the new interest in distributed capabilities, technologies for rapid scaling, and net-centric warfare. Reduced funding and a shifting strategic context for large capital projects also made the larger government projects seem of uncertain merit. The rise in importance of knowledge management, including inferencing engines for fusing huge volumes of information into meaningful messages and communications capabilities that permit appliances to talk to each other, have redefined the relationship between government—now in catch-up mode—and industry, which is now shaping as much as responding to the new military environment. Controlling such commercial technologies had once seemed less feasible than beating adversaries in applying them. Yet even before the 9/11 attacks, Washington recognized that individual terrorists could adopt these commercial capabilities faster than US government agencies could do so. What had long made US industry exceptional—a capacity to tinker, innovate, and sell—is now making terrorists exceptionally powerful; but crippling the latter through constraints on the former is neither feasible nor desirable. In such an environment, the influence of industry on government is both increasingly powerful and potentially disruptive. Larger defense-oriented firms are fighting for niches as prime contractors, but they also recognize that the commercial winners will be those that identify the best start-ups and commercial technologies to adapt to military needs.

Elites, Interest Groups, and Public Opinion

Arms control involves two parallel political processes: negotiations with foreign powers and internal negotiations among competing domestic interest groups and bureaucracies. Military dictatorships may have the easiest time dealing with this problem; they control the arms control process, the influence of advisers, and the reaction of the press (if it exists) by fiat. In contrast, democracies with protected speech and an independent media can be heavily affected by expressions of public interest.[29] The complicated politics and economics of arms control draw the attention of interest groups from all parts of the political spectrum and private industry. Depending on the stakes involved and these groups' organizational skills and resources, a marketplace for ideas can emerge that results in imaginative and often controversial arms control solutions.

Technological changes have expanded the organizational capacities of interest groups to affect governmental decisionmaking beyond traditional state boundaries. The rise of what some have called "civil society" and others have called "smart mobs" was perhaps best symbolized by the grant of the Nobel Peace Prize to the International Campaign to Ban Landmines (ICBL).[30] In bringing about a ban on landmines in less than five years, the ICBL marked a new stage in the role of transnational interest groups in arms control policy. Yet the receipt of the prize money was delayed by almost a year because the ICBL was not a legal entity. "It was an amorphous network of nongovernmental organizations (NGOs), not registered as an entity anywhere in the world."[31] These highly diverse, networked, and mobile interest groups use the Internet to acquire information quickly and assemble subject matter experts rapidly on emerging issues.

Civil groups of this kind are taking a growing place alongside more traditional research institutions devoted to defense-related issues such as arms control. The arcane nature of weapons-related issues during the Cold War generally meant that the most influential private sector opinion leaders on arms control were well-known scientific and technical experts. The better the ties these individuals had within their governments, the more influential their views tended to be. In democracies and the United States in particular, this reliance on expertise for making and marketing arms control as well as larger defense policy led to the proliferation of advisory institutes affectionately known in Washington as think tanks.

The US case. In the United States, private research organizations increased dramatically in number during the Cold War, helping to frame often arcane and technical debates in lay terms. The impetus for their creation came from a concerned citizenry (that formed groups such as Ground Zero and the Federation of American Scientists), military services interested in linking strategic concepts to force planning (via studies done at research centers such as the RAND Corporation), and former bureaucrats turned policy advocates who were waiting for their chance to return to the executive branch. Some of these institutes were created specifically to support or counter the arms control process. These issue-based organizations have blanketed Capitol Hill with leaflets and briefings detailing positions and talking points on particular accords. Some have acted in quiet ways to prevent presidents from either intentionally or unintentionally killing negotiations or treaties. For example, the prospects for timely ratification of the CWC were substantially improved by the role that the Washington-based think tanks played in informing the congressional staff, thereby keeping the CWC alive between the George H. W. Bush and Clinton administrations. The Henry L. Stimson Center, in particular, provided a repository of expertise on the CWC that likely would have been lost when Democrats in the Clinton administration cleaned house within the executive branch after twelve years of Republican rule.

In the rough and tumble of intragovernmental negotiations on arms control, the primary facilitator and sometimes agitator has been the media. The media report on developments in negotiations, characterize the issues at stake, report on the outcome of hearings, and publish leaks. Informally, the press helps power brokers make contact with one another.[32] The press also shapes public attitudes to treaties. Although the American public is sympathetic to arms control purposes in general, it can strongly oppose particular treaties if they are characterized as sacrificing a US strategic advantage or are concluded by an administration that appears weak or untrustworthy on other grounds.

The Politics of Arms Control in an Age of Transitional Threat

The serious strategic threat that provided the backdrop for all post–World War II US arms control debates dissipated in 1991. With the international distribution of power in flux, the United States faces an era in which domestic and transnational trends will shape arms control and national security policies in new and potentially disturbing ways. Three of the more salient trends include: (1) the new dominance of the US unilateralist impulse, tempered by an uncharacteristic American pessimism since the attacks in 2001 and the launching of the war in Iraq; (2) the revolutions in information, biogenetic, and materials technologies; and (3) the merging of law enforcement with private sector surveillance for national security purposes.

Unilateralism and Pessimism

Recent US foreign policy reflects a new preference for going it alone on matters of international importance. This trend was evident in the George W. Bush administration's approaches to global warming, the Balkans, and national missile defense, and, arguably, its launching of the war against Saddam Hussein's regime in Iraq.

The return of the US preference for independent action is not simply a reflection of a unipolar international system. It is, in part, a reaction to the advent of what might be an emerging international political culture that is sometimes at odds with US preferences. The international institutions that Washington helped build after World War II have developed a measure of independence from US control. Multilateral regimes in the areas of arms control, human rights, international law, trade, and environmental affairs have begun to generate transnational norms backed by international organizations with growing authority overseas. Other states, including traditional US allies, are increasingly emboldened to levy judgments on US preferences and actions that most Americans believe remain their sovereign concern.

The preference for unilateral action also reflects a new existential fear in the American body politic—a fear that has led to a measure of apathy regarding federal incursions into local affairs and complacency regarding loss of privacy for the purposes of national security. In the age of terror, public passions for security have seemed more important than long-held beliefs in privacy, expertise, and even entrepreneurialism.

The implications of this trend for arms control are fairly clear, albeit controversial. To the extent that the political leadership in Washington ties its opposition to arms control treaties to the instinct to resist binding ties, it may succeed in gaining public support for eschewing formal arms control in favor of unilateral action. Yet the need to reduce the threat from rogue states and terrorists will keep arms control issues alive and, in the changing international system, drive the United States to multilateral solutions to problems posed by North Korea and Iran—both past dealers in terrorism. Moreover, the need to reduce military costs while fighting worldwide terror seems to be driving the Barack Obama administration to seek new partnerships that require compromising arms control precepts, such as those embedded in the deals with India and Pakistan, while continuing to seek arms reductions through reciprocal unilateral measures. The chance this shift will be enduring will increase if political leaders successfully ascribe faith in the feasibility of reciprocal unilateralism to the public's remaining faith in US exceptionalism—that is, the belief that, in any unconstrained competition, the United States can triumph by dint of pluck and skill.

Yet this case may be getting harder to make. Whereas in 2002, 74 percent of Americans agreed that "we can always find a way to solve our problems and get what we want," that percentage had fallen to 58 percent by 2007.[33] The collapse of the World Trade Center on 9/11, the government's failed response to Hurricane Katrina, the war in Iraq, and even the I-35W bridge collapse in Minnesota, which cast doubt on the stability of bridges in general, have lent a deep pessimism to what has traditionally been an optimistic American national self-image. To the extent that Americans perceive that they cannot face their existential threats alone, the idea of cooperative security bolstered by arms control regimes may gain more adherents.

Technological Change, Law Enforcement, and National Security

The effects of the technological revolution under way are profound in multiple arenas, including information, bioengineering, and commercial space-based technologies and manufacturing. In some ways, this revolution is likely to improve the prospects for arms control. The Internet offers new ways to collect open source (unclassified) information. Such advances can improve the capacity of governments and individuals to monitor and verify agreements. To the extent that the United States continues to favor unilateralist approaches to arms control, a rebalancing of collection efforts will be necessary; absent the data exchanges involved in more formal accords, demands on intelligence gathering to monitor tacit agreements are high.

The expansion of the Internet and related information technologies, however, is also creating new vulnerabilities for the United States. National networks such as the nation's electrical grid, air traffic controls, border security, and communications have become computer dependent. If the public and policymakers become convinced that the primary threats to US security will be unconventional attacks against these vulnerable nodes and not traditional battlefields, classic arms control negotiations may become, if not irrelevant, something of a sideshow. In their place will likely evolve complex transnational approaches to cooperative security. For example, advances in biotechnology will likely make germs increasingly susceptible to tinkering in any country's domestic laboratories. Industries developing these technologies also will be at the cutting edge of advances in health, agriculture, and environmental protection. Thus, arms controllers' efforts to constrain the threat will involve capabilities that are, more than ever before, tied to concepts of public good as opposed to militarism. And monitoring accords will involve civilian industries, not only defense-related ones. Controls on biological weapons (BW) will require unprecedented cooperation between civilian entities and national security establishments worldwide.

The United States will likely find that its arms control efforts increasingly involve negotiations with collaborators—governments wrestling with their own industrial interests, weapons precursors, and porous borders—and not just adversaries. Alliances with civilian groups, including NGOs and more elusive networks such as the ICBL, will grow in importance. Such allies will be needed because the steps that must be taken to control and ultimately defend against chemical and biological weapons (CBW) and their precursors will require rethinking the operations of institutions largely regarded as civilian, including law enforcement. National security and domestic policies, increasingly overlapping, will generate broad national concern about federal prerogatives, as has already been apparent with the creation of the Department of Homeland Security and recent talk of building a more robust domestic intelligence capability.

Conclusion

Although international politics help to explain why states conclude arms control agreements, the particulars—including the content and timing of negotiations—turn on domestic politics and processes. In democracies great ideas do matter, particularly if they resonate with the popular political culture. If policymakers are to rely on an appreciation of strategic culture in framing approaches to national security policy and arms control, they must recognize the importance of strategic culture while avoiding the fallacy that such cultures are immutable. The art of leadership in the national security domain involves more than salesmanship; it can be transformative.

The foregoing discussion includes only some of the political forces and trends that will challenge US arms control and national security policymakers during the coming decades. Of course, other features may again come to the fore. An appreciation of how arms control policy is framed within any state requires analysis of generic factors (such as bureaucratic politics and economic drivers) as well as the unique (such as a nation's strategic culture). The weaving of these threads will produce, for every state, a fabric of strength, elasticity, or weakness in which basic patterns tend to repeat themselves and certain qualities seem dominant. The best negotiators are the ones who have a feel for not only the fabric of their collaborators' and their enemies' polities, but also their own.

Notes

1. Wade Boese, "Bush Promises India Nuclear Cooperation," *Arms Control Today* (September 2005), available at www.armscontrol.org/act/2005_09/USIndia 9-05.

2. Emphasis added by the author. Draft doctrine available in *Arms Control Today* (July/August 1999), available at www.armscontrol.org/act/1999_07-08/ffja99.

3. Arguably, this careful balancing of needs was accomplished in the 1994 Agreed Framework Between North Korea and the United States: the United States "won" a freeze and monitoring of Pyongyang's nuclear weapons program; North Korea "won" enhanced international standing and desperately needed domestic energy supplies. A conflict that seemed irresolvable gave way to a bargain that defined security needs broadly enough to take domestic factors into account. Although the incoming George W. Bush administration disliked the implicit trade, it struck a similar deal in early 2007.

4. These factors interact with each other in important ways. For example, a representative democracy with a legalistic strategic culture may take longer to ratify a treaty or to extract itself from prior commitments than will a dictatorship. The "stickiness" of arms control policies in legalistic democracies like the United States will be more apparent in a rapidly changing strategic environment than in a more static one. Whereas US arms control critics are troubled by the resulting lags in military responsiveness to changing international conditions, advocates have noted that having institutionalized rules of the road can help in the management of what would otherwise be an unpredictable and potentially threatening strategic environment. Arguably, the collapse of the Soviet Union would have been more destabilizing if strategic arms control accords had not been in place, the monitoring of which indicated that the former Soviet republics intended to abide by the Soviet Union's international commitments.

5. Joseph Cirincione, *Bomb Scare: The History and Future of Nuclear Weapons* (New York: Columbia University Press, 2007), pp. 52–53. Cirincione cited Avner Cohen who had made the same point in *Israel and the Bomb* (New York: Columbia University Press, 1988), p. 10.

6. Cirincione, *Bomb Scare*, pp. 52–53.

7. Husain Haqqani, *Pakistan: Between Mosque and Military* (Washington, DC: Carnegie Endowment for International Peace, 2005), pp. 1–3.

8. The concept of mutual assured destruction suggested that each of the two strategic nuclear powers (the Soviet Union and the United States) needed only enough nuclear weapons to strike back with a devastating (incapacitating) blow if struck first by the other. It was a doctrine designed to describe what level of capacity was enough, not how that capacity would in fact be used.

9. William C. Widenor, "The League of Nations Component of the Versailles Treaty," in Michael Krepon and Dan Caldwell, ed., *The Politics of Arms Control Treaty Ratification* (New York: St. Martin's Press, 1991), pp. 17–64.

10. The guidelines for the US strategic building program designed to assure US deterrence at a reasonable cost became, when projected onto a bipolar map, arms control's formula for strategic stability: MAD. The formula for raising the nuclear threshold to minimize the prospect of a strategic exchange included the deployment of significant conventional and tactical nuclear forces to Europe (the doctrine of flexible response) and a vigorous nonproliferation program. Force building and weapon restraint went hand in hand.

11. Hans J. Morgenthau, *Scientific Man Versus Power Politics* (Chicago: University of Chicago Press, 1946), p. vi.

12. Jennifer E. Sims, *Icarus Restrained: An Intellectual History of Nuclear Arms Control, 1945–1960* (New York: Westview, 1991), p. 61. See also Hans J. Morgenthau, "The H-Bomb and After," *Bulletin of Atomic Scientists* (March 1950): 76–79.

13. Grigori Aleksandrovich Potemkin (1739–1791) was a Russian statesman and field marshal who reportedly constructed fake building facades so that Catherine the Great would not see the poverty of the towns through which she was traveling.

14. John H. Gill, "India and Pakistan: A Shift in the Military Calculus?" in Ashley J. Tellis and Michael Wills, eds., *Strategic Asia 2005–06: Military Modernization in an Age of Uncertainty* (Seattle: National Bureau of Asian Research, 2005), p. 253.

15. Unlike treaties, congressional-executive agreements may be ratified by majorities of both houses of Congress. The Supreme Court has found such agreements to have the same domestic legal authority as treaties. Presidential agreements, which are based on powers that inhere only in the executive, do not.

16. For excellent legal background on the treaty-making process and other matters of law related to arms control, see John Norton Moore, Fredrick S. Tipson, and Robert E. Turner, *National Security Law* (Durham, NC: Carolina Academic Press, 2006).

17. The White House, citing executive privilege, had often denied Congress important information while the Departments of State and Defense have tended to relegate arms control to a second-order priority.

18. Duncan L. Clarke, *Politics of Arms Control: The Role and Effectiveness of the US Arms Control and Disarmament Agency* (New York: Free Press, 1979), pp. 22–23.

19. Thus, Christopher R. Hill, assistant secretary for East Asian and Pacific affairs had the lead in negotiations with North Korea over its nuclear weapons program.

20. Such charges were evident during the debate over whether to sanction Pakistan under the Symington amendment for having developed a nuclear explosive device. The intelligence community repeatedly stressed then, and on other occasions, that its job is to expose what is known, but not to pass judgment on whether any given set of facts is sufficient for triggering sanctions.

21. I was the first coordinator of Intelligence Resources Planning and was given department-wide authorities. Working groups were established to monitor the funding levels for certain sensors deemed crucial for effective verification of strategic arms control treaties.

22. Bargaining chips are assets brought to the negotiating table primarily to be used as items for trade during discussions with one's competitor.

23. Federal Bureau of Investigation and Defense Department counterintelligence operations are also engaged in protecting US military and industrial secrets from foreign spies who might be participating in such inspections.

24. The role of Congress in this regard is not always altruistic; committees (and individual senators and representatives) have been known to redirect monies and programs from one agency to another, more in the interest of wresting legislative power from other, weaker committees than in the interest of broader national purpose. For example, after 9/11, Congress moved rather swiftly to reform intelligence agencies as recommended by the 9/11 Commission, but was unable to ration-

alize their oversight on Capitol Hill, arguably because of competing jurisdictional interests. See L. Brit Snider, "Congressional Oversight of Intelligence after September 11" in Jennifer E. Sims and Burton Gerber, eds., *Transforming US Intelligence* (Washington, DC: Georgetown University Press, 2005), pp. 239–258.

25. Although legal opinions have varied on the subject, it is generally agreed that the House may not refuse to pass laws or appropriate funds for treaties signed by the president and ratified by the Senate. However, in practice, the senators' close consultations with House colleagues have meant that controversial funding and legal provisions have been dealt with collegially and as part of the ratification process to avoid congressional division and abrogation of obligations. Moore, Tipson, and Turner, *National Security Law*, pp. 792–796.

26. Security assistance generally refers to programs associated with the Arms Export Control Act and Part 2 of the Foreign Assistance Act (22 USC SS 2751-276c, 1982 and SS2301-2349aa-b 1982). These programs have changed in scope, character, and geographic orientation since World War II. Although their scope has grown overall, grants have given way to sales on credit, and assistance has spread from Europe to East Asia and the Middle East. Michael John Matheson, "Arms Sales and Economic Assistance," in Moore, Tipson, and Turner, *National Security Law*, pp. 1111–1125.

27. This particular list of desirable, yet troubling, technologies was suggested by Henry Crumpton, former counterterrorism coordinator at the State Department from 2005 to 2007.

28. For example, Thomas Friedman has suggested that Indian firms weighed in heavily to damp down rising tensions between New Delhi and Islamabad over Kashmir. See Thomas L. Friedman, *The World Is Flat: A Brief History of the Twenty-first Century* (New York: Farrar, Strauss and Giroux, 2005), pp. 425–429.

29. For an important study of the impact of public opinion on arms control, see Jeffrey Knopf, *Domestic Society and International Cooperation: The Impact of Protest on US Arms Control Policy* (Cambridge: Cambridge University Press, 1998).

30. See Howard Rheingold, *Smart Mobs: The Next Social Revolution* (Cambridge, MA: Perseus, 2002); Ann M. Florini, ed., *The Third Force: The Rise of Transnational Civil Society* (Washington, DC: Carnegie Endowment for International Peace, 2000).

31. Motoko Mekata, "Building Partnerships Toward a Common Goal: Experiences of the International Campaign to Ban Landmines," in Florini, *The Third Force*, pp. 143–176.

32. Members of the press sometimes brought players in the SALT negotiations together for a back-channel reconciliation or joining of the issues, which occasionally led to resolutions. Strobe Talbott, *The Master of the Game: Paul Nitze and the Nuclear Peace* (New York: Alfred A. Knopf, 1988), pp. 151, 353.

33. The polls were conducted by Pew Research with backup annual data by Marist College Institute for Public Opinion. See John McQuaid, "The Can't Do Nation: Is American Losing Its Knack for Getting Big Things Done?" *Washington Post,* 5 August 2007, p. B1.

Suggested Readings

Caldwell, Dan, *The Dynamics of Domestic Politics and Arms Control: The SALT II Treaty Ratification Debate* (Columbia: University of South Carolina Press, 1991).

Florini, Ann, *The Third Force: The Rise of Transnational Civil Society* (Washington, DC: Carnegie Endowment for International Peace, 2000). A general read on the impact of transnational forces on domestic politics.

Graham, Thomas Wallace, "The Politics of Failure: Strategic Nuclear Arms Control, Public Opinion, and Domestic Politics in the United States, 1945–1980" (Ph.D. diss., Massachusetts Institute of Technology, June 1989), available at http://dspace.mit.edu/bitstream/1721.1/13981/1/23072110.pdf.

Knopf, Jeffrey, *Domestic Society and International Cooperation: The Impact of Protest on US Arms Control Policy* (Cambridge: Cambridge University Press, 1998). See, particularly, Chapter 2, "Protest and Arms Control: A First Look," and Chapter 3, "A Framework for Assessing Activism's Influence," pp. 28–78.

Krepon, Michael, and Dan Caldwell, *The Politics of Arms Control Treaty Ratification* (New York: Palgrave Macmillan, 1992).

Nacht, Michael, "The Politics: How Did We Get Here?" in Alexander T. J. Lennon, ed., *Contemporary Nuclear Debates: Missile Defenses, Arms Control, and Arms Races in the Twenty-First Century* (Cambridge: MIT Press, 2002), pp. 3–11.

Platt, Alan, *The Politics of Arms Control and the Strategic Balance* (Santa Monica, CA: RAND, 1982).

Sims, Jennifer E., *Icarus Restrained: An Intellectural History of Nuclear Arms Control, 1945–1960* (Boulder: Westview, 1990).

5

New Directions in Strategic Nuclear Arms Control

Forrest E. Waller Jr.

In June 2007, the Ronald Reagan Building in Washington, DC, was the site of the world's largest conference of experts on nonproliferation and arms control. At the conference, the UK's secretary of state for foreign and commonwealth affairs, the Right Honourable Margaret Beckett, challenged the international community to recommit itself to an old vision: the total abolition of nuclear weapons. In proclaiming this vision as the objective of British foreign and national security policy, she acknowledged the difficulty of achieving this goal and admitted that the underlying political conditions for nuclear disarmament do not currently exist. Nevertheless, Beckett equated the need to shape the international security environment in favor of nuclear disarmament with humanity's effort to end one of its greatest evils—chattel slavery—and said it was time for the nuclear powers to restore humanity's faith in nuclear disarmament. Beckett stated:

> There are some who are in danger of losing faith in the possibility of ever reaching that goal. That would be a grave mistake. The judgment we made forty years ago, that the eventual abolition of nuclear weapons was in all of our interests, is just as true today as it was then. For more than 60 years, good management and good fortune have meant that nuclear arsenals have not been used. But we cannot rely on history just to repeat itself. It would be a grave mistake, too. It underestimates the power that commitment and vision can have in driving action. A parallel can be drawn with some of those other decades-long campaigns conducted as we strive for a more civilized world.
>
> When William Wilberforce began his famous campaign, the practice of one set of people enslaving another had existed for thousands of years. He had the courage to challenge that paradigm; and in so doing he helped to bring an end to the terrible evil of the transatlantic slave trade. Would he have achieved half as much, would he have inspired the same fervour in others if he had set out to "regulate" or "reduce" the slave trade rather than abolish it? I doubt it.[1]

No senior US officials were present to hear Beckett's speech. No senior US official attended the conference. In that regard, the conference stands as a metaphor for US strategic arms control policy at the beginning of the twenty-first century. After two generations of effort to control and reduce nuclear weaponry, and after conspicuous success in doing so, US national security policy has largely abandoned traditional nuclear arms control as a tool of security policy and an objective of US diplomacy.

For fifty years, the reduction of strategic nuclear arms was the crown jewel of US arms control efforts. The Cold War ideological and military standoff between the United States and the Soviet Union made arms control nearly impossible, but also clarified why the effort was essential. Eventually, perseverance paid off. Strategic nuclear arms control became one of the most successful arenas of US-Soviet cooperation. Moreover, the effects of that cooperation contributed to an unanticipated boon. When the Soviet Union dissolved unexpectedly, enough confidence had developed between the leadership of both societies that an international crisis over Soviet survival never occurred.

Although the Cold War ended almost two decades ago, two great paradoxes have arisen since its conclusion. First, more states than ever before are interested in nuclear weapons, and, second, the United States and Russia have abandoned strategic nuclear arms control and have begun to dismantle their arms control accomplishments. We are obliged to ask, Why? Why has an enterprise so spectacularly successful only a short time ago ended so unceremoniously? Is abandonment the new direction that strategic nuclear arms control will take? Or, will Beckett's vision mark a new course change?

This chapter explores the history and future of strategic nuclear arms control. It examines contemporary arguments against pursuing additional nuclear arms control arrangements with Moscow as well as alternate futures for the entire arms control enterprise. The purpose of such a forecast is analytic and didactic. Four plausible directions describe the objectives, expected outcomes, and strengths and weaknesses of a spectrum of arms control futures. By understanding them, we can see an integrated picture of strategic nuclear arms control—past, present, and future.

The Problem of Terminology

When discussing strategic nuclear arms control, one faces the immediate problem of defining the relevant terms. This chapter uses two terms interchangeably—*strategic nuclear arms control* and *strategic offensive arms control.*

International arms control specialists cannot always agree on a precise definition for the terms strategic nuclear arms and strategic offensive arms. So the term, strategic nuclear arms control, means different things to different people.[2] For some, the word *nuclear* is the key to the definition. Explosive nuclear yield is the operative element describing the weapons that must be controlled. For others, the *arm or delivery platform* is the key. Strategic nuclear arms, for example, are intercontinental delivery systems equipped to carry nuclear weapons. For another group, the *target* is the operative element. A strategic nuclear weapon is one targeted to explode on one's homeland or the homeland of the opponent. For a final group, the term *offensive arms* is crucial. Those who build nuclear bombs fear that nuclear arms control negotiations inevitably will reveal sensitive information about nuclear weapon designs. They would prefer to avoid reference to nuclear arms altogether and simply list the weapon systems under political control (e.g., the US B-2 heavy bomber).

The US government combines approaches to reach its definition of what is to be addressed in negotiations. Strategic offensive arms are intercontinental delivery vehicles equipped to deliver nuclear weapons. The United States identifies these systems by name (e.g., Russia's SS-27 intercontinental ballistic missile and the US Minuteman III intercontinental ballistic missile). As used in this chapter, strategic nuclear arms control and strategic offensive arms control refer to the same thing: the imposition of political or legal constraints on the arms designated to carry out intercontinental nuclear warfare.

The History of Strategic Arms Control Policy

An American college student studying international affairs today probably has no recollection of the Cold War and has not lived a day during which the United States was not the most powerful nation on Earth. Earlier generations of Americans, however, had a different experience.

Beginning in the mid-1940s, even before World War II had ended, the United States and the Soviet Union became rivals in a struggle for global political hegemony. Each society saw the struggle as a contest for national survival. Even though the United States had emerged as the strongest of the victors at war's end, a pervasive sense of decline in relation to the Soviet Union assaulted Americans with each news headline. The evolution of US strategic arms control policy reflected the intensity of the struggle between the two superpowers. Nuclear weapons affected nearly every aspect of US-Soviet relations, making normal bilateral relations nearly impossible. In particularly tense times, nuclear arms control talks occasionally were the only diplomacy taking place between the two antagonists.

Multilateral Efforts to Control Nuclear Arms (1945–1967)

On 16 July 1945, the United States detonated the world's first nuclear explosive device at the Trinity Test Site near Alamogordo, New Mexico. The detonation, small by current standards, was the equivalent of 21,000 tons of high explosives. Among the handful of US political, military, and scientific leaders who knew about the test, the atomic bomb caused grave concern about the future. Most understood that the United States could not base its security indefinitely on its monopoly of atomic weapons. Eventually, other states would develop them and pose a threat to national survival.

The Truman and Eisenhower administrations. In September 1945, Secretary of War Henry L. Stimson proposed to President Harry S. Truman that the United States discuss the control and limitation of atomic weapons with the Soviet Union. In March 1946, an interagency group met at Dumbarton Oaks in Washington, DC, to develop the first US nuclear arms control proposal, one calling for complete nuclear disarmament. The major alternative to arms control was nuclear deterrence—peace through the threat of devastating nuclear retaliation.

When confronted with the difficult choice between a path of nuclear arms control and a path of nuclear deterrence programs, President Truman set a precedent that other presidents would follow for decades: he chose both. In mid-1946, Truman approved the Dumbarton Oaks disarmament proposal. And in early 1947, he ordered the largest nuclear weapon modernization effort in US history.

On 14 June 1946, US Ambassador Barnard Baruch introduced the Dumbarton Oaks disarmament proposal at the first session of the UN Atomic Energy Commission (UNAEC). Thereafter, the proposal was known as the Baruch Plan. It called for the complete transfer of all US atomic weapons, atomic power facilities, and atomic know-how to an international organization responsible for all aspects of the development and use of atomic energy. The plan denied the UN Security Council a veto right on matters of compliance with atomic energy restrictions. Most importantly, the plan gave the UN authority to compel national compliance, supported by the use of force.[3]

The Soviets rejected the US proposal immediately, calling it a transparent effort to monopolize nuclear weapon technology. They counterproposed that the United States disassemble its nuclear weapon infrastructure and completely disarm before an international agreement was negotiated on the multinational control of nuclear weapons. US allies in Western Europe were equally unwilling to accept the Baruch Plan. By the end of 1946, the United States could convince only China to put the Baruch Plan to a test vote. For ten years, the United States advanced its nuclear disarmament initiative at the UN Disarmament Commission without the slightest success.

The failure of the Baruch Plan led the Dwight D. Eisenhower administration to abandon nuclear disarmament. Instead, the United States tried to negotiate multilateral agreements dealing with discrete arms control opportunities. The United States was looking for arms control successes; therefore, it selected its initiatives carefully. Most of them were uncontroversial. They had low risk of failure. Many were based on the assumption that it was easier to ban a practice before it appeared than to control it once it began. It also helped the success of the negotiations that the initiatives prohibited nothing the United States or the Soviet Union really wanted to do. Nevertheless, negotiations took many years under three presidential administrations. Three treaties prohibited nuclear weapon deployment in environments that were extremely inhospitable (Antarctica, outer space, and the ocean seabed). Deployments in any of those areas would have inflated program costs and would have raised nearly insurmountable problems for nuclear warhead maintenance and security. The treaties represented successes, but their contributions to national security were modest.

The Kennedy and Johnson administrations. Two multilateral treaties negotiated during this period were clear exceptions to the rule that early arms control efforts tended to outlaw weapons procurement or deployment decisions that were unlikely to occur in the first place; that is, their contributions to national security were significant. The first was the Limited Test Ban Treaty (LTBT) of 1963, which was negotiated during the John F. Kennedy administration. The LTBT forbade nuclear testing anywhere on Earth except underground and under conditions prohibiting the spread of radioactive debris across international boundaries. The LTBT negotiations attracted and sustained considerable public and international interest due to the danger that atmospheric nuclear testing posed to public health and the environment. The LTBT, however, shared at least one commonality with the Antarctica, outer space, and seabed agreements. Ending atmospheric testing was uncontroversial and it played only a modest part in curbing the arms race. Neither the United States nor the Soviet Union wanted to poison the environment with their nuclear tests, and both could accommodate these new restrictions by moving their nuclear test programs underground.

The second exception was the Nuclear Nonproliferation Treaty (NPT) of 1968, which was negotiated during the Lyndon B. Johnson administration. The NPT forbade providing nuclear weapons and nuclear weapon technology to other states. Neither the United States nor the Soviet Union wanted to see other states deploy nuclear weapons. Multiple nuclear adversaries added uncertainty and unpredictability to nuclear relationships. By the mid-1960s, three other states—the United Kingdom, France, and the Peoples

Republic of China—had already detonated nuclear devices. The United States and Soviet Union led the effort to negotiate the NPT to stop what appeared to be an accelerating process of nuclear proliferation. Non–nuclear weapon states (NNWS), however, demanded that the five nuclear powers accept balanced obligations. In return for giving up the legal right to build nuclear weapons, NNWS insisted that the nuclear powers allow them access to peaceful nuclear technology and achieve universal nuclear disarmament. The five nuclear powers accepted the obligations, and the NNWS have never let them forget that they hold the weapon states accountable for a nuclear disarmament agreement.

Bilateral Nuclear Arms Control (1968–1993)

In the late 1960s, the United States gradually abandoned its successful strategy of multilateral agreements to enter direct, bilateral nuclear arms control negotiations with the Soviet Union. Negotiations to limit strategic offensive arms had become a necessity for the United States due to Soviet deployment of hundreds of intercontinental ballistic missiles (ICBMs). The emergence of a significant Soviet nuclear arsenal was not a surprise. US national security specialists had predicted nuclear stalemate for twenty years. National Security Council Memorandum 162/2, the analysis on which the doctrine of massive retaliation was based, had predicted the loss of US nuclear superiority. Some in the United States, however, began to wonder whether their Soviet counterparts had made the same prediction to their leaders. Soviet strategic offensive arms modernization programs went beyond the quantitative requirement for equality. For the first time it appeared that Moscow might deploy enough nuclear weapons of sufficient power to threaten the survivability of US retaliatory forces—undermining the conditions necessary for US security in the nuclear age. At roughly equal numbers, there was rough balance between the sides. Nevertheless, if either side could eliminate the retaliatory forces of the other in a first strike, there might be an incentive to strike first in a crisis. US political figures considered such a situation unstable and intolerable.

The Nixon-Ford and Carter administrations. President Richard M. Nixon came into office in January 1969 hoping to restore US nuclear supremacy. Once in office, however, he came to understand that there was no hope of deploying more forces than the Soviet Union. President Nixon turned to arms control for help. Although he had a reputation as a hardened anticommunist, Nixon did much to change the atmosphere of tension between Washington and Moscow. In late 1971, Nixon and Soviet General Secretary Leonid Brezhnev signed the Accident Measures Agreement. In it, the United States and the Soviet Union pledged to improve technical safeguards against accidental and unauthorized use of nuclear weapons, notify each other should the risk of nuclear war arise, and provide advance notification of missile launches into international airspace or waters. The Accident Measures Agreement also expanded the 1963 US-Soviet memorandum establishing the hotline direct communications system. In 1972, the United States and Soviet Union signed the Incidents at Sea Agreement, committing the US and Soviet navies to follow safe practices when their warships operated in close proximity. In 1973, Nixon and Brezhnev signed the Prevention of Nuclear War Agreement. In it, both sides committed to avoid confrontations likely to lead to nuclear war and, if such crises arose anyway, to consult with each other on ways to solve differences peacefully.

During the Nixon administration, arms control policy became a full partner in achieving US national security objectives. The administration defined its security requirements in terms that facilitated arms control. Weapon system requirements and arms control planning were closely integrated.[4] The objective of US strategic nuclear arms control was to ensure strategic stability by assuring the ability of the United States to destroy the Soviet Union under all conditions.

The Nixon administration negotiated three strategic arms limitation agreements: the Anti-Ballistic Missile Treaty (ABM Treaty) of 1972 and two agreements limiting strategic offensive arms. The forum for negotiating all three of these agreements was the Strategic Arms Limitation Talks (SALT). The first strategic offensive arms agreement (SALT I) was a temporary agreement limiting the growth of strategic forces, whereas the more detailed second treaty (SALT II) froze the level of deployed strategic weapons. SALT II froze forces at unequal levels, placing the United States at a slight numerical disadvantage in deployed delivery systems. The numerical difference was militarily meaningless at the time it was signed. As the quality of Soviet ballistic missiles improved, however, the vulnerability of US strategic nuclear forces to destruction in a preemptive strike would become an urgent concern.

President Jimmy Carter inherited the SALT negotiations. His administration wanted to redefine the objectives of the nearly complete SALT II to require deep weapon reductions. The Soviets, however, refused to renegotiate the objectives of the pact so late in the talks. SALT II was supposed to help the US force vulnerability problem, but conservative critics pointed out that the treaty did nothing to improve the survivability of US retaliatory forces. They complained that SALT II made matters much worse by granting the Soviets unilateral advantages in heavy ICBMs. They also questioned whether SALT II was verifiable. Liberal critics pointed out that SALT II did not limit deployed warheads, and they predicted that deployed nuclear weapons would grow in number as modern multiple-warhead ballistic missile systems replaced older ones carrying single warheads.

The critique of SALT II was bitter medicine for the Carter administration. Paradoxically, the US Joint Chiefs of Staff were the only officials to testify in favor of SALT II. Most of the chiefs supported it only because ratification was attached politically to US nuclear force modernization programs in every category of military nuclear power. Congress appeared ready to support both the treaty and the modernization programs. This support came to an end in December 1979, however, when the Soviets invaded Afghanistan. Understanding that the US Senate would never ratify SALT II following the invasion, the Carter administration withdrew the treaty from consideration.

The Reagan and George H. W. Bush administrations. The critiques of SALT II resonated with California governor and presidential candidate Ronald Reagan. He considered SALT II "fatally flawed" and made arms control a major issue in his 1980 presidential campaign. When he became president in 1981, he refused to resubmit SALT II to the Senate for advice and consent to ratification. Reagan proposed entirely new bilateral negotiations whose objective was deep reduction of nuclear arms. The US nuclear arms control efforts begun during the Reagan years succeeded spectacularly. The 1987 Intermediate-Range Nuclear Forces Treaty (INF Treaty) eliminated an entire class of US and Soviet nuclear arms. The INF Treaty also set new standards in verification, data exchange, and on-site inspection.

President George H. W. Bush inherited the Reagan arms control agenda and completed the greatest strategic arms reduction agreements in history. The Strategic Arms Reduction Treaty (START) of 1991 reduced US and Soviet strategic offensive forces by one-third, limiting both sides to no more than 1,600 deployed delivery systems and 6,000 deployed warheads. START built on the INF Treaty precedents in verification, establishing a regime for data exchange, open telemetry, and several kinds of on-site inspection. The START Treaty, at 400 pages, was the longest and most complex treaty of its kind. US and Soviet delegations negotiated for nine years to complete it. By the time START was finished, the Cold War had ended, and the Soviet Union was on the verge of political and economic collapse.

As the START Treaty was being prepared for signature, the US Department of Defense (DoD) prepared a list of operational practices, nuclear systems, and nuclear modernization programs that it no longer considered necessary. The department recommended to the White House that the United States seek parallel cuts in Soviet nuclear programs. The recommendation resulted in the Presidential Nuclear Initiatives (PNI) of 1991–1992. In September 1991 and January 1992, President Bush announced several unilateral US steps to further reduce nuclear tensions and invited Moscow to match them. Soviet President Mikhail Gorbachev and, later, Russian President Boris Yeltsin responded with unilateral initiatives of their own. As a result of these initiatives, both sides withdrew substantial numbers of theater nuclear weapons from forward deployment sites, canceled a variety of strategic and theater nuclear force modernization programs, and relaxed considerably the alert postures of their respective strategic retaliatory forces. The United States reduced the number of nuclear ballistic missile submarines it kept on patrol, and it ended the practice of keeping its heavy bombers on quick-reaction alert.

The dissolution of the Soviet Union in December 1991 left its successor, the Russian Federation, destitute. As the scope of Russia's economic plight became clear, the United States recognized that Moscow could not afford to deploy the number of strategic offensive arms permitted under START. Sensing an opportunity to reduce the threat posed by Russia's nuclear arsenal and to lessen the expense of US strategic forces, the Bush administration proposed a second round of START negotiations. In January 1993, after only six months of negotiation, the two sides signed START II, which reduced the ceilings on strategic offensive warheads from 6,000 to 3,000–3,500. Bush submitted the treaty to the Senate for advice and consent to ratification on his last day as president of the United States.

Post–Cold War Nuclear Arms Control (1994–2008)

START II encountered difficulties in the Russian parliament. The treaty was very favorable to the United States. Nationalist members of the Russian parliament objected to what they saw as an unbalanced treaty. Although the Soviet Union no longer existed and the Communist Party was in tatters, habits of mind developed over generations of distrust from the Soviet era had not disappeared. (They still exist today, in fact.) While US national security strategy documents crowed about the positive effects that the Soviet collapse had wrought in the international security environment, Russian nationalists painted a different portrait of the collapse, blaming the West for the dire conditions that ordinary Russians faced daily. START II would never enter into force.

Foreign and national security policies played an insignificant role in the 1992 presidential election in the United States. The principle election issue was the economy, not the state of international security or the US role in the world. For centuries, Western statesmen had regarded foreign security affairs as "high politics," the pinnacle of international relations. International economic and commercial matters were "low politics" and enjoyed less stature and priority. The Clinton administration turned the order of international politics on its head, elevating economic summitry to new heights.

Nuclear policy matters repeatedly caught the Clinton administration by surprise. When the new civilian leadership of DoD tried to revise US nuclear policy to lessen the chances of an accidental nuclear exchange and reset nuclear weapon requirements at a lower level, it was surprised to find the civilian and military bureaucracy skillfully opposing it. It was surprised again when the opportunity to affiliate the United States with the African Nuclear Weapon Free Zone shattered consensus within the national security interagency over a seemingly indefensible proposition—that the United States must reserve the right to deploy nuclear weapons against Africa.

The Clinton administration built on the Presidential Nuclear Initiatives of the George H. W. Bush–Gorbachev–Yeltsin period. Clinton and Yeltsin agreed to retarget their ICBMs and submarine-launched ballistic missiles (SLBMs), aiming those missiles on open areas of the ocean, rather than on targets in Russia and the United States, to reduce the chance of a catastrophic accident. They agreed later to establish a US-Russian Joint Data Exchange Center in Moscow to share ballistic missile early warning data. The purpose of the center was to prevent false alarms, misjudgments, and accidents as Russia's ballistic missile early warning system slowly decayed. The center has yet to begin operations. In 1997, Clinton and Yeltsin set goals for deeper nuclear reductions, to levels of 2,000 to 2,500 deployed strategic warheads, in a third set of START negotiations. The timing of the negotiations depended on entry into force of START II.

Most of the Clinton arms control efforts never resulted in tangible accomplishments. Moscow backed out of the data center. Although the Russian parliament ratified START II, it would not allow the treaty to enter into force until modified, and the modifications were never completed. So, negotiations on START III never began. The Clinton years ended having accomplished virtually nothing in nuclear arms control.

George W. Bush had little experience, and seemingly little interest, in foreign and national security affairs when he became president in January 2001. Although President George H. W. Bush had signed the most important nuclear arms control agreements in history, President George W. Bush appeared determined to dismantle much of the existing arms control framework.

George W. Bush had run on a platform calling for a national missile defense to protect the United States and its allies from rogue state ballistic missile attack. When the Bush administration announced its plan to field an antiballistic missile test bed with limited operational capability, the intention of the administration to withdraw from the ABM Treaty became clear. The Russians and US European allies protested, arguing that the treaty was the cornerstone of global nuclear stability. Moscow did again what it had done repeatedly during the Cold War: it pressured Washington to change US policy by threatening Europe. Vladimir Putin's government reminded Western European governments that Russian nuclear missiles could strike

European cities, hoping that fearful allies would push the Bush administration to change direction on the ABM Treaty. The allies tried hard to get the administration to reconsider its plans to deploy missile defenses. But the administration rejected the Russian and European arguments, explaining that the Cold War was over and its end demanded new thinking. The United States exercised the "supreme national interests" clause of the ABM Treaty and withdrew in May 2002.

When its strong-arm tactics regarding the ABM Treaty failed, Moscow announced that it would withdraw from START II. Confident that the Russians could not afford to maintain the force structure permitted in START I, the George W. Bush administration announced that it was prepared to go to levels of arms lower than those contemplated for a possible START III. At the Moscow summit of 2002, presidents Bush and Putin signed an agreement lowering levels of strategic offensive arms to 1,750 to 2,200 warheads in a nuclear arms control treaty unlike any other. The Moscow Treaty had no verification provisions, no data exchange requirements, and no milestones for elimination. It had no provisions to make reductions permanent, although that had been an US objective for a START III.

The end of the ABM Treaty did not cause the collapse of nuclear stability, but it did create conditions for increased uneasiness about it. In June 2006, the US-Russia nuclear relationship received an unexpected shock from a surprising source. *Foreign Affairs* magazine, one of the most respected publications in the world on international affairs, published an article entitled, "The Rise of US Nuclear Primacy," written by two junior academics.[5] Using a force-on-force nuclear exchange model of their own design, Karl Lieber and Daryl Press concluded that the United States had achieved, or was on the cusp of achieving, first-strike nuclear supremacy in spite of the arms control agreements designed to preserve stability. The article prompted denials from US officials, official requests for explanation from Moscow, and an orgy of caloric commentary from Russian nationalists. *Foreign Affairs* invited internationally respected US and Russian national security specialists to comment on the Lieber-Press article in a subsequent edition of the magazine, but the original article had caused deep uncertainty in Russia regarding its ability to deter the United States. About the same time, one of the Armed Services received a commissioned study of the prospects for a START I extension. On the service's behalf, a contract research organization had interviewed key national security specialists in the US government, the North Atlantic Treaty Organization (NATO), and nongovernmental national security experts in Russia. The researchers asked if the officials and nongovernmental experts thought the treaty should be extended in 2009. The vast majority of interviewees believed that treaty extension had little utility.[6]

Why Has Traditional Strategic Nuclear Arms Control Ended?

For some, the end of formal strategic nuclear arms control negotiations is long overdue. Many national security experts consider it an anachronism for several reasons. First, the international security environment has changed dramatically. The Soviet Union is gone, its empire has crumbled, and Moscow is unlikely to ever reemerge as a peer competitor. Second, the United States and Russia are no longer enemies. They cooperate on many fronts. On other fronts, they compete. In short, their relations are normal and war between them is nearly unimaginable. Third, today's security threat to the United States arguably comes from rogue states and the international terrorist groups associated with them. For some of these adversaries, the United States is the only real obstacle to their ambitions. The rogues are acquiring ballistic missiles and nuclear, biological, and chemical (NBC) weapons to deter outside military intervention to stabilize their regions. Fourth, strategic offensive arms control contributes, some say, to an adversarial atmosphere between the United States and Russia. It perpetuates Cold War attitudes and perspectives. Some even claim that formal arms control actually interferes with unilateral arms reduction because the United States and Russia habitually hang on to weapons they do not need in order to trade them in future arms control negotiations. Finally, formal strategic offensive arms control may inhibit defense programs that US security interests urgently require.

These analysts conclude that the United States and Russia ought to act unilaterally to reach the strategic nuclear force levels that make sense for each. Parity of forces is not required for stability. The implication for US national security policy is that additional strategic offensive arms control is unnecessary and that some existing bilateral arms control agreements, like the ABM Treaty, should be discarded. Formal strategic offensive arms control has come to an end, it is said, because US national security strategy during the Cold War worked. Cold War arms control played its part, but now its part is over. Different threats face the United States, and future US administrations need tools tailored to meet those threats. Seemingly, the Putin government agrees. In 2007, it suspended its adherence to the Conventional Forces in Europe Treaty (CFE Treaty), a key Cold War agreement on conventional forces, and threatened to withdraw from the INF Treaty.

For other national security experts, the work of strategic offensive arms control is unfinished. Even though the likelihood of war between the United States and Russia is remote, a balanced nuclear relationship between them has been brought into question with enough force for each side to begin thinking in familiar Cold War terms. There is always the risk that conflict could result from accident, miscalculation, misjudgment, or unauthorized use of nuclear weapons. There is persistent concern in the United States about the alert postures, safety, and security of Russian nuclear weapons. Not even the most ardent believer in strategic arms control's success would claim that US-Russian agreements have finished the job of nuclear weapon reduction and elimination. Many hundreds of warheads are in storage even though the delivery systems for them no longer exist. Thousands of theater nuclear weapons remain in the US and Russian inventories. According to this school of thought, formal strategic nuclear arms control retains an urgent purpose.

To many, the assertion that arms control negotiation gives rise to Cold War attitudes is deeply cynical. These individuals point out that the United States has reneged on solemn security assurances made to Russian leaders early in the post–Cold War period. They have pointed to US plans to deploy antiballistic missile systems in Central Europe despite Russian concerns about the impact on the strategic nuclear balance. They cite the record of US dismissal of the legitimate security interests of the Russian Federation during its period of grave national distress. These actions, they claim, have caused Moscow to join with like-minded states to counterbalance US military power and contain US expansion. It is difficult to believe, some say, that arms control negotiations could have made bilateral US-Russia relations any worse.

Visions of the Future

Given the divergence of expert views, what might be the future direction of strategic nuclear arms control? This subsection examines the objectives, characteristics, strengths, and weaknesses of four alternate arms control futures: (1) continuation of the present, limited formal approach to strategic nuclear arms control; (2) abandonment of formal arms control in its entirety; (3) reorganization of the nuclear arms control enterprise emphasizing a few key principles and objectives; and (4) transformation of strategic nuclear arms control into something entirely different.

Continuation of a limited formal approach. The reason for continuing the strategic arms reductions begun twenty years ago is to complete unfinished business. That business includes implementing the 2002 Moscow Treaty, reducing ceilings to perhaps 1,000 to 1,500 warheads, and making the reductions more difficult to reverse. The Moscow Treaty has no verification procedures. Perhaps it should have. Verification of the Moscow Treaty will require a different approach than the one found in START I. START's verification provisions, while extensive, cannot verify the key unit of account in the Moscow Treaty: operationally deployed warheads. By any standard, these are important arms control goals.

The reasons for continuing the current approach are the recognized strengths of the ritual arms control process. The process itself is deeply dignified. It is cautious. It is respectful of the rights of states parties. It confers status on the participants. It reflects the prerogatives of legislative institutions and constitutional forms. It is observable to third parties, including the public, but it is not so public that observers can interfere with it. It is the most predictable process for arms reduction and provides a forum for participants to exchange their views about their own, and their competitors', strategic programs.

The reasons for ending the limited formal approach to arms control are to avoid its collateral consequences. Strategic nuclear arms control is likely to prohibit conventional ICBMs and SLBMs, concepts important to future US global power projection. It is likely to control future heavy bombers even though they may not be equipped for nuclear weapons. Strategic offensive arms control is likely to require the parties to allow inspection of advanced "new kinds" of weapon systems even though they are entirely nonnuclear. These kinds of restrictions are likely to be intolerable to the United States because they almost certainly will constrain US conventional military superiority.

Abandonment of strategic nuclear arms control. The reasons to abandon strategic nuclear arms control are to eliminate the artifacts of the Cold War: mutual assured destruction and the notion that Russia is an equal to the United States. This approach is distinguished by continued observance of existing nuclear arms control agreements until they end, the absence of formal arms control negotiations whose purpose is legally binding arms control agreements, and increased reliance on transparency and other measures to encourage nuclear stability. Favoring the abandonment of strategic offensive arms control requires one to believe that improved US-Russia relations are irreversible, Russian nuclear arms no longer pose a dire threat to US security, and addressing rogue states and terrorism is more important to US vital national interest than attending to nuclear stability with the Russians. The first two reasons are difficult to take seriously, and even those most opposed to traditional nuclear arms control almost certainly do not believe them to be true.

The strengths of this approach are its flexibility in arranging force structures. Both sides could build nuclear forces as they pleased if the security environment were to deteriorate. If the environment improved, both sides could reduce their arsenals without delay. This is the approach that the George W. Bush administration championed and the Putin administration accepted.

The weakness of this approach is its unpredictability. Absent negotiated arms control arrangements, neither the United States nor Russia has an obligation to follow the other to lower levels of strategic nuclear arms or to provide the other any insight into future deployment plans. Unilateral arms control reductions may not be appreciated or matched, causing the presumed unimportance of the nuclear balance to wear thin. Inevitably, such an approach will cause both sides to behave more cautiously about reductions than they might have done with a treaty in place. This approach is also likely to dishearten third parties who expect Washington and Moscow to make progress toward nuclear disarmament.

Reorganization around a few key principles. The reason for reorganizing strategic nuclear arms control is to focus on the nuclear arms control issues that matter the most. For two generations, US policymakers have pursued strategic arms control for security, stability, and predictability. During the Cold War, all three objectives were judged to be equally important. Today, that is no longer true.

The risk of premeditated nuclear war between the United States and Russia is very low. New strategic offensive arms control initiatives might focus on other problems—for example, reducing the risk of accidental launch or unauthorized use of nuclear weapons; or making reduction of nuclear arms more difficult to reverse by eliminating warheads removed from active service; or, if the security of remaining nuclear weapons is a concern, exchanging threat information and sharing security technology. The principles around which the initiatives could form are open and flexible. They could involve any aspect of the force thought to present a problem. The strengths of reorganizing arms control initiatives around a few key principles are its flexibility and focus.

Transforming strategic nuclear arms control. The reason for transforming nuclear arms control is to set an entirely new direction for strategic arms reductions and limitations and to accomplish something ambitious. This approach would define new organizational principles, new objectives, and new institutional agreements for arms control. The strength of transforming the US approach to arms control is that it is likely to lead to a renaissance of activity focused in those areas where arms control is best able to make a contribution to security. Where it cannot contribute, arms control will wither and die. Transformation is a direct answer to the indictment aimed at arms control by those who believe it to be out of step with the times. The weakness of the transformation paradigm is that government does not transform easily, particularly privileged activities like national defense. However, even in the defense arena, arms control may be transformed to help solve a critical problem. For example, a transformed approach to arms control might seek to free limited budget resources and allow them to be reallocated where they are needed most. A practical example exists from our recent past.

START allowed DoD to redirect a significant part of its budget from nuclear arms to other activities. During the Cold War, DoD routinely spent nearly 20 percent of the defense budget on nuclear forces. Thanks to START, the percentage of the defense budget allocated to nuclear forces quickly fell to 7 percent. Thus, 11 percent of the defense budget, a huge reallocation of resources, was freed permanently for investment in other capabilities. START contributed to resource reallocation by reducing nuclear force structure, personnel strength, and base infrastructure. It soothed legitimate concerns about Russian strategic programs and allowed national security managers to take acceptable risks when they reduced investment in nuclear forces. START provided tools that allowed the United States to assess confidently what Moscow was doing in its programs and forces for intercontinental nuclear conflict. An unpublished study completed for one of the armed services in 2006 predicted that a transformational arms control strategy might free up to 5 percent of today's defense budget over the next twenty-five years, potentially allowing reallocation of up to $600 billion. There are many resource-constrained programs in DoD and the ability to reallocate hundreds of billions of dollars would provide welcome relief.

The objectives sought through new types of arms control, resource reallocation, and risk mitigation, and the institutional accords regarding them, would be unlike those of the traditional arms control era. They would require new institutional agreements within DoD and between the executive and legislative branches. The agreements would be transformational and would mark the beginning of a new era of arms control.

Nuclear disarmament also would represent arms control transformation. In September 2006, Stanford University gathered a bipartisan group of senior US statesmen to commemorate the 1986 Reykjavik summit at which President Reagan and President Gorbachev discussed the possibility of moving beyond nuclear arms reduction and pursuing nuclear disarmament. This group recommended that US arms control policy embrace the Reykjavik vision as a long-term goal while pursuing a series of discrete, short-term objectives. Four members of the group published an editorial in the *Wall Street Journal* calling for the United States to adopt a policy of nuclear disarmament and begin shaping the political environment to make disarmament possible.[7] There are no illusions, however, among those advocating disarmament. The political conditions for nuclear weapon abolition do not yet exist. The transformational dimension of the Stanford group's recommendation is the proposal to begin shaping the security environment to achieve a disarmament objective in the future.

Conclusion: Back to the Future

When one considers the sixty years of US strategic nuclear arms control experience, the contemporary international security environment, and the spectrum of plausible arms control futures, several connected themes emerge.

First, arms control policies must be appropriate for their environment. They cannot succeed if divorced from the reality of power relationships among major states. If the relationships are unsettled, as they are today, the prospects for successful nuclear arms control diminish. US efforts to reduce reliance on nuclear weapons and advance the objectives of the NPT, however, still can accomplish important things. When the Moscow Treaty reductions are complete in 2012, the US nuclear inventory will be smaller than at any time since the Eisenhower administration. The United States no longer produces fissile material for nuclear weapons thanks to the strategic arms reductions that have already taken place. By using the fissile materials from deactivated bombs, the Department of Energy (DoE) has eliminated the need to produce nuclear reactor fuel for the navy for at least fifty years. DoE has consolidated fissile material in fewer locations to improve physical security. It has a program to down-blend over 350 metric tons of US and Russian weapon-grade fissile material for use in civil reactors in the United States. Although not an era of startling new arms control agreements, it is wrong to believe that worthwhile arms control activity has ended. It continues in ways that are appropriate for the times.

Second, the history of strategic offensive arms control is one of abandonment. The United States abandons arms control initiatives when they fail. It abandons successful initiatives to achieve more ambitious ends. Thus, there is reason to believe that the current course of US arms control policy eventually will be abandoned in favor of one taking a new direction, perhaps one seeking ambitious new objectives.

Third, the international security environment radically changed for the United States on 11 September 2001, and it will continue to change even more in the years ahead. Russia has emerged from a period of radical social, economic, and political decline and has begun to reassert its interests. Moscow has suspended arms control agreements with the West that it deems incompatible with its interests. It has threatened to follow the US example by dismantling further the agreements underpinning Cold War nuclear stability. Sooner or later, neither party will be able to ignore the consequences of these actions, especially the long-term uncertainty they already have created.

Fourth, strategic nuclear arms control has more leaders today than ever before. The UK has adopted officially a vision of the future free of nuclear weapons. The vision has many supporters among US allies, strategic partners, and at home, including influential senior statesmen from both major political parties. It cannot be assumed that Americans will control the direction of strategic nuclear arms control indefinitely.

Although there is much unfinished business in bilateral arms control negotiations between the United States and Russia that offers several potential new directions for strategic nuclear arms control, the logic of nuclear arms reduction and nuclear nonproliferation leads ultimately to one global numerical limit on nuclear warheads. That limit is zero—the limit sought in the Baruch Plan more than sixty years ago. And powerful allied governments, influential statesmen, obscure academics, and informed citizens almost certainly will ask why the next new direction we choose cannot lead to global nuclear zero.

Notes

1. "A World Free of Nuclear Weapons?" keynote address, secretary of state for foreign and commonwealth affairs, United Kingdom, Margaret Beckett, Carnegie International Nonproliferation Conference, 25 June 2007.
2. The reasons for the lack of a definition are complicated. The United States did not want to define *strategic nuclear weapon* in a way that would include its theater nuclear weapons located in Europe and the Far East. In addition, the agency responsible for building US nuclear weapons never wanted to define what a *nuclear weapon* was for fear of revealing critical nuclear weapon design information.
3. R. Joseph DeSutter, "Strategic Arms Control: Theory and Practice," in Schuyler Foerster and Edward Wright, eds., *American Defense Policy,* 6th ed. (Baltimore: Johns Hopkins University Press, 1993), p. 352.
4. Jerome H. Kahane, *Security in the Nuclear Age* (Washington, DC: Brookings Institution Press, 1975), p. 171.
5. Karl A. Lieber, and Daryl G. Press, "The Rise of US Nuclear Primacy," *Foreign Affairs* March/April (2006).
6. *START I Treaty Extension: An Air Force Emerging Issues Project,* prepared by the Strategies Group, Science Applications International Corporation, June 2006.
7. George P. Shultz, et al., "A World Free of Nuclear Weapons," *Wall Street Journal,* 4 January 2007.

Suggested Readings

Cimbala, Stephen J., and James Scouras, *A New Nuclear Century: Strategic Stability and Arms Control* (Westport, CT: Praeger, 2002).

Cirincione, Joseph, *Bomb Scare: The History and Future of Nuclear Weapons* (New York: Columbia University Press, 2007).

Drell, Sidney D., *Nuclear Weapons, Scientists, and the Post–Cold War Challenge: Selected Papers on Arms Control* (Hackensack, NJ: World Scientific, 2007).

Feiveson, Harold A., ed., *The Nuclear Turning Point: A Blueprint for Deep Cuts and De-alerting of Nuclear Weapons* (Washington, DC: Brookings Institution Press, 1999).

Gaddis, John Lewis, *Cold War Statesmen Confront the Bomb: Nuclear Diplomacy Since 1945* (New York: Oxford University Press, 1999).

6

The Future of the Nonproliferation Regime

Leonard S. Spector

Since the early 1990s, the contours of the nonproliferation regime have been slowly, but significantly, changing. What might be called the classic nonproliferation regime was composed of four distinct subregimes—three of them anchored by widely adopted international treaties—each focused on curbing the spread of a specific weapon of mass destruction or advanced delivery systems to states. Since the mid-1990s, however, growing concerns over a series of new challenges have led to the emergence of important new regime components that seek to curb the spread of all weapons of mass destruction (WMD) to both state and nonstate actors. Today, the *nonproliferation regime* is best defined as: a set of treaties, institutions, and other arrangements, with wide international acceptance, whose purpose is to slow the acquisition by states and nonstate actors of nuclear weapons, chemical weapons (CW), and biological weapons (BW), and/or advanced WMD delivery systems.

As broad as it is, the current nonproliferation regime remains a subset of a larger constellation of international efforts to curb the spread of WMD and advanced delivery systems, an enterprise that encompasses many other components in addition to the regime itself. Nonregime elements encompass such activities as ad hoc, country-specific diplomatic initiatives, economic sanctions, intelligence gathering, and even the use of military force against states or terrorist groups, including the global, US-led effort to combat terrorism. Because the regime is so widely supported, it has gradually created a deeply etched international norm against the acquisition and use of WMD. This framework provides the political and moral foundation for many nonproliferation activities that fall outside the formal regime.

Today, the vast majority of states, as parties to relevant nonproliferation treaties, have renounced all three weapons of mass destruction. They also have accepted wide-ranging inspections by international monitoring organizations over their nuclear and chemical facilities, although there are no comparable inspection systems for verifying that states are not developing BW or WMD-capable missiles. Of the UN's 192 member states, fewer than 10 are thought to possess nuclear weapons and only a handful are thought to have offensive CW or BW programs.[1] Although nonstate actors, including Al-Qaida, are known to be seeking WMD, none is known to possess such weapons.[2] Groups in Iraq, however, have used the industrial chemical chlorine in truck bombs and other explosive devices. Authorities have also disrupted attempts by Al-Qaida in Jordan to use explosives that would have dispersed toxic chemicals. The malicious dispersal of anthrax through the US mail in November 2001 appears to have been the work of a single individual rather than a terrorist organization.[3]

This chapter describes the classic, state-focused nonproliferation subregimes and reviews their limitations. It then identifies how these regimes have been augmented by related efforts to address the dangers posed by the Soviet WMD legacy, the possible spread of WMD to violent nonstate actors, and the emergence of private international WMD smuggling networks.

The Classic Regime: State-focused Nonproliferation Subregimes

The nonproliferation subregimes focused on states are usually built around a widely adopted international treaty. These agreements often include inspection provisions, to verify states' compliance with the treaty's most important provisions, and associated export control systems to restrain the spread of enabling technologies to states that may harbor intentions to develop WMD.

Core Components

The cornerstone of each of the three major state-oriented nonproliferation subregimes is a widely accepted treaty prohibiting the states that have joined it from acquiring and possessing a specific weapon of mass destruction and from assisting other states to acquire such weapons. The core treaties are: the Nuclear Nonproliferation Treaty (NPT), which opened for signature in 1968 and entered into force in 1970; the Chemical Weapons Convention (CWC), which opened for signature in 1993 and entered into force in 1997; and the Biological Weapons Convention (BWC), which opened for signature in 1972 and entered into force in 1975.[4] The Comprehensive Test Ban Treaty (CTBT), which was opened for signature in 1996 but has not yet entered into force, is a powerful constraint on states possessing nuclear weapons and is seen as an important complement to the

NPT.[5] Also supporting the NPT are five nuclear-weapon-free zone (NWFZ) treaties covering Africa (not yet in force), Central Asia, Latin America and the Caribbean, the South Pacific, and Southeast Asia.[6] Under these treaties, regional states parties reiterate their pledges not to develop nuclear weapons and, through protocols to the treaties, the NPT nuclear weapon state(s) agree not to use or threaten to use nuclear weapons against parties to the treaties.[7] The Geneva Protocol of 1925 bans the use in war (but not the development, production, possession, or transfer) of chemical and biological warfare agents.[8]

The missile nonproliferation regime, known as the Missile Technology Control Regime (MTCR), which was established in 1987, is not associated with a prohibitory treaty.[9] In November 2002, however, the Hague International Code of Conduct Against Ballistic Missile Proliferation was opened for signature. Although the code does not ban the development, possession, or use of ballistic missiles (and, unlike the MTCR, does not extend to cruise missiles), it endorses the principle of limiting the spread of ballistic missiles to states that might use them to deliver WMD in violation of international norms established by various nonproliferation treaties, and it calls on all states to exercise restraint in the development of ballistic missiles. Signatories also agree to provide advance notice of missile launches, to reduce their ballistic missile holdings, and to report annually on their inventories of such missiles.[10] Some 123 states have signed the code.[11]

In early 2009, the CWC had 187 states parties and the BWC had 163.[12] The prohibitions in both treaties apply to all states that have signed and ratified (or acceded to) these treaties, without exception. When the NPT was negotiated, however, the states then possessing nuclear weapons were unwilling to eliminate their arsenals, given the military importance of those weapons during the Cold War. Thus, the NPT was drafted to allow those states that had detonated a nuclear explosion prior to 1 January 1967 to retain their nuclear arsenals and nuclear weapon production programs. These states are the United States (first test 1945), the Soviet Union (now Russia) (1949), the UK (1952), France (1960), and China (1964).[13] These countries, defined as nuclear weapon states (NWS) under the NPT, are, however, required by Article VI of the treaty "to pursue negotiations in good faith on effective measures relating to cessation of the nuclear arms race at an early date and to nuclear disarmament, and on a treaty on general and complete disarmament under strict and effective international control."

As of early 2009, the NPT had 184 non–nuclear weapon states parties and five NWS parties, making it the most widely adhered to of all the nonproliferation treaties. Three additional states that are known or believed to have nuclear weapons (India, Israel, and Pakistan) have never joined the treaty. In addition, North Korea, which also possesses nuclear weapons, ratified the NPT in 1985, but withdrew from the pact in January 2003.[14] (In understandings reached in September 2005 and February 2007 with China, Japan, Russia, South Korea, and the United States—negotiations known as the Six-Party Talks—North Korea agreed to renounce its nuclear arms. Although Pyongyang has taken several important steps to fulfill these agreements, whether it will fully implement them remains in doubt.[15])

Inspections

The nuclear weapon and CW regimes include extensive inspection systems to verify that any development and production activities that states parties undertake in these sectors, such as the operation of nuclear power plants or chemical production facilities, are not misused for weapon purposes. The NPT specifies that non–nuclear weapon state (NNWS) parties to the treaty must place all of their nuclear materials under the accounting and inspection system of the Vienna-based International Atomic Energy Agency (IAEA), which verifies through its accounting and inspection procedures that none of these materials are being diverted for nuclear explosive purposes.[16] This inspection arrangement is known as "full-scope IAEA safeguards." NWS parties to the treaty are not required to submit to such inspections but, as a gesture of support for the treaty, all have voluntarily agreed to allow IAEA safeguards on some of their civilian nuclear activities. During 2006, the agency conducted 2,142 inspections in 162 states.[17]

Under states' agreements with the IAEA for the implementation of full-scope safeguards, the IAEA director general has the right to request a "special inspection" of any facility within an NPT NNWS if the facility is believed to be engaged in undeclared activities involving nuclear materials.[18] The IAEA has invoked this authority on at least one occasion, to seek access to an undeclared site in North Korea where it believed wastes from clandestine plutonium separation ("reprocessing") activities were stored. Analysis of the wastes might have allowed the agency to deduce the quantity of plutonium North Korea had separated. Pyongyang refused the agency's demand, however, triggering an international crisis whose repercussions continued into 2008.[19]

The CTBT also has an elaborate verification mechanism to ensure that parties do not circumvent the treaty by conducting clandestine nuclear tests.[20] To this end, the treaty establishes an International Monitoring System (IMS)—an extensive network currently made up of 337 monitoring stations using seismic, hydroacoustic, infrasound, and radionuclide detectors. The system is currently operated by the Vienna-based Preparatory Commission to the CTBT and will be run by the Comprehensive Test Ban Treaty Organization (CTBTO) once the treaty enters into force. At that time, if a state party believes, based on information provided by the IMS and other information available to it, that another state party has conducted a nuclear explosion in violation of the treaty, the concerned state party will be able to demand an on-site inspection of the location where it believes the test occurred, for the purpose of determining whether a violation of the treaty has taken place. Before the inspection will be able to proceed, however, it will have to be approved by thirty parties of the fifty-one-party CTBT Executive Council. The Technical Secretariat of the CTBTO will carry out the inspection, but the requesting party will have the right to send an observer to accompany the inspection team.

The CWC also contains provisions for comprehensive inspections in states parties that cover all CW stockpiles, former CW production facilities, and industrial manufacturing facilities that produce certain dual-use chemicals listed in "Schedules" in the treaty above specified quantitative thresholds.[21] The inspections are conducted by an international body created by the CWC, the Organisation for the Prohibition of Chemical Weapons (OPCW), based in The Hague. As of 2007, the organization had conducted 3,000 inspections in seventy-nine member states. In contrast to the NPT verification scheme, all parties to the CWC are subject to these inspections. The CWC also contains a provision not found in the nuclear inspection system: it authorizes a state party, rather than the inspection agency, to demand a "challenge inspection" of a location within another state party where the challenger believes that the second party is engaged in prohibited activities.[22] The challenge inspections themselves, however, are conducted by OPCW inspectors. To rule out frivolous or abusive challenge inspections, a challenge inspection request can be blocked by a vote of three-fourths of the Executive Council of the OPCW. To date, no party has used the CWC challenge inspection authority.

Unlike the NPT and CWC, the BWC has no on-site inspection system, a reflection of the difficulty of confirming that development and manufacturing activities in this sector are being devoted solely to peaceful or permitted defensive purposes. Factors including the dual-use nature of the equipment involved in manufacturing biological products such as vaccines, the ease of covering up prohibited BW activities at specific sites through rapid cleanup activities, and the feasibility of hiding small-scale bioweapon facilities contributed to this decision. Soviet opposition to on-site inspections of any kind, at the time the convention was being negotiated, was another factor influencing this outcome.

Because no treaty bans the possession of longer-range missiles, there is no basis for inspections to confirm state renunciation of these systems, and none are provided for as part of the MTCR. The Hague International Code of Conduct Against Ballistic Missile Proliferation calls on all signatories to disclose their holdings of ballistic missiles, but it does not provide for verification of these declarations.[23]

Export Controls

The NPT, CWC, and BWC also contain restrictions on exports, implemented through export licensing procedures in member states. The goal of these restrictions is to prevent additional states from acquiring from outside sources the advanced technologies and materials needed for the development of WMD and related delivery systems. The CWC imposes restrictions on trade in treaty-controlled (scheduled) chemicals with states not party to the convention, and the NPT and the BWC contain similar obligations, also to be implemented through the application of national export controls. The NPT, CWC, and BWC also contain provisions guaranteeing the right of parties to enjoy the benefits of the peaceful use of these technologies such as nuclear electric power reactors, modern chemical industries, and advanced biomedical capabilities.

In addition to a general prohibition barring NWS parties from aiding NNWS to develop nuclear weapons, the NPT requires that all nuclear exports by parties to states considered NNWS under the treaty be placed under IAEA inspection in the recipient states, a step designed to limit the danger that such exports might be used for nuclear weapons.[24] The CWC similarly prohibits exports to nonparties of chemical warfare agents and precursor chemicals listed on two of the treaty's Schedules. Because many of the latter substances have important industrial as well as military uses, this restriction not only impedes the development of CW by nonparties, but also imposes a significant trade sanction for their unwillingness to join the CWC.[25] The BWC bans exports of BW, defined as biological agents and toxins "of types and in quantities that have no justification for prophylactic, protective or other peaceful purposes," as well as equipment "designed to use such agents for hostile purposes or in military conflict."[26] Export controls in this case focus on dual-use items that are suitable both for peaceful commercial production and for military applications, such as biocontainment systems for laboratories, large-volume fermentation tanks, and samples of dangerous bacterial and viral agents.

Incentives

To encourage states to join the three nonproliferation treaties and renounce potentially valuable military capabilities, each of the treaties includes provisions guaranteeing the right of all parties to use the technology in question for peaceful purposes and calling on the more advanced states to help less developed nations to exploit the technology for peaceful purposes.[27] These provisions have been controversial because some advanced states, fearing the potential for proliferation, have sought to restrict access to sensitive nuclear, chemical, or biological technologies while developing countries have demanded unrestricted access to them.[28]

The clash of views on access to dual-use technologies is at the center of the controversy concerning the Iranian nuclear program. This controversy arose in mid-2002, when it was learned that for many years Iran, a party to the NPT, had secretly pursued the enrichment of uranium and the production and separation of plutonium, technologies that can support civilian nuclear energy programs but also can be used to produce material for nuclear weapons. Iran has insisted that it has the legal right under Article IV of the NPT to pursue all aspects of nuclear power for peaceful purposes, including uranium enrichment and plutonium production. The UN, however, citing suspicions raised by Iran's history of clandestine nuclear activities, has demanded that it halt activities related to uranium enrichment and plutonium separation, noting that Article IV of the NPT guarantees the right to pursue peaceful nuclear energy only when such activities are "in conformity" with the basic NPT prohibition against the development of nuclear weapons.[29]

The three nonproliferation treaties also contain additional incentives to encourage states to renounce WMD. For example, under the NPT, the NWS parties have agreed to pursue negotiations toward the elimination of nuclear weapons. This step could eventually eliminate the discriminatory nature of the treaty, which allows some states to retain nuclear weapons while requiring others to renounce them. The CWC and BWC, which are nondiscriminatory, contain incentives of a different type. For example, the CWC imposes trade restrictions on nonstate parties, while parties to the CWC and the BWC agree to aid parties that may be the victims of a CW or BW attack, respectively.

Enforcement

The three nonproliferation treaties include explicit or implicit provisions to address violations. The NPT delegates the implementation of its inspection system to the IAEA, and the statute of that organization empowers the agency to refer instances of noncompliance with IAEA safeguards to the UN Security Council as the "organ bearing the main responsibility for the maintenance of international peace and security."[30] The IAEA used this authority to refer noncompliance by North Korea to the Security Council in 2003 and noncompliance by Iran in 2006.[31] Further developments in both cases led the Council to require all UN member states to impose economic sanctions on the two countries.[32] Whether these steps, combined with related diplomatic initiatives, will ultimately prove effective in altering the behavior of North Korea and Iran remained unresolved in early 2009.

The CWC takes a somewhat different approach. It authorizes the OPCW Conference of the States Parties to recommend to all CWC states parties the implementation of "collective measures" in cases "where serious damage to the object and purpose of this Convention may result from activities prohibited under this Convention." These collective measures potentially include the imposition of sanctions through the OPCW, without the need to refer a state that violates the CWC to the Security Council. In cases of "particular gravity," however, the OPCW Conference of the States Parties is given the authority to refer the issue to the UN General Assembly and Security Council.[33] Like the CWC's challenge inspection provisions, the OPCW's authority to impose sanctions or refer matters to the UN has never been invoked.

Article VI of the BWC provides that any party that believes another party is in breach of the convention may lodge a complaint with the Security Council, which would then investigate the matter and take action as appropriate under the UN Charter.[34] No party has used this provision to date. There also are provisions under Article V of the BWC for bilateral or multilateral consultations to address compliance concerns.

Supplier Organizations: The Nuclear Suppliers Group, the Australia Group, and the MTCR

As the three state-focused nonproliferation regimes have evolved, key supplier states (i.e., countries capable of supplying equipment, material, or technology needed for the production of the various WMD) have established informal (non-treaty-based) organizations to reinforce and expand the national export controls required by the nonproliferation treaties. These organizations are the forty-five-member Nuclear Suppliers Group, founded in 1976, covering nuclear-related transfers, and the forty-one-member Australia Group, founded in 1985, covering CW- and BW-relevant transfers.[35]

In 1987, the Missile Technology Conrol Regime, which now has thirty-four partners, was established to limit the spread of ballistic and cruise missiles capable of delivering WMD, with a particular focus on missiles able to carry a 500-kilogram payload to a distance of 300 kilometers or more. The regime also targets transfers of shorter-range systems in cases where there is reason to believe that they may be used for the delivery of WMD.[36]

The supplier organizations develop and maintain guidelines for national export controls, including general standards for issuing export licenses and "core lists" of controlled items that might contribute to the manufacture of the respective WMD and advanced delivery systems. For example, the MTCR Guidelines specify that there shall be a "presumption of denial" for licenses to export missile production facilities, and the Nuclear Suppliers Group has a set of key requirements and guarantees that must be satisfied by a proposed recipient nation before an export can be made to that recipient by a member state. The licensing rules and commodity lists are negotiated among member states or partners by a process of consensus, but they become legally binding only when voluntarily enacted by each member and made part of its respective domestic export licensing regulations. Although there are no treaties or other formal undertakings requiring members to adhere to each group's export guidelines, states join the groups in the expectation that they will contribute to the formulation of new provisions and implement the agreed rules domestically.

Gradually, the export restrictions adopted by the supplier organizations have become more stringent than those required by the related nonproliferation treaty, reflecting the desire of the supplier states to reinforce controls over sensitive technologies. The Nuclear Suppliers Group Guidelines, for example, provide for export controls not only over equipment specially designed or prepared for nuclear weapon use, as required under the NPT, but also over dual-use items such as high-strength maraging steel and certain types of aluminum (items that can be used both to make components for uranium enrichment centrifuges and for non-weapon-related industrial purposes).

The Nuclear Suppliers Group rules also require that, as a condition for receiving nuclear commodities, NNWS recipient countries (including states that are not party to the NPT) place all of their nuclear activities under IAEA safeguards. In contrast, the NPT requires only that the exported item itself (and nuclear materials produced through its use) be placed under IAEA monitoring. The Nuclear Suppliers Group rule has the effect of barring civil nuclear exports to Israel, North Korea, and Pakistan, all of which have declined to place some of their nuclear installations under IAEA monitoring. (A special exception to this rule was granted to India in 2008 at the urging of the United States, in conjunction with a US-Indian agreement on nuclear trade.[37]) Similarly, the Australia Group requires stringent export licensing reviews for transfers of several CW precursor chemicals listed on Schedule 2 of the CWC to countries, such as Iran, that are nonmembers of the Australia Group, but are parties to the CWC and thus not barred by the treaty from receiving these commodities.[38] Although there is overlap between the Australia Group list of CW precursors and the CWC Schedules, the two lists are not identical because they serve different purposes: whereas the Australia Group list is a nonproliferation measure that focuses exclusively on CW precursors, the CWC Schedules provide the basis for CWC verification and hence focus both on CW agents and CW precursors. There are no restrictions in the CWC itself on the export of Schedule 3 chemicals to nonstate parties to the treaty, except for the requirement for an end-use declaration. (The Australia Group also covers pathogens and toxins of BW concern as well as dual-use biological production equipment.)

Although supplier states consider the Nuclear Suppliers Group and the Australia Group to be essential elements of the nonproliferation regimes, countries outside of these groups, in particular those from the developing world, have complained that the supplier arrangements are discriminatory and restrict their rights to have access to peaceful nuclear, chemical, or biological technology.[39]

The supplier groups have developed informal rules regarding the admission of new members, usually requiring that they have strong nonproliferation "credentials." In other words, they have to be members in good standing of the NPT, CWC, or BWC; they cannot be suspected of engaging in proliferative activities; and they must be committed to active nonproliferation efforts. Russia, suspected by the United States of not being in full compliance with the CWC and the BWC, has not been invited to join the Australia Group, and China, which has reportedly continued to allow transfers to Pakistan's missile program, has not been invited to join the MTCR.

Regime Evolution

The state-oriented nonproliferation subregimes have evolved, in large part, as responses to related international developments. The Nuclear Suppliers Group, for example, began with seven members but now has forty-five, and its list of controlled items has expanded over the years. Similarly, the Australia Group has grown from fifteen participating states in 1985 to forty states plus the European Commission today. In 2005, the Australia Group, recognizing the danger of BW against livestock and crops, for the first time adopted stronger controls over transfers of strains of pathogens suitable for use in antiagriculture attacks. The MTCR also has been adapted to increase controls over exports of shorter-range cruise and ballistic missiles in cases where concerns have been raised that they might be used to deliver WMD. Figure 6.1 summarizes the basic elements of the four state-oriented nonproliferation subregimes.

The regime reached a moment of particular cohesion in the mid-1990s:

- in 1993, the CWC was opened for signature;
- in 1995, the parties to the NPT agreed by consensus to extend the treaty indefinitely at a conference called for by the treaty at its twenty-fifth anniversary;
- in 1996, the UN General Assembly voted to open the CTBT for ratification, an action seen as an important step toward fulfilling the obligation set forth in the NPT for the NWS parties to work toward ending the nuclear arms race; and
- in 1997, the CWC entered into force.

In 1999, however, the US Senate voted not to give its advice and consent to ratification of the CTBT and, by the early 2000s, the administration

Figure 6.1 Basic Elements of the State-oriented Nonproliferation Regimes

Subregime	Treaty	Treats States Equally	Verification System	Inspection Agency	Export Controls/ Suppliers Group	Incentives	Enforcement
Nuclear	Nuclear Nonproliferation Treaty (NPT)	No (China, France Russia, UK, United States exempt; required only to pursue nuclear disarmament)	Yes	International Atomic Energy Agency (IAEA)	NPT + Nuclear Suppliers Group	Nuclear states pledge negotiations on disarmament; aid for nuclear energy	IAEA referral to UN Security Council; used against North Korea and Iran
Chemical	Chemical Weapons Convention (CWC)	Yes	Yes	Organisation for the Prohibition of Chemical Weapons (OPCW)	CWC + Australia Group	Access to chemical technology; assistance to victims of an attack	OPCW members may take collective measures; referral to UN Security Council for most serious cases (never used)
Biological	Biological and Toxin Weapons Convention	Yes	No	None	Australia Group	Access to biotechnology; assistance to victims of an attack	Party may lodge complaint with UN Security Council
Missile	None	Rules sometimes applied more leniently to member states	No	None	Missile Technology Control Regime	Members sometimes obtain assistance to peaceful space programs, missile defenses	None

of President George W. Bush was expressing great dissatisfaction with the effectiveness of the regime and the process of multilateral treaty negotiations. The regime also suffered from considerable internal dissention. Concerned that the Bush administration now opposed promotion of the CTBT in international fora, contrary to understandings reached at the 1995 NPT Extension Conference and the 2000 NPT Review Conference, and fearing that the United States was lowering the threshold for nuclear weapon use by developing new low-yield warheads, many NNWS parties to the NPT complained that the NWS parties were not living up to their treaty obligation to work toward disarmament.[40] The US decision in 2001 to withdraw from negotiations on a compliance protocol for the BWC was an added source of acrimony.[41]

Another major point of contention was the accusation that the advanced industrial states had not met the requirements of the NPT, CWC, and BWC to share the benefits of nuclear, chemical, and biological technology, respectively, with less advanced parties to these treaties. The imposition of controls on technology transfers through the Nuclear Suppliers Group and the Australia Group that were more restrictive than those in the NPT, CWC, and BWC was a particular sore point in this regard.[42] Reflecting such tensions, the April–May 2005 NPT Review Conference ended in a deadlock that made it impossible to issue a consensus final declaration endorsing the importance of the treaty.

On-going Challenges to the State-oriented Nonproliferation Subregimes

Despite their breadth, the state-focused nonproliferation regimes have significant weaknesses, a number of which have been or are being exploited by states pursuing WMD capabilities.

Treaties Not Universally Adopted

None of the nonproliferation treaties has been universally accepted. India, Israel, and Pakistan, for example, never joined the NPT, and North Korea withdrew from the treaty in 2003. All four of these states are known or believed to possess nuclear weapons, although in early 2007, North Korea declared it would eliminate its nuclear arms as part of an agreement with China, Japan, South Korea, Russia, and the United States.[43] Moreover, the NPT exempts its five NWS parties from the obligation to relinquish their nuclear weapons, provided they pursue good faith negotiations toward this goal. Thus, while the NPT may help slow further proliferation, it is unlikely to lead to the early abolition of these weapons.

Although the CWC and BWC prohibit all states parties, without exception, from possessing chemical and biological weapons (CBW), a number of important states have not joined these treaties. North Korea and Syria, both thought to have large stocks of CW, have not joined the CWC, nor have two other important Middle Eastern states: Israel and Egypt.[44] In addition, the United States is a party to the CWC but, in the process of ratifying the treaty, adopted unilateral conditions that restrict the treaty's implementation in that country.[45] Syria, Israel, and Egypt, along with a number of smaller states, are not parties to the BWC.[46]

Inspection Systems Incomplete

NPT regime. IAEA safeguards are based on monitoring and accounting for the use of all nuclear materials in NNWS. Nuclear materials include uranium in various forms, such as fuel for nuclear power plants and research reactors, and plutonium, which is produced when uranium is irradiated in a reactor. Traditionally, the IAEA began with a declaration by an NPT member state of its nuclear materials and the facilities using or processing them. The agency then tracked the changes in the inventory to confirm that the materials were used exclusively for peaceful purposes.

During the 1980s, however, Iraq, a NNWS party to the NPT, defeated the system by failing to declare numerous facilities and their inventories of nuclear material. Some of the facilities were intended for the production of nuclear weapons. After the first Gulf War in 1991, these activities as well as Iraq's offensive CW and BW programs were investigated by the UN Special Commission (UNSCOM) and a specially established IAEA Iraq Action Team, both created by the Security Council to expose and eliminate Iraq's WMD programs. UNSCOM and Iraq Action Team inspectors, unlike traditional IAEA inspectors, had authority to go anywhere in Iraq at any time, to interview scientists and engineers and to seize documents. The team was supported by high-altitude U-2 reconnaissance aircraft and intelligence provided by UN member states. Eventually UNSCOM and IAEA uncovered and eliminated Iraq's WMD programs, although the extent of their success was not clear until after the US-led invasion of Iraq in 2003. This led to the determination that all of Iraq's WMD programs had, in fact, been eliminated in the 1990s, except for some innocuous remnants.[47]

The IAEA, recognizing the deficiencies in its classic nuclear safeguards, began in 1993 to develop an upgrade of the safeguards system. This enhanced system was subsequently embodied in a document, approved by the IAEA's Board of Governors in 1997, that was known as the Model Additional Protocol.[48] All NPT parties were asked to adopt the Additional Protocol as an amendment to their preexisting safeguards agreements with the IAEA. The Additional Protocol empowered the agency's inspectors to take "environmental samples" (e.g., swipes) at inspected sites in NNWS, to have free access to all buildings at such locations, and to demand "special inspections" at undeclared sites where it had reason to suspect that undeclared activities involving nuclear materials were taking place. Even so, these new authorities fell far short of those available to UNSCOM, in part because of the concerns of advanced industrial states that open-ended inspections would place too great a burden on their legitimate use of nuclear energy.[49]

As of early 2009, ninety states had adopted the Additional Protocol, but many others, including Iran and Syria, had not done so. Moreover, developments in Iran raise doubts that even the Additional Protocol provides sufficient authority to the IAEA to expose clandestine nuclear weapon programs in NPT NNWS. In 2002, for example, an Iranian opposition group revealed that for the previous eighteen years, Iran had secretly pursued clandestine programs to enrich uranium and produce plutonium without informing the IAEA.[50] Under international pressure to clarify that these past activities were not part of a nuclear weapon program, Iran agreed informally to grant the IAEA the inspection rights that the agency would enjoy under the Additional Protocol, and then agreed to additional measures by allowing IAEA inspectors access to Iranian scientists and documents. Even then, the agency reported that it was unable to fully clarify the history of the Iranian nuclear program. Subsequent political developments caused Tehran to withdraw these voluntary measures in 2005 and 2006, exacerbating uncertainties about its nuclear activities. These developments led the IAEA to declare Iran in breach of its inspection obligations in September 2005 and to refer the matter to the UN Security Council in February 2006. In December 2006, March 2007, and April 2008, the Security Council adopted Resolutions 1737, 1747, and 1803, respectively, imposing a range of economic sanctions on Iran and demanding that it cease its work on uranium enrichment and plutonium production.[51]

As of early 2009, the matter remained unresolved. Iran continued to pursue its uranium enrichment and plutonium production nuclear activities, which it claimed were intended solely for peaceful purposes.[52] Whatever the outcome, the Iran case provides a benchmark suggesting that, even when augmented by measures such as the Additional Protocol, IAEA inspections may be insufficient to resolve cases of clandestine nuclear proliferation and may need additional strengthening.

In April 2008, the US Central Intelligence Agency declared that, like Iraq and Iran, Syria had also pursued a clandestine nuclear program, apparently intended to produce plutonium for nuclear arms through the operation of a reactor built with North Korean assistance beginning in 2001. The Syrian reactor, modeled on the one used by North Korea to produce plutonium used in its nuclear weapons, was destroyed by Israeli warplanes in

September 2007, but details as to the nature of the facility Israel attacked were not revealed until eight months later.[53]

CWC regime. Inspections under the CWC also confront difficulties. The treaty's schedules of toxic chemicals and precursors whose manufacture is subject to declaration and inspection obligations have not kept pace with developments in the global chemical industry, leaving gaps in the verification system. OPCW resources have been focused on monitoring the elimination of CW stockpiles in six CWC member states (Albania, India, Libya, Russia, South Korea, and the United States), limiting the routine inspections of the chemical industry. Inspection protocols also have not been adapted to deal with the advent of small, multipurpose chemical manufacturing facilities. On-site sampling at inspected facilities has been constrained because of objections by plant operators that such sampling could disclose proprietary information.[54]

In addition, the CWC challenge inspection system has yet to be used, raising questions about the viability of this tool over the long term.[55] The United States has repeatedly accused Iran, a party to the CWC, of having an offensive CW program.[56] Despite these public allegations, however, Washington has not attempted to resolve them by invoking the challenge inspection provisions of the treaty. Uncertainties about the ability of US intelligence agencies to pinpoint the precise locations of illicit CW stockpiles or clandestine production facilities in Iran and reluctance to divulge the extent of US knowledge (which might compromise intelligence sources and methods), have likely contributed to this decision. The United States also may be mindful that, when it ratified the CWC in 1997, it reserved the right to deny OPCW inspectors access to particular sites on the grounds of national security. The United States is the only state to date to have insisted on this right. If pressed, however, Iran might seek to invoke a similar exclusion, seriously weakening the CWC verification system.

BWC regime. No inspections or other mechanisms are provided under the BWC to verify states' compliance with its provisions. An effort over six and one-half years to negotiate an inspection protocol to the BWC was abandoned in 2001, after the United States rejected the draft protocol and withdrew from the talks, claiming that any such instrument could not be effective and would be unduly intrusive.[57] This gap leaves uncertainty about whether or not states may be developing BW. The situation is exacerbated by provisions of the BWC that allow states to pursue defensive BW research and related activities, many of which could have offensive applications. The United States has accused Iran and North Korea, both of which have signed and ratified the BWC, and Syria, which has signed but not ratified the convention, of maintaining offensive biological warfare programs.[58] In the past, the United States has also expressed concern that Russia has maintained elements of the offensive BW program that it inherited from the Soviet Union.[59] Thus, although the BWC reinforces the international norm against the possession and use of BW, it has little ability to deter states from developing these capabilities by the threat of exposure.

The "Break-out" Option

Because the nonproliferation treaties allow states to exploit WMD-relevant technologies for peaceful purposes, states can take significant steps toward the acquisition of WMD without explicitly violating the rules laid out in the treaties. In addition, the treaties permit a party to withdraw on several months notice if it decides that "extraordinary events, related to the subject matter" of the treaty or convention "have jeopardized its supreme interests."[60] Taken in combination, these two features of nonproliferation treaties allow states to come close to acquiring WMD—for example, by stockpiling highly enriched uranium or plutonium as part of a peaceful nuclear energy program and secretly fabricating the nonnuclear components of nuclear weapons. If the country were then to break out of the treaty, it could rapidly produce the banned weapon and present the world community with a fait accompli before a preventive diplomatic (or military) response could be mounted.[61]

Japan, for example, has insisted on pursuing uranium enrichment and plutonium separation technologies to support its energy independence. Because of Japan's strong nonproliferation credentials, the matter has not raised significant international concerns, even though Japan's uranium enrichment and plutonium recycling programs undoubtedly give it a latent nuclear weapon capability.

Iran also is asserting the right to develop uranium enrichment and plutonium production technologies for peaceful purposes. In view of Iran's years of hiding these programs from IAEA inspectors, the lack of economic justification for these activities, and its revolutionary Islamist ideology, the international community has become increasingly persuaded that Iran's pursuit of these technologies is intended to support a nuclear weapon program. Such concerns led the Security Council to demand that Tehran cease its sensitive nuclear activities and to impose sanctions against Iran in late 2006, early 2007, and early 2008.

Production of CW in amounts sufficient to be militarily useful to states on the battlefield requires large-scale CW agent production facilities. The CWC bans all such facilities, which must either be dismantled or converted to peaceful purposes in a verifiable manner. Nevertheless, CWC parties can produce stocks of dual-use precursor chemicals under the guise of peaceful industrial activity. Thus, even though large-scale CW agent production could not be started overnight, steps down this road could be taken within the bounds of the CWC. In particular, highly flexible chemical plants that can manufacture a variety of products in response to changing market conditions, and emerging technologies such as microreactors, may permit the rapid production of large quantities of CW agents without the need for dedicated industrial-scale facilities. CWC parties could acquire the key components of a CW program while complying with the treaty, and then withdraw and rapidly begin the large-scale production of a chemical weapon agent. Even so, it would take several months to produce and weaponize the hundreds of tons of agent required for a militarily significant CW capability.

The quantity of a BW agent, such as anthrax bacterial spores, that is needed to cause massive harm can be quite small—tens to hundreds of kilograms—and scaling up from laboratory production to these larger quantities can be quickly accomplished. Weaponization activities, such as spray drying and formulation, can be conducted secretly on a small scale without fear of detection because the BWC has no inspection component. Moreover, BWC parties are specifically prohibited only from producing agents "of types and in quantities that have no justification for prophylactic, protective or other peaceful purposes," allowing parties to pursue defensive research that can involve many agents and technologies relevant to offensive biowarfare programs. For example, the study of dispersion patterns, intake pathways, and minimum lethal dosages for various BW agents could legitimately be pursued as part of a program to develop protective measures and antidotes. Indeed, some have argued that the development of vaccine- or antibiotic-resistant strains of BW pathogens might be permissible for the purpose of testing the efficacy of medical countermeasures. The offensive potential of such agents is obvious. In the 1990s, the United States conducted a number of investigations of this kind.[62] Although Washington has argued that the activities were permitted under the BWC, some outside observers have challenged this view.[63]

The CW nonproliferation regime has not attempted to address the break-out issue directly, and the BW regime lacks the tools to do so. The nuclear regime, however, has attempted to deal with this challenge since the 1970s by seeking new technologies to harness plutonium's energy value without making the material potentially available for nuclear weapon use.[64] Indeed, this goal is a focal point of the Global Nuclear Energy Partnership, a multimillion-dollar research and development program initiated by President Bush in February 2006, and it is the target of a second US initiative to discourage additional states from pursuing uranium enrichment and plutonium separation technologies.[65] IAEA Director General Mohamed El-Baradei also has pressed for restraint in the development of a full nuclear fuel cycle by additional states.[66] Iran has rejected such restraints, and it is not clear whether other states planning nuclear energy programs would accept such limitations on their nuclear activities, although Qatar and the United Arab Emirates have done so.[67]

Enforcement

The cases of the North Korean and Iranian nuclear programs highlight the difficulties of enforcing regime rules against intransigent states. Pyongyang's refusal to allow a special inspection demanded by the IAEA in 1993 led to a crisis that was resolved by a compromise, but only after the United States threatened military intervention. Under that compromise, embodied in an October 1994 arrangement called the Agreed Framework, North Korea froze the known elements of its nuclear program in return for a range of incentives. By this time, however, North Korea was thought to possess enough clandestinely separated plutonium for two nuclear devices. The Agreed Framework deferred unrestricted IAEA inspections, which might have required North Korea to place this material under safeguards, until a later date.[68]

In 2002, the Bush administration accused North Korea of cheating on the Agreed Framework by secretly pursuing a uranium enrichment program. This allegation led North Korea to withdraw from the NPT, citing the treaty's "supreme national interest" clause. In September 2005, the Six-Party Talks led to an agreement in which North Korea agreed to eliminate its nuclear weapon program in return for economic and political inducements. Soon after the September 2005 agreement was announced, however, the United States imposed new economic sanctions that had the effect of freezing some of North Korea's financial assets. This step apparently led Pyongyang to conduct a series of long-range missile tests in July 2006, ending a seven-year moratorium on such launches, and to conduct its first nuclear weapon test in October 2006 (an underground detonation).

The nuclear test caused the Security Council to adopt a binding resolution requiring North Korea to eliminate its nuclear weapon program and rejoin the NPT, and imposing an international embargo on conventional arms transfers and nuclear- and missile-related transfers to Pyongyang.[69] Thereafter, the Six-Party Talks resumed. In exchange for the release of its frozen assets and other incentives, North Korea once again agreed to end its nuclear weapon program, beginning by halting operations at its plutonium production complex at Yongbyon and permanently disabling the facilities at that site. As of early 2009, North Korea had implemented the freeze at Yongbyon and was taking steps to disable facilities at the site, but it remained unclear whether Pyongyang would implement all facets of the proposed new arrangement.[70]

Enforcing nuclear nonproliferation regime rules in Iran has been equally challenging. Tehran refused to comply with Security Resolutions 1737 and 1747, which demanded that Iran cease its sensitive nuclear activities and imposed sanctions against Tehran. These sanctions included banning transfers of nuclear- and missile-related matériel to Iran and freezing the assets of individuals and entities contributing to the country's nuclear and missile programs. Resolution 1747 also called on all states to exercise restraint in selling Iran conventional arms. Tehran, however, continued to defy the Security Council's demands. This standoff led the United States to seek the adoption of a third, more powerful set of sanctions, but it faced difficulty in obtaining the support of Russia and China, two states with the power to veto any Security Council action. Russian and Chinese opposition to additional sanctions was reinforced by Iran's agreement with the IAEA to establish a timetable for resolving the outstanding questions about Tehran's nuclear program. These developments led the United States to work with France and the United Kingdom on the imposition of new sanctions independent of action at the UN while, at the same time, seeking a more limited set of penalties for enforcement by that body that resulted in Resolution 1803 in March 2008.[71]

Through early 2009, however, Iran had refused to curtail its uranium enrichment program, although it had agreed to a timetable for resolving outstanding IAEA questions concerning the precise scope of its nuclear activities.[72] It is not clear, however, whether this is a first step toward complying with UN demands that it cease its pursuit of sensitive nuclear technologies, or merely a delaying tactic to enable it to gain added mastery of enrichment and plutonium production while avoiding the further imposition of UN-mandated sanctions.

The North Korean and Iranian cases illustrate that, although the tools exist for enforcing nonproliferation rules, using them to achieve compliance is a contentious process that has yet to show success.

New Regime Elements: Focusing on Both State and Nonstate Actors

The dissolution of the Soviet Union following the coup of late 1991, growing awareness of the danger of WMD terrorism during the 1990s (which became a profound concern after 9/11), and the exposure of the global nuclear smuggling network led by Pakistani nuclear scientist Abdul Qadeer Khan have resulted in the development of new nonproliferation mechanisms focused on both state and nonstate actors and on all categories of WMD. Some of these new efforts have gained such wide acceptance and legitimacy that they are now properly included in the nonproliferation regime while others are fast approaching this status.

The principal elements of this new dimension of the nonproliferation regime are:

- cooperative threat reduction (CTR) programs (initially launched in 1992), including bilateral programs and multilateral programs, such as the G8 Global Partnership Against the Spread of Weapons and Materials of Mass Destruction (Global Partnership);[73]
- the Proliferation Security Initiative ([PSI], announced in 2003), which seeks to build an international network of like-minded states to interdict WMD cargoes;[74]
- UN Security Council Resolution 1540, adopted in April 2004, requiring all states to adopt effective controls over WMD-related assets and to impose criminal penalties against individuals and groups that attempt to develop or assist in the development of WMD;[75]
- the Financial Action Task Force and the Egmont Group, international bodies that seek to combat money laundering and that, since 2005, have begun to adapt these tools to disrupt WMD transactions;[76]
- amendments to the Convention on the Suppression of Unlawful Acts at Sea (opened for ratification in 2005, but not yet in force), authorizing all treaty parties to interdict WMD cargoes on the vessels of other parties;[77] and
- several more narrowly focused initiatives, including the opening for signature of amendments to the Convention on the Physical Protection of Nuclear Materials, extending its requirements, initially applicable only to international transport of nuclear materials, to materials within the borders of individual parties;[78] the International Convention for the Suppression of Acts of Nuclear Terrorism (which opened for signature in 2005, and entered into force in July 2007);[79] the Global Initiative to Combat Nuclear Terrorism, launched in 2006, aimed at reinforcing controls over WMD-related assets;[80] and evolving biosafety and biosecurity standards adopted by the World Health Organization.[81]

Three of these programs—CTR, the PSI, and UN Security Council Resolution 1540—can illustrate the new nonproliferation efforts that are directed against nonstate actors, but also reinforce global nonproliferation efforts against states.

Cooperative Threat Reduction

The dissolution of the Soviet Union introduced a nonproliferation challenge of a new sort: the danger that material, equipment, or technology from the vast legacy of Soviet WMD programs might leak to proliferant states or violent nonstate actors. This threat led the United States in the mid-1990s to begin a series of programs with the Soviet successor states to secure dangerous WMD materials and engage former Soviet WMD scientists in order to reduce the risk that they would share WMD technology with foreign states or entities. The United States has contributed more than $10 billion to this effort, known as the cooperative threat reduction programs, which now includes many donor states who participate through the G8 Global Partnership.[82] Specific CTR programs include:

- the transfer to Russia, between 1992 and 1996, of all Soviet nuclear weapons remaining on the territory of Belarus, Kazakhstan, and Ukraine;[83]
- assisting these four countries to destroy missiles, missile silos, strategic bombers, and ballistic missile-firing submarines to permit these states to comply with the Strategic Arms Reduction Treaty (START I);[84]
- securing nuclear weapons in Russia and nuclear weapon materials throughout the newly independent states (NIS);[85]
- eliminating hundreds of tons of Soviet-made weapon-grade uranium;[86]
- assisting Russia in the destruction of large quantities of CW, as required under the CWC;[87]
- helping the former Soviet republics secure dangerous BW pathogens;[88] and
- establishing new institutions, such as the International Science and Technology Center (ISTC) in Moscow, the Science and Technology Center–Ukraine in Kiev, and other mechanisms to employ former Soviet WMD scientists in peaceful activities and thereby reduce incentives for them to sell their services abroad.[89]

Despite considerable accomplishments, these efforts have not been universally successful. Security over large quantities of weapon-usable nuclear material remains below international standards.[90] Moreover, a number of episodes involving the smuggling of weapon-grade nuclear materials from Russia have surfaced since the onset of these programs, and Russian or Ukrainian missile scientists are rumored to have assisted foreign missile programs. There also have been reports that, soon after its independence, Ukraine sold advanced nuclear-capable Kh-55 cruise missiles to China and Iran, and that elements of the Russian military production complex may have sold technology, including a sample of the Soviet SS-N-6 submarine-launched ballistic missile, to North Korea.[91]

Nonetheless, the CTR program is now more than a decade old, has many international sponsors and supporters, and is widely viewed as crucial to the international nonproliferation effort. CTR also is being adapted to new threats such as managing the legacy of the former Iraqi and Libyan WMD programs. Thus, even if CTR is unique in many respects, it fits easily within the definition of the nonproliferation regime provided above.

Proliferation Security Initiative

The PSI is an effort by a group of like-minded states, launched under US leadership in May 2003, to collaborate in interdicting cargoes containing WMD commodities by exploiting existing legal authorities such as the right of states to board vessels in their territorial waters or vessels flying their flag.[92] As of early 2009, more than ninety states were participating in or were affiliated with the PSI. States become participants by declaring their support for a set of interdiction principles, which commit them to work to interrupt transactions involving WMD commodities. Other states are less closely affiliated with the PSI, agreeing only that they may be called on to assist in specific interdiction activities involving their nationals or territory. One noteworthy adjunct of the PSI is a set of agreements under which many of the major vessel registry states have agreed to permit the United States, following notification to their country, to board vessels sailing under their flag, if the United States has reason to believe they are carrying WMD commodities.[93]

The PSI achieved its greatest success in late 2003 with the seizure of a massive shipment, destined for Libya, of equipment for the construction of a uranium enrichment plant. In May 2005, Secretary of State Condoleezza Rice announced that under the PSI, participating states had engaged in eleven successful interdictions. But she declined to reveal the details of these episodes, which remain classified.[94]

Although, at first, the PSI met with international criticism because it appeared to authorize the use of military force to seize vessels on the high seas, the commitment of participants to operate within existing legal authorities has gained it gradual acceptance. Indeed, the importance of restricting the transportation of WMD commodities has been recognized in a series of subsequent Security Council resolutions calling on all states to ensure that their vessels and aircraft are not used to support WMD programs in North Korea and Iran, and to inspect cargoes going to and from the two states.[95] Nonetheless, with its informal membership and affiliation arrangements and the secrecy surrounding the identity of its participating states and interdiction operations, the PSI is a unique element of the nonproliferation regime. Indeed, some might argue that it has not yet attained the level of international legitimacy or permanence to be recognized as a fully fledged component of the regime and is better thought of as a candidate for such status.

UN Security Council Resolution 1540

Resolution 1540 was unanimously adopted by the Security Council in April 2004 under Chapter VII of the UN Charter, which makes it legally binding on all states.[96] The resolution requires all UN member states to adopt effective domestic and export controls over weapons or commodities that might contribute to the development of WMD or advanced delivery systems, particularly by terrorist organizations. It also requires all states to criminalize acts within their territories that could contribute to the acquisition of WMD and advanced delivery systems by states and nonstate actors. Security Council Resolution 1540 was a reaction to the exposure of the A. Q. Khan network through which Khan sold technology for the enrichment of uranium, capable of producing nuclear weapon material, to Iran, North Korea, and Libya. Khan is known to have provided a nuclear weapon design to Libya, and he may have also provided it to the others.[97]

Recognizing that many developing countries had not established effective controls over WMD- and missile-related commodities, Security Council Resolution 1540 called on member states to provide assistance to enable them to do so. It also established a Security Council committee to monitor implementation of the resolution. Many states have reported substantial progress in establishing the necessary controls, but others have indicated they still have far to go and some have not even filed the required reports on the status of their programs. The mandate of the Security Council Resolution 1540 committee was renewed for three years in April 2008 as a means of sustaining pressure for compliance with the resolution.[98] Despite these challenges, as a mandatory Security Council measure to build capacity for controlling WMD and related delivery systems, the resolution is likely to remain an important and enduring feature of the nonproliferation regime.

A New Approach to Multilateralism

The central components of the nonproliferation regime were built on the principle of universality, under which all nations had the opportunity to participate in designing the rules to limit the acquisition of WMD. Moreover, all such decisions were adopted by consensus, giving individual states the opportunity to veto provisions they opposed. In most instances this approach meant that the core nonproliferation treaties were negotiated in a UN-affiliated forum, the Conference on Disarmament (CD) in Geneva, although there have been some exceptions. (The CTBT, for example, was finalized in the UN General Assembly.[99])

The CD has been deadlocked since the late 1990s.[100] In addition, many of the new regime elements have been targeted on nonstate actors and specific states (in particular, Iran and North Korea) that are accused of supporting terrorists or of directly threatening the United States or its allies. These factors led the Bush administration to pursue an alternative approach to building new elements of the nonproliferation regime. Rather than negotiate a new restraint in a universal forum where progress could be blocked by a single state—including one that might be an implicit target of the new initiative—the Bush administration followed the model that had been used to create the Nuclear Suppliers Group, the Australia Group, and the MTCR: it started with a core of like-minded states to establish a new restraint and then, by a variety of mechanisms, invited additional states to participate in the initiative.

The United States used this approach to engage additional states as project sponsors in the CTR program. The members of the G8 agreed to participate in the Global Partnership at their 2002 summit in Kannanaskis, Canada, after which other states were invited to join. In the end, more than thirty interested states, some as distant as South Korea and Australia, agreed to participate.[101] The United States used a variant of this model to develop the PSI, which began with eleven core members and was slowly enlarged.[102] The US-Russian Global Initiative to Combat Nuclear Terrorism, aimed at strengthening controls over WMD-relevant materials and hardware, also used this approach.[103]

Security Council Resolution 1540 also bypassed the multilateral negotiating process in the CD. In this instance, the Security Council, which is comprised of ten rotating members (selected to ensure regional representation) and five permanent members (China, France, Russia, the United Kingdom, and the United States), developed the resolution. The Security Council then adopted the resolution under Chapter VII of the UN Charter, making it binding on all UN member states. Washington adopted yet another variant in the case of the Egmont Group, gaining the agreement of that organization—comprised of more than 100 national financial intelligence units and focused on suppressing money laundering by criminals and terrorist organizations—to expand its activities to include the disruption of financial transactions supporting WMD programs.[104] The Financial Action Task Force, made up of the banking authorities of thirty-four leading economic powers that seek to prevent money laundering in support of criminal and terrorist activities, is also considering the expansion of its focus to constrain financial transactions that support WMD programs.[105]

Although some criticize the mechanisms for regime building based on ad hoc groups of like-minded states, more than 100 countries are participating in one or more of these initiatives. US officials have characterized this approach as "effective multilateralism," an implicit criticism of the traditional approach of developing nonproliferation measures through traditional multilateral forums such as the deadlocked CD.[106]

The Future

The effectiveness of the nonproliferation regime in curbing the spread of WMD to states is a matter of considerable debate. Proponents believe the regimes have played a crucial role in slowing the proliferation of these weapons by reinforcing norms against their acquisition, sounding alarms when cheating has taken place, and imposing significant political and economic costs on states that defy regime norms. Proponents argue that the existence of the regimes contributed significantly to the decision of South Africa to eliminate its nuclear weapons in 1991; the decisions by Belarus, Kazakhstan, and Ukraine to transfer all nuclear weapons on their territory to Russia in the mid-1990s; and the decision of Libya to renounce all of its WMD programs in 2003. The regimes, they contend, also helped to expose undeclared nuclear weapon relevant activities in North Korea in 1992 and similar activities in Iran after 2002, and provided the political basis for developing strong international responses to these threatening nuclear programs. The regimes, proponents argue, also have reinforced norms against the possession and use of CBW.

Critics charge that the regimes are unreliable because determined proliferators can defeat them. Citing the above cases, they argue that states can bypass the nonproliferation regimes by refusing to participate in the regimes altogether, secretly violating their rules, exploiting those rules to develop sensitive technologies under the guise of "peaceful uses," or withdrawing from the regimes.

Although there is evidence to support both views of the nonproliferation regimes, there appears to be a consensus that, however imperfect, the regimes are worth preserving and strengthening. Moreover, the international community appears unified in its commitment to new regime initiatives aimed at preventing terrorists from gaining access to WMD.

Since the period of turmoil that the nonproliferation regime experienced in the early 2000s, however, the differences among participants in the regimes appear to have moderated. For example, the December 2006 BWC Review Conference, which was expected to be particularly contentious, resulted in a consensus declaration, and the Inter-sessional Meetings of BWC experts, which have been pursued as an alternative to the formal negotiation of a compliance protocol, have proceeded without rancor.[107] In the area of export controls, the adoption of UN Security Council Resolution 1540, mandating that all states implement such controls, has begun to take the edge off this area of contention, particularly as many additional states have adopted the export control lists of the Nuclear Suppliers Group and the Australia Group. Moreover, unanimous resolutions of the Security Council sanctioning North Korea and Iran require all states to halt transfers to both states of sensitive nuclear- and missile-related commodities and to use the

Nuclear Suppliers Group and MTCR lists to identify the specific commodities to be embargoed, further validating the lists as the international norm for export controls. The rejection by the US Congress of the development of new, low-yield nuclear weapons and the departure of the most vocal Bush administration critics of the nonproliferation regime have also reduced intraregime tensions. The participation of many previously disaffected states in new elements of the nonproliferation regime, such as the PSI, the Global Initiative to Combat Nuclear Terrorism, and the Egmont Group, has helped to strengthen and modernize the overall regime.[108]

This gradual movement toward restoration of the international consensus on the need to restrict the spread of WMD, advanced missile delivery systems, and related commodities to additional states and to nonstate actors, together with the gradual expansion of the scope of nonproliferation measures, leaves little doubt that, despite the flaws of the regime, the international community supports its application to new areas as circumstances demand. The history of the nonproliferation regime over the past decade, and indeed since its inception, demonstrates its ability to absorb shocks and adapt to new circumstances.

As this book goes to press, North Korea is moving toward the elimination of its nuclear weapon capability in response to a combination of pressures applied under the umbrella of the nonproliferation regime and incentives offered through the creative diplomatic initiative of the Six-Party Talks. If these negotiations succeed, the effectiveness and importance of the nonproliferation regime will be validated and greatly reinforced. If the negotiations fail, critics may draw lessons about the limits of the regime. Under any circumstances, however, the nonproliferation regime will continue as an element of the international order. How central and how effective a role it will play in the future is a matter for continuing assessment by students of unfolding events.

Notes

The author would like to express his appreciation to Dr. Jonathan B. Tucker for his editorial suggestions and contributions to analyses in this chapter on the chemical and biological weapons regimes.

1. States that have declared their possession of nuclear weapons are: China, France, India, North Korea, Pakistan, Russia, the United Kingdom, and the United States. Israel is also widely believed to possess them. According to the Organisation for the Prevention of Chemical Weapons (OPCW), states that are party to the Chemical Weapons Convention (CWC) that have declared chemical weapons (CW) production facilities (and associated CW stocks) that are now in the process of being eliminated are: "Bosnia and Herzegovina, China, France, India, the Islamic Republic of Iran, Japan, the Libyan Arab Jamahiriya, the Russian Federation, Serbia, the United Kingdom of Great Britain and Northern Ireland, the United States of

America, and another State Party." OPCW, "Chemical Weapons Destruction Under Way" (August 2007), available at www.opcw.org/factsandfigures/index.html#CWDestructionUnderWay. The unnamed "state party" is widely understood to be South Korea. States most often identified as having offensive CW programs are Syria and North Korea, and the United States has accused Iran of having the potential for rapid production of CW. See, for example, "Current and Projected National Security Threats to the United States, Lieutenant General Michael D. Maples, US Army Director, Defense Intelligence Agency, Statement for the Record, Senate Select Committee on Intelligence Committee, January 11, 2007," available at http://intelligence.senate.gov/070111/maples.pdf. Israel is also sometimes reported to have CW. See Avner Cohen, "Israel and Chemical/Biological Weapons: History, Deterrence, and Arms Control," *The Nonproliferation Review* 8, no. 3 (2001): 29. Information on biological weapons (BW) programs is more limited. The United States believes that Iraq and Iran are pursuing BW capabilities, that North Korea has the ability to produce BW, and that Russia and China are engaged in activities relevant to the possible future production of BW. See "Current and Projected National Security Threats to the United States." Israel has been reported to have conducted research and development related to BW. See Cohen, "Israel and Chemical/Biological Weapons."

2. "Annual Threat Assessment of the Director of National Intelligence for the Senate Armed Services Committee, Statement by the Director of National Intelligence, John D. Negroponte, the Senate Armed Services Committee, February 28, 2006," available at www.globalsecurity.org/intell/library/congress/2006_hr/060228-negroponte.htm.

3. David Blair, "Al-Qaeda Plot Would Have Killed 20,000," *Daily Telegraph* (London), 19 April 2004, p. 11; see also "Chemical Attack Said Thwarted on Jordan Security HQ, US Embassy," *BBC Monitoring International Reports*, 16 April 2004; "Jordan 'Was Chemical Bomb Target,'" *BBC World News*, 17 April 2004. These sources cited in Margaret E. Kosal, "Near Term Threats of Chemical Weapons Terrorism," *Strategic Insights* 5, no. 6 (2006), which notes other cases of possible CW terrorism. See also Richard Weitz, "Chlorine as a Terrorist Weapon in Iraq," *WMD Insights* (May 2007). David Willman, "Anthrax Blend Led FBI to Ivins," *Los Angeles Times,* 4 August 2008, available at www.latimes.com/news/nationworld/nation/la-na-anthrax4-2008aug04,0,5223525.story; for additional details, see FBI www.fbi.gov/anthrax/amerithraxlinks.htm.

4. The texts of the treaties may be found, respectively, at the International Atomic Energy Agency (IAEA) www.iaea.org/Publications/Documents/Treaties/npt.html; the OPCW www.opcw.org; the Organization for the Prevention of Biological Weapons, an ad hoc organization established during the Sixth Review Conference of the Biological Weapons Convention, www.opbw.org; and "The Biological Weapons Convention," providing current official list of BWC states parties, (UN Office in Geneva), available at www.unog.ch/80256EE600585943/(httpPages)/04FBBDD6315AC720C1257180004B1B2F?OpenDocument.

5. For the text of the treaty, see the website of the Comprehensive Test Ban Treaty Organization ([CTBTO] established under the treaty to implement the treaty's International Monitoring System [IMS]) at http://www.ctbto.org. For the treaty to enter into force, forty-four states identified in an appendix to the treaty—states that possessed nuclear research or power reactors—must ratify it. Among these forty-four states, China, India, Israel, North Korea, Pakistan, and the United States have not taken this step (the US Senate voted against giving its advice and consent for the ratification of the pact in October 1999). Ibid.

6. For a compilation of texts of the treaties and details concerning their

implementation, see *Inventory of International Nonproliferation Organizations and Regimes* (Monterey, CA: James Martin Center for Nonproliferation Studies, 2008), available at www.cns.miis.edu/pubs/inven/pdfs/psi.pdf.

7. Ibid. Some protocols regarding the use or threat of use of nuclear weapons against parties to the nuclear-weapon-free zone (NWFZ) treaties have not been signed by all of the NPT nuclear weapon states (NWS) recognized by the NPT (China, France, Russia, the UK, and the United States). The protocols are not open for signature by the four other states possessing nuclear weapons (India, Israel, North Korea, and Pakistan).

8. For the text of the Geneva Convention, see OPCW, "Relevant Conventions," available at www.opcw.org/html/db/cwc/more/relconv_frameset.html.

9. See Missile Technology Control Regime (MTCR), available at www.mtcr.info/english/index.html.

10. For the text of the code, see Canadian Ministry of Foreign Affairs and International Trade, "International Code of Conduct Against Ballistic Missile Proliferation," available at www.dfait-maeci.gc.ca/arms/missile-hcoc-en.asp.

11. Ibid.

12. See references in notes 4 and 5.

13. See Nuclear Nonproliferation Treaty (NPT), Art. IX.

14. "Text of North Korea's Statement on NPT Withdrawal," North Korea Special Collection (Monterey, CA: James Martin Center for Nonproliferation Studies, 10 January 2003), available at http://cns.miis.edu/research/korea/nptstate.htm.

15. US Department of State, Office of the Spokesman, "North Korea–Denuclearization Action Plan, Statement by President Bush on the Six Party Talks," 13 February 2007, available at www.state.gov/r/pa/prs/ps/2007/february/80479.htm; Choe Sang-Hun, "North Korea Destroys Tower at Nuclear Site," *New York Times*, 28 June 2008, available at http://www.nytimes.com/2008/06/28/world/asia/28korea.html?_r=1&hp&oref=slogin.

16. IAEA, available at www.iaea.org/About/index.html. The IAEA was founded in 1957 and predates the NPT. The precise phrasing of the NPT provides that all non–nuclear weapon state (NNWS) parties must place all of their nuclear materials that are used in peaceful nuclear activities under IAEA inspection. The phrasing would permit states to exclude materials used in military (naval) propulsion systems but, to date, no state has exercised this option. Doing so could create uncertainty as to whether uninspected nuclear material was being diverted to a nuclear weapon program.

17. IAEA, "IAEA by the Numbers," available at www.iaea.org/About/by_the_numbers.html.

18. "The Structure and Content of Agreements Between the Agency and States Required in Connection with the Treaty on the Non-Proliferation of Nuclear Weapons," IAEA Information Circular (INFCIRC) 153 (corrected) (1972), paras. 73 and 77, available at www.google.com/search?q=iaea+infcirc%2F153&hl=en&sourceid=gd&rls=GGLD,GGLD:2005-41,GGLD:en.

19. IAEA, "In Focus: IAEA and DPRK: Fact Sheet on DPRK Nuclear Safeguards" (March 2007), available at http://www.iaea.org/NewsCenter/Focus/IaeaDprk/fact_sheet_may2003.shtml.

20. CTBT, Art. V.

21. CWC, Annex on Implementation and Verification ("Verification Annex").

22. Ibid., Part X.

23. See notes 9 and 10.

24. See NPT, Art. III.2.

25. See CWC, Annex on Implementation and Verification, Part VI.

26. BWC, Art. III.

27. See NPT, Art. IV; CWC, Art. XI; BWC, Art. X.

28. See, for example, "Foreign Minister of Iran Defends Country's Inalienable Right to Nuclear Technology for Peaceful Purposes," Conference on Disarmament press release DCF/433, 29 January 2004, available at www.un.org/News/Press/docs/2004/dcf433.doc.htm; "The US Position on the Biological Weapons Convention: Combating the BW Threat, Remarks of John R. Bolton, undersecretary for arms control and international security, Tokyo America Center, Tokyo, Japan, August 26, 2002," available at www.state.gov/t/us/rm/13090.htm.

29. Art. IV.1, "Nothing in this Treaty shall be interpreted as affecting the inalienable right of all the Parties to the Treaty to develop research, production and use of nuclear energy for peaceful purposes without discrimination and in conformity with articles I and II [the basic nonproliferation undertakings] of this Treaty." (Article I prohibits all parties from assisting others to acquire nuclear weapons; Article II prohibits NNWS from developing nuclear weapons.)

30. IAEA Statute, Art. III (B)(4) and Art. XII (C), available at www.iaea.org/About/statute_text.html.

31. See various periodic reports by the director general to the IAEA Board of Governors and to the UN Security Council, available at www.iaea.org.

32. See UN Security Council Res. 1718 (14 October 2006) imposing sanctions on North Korea, and Res. 1737 (23 December 2006), Res. 1747 (24 March 2007), and Res. 1803 (3 March 2008) imposing sanctions on Iran.

33. CWC, Art. XII.

34. BWC, Art. VI.

35. See the Nuclear Suppliers Group website at www.nuclearsuppliersgroup.org/; Australia Group website at http://www.australiagroup.net/index_en.htm. The Nuclear Suppliers Group was established after India's first nuclear test in 1974 highlighted the proliferation risks posed by imported civilian nuclear facilities. At the time, a number of major nuclear supplier states, including France, were not parties to the NPT, leading to the establishment of an organization separate from that treaty. The Australia Group was founded before the advent of the CWC, following Iraq's extensive use of CW in the 1980–1988 Iran-Iraq war, a capability developed in part through the acquisition of equipment and precursor materials from firms based in the West.

36. See the MTCR website at www.mtcr.info/english/index.html. The regime was founded at a time when numerous states thought to be pursuing weapons of mass destruction capabilities were also acquiring or developing ballistic missiles able to deliver such weapons. The regime initially focused on missiles deemed capable of carrying a nuclear warhead, nominally estimated to weigh 500 kilograms, to a range of 300 kilometers or more—roughly the capabilities of the Soviet-made Scud. At this time, the Soviet Union was supplying Scud missiles to a number of states thought to be interested in developing WMD, including Iraq, Libya, Syria, and North Korea. Also at this juncture, a number of other states with potential interest in WMD, including Egypt, Argentina, and Brazil, as well as Iraq, were pursuing indigenous programs to develop WMD-capable missiles, often relying on equipment and technology imported from Western firms. See Robert Shuey et al., "Missile Proliferation—Survey of Emerging Missile Forces" (Congressional Research Service, 3 October 1988, rev. 9 February 1989).

37. Under a July 2005 agreement between the United States and India, Washington sought a change in the Nuclear Suppliers Group rules to end the application of the full-scope safeguards requirement for India, so as to permit Nuclear Suppliers Group members to engage in civilian nuclear trade with it. See Somini Sengupta and Mark Mazzeti, "Nuclear Suppliers Group Ends Ban on Trade with India," *International Herald Tribune,* 7 September 2008. See also Dennis M. Gormley and Lawrence Scheinman, "Implications of Proposed India-US Civil Nuclear Cooperation" (Monterey, CA: Monterey Institute of International Studies, Center for Nonproliferation Studies, July 2005), available at www.nti.org/e_research/e3_67a.html.

38. "The Australia Group: Activities," available at http://www.australiagroup.net/en/activities.html.

39. See, for example, Henrietta Wilson, "The Biological Weapons Convention Protocol: Politics, Science and Industry," in *Verification Matters* (Verification Research, Training and Information Centre, December 2001), available at www.vertic.org/assets/VM02Intro_Wilson.pdf.

40. See, for example, "White Papers of the Non-Aligned Movement and the New Agenda Coalition, 2002 Nonproliferation Treaty Preparatory Commission, April 8–19, 2002," available at www.basicint.org/nuclear/NPT/2002prepcom/official.htm#One.

41. Jonathan B. Tucker, "Issue Brief: The Biological Weapons Convention (BWC) Compliance Protocol," Nuclear Threat Initiative, available at www.nti.org/e_research/e3_2a.html.

42. See references in note 27 and 28.

43. Glenn Kessler and Edward Cody, "US Flexibility Credited in Nuclear Deal with N. Korea," *Washington Post*, 14 February 2007, available at www.washingtonpost.com/wp-dyn/content/article/2007/02/13/AR2007021300130.html; see also note 15.

44. Regarding Syria and CW, see, for example, "Syria Profile, Chemical Weapons Overview," Nuclear Threat Initiative, available at www.nti.org/e_research/profiles/Syria/Chemical/2973.html; "Syria—Chemical Weapons," (GlobalSecurity.org), available at www.globalsecurity.org/wmd/world/syria/cw.htm; "Unclassified Report to Congress on the Acquisition of Technology Relating to Weapons of Mass Destruction and Advanced Conventional Munitions, 1 January Through 30 June 2003" (Central Intelligence Agency, 10 November 2003), available at www.acronym.org.uk/docs/0311/doc14.htm. For a list of CWC parties, see OPCW, available at www.opcw.org/html/db/members_frameset.html.

45. See Arms Control Association, "Summary of the Senate Resolution of Ratification to the Chemical Weapons Convention" (April 1997), available at www.armscontrol.org/act/1997_04/cwcanal.asp.

46. For current BWC members, see "The Biological Weapons Convention" (UN Office in Geneva). See also "Increasing Universal Adherence to the BTW Convention," BTWC 6th Review Conference 2006, EU Paper (Italy: 19 September 2006), available at www.opbw.org/rev_cons/6rc/docs/adv/BWC.Conf.VI_EU_WP_05_en.pdf.

47. See UN Special Commission website (maintained through 1999) at www.un.org/Depts/unscom.

48. Model Protocol Additional to the Agreement(s) Between State(s) and the International Atomic Energy Agency for the Application of Safeguards, IAEA INFCIRC/540 (1997), available at www.iaea.org/Publications/Documents/Infcircs/1998/infcirc540corrected.pdf.

49. Trevor Findlay, "Looking Back: The Additional Protocol," *Arms Control*

Today (November 2007), available at www.armscontrol.org/act/2007_11/Lookingback.asp.

50. "New Mullahs' Nuclear Site Under Scrutiny by International Media" (Foreign Affairs Committee National Council on Resistance of Iran), available at www.ncr-iran.org/index.php?option=com_content&task=view&id=4142&Itemid=152.

51. See note 32.

52. "Implementation of the NPT Safeguards Agreement and Relevant Provisions of Security Council Resolutions 1737 (2006) and 1747 (2007) in the Islamic Republic of Iran" Report of the Director General, GOV/2007/58 (15 November 2007), available at www.iaea.org/Publications/Documents/Board/2007/gov2007-58.pdf. In early December 2007, the US National Intelligence Council released a National Intelligence Estimate stating that, in 2003, Iran had halted its efforts to design a nuclear weapon and ready its components. The document and subsequent statements by US officials emphasized, however, that other aspects of Iran's nuclear program continued to raise concerns that it might be seeking to develop nuclear weapons. See Mark Mazzetti, "US Says Iran Ended Atomic Arms Work," *New York Times*, 3 December 2007, available at www.nytimes.com/2007/12/03/world/middleeast/03cnd-iran.html?ex=1354424400&en=d05bba4ef40f63b7&ei=5088&partner=rssnyt&emc=rss. Testifying in early 2009, newly appointed US director of national intelligence Dennis Blair declared that Iran remained several years away from possessing nuclear weapons, and that while it had continued to advance its overall nuclear capabilities it had not yet made the decision to build such weapons. See Peter Finn, "US, Israel Disagree on Iran Arms Threat," *Washington Post*, 3 March 2009, available at www.washingtonpost.com/wp-dyn/content/article/2009/03/10/AR2009031003626.htm.

53. "Background Briefing with Senior US Officials on Syria's Covert Nuclear Reactor and North Korea's Involvement" (24 April 2008), available at http://dni.gov/interviews/20080424_interview.pdf.

54. Jonathan B. Tucker, "Verifying the Chemical Weapons Ban: Missing Elements," *Arms Control Today* (January-February 2007), available at www.armscontrol.org/act/2007_01-02/Tucker.asp.

55. Ibid.

56. US Central Intelligence Agency, "Unclassified Report to Congress on the Acquisition of Technology Relating to Weapons of Mass Destruction and Advanced Conventional Munitions, 1 January Through 30 June 2003," available at www.cia.gov/library/reports/archived-reports-1/jan_jun2003.htm#iran; "Current and Projected National Security Threats to the United States, Lieutenant General Michael D. Maples, US Army, Director, Defense Intelligence Agency, Statement, Senate Armed Services Committee, February 28, 2006," available at www.dia.mil/publicaffairs/Testimonies/statement24.html.

57. "The US Position on the Biological Weapons Convention: Combating the BW Threat," speech by John Bolton, US undersecretary of state for arms control and international security, Tokyo American Center, 27 August 2001, available at www.acronym.org.uk/docs/0208/doc02.htm#02.

58. "Current and Projected National Security Threats to the United States," 2006; US Department of State, "Adherence to and Compliance with Arms Control, Nonproliferation, and Disarmament Agreements and Commitments" (30 August 2005), available at www.state.gov/t/vci/rls/rpt/51977.htm#chapter6.

59. US Department of State, "Adherence to and Compliance with Arms Control, Nonproliferation, and Disarmament Agreements and Commitments."

60. NPT, Art. X; CWC, Art. XVI (2); BWC, Art. XIII (2).

61. Modern nuclear power reactors require low-enriched uranium (LEU) for fuel, and this has led some states to assert that they have the right to produce that material domestically rather than purchase it on the international market. Once a state masters the ability to enrich uranium, however, it can use that technology to enrich uranium to the higher levels used in nuclear weapons. States can also claim the right to separate and reuse (or "recycle") the plutonium created in spent nuclear reactor fuel; fuel made from recycled plutonium and natural (unenriched) uranium can be used as a substitute for LEU fuel. Again, however, plutonium, once separated from spent reactor fuel, can also be used for nuclear weapons.

62. Judith Miller, Stephen Engelberg, and William J. Broad, "US Germ Warfare Research Pushes Treaty Limits," *New York Times*, 4 September 2001, available at http://query.nytimes.com/gst/fullpage.html?res=9E02E1D71639F937A3575AC0A9679C8B63&sec=health.

63. Jonathan B. Tucker, "Biological Threat Assessment: Is the Cure Worse Than the Disease?" *Arms Control Today* (October 2004): 13–19, available at www.armscontrol.org/act/2004_10/Tucker.asp.

64. See R. W. Jones, "Next Steps after INFCE: US International Nuclear and Nonproliferation Policy," OSTI ID: 6631667; DE84015111 (Oak Ridge National Laboratory, 1 March 1980), available at www.osti.gov/energycitations/product.biblio.jsp?osti_id=6631667.

65. See US Department of Energy, Global Nuclear Energy Partnership website at www.gnep.energy.gov. See also Sean Lucas, "The Bush Proposals: A Global Strategy for Combating the Spread of Nuclear Weapons Technology or a Sanctioned Nuclear Cartel?" Nuclear Threat Initiative, November 2004, available at www.nti.org/e_research/e3_58a.html.

66. Statement of Mohamed El-Baradei, director general, International Atomic Energy Agency, "Treaty on the Non-proliferation of Nuclear Weapons, 2005 Review Conference, available at www.un.org/events/npt2005/statements/npt02iaea.pdf.

67. Leonard S. Spector and Benjamin Radford, "Algeria, Emirates Plan Nonproliferation-Friendly Nuclear Programs; Egypt Keeps Fuel Cycle Options Open, Rejects Expanded IAEA Monitoring," *WMD Insights* (June 2008), available at http://wmdinsights.org/I25/I25_ME1_AlgeriaEmirates.htm.

68. See, for example, Daniel B. Poneman, Joel S. Wit, and Robert L. Gallucci, *Going Critical: The First North Korean Nuclear Crisis* (Washington; DC: Brookings Institution Press, 2004).

69. UN Security Council Res. 1718 (14 October 2006).

70. See notes 15 and 43.

71. John Heilbrin, "UN Powers Agree on More Iran Sanctions," Associated Press, 24 January 2008, available at http://ap.google.com/article/ALeqM5hCI7RGA8YSn3o9e4l_JdWzN_ju4AD8UCLMG00. For the text of Security Council Resolution 1803, see Security Council, "UN Security Council Resolutions—2008," available at www.un.org/docs/sc/unsc_resolutions08.htm.

72. "Report by the Director General, Implementation of the NPT Safeguards Agreement and Relevant Provisions of Security Council Resolutions 1737 (2006) and 1747 (2007) in the Islamic Republic of Iran," GOV/2007/58 (15 November 2007), available at www.iaea.org/Publications/Documents/Board/2007/gov2007-58.pdf.

73. See note 82.

74. See note 92.

75. See note 97.

76. Financial Action Task Force, available at www.fatf-gafi.org/pages/0,2987,en_32250379_32235720_1_1_1_1_1,00.html; Egmont Group website at

www.egmontgroup.org/; Andrew K. Semmel, deputy assistant secretary for nuclear nonproliferation, US Department of State, "Effective Multilateralism: The US Strategy for Dealing with Global Nuclear Proliferation," address at the National Strategy Forum, Chicago, 14 November 2005, available at www.state.gov/t/isn/rls/rm/56942.htm.

77. See "Revised Treaties to Address Unlawful Acts at Sea Adopted at International Conference; Diplomatic Conference on the Revision of the SUA Treaties: 10–14 October 2005," International Maritime Organization, available at http://194.196.162.45/Newsroom/mainframe.asp?topic_id=1018&doc_id=5334; Douglas Guilfoyle, "Maritime Interdiction of Weapons of Mass Destruction," *Journal of Conflict and Security Law* 12, no. 1 (2007): 36, available at http://jcsl.oxfordjournals.org/cgi/content/abstract/12/1/1.

78. IAEA, "Convention on the Physical Protection of Nuclear Materials (CPPNM) and Amendment thereto," available at www-ns.iaea.org/security/cppnm.htm.

79. "International Convention for the Suppression of Acts of Nuclear Terrorism" (Monterey, CA: James Martin Center for Nonproliferation Studies), available at http://cns.miis.edu/pubs/inven/pdfs/nucterr.pdf.

80. See "Cooperative Nonproliferation: The Global Initiative to Combat Nuclear Terrorism," (Henry L. Stimson Center, 2007), available at www.stimson.org/cnp/?SN=CT200705181262.

81. World Health Organization, "Biorisk Management—Laboratory Biosecurity Guidance," WHO/CDS/EPR/2006.6 (September 2006), available at http://www.who.int/csr/resources/publications/biosafety/WHO_CDS_EPR_2006_6.pdf.

82. The Global Partnership was established in 2002. At that time the United States pledged to spend an additional $10 billion over the coming decade on Cooperative Threat Reduction (CTR) programs, and the other members (Canada, France, Germany, Italy, Japan, Russia, and the United Kingdom) pledged a similar amount over the same period. Since 2002, a number of other states have joined the Global Partnership. See "Global Partnership Resource Page" (Monterey, CA: James Martin Center for Nonproliferation Studies, 2008), available at http://cns.miis.edu/research/globpart/; "The G8 Global Partnership Against the Spread of Weapons and Materials of Mass Destruction" (Henry L. Stimson Center), available at www.stimson.org/cnp/?SN=CT200705231266.

83. See US Defense Threat Reduction Agency, "Cooperative Threat Reduction Scorecard," 2009, available at www.dtra.mil/oe/ctr/scorecard.cfm.

84. Ibid.

85. For a review of the current status of the nuclear aspects of CTR programs and the Global Partnership, see Matthew Bunn, *Securing the Bomb 2007* (Washington, DC: Nuclear Threat Initiative, 2007), available at www.nti.org/e_research/securingthebomb07.pdf.

86. Ibid.; United States Enrichment Corporation (USEC), "Megatons to Megawatts Program," 2009, available at www.usec.com/v2001_02/HTML/megatons.asp.

87. See Richard Weitz, "Russia Chemical Weapons Dismantlement: Progress with Problems," *WMD Insights* (June 2007), available at www.wmdinsights.com/I16/I16_RU1_RussianChemical.htm.

88. See *The Biological Threat Reduction Program of the Department of Defense: From Foreign Assistance to Sustainable Partnerships* (Washington, DC: National Academy of Sciences, 2007).

89. See International Science and Technology Center (ISTC) website at

www.istc.ru; and the Science and Technology Center (Ukraine) website at www.stcu.int.

90. Bunn, "Executive Summary," Securing the Bomb 2007, available at www.nti.org/e_research/exsummary_stb07.pdf.

91. Richard Weitz, "Uranium Smuggling Incident Reinforces Concerns About Nuclear Trafficking in South Caucasus," *WMD Insights* (March 2007), available at www.wmdinsights.com/I13/I13_R2_UraniumSmuggling.htm; IAEA, "Trafficking in Nuclear and Radioactive Material in 2005," available at www.iaea.org/NewsCenter/News/2006/traffickingstats2005.html; Nuclear Threat Initiative, "NIS Nuclear Trafficking Database: What's New," available at www.nti.org/db/nistraff/update.htm (website currently down.); Nikolai Sokov, "Ukraine Rejects Russian Accusations of Missile Technology Control Regime Violation," *WMD Insights* (September 2006), available at www.wmdinsights.org/I8/I8_R2_UkraineRejects.htm; Jennifer Kline, "Special Report: Challenges of Iranian Missile Proliferation, Part I—Partnership with North Korea," *WMD Insights* (October 2006), available at www.wmdinsights.org/I9/I9_ME1_ChallengesofIran_1.htm; Sonny Enron, "N. Korea Working on Missile Accuracy" (GlobalSecurity.org), 2003, available at www.globalsecurity.org/org/news/2003/030912-nk01.htm.

92. Proliferation Security Initiative (PSI) website at www.state.gov/t/isn/c10390.htm; "Proliferation Security Initiative," *Inventory of International Nonproliferation Organizations and Regimes.*

93. As of late 2007, Belize, Croatia, Cyprus, Liberia, Malta, the Marshall Islands, Mongolia, and Panama had signed boarding agreements with the United States.

94. US Department of State, "Remarks on the Second Anniversary of the Proliferation Security Initiative," Secretary of State Condoleezza Rice, Washington, DC, 31 May 2005, available at www.state.gov/secretary/rm/2005/46951.htm.

95. See UN Security Council Res. 1718, Res. 1737, Res. 1747, and Res. 1803.

96. UN Security Council Res. 1540 (28 April 2004).

97. Mark Fitzpatrick, ed., *Nuclear Black Markets: Pakistan, A. Q. Khan and the Rise of Proliferation Networks* (London and Washington, DC: International Institute of Strategic Studies, 2007).

98. UN Security Council Res. 1810 (25 April 2008), "UN Security Council Resolutions—2008," available at www.un.org/docs/sc/unsc_resolutions08.htm.

99. "Comprehensive Nuclear Test Ban Treaty," UN Office of Disarmament Affairs, available at http://disarmament.un.org/wmd/ctbt/index.html.

100. See, for example, Rebecca Johnson, "CD Update—Conference Remains Deadlocked after First Part of 2002 Session," *Disarmament Diplomacy* no. 64, May–June (2002), available at www.acronym.org.uk/dd/dd64/64cd.htm; "Conference on Disarmament Hears Comments on President's Non-Paper on Debate on Nuclear Disarmament" (UN Office in Geneva, 16 March 2006), available at www.unog.ch/80256EDD006B9C2E/(httpNewsByYear_en)/86286735EA6826E4C12571320054D685?OpenDocument; "Conference on Disarmament Hears Statements from Dignitaries from Ecuador and Venezuela, March 12, 2007," (UN Office in Geneva), available at www.unog.ch/80256EDD006B9C2E/(httpNewsByYear_en)/D4FAEF4EE5AE2673C125729C0056F4F7?OpenDocument.

101. See "Report on the G8 Global Partnership," St. Petersburg G8 Summit, 16 July 2006, available at http://en.g8russia.ru/docs/22.html; "Report on the G8 Global Partnership," G8 Heiligendamm Summit, 8 June 2007, available at www.g-8.de/Content/EN/Artikel/__g8-summit/anlagen/gp-review-final,templateId=raw,property=publicationFile.pdf/gp-review-final.

102. "The Proliferation Security Initiative" (US Department of State, June 2004), available at http://usinfo.state.gov/products/pubs/proliferation/.

103. See "Cooperative Nonproliferation: The Global Initiative to Combat Nuclear Terrorism."

104. See note 76.

105. See note 76.

106. See Semmel, "Effective Multilateralism."

107. Final Documents, Sixth Review Conference of the States Parties to the Biological Weapons Convention, Geneva, 20 November to 8 December 2006, available at www.unog.ch/80256EE600585943/(httpPages)/3496CA1347FBF664C125718600364331?OpenDocument.

108. Regarding the Global Initiative to Combat Nuclear Terrorism, see note 80. See also "Effective Multilateralism."

Suggested Readings

Arms Control Today offers excellent current coverage of issues pertaining to the nonproliferation regimes. For example, *Arms Control Today* 38, no. 2 (2008) addresses key issues surrounding the "Chemical Weapons Convention at 10." See articles by John Hart, "The Continuing Legacy of Old and Abandoned Chemical Weapons"; Oliver Meier, "Chemical Weapons Parlay's Outcome Uncertain"; Ralf Trapp, "Advances in Science and Technology and the Chemical Weapons Convention"; Daniel Feakes, "Getting Down to the Hard Cases: Prospects for CWC University."

Australia Group website at www.australiagroup.net/index_en.htm.

Dossiers prepared by the International Institute of Strategic Studies, London, on *The North Korean Nuclear Program,* the *Nuclear Black Market,* and *Nuclear Programs in the Middle East,* available at www.iiss.org/publications.

International Atomic Energy Agency website at www.iaea.org/About/index.html.

Inventory of International Nonproliferation Organizations and Regimes (Monterey, CA: James Martin Center for Nonproliferation Studies, 2008), available at www.cns.miis.edu/pubs/inven/index.htm.

Nuclear Suppliers Group website at www.nuclearsuppliersgroup.org.

Organisation for the Prevention of Chemical Weapons website at www.opcw.org.

Organization for the Prohibition of Biological Weapons website at www.opbw.org.

Scheinman, Lawrence, *International Atomic Energy Agency: A Critical Assessment* (Washington, DC: Resources for the Future Press, 1985).

Thränert, Oliver, *Enhancing the Biological Weapons Convention* (Bonn: Verlag J. H. W. Dietz Nachf. GmbH, 1996).

Wright, Susan, *Biological Warfare and Disarmament: New Problems/New Perspectives* (New York: Rowman and Littlefield, 2002).

7

Regional Perspectives on Arms Control

Michael Moodie

Any chapter that addresses regional perspectives on arms control in the first decade of the twenty-first century must come to grips with several difficult questions. First, what constitutes arms control? Is it the traditional agenda and processes to regulate weapons that have been of concern to the international community for the past fifty years? Or does it go beyond that focus to include new issues, new processes, and new measures that have emerged since the end of the Cold War and the tragedies of 9/11?

Second, what constitutes a region? Is it the Cold War groupings seen in past multilateral negotiations defined by the Warsaw Pact, Western Europe, and the Non-Aligned Movement (NAM)? Or is it more broadly defined, based on geography, to include Europe, North America, South America, the Middle East, Asia, and Africa? Or should it be more precisely defined in terms of subregions such as South and Southeast Asia or northern and sub-Saharan Africa?

Third, what constitutes a regional perspective? Should it address the tangible arms control measures in operation in various regions? Or should it stress regional perspectives on arms control as an item on the global security agenda?

Fourth, does a regional perspective really matter, and do all regional perspectives matter the same? Neither the security challenges in various regions nor the measures taken to address them have the same salience. The result is that arms control is not equally important everywhere. Even establishing a metric to determine what is important is hard to do. The Middle East, for example, witnesses severe security challenges, but arms control has done little to address them. In contrast, Latin America does not have security problems of a comparable urgency, but arms control processes are reasonably well established in that part of the world. Which of these should be the focus of a chapter addressing regional arms control perspectives?

This chapter does not provide definitive answers to these questions, but considers all of them in some way or another. In doing so, it becomes clear that the arms control agenda from a regional perspective is a mix of old and new, familiar and unusual, reflecting a phenomenon with strong elements of both continuity and change. It is an agenda that involves the interplay of issues at varying levels—national, regional, and global. From a regional perspective, arms control has become a more complex phenomenon whose dimensions intertwine to create a skein of interactive challenges.

Preliminary Understandings

The term *arms control* has largely disappeared from the political lexicon (almost all references to the term, for example, have been excised from the names of US State Department bureaus and departments in recent years). Nevertheless, efforts persist to achieve international cooperation to regulate aspects of the development, production, and use of weapons or associated technologies as a means for diminishing conflict and fostering better political relationships. Many activities thus can be considered to be arms control, whether they are called arms control or not. Examining such initiatives in a broad context makes sense for several reasons. Shifts in the geostrategic environment and the security agenda have pushed efforts to control weapons in different directions, especially toward the use of less traditional diplomatic instruments.[1] Concern about the activities of nonstate actors since 9/11, for example, has inspired a number of new approaches that have expanded the range of choices available to governments in seeking to regulate the instruments of violence.[2] This trend has been reinforced by the need to shift from a focus on the conventional or unconventional arsenals of states to weapon technologies themselves.[3] Much of the regional and global arms control agenda today has to do with managing risks associated with dual-use technology.

Another reason for employing an expansive concept of arms control is based on the recognition that policymakers have not devoted much energy to improving or even maintaining the achievements of arms control since the mid-1990s.[4] Focusing solely on traditional arms control, especially in regional contexts, would make this a very short chapter indeed.

A broad approach to the notion of arms control also allows for consideration of a perspective that is often missing from contemporary studies. Arms control assessments are usually written from the viewpoint of leading arms control players, particularly the United States. An alternative arms control narrative exists, however, for many countries, especially those in the developing world. That alternative narrative relates both to past arms control initiatives and to the type of diplomatic and cooperative initiatives that could be undertaken in the future. It also reflects that fact that the future arms control narrative will incorporate significant elements of both continuity and change.

Continuity: A Lingering Old Agenda

Countries around the world continue to devote attention to traditional arms control concerns at both the regional and global levels. Some of these issues command attention because they reflect long-standing commitments to legally binding treaties. Others receive periodic scrutiny because they demonstrate a frustrating lack of progress in often decades-old efforts to secure acceptable political arrangements. This lack of progress betrays an inability in virtually every region of the world outside Europe to carry the arms control agenda beyond its usual focus either on weapons of mass destruction (WMD) or low-level technologies banned for humanitarian reasons (such as landmines).[5]

The regions currently of greatest concern are the Middle East and Asia because of their potential for violent conflict, the significant weapon inventories to which they are home, and the prospect that they could become areas of cascading proliferation. Although both areas pose several similar challenges for regional actors and the global community, a closer look reveals notable differences. To the extent that arms control issues have received any attention at all beyond the Middle East and Asia, the result has been a bifurcated approach. On one hand, attention has been given to the use of arms control measures to ameliorate emerging security challenges. On the other, to the degree that traditional arms control has been considered, it has reflected issues at play at the global level as opposed to issues of regional relevance.

The Middle East. Arms control progress in the Middle East has largely been hostage to a "Gordian knot of linkages."[6] Those linkages derive from alternative security perspectives. For Israel, national security can be achieved only by following the establishment of peaceful relations with its Arab neighbors, mutual recognition, and good neighborliness. Until such time, Israel will maintain its national security by maintaining a conventional military capability that is superior to that of any potential combination of its neighbors and, ultimately, a nuclear arsenal. For Arab states, Israel's nuclear weapons are the primary concern and must be "on the table" at the outset of any search for a stable regional security arrangement. These attitudes are complicated by efforts of some states to provide themselves with some minimal military response to Israel's nuclear weapons, such as Syria's chemical weapons (CW) program.[7] Additionally, Iran's nuclear ambitions, which Tehran claims are peaceful, are interpreted by some analysts as a counter to Israel. If Tehran is actually seeking to develop a nuclear deterrent or warfighting capability vis-à-vis Tel Aviv, the emergence of a nuclear arms race in the Middle East would have profound implications for the broader security environment not only in the Arab-Israeli context, but for the entire Persian Gulf and beyond.

These perspectives and linkages have influenced national policies relating to arms control. Israel is not a party to the Nuclear Nonproliferation Treaty (NPT) or the Biological Weapons Convention (BWC). Although Israel has signed the Chemical Weapons Convention (CWC), it has not ratified it. Iran is a party to all these agreements, but the United States alleges that Tehran is not complying with obligations related to any of these treaties. Another key regional arms control player, Egypt, is a party to the NPT, but not to either the BWC or the CWC. Cairo not only refrained from signing the CWC, arguing that it will not do so until Israel signs the NPT, but it led a boycott of Arab states when the treaty was initially opened for signature in 1993. This effort has eroded over the past decade and most Arab nations are now CWC states parties, although Syria has joined Egypt as a key holdout.

Several efforts have been made both in the region and extraregionally to address these interrelated problems. One of the most prominent has been pursuit of a region-wide zone free of WMD. This initiative had its origins in a 1974 Iranian proposal, backed by Egypt, for a regional nuclear-weapon-free zone (NWFZ). In 1990, the United Nations created an expert group to identify how such a goal could be achieved.[8] At about the same time, Egypt proposed expanding the initiative to include all weapons of mass destruction. UN Security Council Resolution 687, which ended the 1991 Gulf War, supported this idea.[9] In theory, the goal of eliminating WMD from the Middle East has been embraced by all the regional states, including Israel. Theory, however, has not translated into practice. The linkages between issues and differences over when Israel's nuclear weapons should be addressed in any negotiations have proven too difficult to overcome.

The severity of the barrier created by those attitudes and perspectives was demonstrated by another major Middle East arms control initiative that emerged at the end of the Cold War, the Arms Control and Regional Security Working Group (ACRS). The ACRS was one of five working groups launched in January 1992 to support the Middle East peace process that had begun three months earlier in Madrid. Its focus was exclusively on military stability and security enhancement in the region as a whole.[10] It held six sessions between May 1992 and December 1994, at which point activities stopped over a dispute about how to proceed on the agenda in the absence of a comprehensive peace accord.

The accomplishments of the ACRS should not be underestimated. They included agreements on a communications network for conveying ACRS-related information, prenotification of certain military activities, guidelines for cooperation to prevent incidents at sea, and principles regarding confidence-building measures (CBMs). The ACRS also held discussions on threat perceptions, definitions of weapon categories, force structures, and a definition of the potential geographic area to be covered in future arms control negotiations.

Ultimately, however, the ACRS could not overcome the barriers that the security perspectives of certain countries posed for its agenda. According to Peter Jones, "some Arab states became increasingly convinced that ACRS was unfairly biased toward the Israeli view of how the nuclear issue should be addressed. Accordingly, key Arab delegations began to block action on other issues. By 1995, it was impossible to hold another plenary."[11] Arms control initiatives could not overcome the fundamental political disagreements that animate Middle East conflicts.

Middle East arms control efforts have been stymied for more than a decade. Periodically, the questions of reviving the ACRS or taking another run at a zone free of WMD resurface.[12] Only arms control specialists will champion such notions until a solid foundation for political progress can be established. The experience in the Middle East shows that, although arms control can be useful in shaping positive relationships among security adversaries, it cannot get too far out in front of the regional political process. Neither a zone free of WMD nor an ACRS-style process will determine a new security paradigm for the Middle East. They each will be products of it.

Asia. Asia reflects the problem of defining what constitutes a "regional perspective" on arms control. "Asia" is too big geographically, politically, and economically to be a useful regional construct. One could argue that at least three subregional perspectives on arms control exist in Asia: Northeast Asia, Southeast Asia, and South Asia. For each of these subregions, the arms control agenda is substantially different. Northeast and South Asia would each have nuclear issues at the top of a potential arms control agenda, but the substance of their security challenges are different. In Northeast Asia, the major focus is the long-term implications of North Korea's nuclear ambitions. In South Asia, the challenge is maintaining stability between India and Pakistan—two historically hostile states that have acquired nuclear weapons.

The nuclear issue has become virtually the only arms control focus in both Northeast and South Asia. This was not always the case. In the early 1990s, for example, the nuclear question, then defined by concerns over the status of North Korea's reactor at Yongbyong, was embedded in a much more comprehensive arms control dialogue between North and South Korea. That dialogue also included discussions of nonnuclear CBMs and even an exchange of ideas on conventional arms control measures. No progress in either of these latter areas has occurred for more than a decade, and North Korea's nuclear program appears to have marched forward relentlessly, consuming the attention of both regional actors and the international community.

In South Asia, the question of nuclear stability between India and Pakistan is theoretically part of a "composite" security dialogue that also is intended to focus on resolving outstanding disputes, most notably over Kashmir, and maintaining a balance of conventional forces.[13] Promoting nuclear restraint also has been part of this composite dialogue. A major milestone in this regard was the February 1999 Lahore Declaration, which followed the summit of prime ministers Atal Bihari Vajpayee and Nawaz Sharif. The declaration noted a number of agreed risk reduction CBMs such as information exchanges on nuclear doctrines and data sharing on nuclear warheads and ballistic missile deployments. The Lahore Declaration also called for advanced notification of ballistic missile test flights and prompt notification of "any accidental, unauthorized, or unexplained incident" regarding nuclear weapons.[14] Unfortunately, the Kargil war of May–June 1999 brought confidence-building between the two countries to a screeching halt, and it has experienced only a desultory resumption in the past few years.

South Asia provides another example of why contemporary security challenges make it difficult to address regional arms control perspectives. India has close ties to Iran, and what Iran does with respect to its nuclear option could have important repercussions for both India and Pakistan. Pakistan and Saudi Arabia also enjoy close links that could further shape the security dynamics in the Middle East. If Riyadh decides to respond to Iran's acquisition of nuclear weapons with a nuclear program of its own, it is virtually certain to ask Pakistan for help.[15] The dynamics among India, Pakistan, Iran, and Saudi Arabia—and between the subregions of South Asia and the Gulf—are impossible to predict as nuclear arsenals emerge. An interlocking arms race across these regions would have profound implications for the global nuclear arms control regime.

Southeast Asia's perspective on arms control is substantially different than that of its neighbors to the north and west. Although the countries of Southeast Asia are concerned about the implications of nuclear proliferation on their flanks, the fact that nuclear proliferation is not occurring in their subregion fosters a less intense sense of urgency regarding arms control. Malaysia's foreign minister, for example, argued that he did not "see any necessity" to sign the Model Additional Protocol to the International Atomic Energy Agency (IAEA) safeguards agreements, despite revelations that a Malaysian firm manufactured some of Libya's nuclear equipment.[16] Another example of this less intense approach to arms negotiations came at the 2007 meeting of the Association of Southeast Asian Nations (ASEAN) Regional Forum. The official communiqué of that meeting reported that the delegates noted a proposal by the United States, China, and Singapore to establish an Inter-sessional Meeting (ISM) devoted to nonproliferation issues. The delegates "expressed widespread support for the principle of a new ISM on this subject, but further consultations on the terms of reference for such a meeting were needed. The Ministers tasked the members to continue consultation on the program for the next inter-sessional year."[17]

This more relaxed perspective is reinforced by the existence of the Treaty on the Southeast Asia Nuclear Weapon-Free Zone (Bangkok Treaty), which entered into force in March 1997, and also by the fact that virtually all Southeast Asian countries are party to both the BWC and the CWC. Moreover, no bilateral or multilateral security relationship in the subregion is sufficiently adversarial that other forms of arms control are deemed particularly necessary.

Member countries of ASEAN do participate with a number of other Asian countries in the Asian Senior-Level Talks on Nonproliferation (ASTOP), an initiative begun in 2003 that is hosted by Japan.[18] Not surprisingly, the primary focus of these talks is nuclear proliferation, notably in North Korea and Iran. At a 2007 meeting, for example, ASTOP participants emphasized "the need to take immediate and rigid measures to implement steadily the United Nations Security Council resolutions" related to both countries.[19] Other key points of discussion included the IAEA's Model Additional Protocol, the concept of assurances of nuclear fuel supply, combating nuclear terrorism, the importance of the Proliferation Security Initiative (PSI), and the need to strengthen export controls. Many Asian states need technical assistance to participate in these initiatives.

ASTOP may hold long-term security benefits for arms control in the Asia Pacific region. According to one assessment, for example, the talks "have facilitated high-level contact between ASEAN members, the United States, and China, allowing them to engage in the type of quiet, non-confrontational, and private dialogue that is consistent with ASEAN diplomatic practices. . . . [T]he fact that contentious and politically sensitive topics are being discussed in a dedicated forum represents significant progress in terms of the development of regional security cooperation."[20] It could be a positive harbinger of diplomatic progress in the region that discussion of the US-initiated PSI within the ASTOP forum has reduced regional resistance to initiatives to interdict the flow of materials related to the production of WMD.

China is a central issue in the arms control processes of all the Asian subregions. The fact that China joined the United States and Singapore in proposing the ASEAN Regional Forum initiative, for example, suggests after decades of assuming a relatively passive posture in most arms control forums—following a period in the 1950s and 1960s of outright opposition and hostility—Beijing is now beginning to play a more activist and, one hopes, positive role.

Suspicions may exist for several reasons, however, with respect to China's commitment to arms control. Not only has Beijing abetted proliferation through nuclear assistance to Pakistan, but the United States has sanctioned Chinese companies for violations of export control norms. On nineteen occasions, the George W. Bush administration imposed sanctions on thirty-two different Chinese entities for transfers related to ballistic and cruise missiles as well as CW, and the director of central intelligence reported to Congress that China remains a "key supplier" of weapon technology, particularly missile and chemical technology.[21] The United States also contends that China maintains some elements of an offensive biological weapons (BW) capability in violation of its BWC obligations, and it has judged that China maintains a CW production mobilization capability, although there is insufficient information to determine whether Beijing maintains an active offensive CW research and development program. Washington argues further that, in violation of its CWC obligations, China has not acknowledged past transfers of CW, and it may not have declared the full extent of its CW-related facilities.[22]

A different view holds that China is doing better with respect to arms control, a view that is shaped less by the rhetoric of China's leaders and more by the actions that the Chinese are taking to demonstrate the seriousness with which they view their international obligations. According to Jing-dong Yuan of the Center for Nonproliferation Studies, since the early 1990s China's arms control and nonproliferation policy has become increasingly compliant with international and multilateral conventions and regimes.[23] This change of policy is a reflection of Beijing's evolving perspectives not just on the importance of arms control and nonproliferation, but in terms of how Chinese policy on these issues could influence the international response to China's emergence as a great power. China's changing attitudes and approaches toward arms control and nonproliferation are a welcome departure from its traditional behavior and practices.[24]

Africa. Nuclear issues are not a regional concern for African states. This is not the result of the Treaty of Pelindaba, which established a NWFZ in Africa. This treaty was opened for signature in April 1996, but has not yet entered into force. Rather, it reflects the fact that, once South Africa abandoned its nuclear ambitions, nuclear weapons have not been of particular interest to African states, especially those south of the Sahara. Neither is there a strong prospect of nuclear proliferation within Africa, regardless of what happens in Iran or North Korea. To the extent that African nations consider nuclear issues, it is in the context of their concern over global nuclear disarmament. A similar observation could be made about Africa's consideration of chemical and biological weapons (CBW) issues. Most African countries are party to the CWC, fewer to the BWC, and neither chemical nor biological weapons are deemed to be much of a regional problem.

African states view intranational, ethnic, tribal, and other localized conflicts to be the security challenges they face that might be ameliorated by arms control. In this environment, small arms and light weapons (SALW) have become the continent's WMD, in the sense that they inflict huge numbers of casualties on an ongoing basis. For many African leaders, these are the weapons that are in greatest need of regulation and control. As a result of this concern, Africa's regional perspective is decidedly oriented toward more novel and less familiar elements of the twenty-first-century arms control agenda.

Latin America. Latin America has not given significant attention to arms control because security challenges in the region have little to do with conflicts that can be mitigated by the control of instruments of violence. Rather, the security challenges of greatest importance in Latin America relate more to socioeconomic issues and include such problems as drug trafficking, social unrest fostered by poverty and inequality, terrorism, some limited guerrilla activity, and fragile political institutions. Latin America, according to Maria Rosas, can be characterized as a region of "generally low military expenditure, a relatively peaceful environment, the existence of democratic governments and reform of the military."[25] This is not to say that the region is without interstate tensions, including border disputes and political rivalries, but in the past two decades, Latin America has been able to emphasize the peaceful and cooperative resolution of disputes.

Arms control agreements and CBMs have contributed to the creation of Latin America's relatively stable security environment. The 1968 Treaty of Tlatelolco was the first regional NWFZ treaty, and all Latin American and Caribbean nations are party to this agreement. In 1991, Argentina, Brazil, Chile, and Uruguay signed the Mendoza Accord, a CW CBM that gave added impetus to the then ongoing CWC negotiations. In that same year, Bolivia, Colombia, Ecuador, Peru, and Venezuela issued the Cartagena Declaration, renouncing their interest in WMD. All states in the Western Hemisphere, except the United States and Cuba, are party to the Ottawa Convention on Landmines. And in 2002, states of the Andean Community issued the Lima Commitment that established principles for establishing a peace zone in the subregion and articulated commitments to combat terrorism, limit defense spending, promote arms control, and eradicate illicit arms trafficking.[26] These are only some of the many security-related agreements that the nations of Latin America and the Caribbean have achieved over the past two decades to promote a more cooperative security environment. The arms control agenda for Latin America, therefore, is more about the maintenance and implementation of these agreements than active pursuit of major new regional initiatives. Latin American states are active in arms control forums, but they focus on global security issues rather than regionally focused initiatives.

Europe. Europe has a richer arms control legacy than most other regions of the world. Largely as a result of the Cold War and the confrontation between the North Atlantic Treaty Organization (NATO) and the Warsaw Pact, European nations extended the region's arms control reach to include instruments of conflict that are neither WMD nor the unsophisticated technology exploited in brutal community conflicts. Rather, Europe gave considerable attention to the conventional instruments of modern war and to how war was waged. In addition to several packages of CBMs, the Treaty on Open Skies and the Conventional Armed Forces in Europe Treaty (CFE Treaty)—both of which were negotiated in the final days of the Cold War in the early 1990s—established Europe's prevailing security architecture. Most of the recent attention given to regional arms control in European capitals has focused on maintenance of these agreements and their adaptation to the region's changing circumstances.

A challenge to this relatively stable regional arms control regime, however, emerged in mid-2007. On 14 July, Russian president Vladimir Putin announced that Russia was suspending its participation in the CFE Treaty. Moscow indicated that it wanted an arrangement more in keeping with the realities of twenty-first-century European security rather than an early post–Cold War agreement whose elements it considered "humiliating and discriminatory."[27] Russia complained that the treaty's "flank arrangements" unfairly forbade it to move its troops and equipment freely within its own borders. President Putin also accused NATO members of "foot dragging" on ratification of an adapted version of the CFE Treaty agreed in Istanbul in 1999, contending that Russia had met its obligations under that agreement.

NATO members have taken a different view, arguing that they will not ratify the treaty until Russia withdraws its military troops, equipment, and ammunition from Georgia and the Trans-Dniester region of Moldova. NATO has acknowledged Moscow's considerable progress in pulling its troops out of Georgia, but it has deplored the continued presence of Russian forces in Trans-Dniester. Russia argues such forces are there for peacekeeping and are thus not covered by the treaty.

It is not clear how this dispute will be resolved. Some analysts are concerned that, if NATO does not move toward the Russian position, Moscow will eventually withdraw from the CFE Treaty. If it does, NATO officials worry that this will undermine a treaty that has become the cornerstone of European security and has facilitated the decommissioning of some 60,000 tanks, armored vehicles, artillery, combat aircraft, and attack helicopters since it entered into force in the early 1990s.

Another legacy of the CFE Treaty in Europe is its role as a template for other agreements. In June 1996, the warring parties in the Balkans agreed to the Agreement on Sub-Regional Arms Control as a key goal of the Dayton Accords that brought conflict there to a halt. Modeled after the CFE Treaty, the agreement established numerical ceilings on tanks, armored vehicles, combat aircraft, attack helicopters, and artillery for Balkan countries, leading to the elimination of thousands of pieces of military equipment in that area. The US State Department called the process a "near total success."[28]

Regional Perspectives on the Traditional Global Arms Control Agenda

With the exception of Europe, most of the nations in the regions considered here are developing countries and members of the Non-Aligned Movement (NAM). Competing with the regional perspective described above for the limited attention that arms control receives is a set of global issues that many NAM members believe are important. Some of these issues carry over from long-standing arms control efforts while others reflect a new agenda for arms control.

Nuclear issues. For many developing countries, the major arms control issue has always been nuclear weapons. During the Cold War, it was the nuclear arsenals of the superpowers that generated the greatest concern. In the post–Cold War era, the core concern has been fostering progress toward the elimination of all nuclear weapons. This view was captured by the Swedish-sponsored Weapons of Mass Destruction Commission, chaired by Hans Blix, which argued that with sufficient political will "even the eventual elimination of nuclear weapons is not beyond the world's reach" and recommended that all nations of the world should "accept the principle that nuclear weapons should be outlawed . . . and explore the political, legal, technical and procedural options for achieving this within a reasonable time."[29]

Many developing countries give their highest priority to what they see as the fundamental bargain of the NPT: in exchange for most countries forgoing a nuclear weapon option, those countries that the treaty allowed to maintain their nuclear status would make good on their promise to achieve nuclear disarmament. In the view of NAM members, the bargain was reinforced by decisions made during the 1995 NPT Review and Extension Conference, at which the treaty was extended in perpetuity, and agreements concluded at the 2000 NPT Review Conference. Many of these states feel let down by what they view as the failure of the nuclear weapon states

(NWS), particularly the United States, to make genuine progress toward nuclear disarmament.

The importance of the nuclear issue to non–nuclear weapon states (NNWS) is reflected during sessions of the UN First Committee and General Assembly. There, resolutions dealing with nuclear nonproliferation and disarmament, though controversial, often receive the greatest number of supporting votes. In the 2006 session, for example, the resolution on Renewed Determination Towards the Total Elimination of Nuclear Weapons garnered the most favorable votes of any resolution (169 in the First Committee; 167 in the General Assembly). Similarly, a resolution on Towards a Nuclear-Free World: Accelerating the Implementation of Nuclear Disarmament Commitments won 157 votes. The United States voted for neither of these resolutions.[30]

The nuclear disarmament issue permeates all multilateral arms control efforts. In discussions of UN Security Council Resolution 1540, for example, a measure designed to prevent terrorists from acquiring nuclear, biological, and chemical (NBC) weapons, some states expressed concern that the resolution addressed only nonproliferation and said nothing about disarmament.[31] South Africa was one of several countries to voice its fear that the resolution could have a negative impact on the disarmament agenda.[32] Some views went even further, suggesting that by passing Resolution 1540, the nuclear weapon states, who are also the Security Council's five permanent members, used their status to require states to take action against nonproliferation without fulfilling their own disarmament obligations.[33]

Nuclear disarmament is not the only nuclear issue of ongoing concern to countries with a more regional perspective. Strong support also exists for the entry into force of the Comprehensive Test Ban Treaty (CTBT), which was negotiated during the Clinton administration, but rejected by the Republican-dominated Senate. It also was opposed by the George W. Bush administration. Another issue that has some support—although not as strong as the CTBT—is conclusion of a Fissile Material Cutoff Treaty (FMCT), whose status is currently caught up in a dispute between Washington and Beijing in the Conference on Disarmament (CD).[34]

Verification. A second ongoing issue that continues to be stressed by many developing countries concerns verification of existing agreements. In particular, these countries continue to call for strong verification measures for any arms control agreement that is or has been concluded.

The verification issue has been most sharply defined in the context of the BWC. For most of the period since the end of the BWC negotiations in 1972, the United States held to the position that the BWC was not verifiable. The Clinton administration took a different view, and throughout much of the 1990s, the Ad Hoc Group of States Parties of the BWC met to negotiate a legally binding protocol to the treaty that included measures intended to strengthen confidence in compliance. Most countries viewed this effort as one of producing a "verification protocol" to fill the gap they saw in the BWC which, as originally negotiated, had no verification or enforcement provisions. The George W. Bush administration rejected the draft protocol and argued that it would oppose any further negotiation of a verification protocol in the Ad Hoc Group or any other forum. The decision created an uproar of opposition and raised questions about the future of the BWC itself.

Although a modus vivendi regarding the BWC was subsequently achieved, the goal of a verification regime continues to receive strong support from many countries. At the Sixth Review Conference held in late 2006, for example, many countries used their opening statements to lament the absence of verification provisions and reiterate their view that such provisions remain necessary.[35] To some extent, these views may be politically motivated. Delegates might simply be exploiting an opportunity to allow the United States to take the heat for an unpopular decision. Some analysts hold the view that a number of countries, including several key NAM states, used the United States as a shield to hide their own opposition to the draft protocol. For other countries, however, verification is a sine qua non for arms control. They seem to believe that, even if highly limited in its effectiveness (as everyone acknowledged the BWC protocol would be), "some verification is better than none." In contrast, the Bush administration's perspective was that "bad verification is worse than none."

The BWC is not the only arms control issue in which verification is a point of contention. The Bush administration challenged a number of countries by arguing, in terms not dissimilar from its position regarding the BWC, that it would prefer an FMCT with few if any verification provisions. Again, the administration was challenging what many countries have taken as "received wisdom" regarding arms control and what is needed for it to be effective. Debate about the importance of arms control verification protocols is an issue that remains far from resolution.

Technology access. A leitmotif of multilateral arms control forums is an ongoing, often contentious dispute between developed countries and many developing nations regarding provisions in most arms control agreements that oblige states parties to provide cooperation and assistance in the promotion of relevant science and technology for peaceful purposes. More strident developing countries argue that these provisions mean that developed countries should disband any non-treaty-based export control arrangements. For example, in their view the Australia Group, an informal organization of more than thirty countries that coordinate policies relating to exports of relevant chemical and biological material and equipment, hampers their economic development. These developing countries contend that such arrangements represent efforts of the technological haves to retain their economic, commercial, and scientific dominance and prevent those without access to such technology from changing their have-not status. In response, developed countries participating in such arrangements argue that treaty-based export control regimes are not sufficiently developed, that many states parties do not have adequate national export control systems, and that such arrangements are needed to fulfill other treaty obligations not to transfer any materials or equipment that could be used to develop banned weapons. Developed countries also contend that such export control arrangements do not interfere with the commercial exchange of relevant technology, material, or equipment and that they engage in a variety of activities that do indeed meet their obligations under various treaties' cooperation and assistance provisions.

This ongoing dispute has impeded arms control progress. In 1992, for example, a group of radical nonaligned states threatened to withhold consensus over the recently concluded draft of the Chemical Weapons Convention until Australia Group members agreed to disband. Although the threat did not materialize, it did create delays and tension in the endgame of the CWC negotiations. The issue has also made itself felt in the context of the BWC. The work of the Ad Hoc Group on the draft BWC protocol, for example, had to include significant measures related to operationalizing the treaty's cooperation and assistance provisions as the price demanded by developing countries for their support of the harder security measures. In the view of some analysts, these cooperation and assistance measures created a serious imbalance between the protocol's security-oriented provisions and those pushed by developing countries, adding to existing concerns about the overall costs and benefits of the full protocol package.[36] More recently, NAM members, led by Iran, raised a demand late in the Sixth BWC Review Conference. Tehran wanted to include the provision that states parties had to agree to an action plan for implementing the BWC's cooperation and assistance provisions, and they tied agreement to this demand to their support for an action plan on national implementation that US officials badly wanted. A consensus could not be reached on whether and how to move both plans forward. As a result, neither plan was approved. Although the best face was put on the result,[37] the fact that national implementation efforts were watered down was disappointing to many participants.[38]

The ongoing dispute over cooperation and assistance obligations resonates beyond the BWC to other arms control agreements as well. Issues of technology transfer also are a constant, if not always highly visible, issue in ongoing work related to the NPT, which is slated to have another Review Conference in 2010.

An Emerging New Agenda for Arms Control

In addition to working on traditional issues, countries with a more regional perspective have begun to stress a set of challenges that are relatively new to the arms control agenda. Several developments have given rise to this new focus. To some extent, this new agenda is related to the emergence of the concept of "human security" and the view of many officials that their major security challenges do not stem from traditional state-to-state dynamics. In the opinion of many regional actors, security is defined not only as a state concern, but also as one relating to individuals who must confront a wide range of challenges to their quality of life. Not the conventional battles between military forces of adversarial nations, but those challenges in which the instruments of violence are used involve other forms of conflict between many different kinds of actors, including perhaps national militaries but also guerrillas, terrorists, warlords, local or ethnic militias, paramilitary forces, and criminal organizations. To address this new conflict environment, arms control must refocus its attention. Those who champion the relevance of arms control to these concerns about human security often point to the internationally agreed constraints on the use of landmines as evidence that formal arms control can improve not only the lot of states, but that of individuals.

Another impetus to the new arms control agenda is the greater attention being given to the potential for nonstate actors to misuse various types of weapons, especially materials related to WMD. Many of the new initiatives have been prompted by concern over nonstate actors acquiring the wherewithal to commit violence at unacceptable levels by using conventional weapons or NBC devices.

States also are increasingly concerned about creating constraints on the ability of other states to use force as an instrument of statecraft. Here, recent US foreign policy, especially the war it launched against Iraq in 2003, comes to mind. Many want to constrain the United States by preventing it from taking unilateral actions that are viewed as detrimental to global peace and security.

New Agenda Issues

Concerns about human security, the threat posed by nonstate actors, and the prospect of additional "unilateralism" on the part of the great powers have combined to foster an agenda and set of initiatives, programs, and measures that go far beyond Cold War arms control. These efforts are likely to be the primary focus of regional actors for years to come.

Small arms and light weapons. More than 600 million SALW are estimated to be in global circulation. Several million more are produced each year in more than ninety countries.[39] The vast majority of these arms are believed to be in private possession. The Small Arms Survey estimates that at least one million civilian-owned small arms are lost or stolen worldwide every year, weapons that can quickly and illegally flow between people and groups with little government oversight or regulation.[40] Not surprisingly, such weapons have become the favorite instruments of violence for insurgents, terrorists, crime syndicates, warlords, bandits, pirates, rustlers, and others who resort to violence to achieve their objectives.

The small arms problem comes in many forms. Although most gun deaths occur in contexts that are unrelated to war, one estimate puts gun deaths in conflicts at between 60,000 and 90,000 per year.[41] Gun violence exacerbates issues of poverty, gender, human rights, humanitarian aid, democratic governance, cultures of violence, and much more. In this sense, it is a quintessential human security rather than national security or military security challenge. For those countries with a more regional perspective, especially in areas where most of the world's gun violence now occurs, securing some regulation and control over these weapons has become a major priority.

From an arms control perspective, the key SALW-related development occurred in 2001 when more than 140 countries agreed to adopt the UN Program of Action (POA) to Prevent, Combat and Eradicate the Illicit Trade in Small Arms and Light Weapons in All Its Aspects. The POA calls on all UN member states to establish a national agency to coordinate relevant activities; engage with civil society in efforts to stop gun violence; harmonize policies at the regional level to strengthen regional agreements on control of small arms; destroy surplus, confiscated, or collected weapons; pass and implement adequate laws to prevent both illegal manufacture and trafficking in small arms; and a range of other measures. It also calls on states to undertake to "cooperate and to ensure coordination, complementarity and synergy in efforts to deal with the illicit trade in small arms and light weapons."[42] This agreement was reinforced by a UN General Assembly resolution that called for the creation of an SALW experts group by 2004.

In 2006, the first five-year review of the POA was undertaken, and the results were disappointing to many. In particular, it was not possible to secure agreement on how the threat of SALW illicit trafficking should be countered at the global level. Although many states argued for the intensification of efforts beyond those called for in the POA, a group of countries, including China, Cuba, India, Iran, Israel, Pakistan, Russia, and the United States, argued that states should implement the obligations they had already undertaken and that further development of the program should not be pursued.[43] Among other issues that sparked controversy were proposed restrictions on transfers to nonstate actors who do not have an import authorization from the government of the recipient state and controls on small arms ammunition or restrictions on civilian arms possession. Both of these regulations have been consistently opposed by the United States.

Despite the lack of movement at the Review Conference, the UN General Assembly considered further steps during its 2006 session. It passed a resolution calling on the Secretary-General to seek the views of member states and establish a group of government experts in 2008 to examine the feasibility, scope, and parameters for a comprehensive and legally binding arms trade treaty establishing common international standards on the import, export, and transfer of conventional arms. The United States was the only country to vote against the resolution.[44]

Expectations were high that the 2008 Biennial Meeting of States on SALW, the third such session, would reestablish momentum. By most accounts it succeeded—partially. Participants at the meeting agreed on a final declaration providing recommendations in four priority areas: (1) international cooperation, assistance, and national capacity building; (2) illicit brokering; (3) stockpile management and surplus disposal; and (4) international tracing. While welcomed, these results were less than hoped because, as one commentator noted, they consisted mainly of rephrased commitments made in 2001.[45] The final report was also weaker than most civil society groups and some delegations would have liked in a number of areas. The recommendations relating to stockpiles, for example, referred only to stocks of weapons but not ammunition supplies. For some, the focus on the four specific issues narrowed the discussion and obscured the "human security" dimension whose holistic, multidimensional character represents a major strength of the effort.[46] Moreover, the meeting participants resorted to an unusual procedure; they voted on the final document rather than requiring consensus. Iran had objected to the "Way Ahead" section of the document. Another source of disappointment was the absence of more than fifty countries from the meeting, including the United States, despite the fact that since 2001 Washington has helped countries around the world to destroy as many as one million SALW and to strengthen their transfer controls and stockpile management.[47]

Some commentators, therefore, concluded the BMS yielded a mixed outcome. It did achieve its primary aim of putting the UN's work on SALW back on track, and it lifted the process out of the stalemate that had continued since 2006. Another positive development was the important role played by developing countries, particularly from Africa and Latin America, in moving the agenda off dead center. The positive view of this result was demonstrated during the 2008 session of the UN General Assembly's First Committee, which passed several resolutions supporting the meeting's outcome by overwhelming majorities. The United States was the only country to vote against the omnibus resolution related to SALW, which recognized the group's results and mandated the convening of an open-ended meeting of governmental experts through 2011 to address key challenges to implementation of the POA. The vote in favor was 166, with no abstentions.[48] The results underscored the difficulty of achieving meaningful regulation. Several of the most contentious issues at the 2006 meeting were not addressed in 2008. Lack of participation remains a source of anxiety. Concerns are also high that most states do not have the capacity to implement effective measures in such a complex area, and, while cooperation and assistance in building those capabilities are welcome, they are deemed inadequate.

Although somewhat stymied at the global level, efforts to address the SALW issue at the regional level have been more enthusiastic. Of particular note is the 2006 Nairobi Protocol for the Prevention, Control and Reduction of Small Arms and Light Weapons in the Great Lakes Region and the Horn of Africa. The protocol is a legally binding agreement committing eleven states in central and eastern Africa to do everything called for in the POA, in addition to strictly regulating civilian possession of firearms and registering and regulating arms brokers. Regional SALW agreements also exist in Central America, the Andean Community, the Pacific Islands Forum, and the Southern African Development Community (SADC). The Economic Community of West African States (ECOWAS) also is expected to adopt a legally binding convention, and the African Union, the League of Arab States, ASEAN, and the Caribbean Community and Common Market (CARICOM) are now working to improve coordination to crack down on small arms trafficking in their respective regions.[49] These developments suggest that a norm might emerge from these regional agreements and activities that will ultimately achieve global scope and relevance with respect to SALW. If this happens, it would be a reversal of the traditional process involving the formation of norms: norms are generally articulated on a global basis only to be refined by regional actors to fit local circumstances.

UN Security Council Resolution 1540. Another issue reflecting the new arms control agenda is UN Security Council Resolution 1540, adopted in April 2004, which aims to prevent nonstate actors from manufacturing, acquiring, possessing, developing, transporting, transferring, or using chemical, biological, radiological, or nuclear (CBRN) weapons. The resolution requires all UN member states to pass legislation and establish effective controls to prevent CBRN weapons, their means of delivery, and related materials and technologies from falling into the hands of nonstate actors and being used for terrorist purposes. Under the resolution, all member states also are required to submit reports to a committee created by the resolution to inform the UN on their efforts.

As of February 2007, 135 member states had submitted their reports and 58 had not.[50] The quality of the submitted reports, however, varied significantly. Some states provided considerable details about their existing or planned efforts to meet the resolution's obligations while others provided little and, in some cases, virtually no information. One assessment pointed out that, as of mid-2006, "no state has fulfilled all of 1540's obligations and the vast majority has only a few of the resolutions' domestic legal requirements in place."[51] To a considerable extent, the limited activity that was reported reflects a lack of capability, resources, or perceived priority. In response, attention has shifted to providing help with implementation by compiling best practices or lessons learned for states to employ in the battle against this type of proliferation and developing voluntary guidelines for them to follow in stopping the spread of CBRN weapons.[52]

One common challenge for many member states is funding. Resolution 1540 calls on more capable states to lend financial, organizational, or technical assistance to those governments requesting such help. More than forty states have requested assistance in such areas as drafting legislation, training, expert advice, technical assistance, and human resources.[53] Most requests have been broad and lacking specific detail, making it difficult for the states that are willing to provide aid to devise meaningful assistance plans.[54]

Out of all the areas identified in Resolution 1540 for action, those that have received the least attention relate to border and export controls. To some extent, this lack of performance reflects insufficient resources. Border and export controls are both expensive and demanding to implement. Some states, however, are opposed to such measures in principle.

For many member states, especially those in the developing world, the threat created by CBRN weapons is just not that serious, especially when compared to other challenges such as SALW, AIDS, poverty, and civil wars. All of these "lesser included threats" have more immediate impact on their social order than CBRN issues and are, therefore, of correspondingly greater political relevance. This sense of lesser priority is reflected in lack of performance. As Peter Crail pointed out, "the most marked discrepancy in the fulfillment of the provisions of the resolution is between the adoption of a legal framework for fulfilling 1540's obligations and the establishment of enforcement mechanisms to deter, identify, and punish violators."[55]

It is not that these states are necessarily indifferent to CBRN issues. Indeed, some countries or regions, such as West Africa, have become deeply involved in at least the illegal trafficking of these kinds of weapons. Troubling, however, was the finding of a 2006 study that determined the regions with the lowest percentage of Resolution 1540 obligations fulfilled by key states were the same regions that have been trouble spots for theft and trafficking, including southeastern Europe, Southeast Asia, and the Middle East.[56]

One approach that has been suggested as a way of giving Resolution 1540 greater salience for many developing countries is to have regional organizations more involved in its implementation. Nana Effah-Apenteng, Ghana's permanent UN representative, for example, has argued that regional organizations are able to "develop more effective and contextually-driven means . . . rather than simply transplanting measures from states with different values and culture."[57] A number of regional seminars to facilitate Resolution 1540 implementation have been organized, and they seem to have been useful in forging a greater sense of ownership among UN member states that are otherwise reluctant to do much to implement the resolution.

Another aspect of Resolution 1540 that reflects a theme of the new agenda is its stress on involving nontraditional players in managing security risks. The resolution calls on all states to work with industry, the public, and academia in implementing its obligations. It suggests that including the private sector will be essential to the resolution's success, and emphasizes that business must become more aware and involved if the resolution is to have a positive impact on global and regional security.

BWC work plan. The need to expand the types of players involved in implementing existing agreements is also a feature of a third example of the new arms control agenda: the new approach that has been taken to strengthen the BWC. Following the US rejection of the draft verification protocol, BWC states parties agreed to an alternative approach proposed by the United States as a way to prevent efforts to strengthen the convention from coming to a complete halt. This alternative entailed the convening between the end of the Fifth Review Conference in 2002 and the opening of the Sixth Review Conference in 2006 of a series of annual meetings of experts to address a specific issue or set of issues. The goal of these meetings was to devise ways to share information and prompt states parties to take action at the national level to implement the BWC. Issues addressed in these meetings included the enactment of national legislation to implement BWC obligations, improvement of biosecurity at relevant scientific and commercial facilities, enhanced disease surveillance, investigations of alleged use, and development of codes of conduct for scientists engaged in advanced research in biology and disease. The findings of the expert meetings were then reviewed at annual meetings of states parties.

Many states parties were reluctant to support this US proposal for a number of reasons. The activities embodied in the proposal were not their preferred mode of operation. Most view the arms control process as the multilateral negotiation of legally binding agreements that are nondiscriminatory in application. The proposed BWC work plan had no negotiating dimension and no commitment to a particular outcome. Moreover, many states thought the meetings would be a waste of time and were suggested by Washington merely as a political ploy to avoid responsibility for bringing the verification protocol negotiations to a halt. They expected little to result.

Many also believed that the subjects to be discussed did nothing to address the major shortcoming that they perceived related to the treaty: the lack of verification provisions.

The intersessional program on which states parties worked from 2003 to 2005, however, came to be seen by most participants and observers to be more successful than anticipated. It demonstrated the value of improving access to information and the benefits of exploring issues in depth rather than in the cursory manner usually undertaken at Review Conferences.[58] For example, many more states parties participated in these information exchanges than were involved in the protocol negotiations. These efforts also galvanized many states parties to begin to improve their national implementation of the treaty, to provide assistance to states parties less capable of effective implementation, and to explore steps that could result in new measures (e.g., codes of conduct) that would add to the mosaic of an effective risk management strategy.

In sum, the intersessional program had the result, in the words of the Review Conference chairman, Masood Khan of Pakistan, of demonstrating that "there was a lot more to an effective BWC than the open-ended debate over whether and how verification should be pursued." The intersessional program moved states parties beyond the sterile and unhelpful debate on the fate of the protocol and shifted their focus to where it actually belonged—on the efforts and actions of states parties themselves. The intersessional program was sufficiently successful that states parties agreed to continue the activity (in a slightly revised mode) in the period leading up to the Seventh Review Conference in 2011.

With respect to the future of arms control, the experience of the intersessional programs suggests that the individual issues to be addressed are less important than the process that has been created to consider them. It is a new mode of operation in the arms control arena, providing information, guidance, assistance, and exchange, but leaving responsibility for action with individual states parties. It has broken out of the standard way of doing business, creating a more flexible tool that can accommodate a variety of associated activities involving a more expansive range of relevant players whose involvement could be crucial to the success of the BWC.

Final Observations

A variety of issues and approaches are embraced in the new arms control agenda: dealing with the explosive remnants of war (e.g., cluster bombs and abandoned landmines), nonlethal weapons, arms control in space (a special concern of China), and the PSI. In light of all these developments, it is clear that arms control retains international support and interest and has not become either moribund or a relic of history. Rather, it is surfacing in nontraditional places to deal with issues that were not of much concern during the Cold War. There is more to arms control than diplomats sitting in a conference room negotiating a legally binding agreement. To appreciate the nature of arms control in the early years of the twenty-first century, we must be willing to expand our horizons, accommodating a wider range of options and operations, more flexible and agile instruments, and less precise boundaries of applicability. The arms control agenda—whether it is termed that or not—is adapting to the evolving security environment. And although change is under way everywhere, the challenges that the world must now confront are emerging in diverse ways in different parts of the world. Therefore, they will have to be addressed in ways that reflect the realities of regional possibilities. Regional perspectives and regional efforts will be essential in promoting the success of the current and future arms control agenda.

Notes

1. Alyson J. K. Bailes, "Arms Control, Disarmament and Non-proliferation: Lessons of the Last Forty Years," speaking notes at the China Arms Control and Disarmament Association, Beijing, 8 May 2007, available at www.sipri.org/contents/director/Beijing20070508.
2. Ibid.
3. Michael A. Levi and Michael E. O'Hanlon, "Arms Control and American Security," *Current History* (April 2005): 168.
4. Bailes, p. 2.
5. Ibid.
6. The term is Baumgart and Müller's. See Claudia Baumgart and Harald Müller, "A Nuclear-Weapons Free Zone in the Middle East: A Pie in the Sky?" *Washington Quarterly* 28, no. 1 (2004–2005): 48.
7. Some analysts also allege that Egypt also maintains at least a limited chemical weapons (CW) and possible biological weapons (BW) program.
8. UN Department of Disarmament Affairs, "Effective and Verifiable Measures Which Would Facilitate the Establishment of a Nuclear-Weapons-Free Zone in the Middle East: Report of the Secretary-General," *Disarmament Study Series* no. 22 (NY: United Nations, 1992).
9. The preamble of the resolution renewed the call for a zone free of WMD and its operative paragraph 14 noted that disarmament in Iraq was an important step in that direction. Baumgart and Müller, p. 47.
10. See Michael D. Yaffee, "Promoting Arms Control and Regional Security in the Middle East," *Disarmament Forum* no. 2 (2001): 9–25.
11. Peter Jones, "Arms Control in the Middle East: Is It Time to Renew ACRS?" *Disarmament Forum* no. 2 (2005): 56.
12. See, for example, "Report on WG2: Weapons of Mass Destruction in the Middle East and the Establishment of a WMD-Free Zone," A Region in Transition: Peace and Reform in the Middle East—The 56th Pugwash Conference on Science

and World Affairs, Cairo, 11–15 November 2006, available at www.pugwash.org/reports/pac/56/working-group2.htm.

13. See, for example, Munir Akram, "Pakistan's Perspective on Arms Control, Disarmament, WMD Proliferation, and Use," presentation at the United Nations, October 2004.

14. Stephen F. Burgess, *India's Emerging Security Strategy, Missile Defense and Arms Control*, INSS Occasional Paper No. 54 (Colorado Springs, CO: USAF Institute for National Security Studies, June 2004), p. 43.

15. Sharad Jashi, "Nuclear Proliferation and South Asia: Recent Trends" (Monterey Institute of International Studies, Center for Nonproliferation Studies, 2007), available at www.nti.org/e_research/e3_91.html.

16. Tanya Ogilvie-White, "Nonproliferation and Counterterrorism Cooperation in Southeast Asia: Meeting Global Obligations Through Regional Security Architectures," *Contemporary Southeast Asia* 28, no. 1 (2006): 11.

17. Association of Southeast Asian Nations, "Chairman's Statement: 14th ASEAN Regional Forum," Manila, 2 August 2007, available at www.aseansec.org/20807.htm.

18. Other participating countries include Australia, Canada, China, New Zealand, the Republic of Korea, and the United States.

19. Ministry of Foreign Affairs of Japan, "The Fourth Asian Senior-Level Talks on Nonproliferation," Tokyo, press release, 1 February 2007.

20. Ogilvie-White, "Nonproliferation and Counterterrorism Cooperation," p. 19.

21. Shirley A. Kan, *China and Proliferation of Weapons of Mass Destruction and Missiles: Policy Issues* (Washington, DC: Congressional Research Service, 9 May 2007), p. 1.

22. Bureau of Verification and Compliance, *Adherence to and Compliance with Arms Control, Nonproliferation, and Disarmament Agreements and Commitments* (Washington, DC: US Department of State, 30 August 2005).

23. Juan-dong Yuan, "China's Proliferation and the Impact of Trade Police on Defense Industries in the United States and China," testimony before the US-China Economic and Security Commission, Washington, DC, 12 July 2007.

24. For more detail, see Evan S. Medeiros, *Reluctant Restraint: The Evolution of China's Nonproliferation Policies and Practices, 1980–2004* (Stanford: Stanford University Press, 2007); Bates Gill, *Rising Star: China's New Security Diplomacy* (Washington, DC: Brookings Institution Press, 2007), chap. 3; Wendy Frieman, *China, Arms Control, and Nonproliferation* (London and New York: Routledge, 2004).

25. Maria Cristina Rosas, "Latin America and the Caribbean: Security and Defense in the Post–Cold War Era," in *Stockholm International Peace Research Institute Yearbook 2005: Armaments, Disarmament and International Security* (Stockholm: SIPRI, 2006), p. 281.

26. Ibid., pp. 264–265.

27. Radio Free Europe/Radio Liberty, "Moscow 'Unhappy' with Outcome of CFE Conference," 15 June 2007.

28. Wade Boese, "Parties Complete Weapons Reduction under Balkan Arms Control Accord," *Arms Control Today* (October 1997), available at www.armscontrol.org/act/1997_10/balkanact.asp.

29. Weapons of Mass Destruction Commission, *Weapons of Terror: Freeing the World of Nuclear, Biological and Chemical Arms* (Stockholm: 1 June 2006), pp. 18, 19, available at www.wmdcommission.org/files/weapons_of_terror.pdf.

30. Jennifer Nordstrom, "Cooperation and Cautious Optimism: Report on the 2006 UN First Committee," *Disarmament Diplomacy* no. 83 (Winter 2006), available at www.acronym.org.uk/dd/dd83/83fc.htm.

31. Mark J. Valencia, "The Proliferation Security Initiative: A Glass Half-Full," *Arms Control Today* (June 2007), available at www.armscontrol.org/act/2007_06/Valencia.asp?print.

32. Lars Olberg, "Implementing Resolution 1540: What the National Reports Indicate," *Disarmament Diplomacy* no. 82 (Spring 2006), available at www.acronym.org.uk/dd/dd82/82lo.htm.

33. Joseph C. Bristol et. al., *A New Urgency for Nonproliferation: Implementing United Nations Security Council Resolution 1540* (Princeton: Princeton University, Woodrow Wilson School, January 2007), p. 12.

34. The Chinese will agree to begin Fissile Material Cutoff Treaty (FMCT) negotiations only if the Conference on Disarmament (CD) also addresses the issue of arms control in outer space, something that the United States opposes. Given that the CD operates by consensus, a deadlock has existed in the CD for years, preventing no work at all. See John Borrie, "Cooperation and Defection in the Conference on Disarmament," *Disarmament Diplomacy* no. 82 (Spring 2006), available at www.acronym.org.uk/dd/dd82/82jb.htm.

35. Graham S. Pearson, "The Biological Weapons Convention Sixth Review Conference," *CBW Conventions Bulletin* no. 74 (December 2006): 5–19.

36. See, for example, Michael Moodie, *The BWC Protocol: A Critique,* Special Report No. 1, (Washington, DC: Chemical and Biological Arms Control Institute, June 2001).

37. See Masood Khan, "The BWC Review Conference: The President's Reflections," *Disarmament Diplomacy* no. 84 (Spring 2007), available at www.acronym.org.uk/dd/dd84/84bwcpr.htm.

38. Richard Guthrie, "Rising Out of the Doldrums: Report on the BWC Review Conference," *Disarmament Diplomacy* 84 (Spring 2007), available at www.acronym.org.uk/dd/dd84/84bwc.htm.

39. Holger Anders, "The UN Process on Small Arms: All Is Not Lost," *Arms Control Today* (March 2007), available at www.armscontrol.org/act/2007_03/Anders.asp?print.

40. Rachel Stohl and Rhea Myerscough, "Sub-Saharan Small Arms: The Damage Continues," *Current History*, May 2007, p. 228.

41. Ibid.

42. Quoted in Kerry Maze and Hyunjoo Rhee, "International Assistance for Implementing the UN Program of Action on the Illicit Trade of Small Arms and Light Weapons in All Its Aspects: Case Study of East Africa" (Geneva: UN Institute for Disarmament Research, 2007), p. 1.

43. Anders, "The UN Process on Small Arms."

44. Twenty-four states, however, abstained, including China, Egypt, India, Iran, Israel, Pakistan, Russia, Saudi Arabia, Sudan, Syria, Venezuela, Yemen, and Zimbabwe. Ibid.

45. Paul Holton, "Combating the Illicit Trade in Small and Light Weapons," *SIPRI Update: Global Security and Arms Control,* July/August 2008.

46. Sejai Vora, "Moving the Small Arms Agenda Forward," *Disarmament Times* 31, no. 3 (Fall 2008): 7.

47. Ibid.

48. The US delegate explained its vote against the resolution by noting that "a perpetual series of costly meetings is not required to achieve this nor do we believe

such meetings are likely to advance the real objectives of this resolution." Mark Marge, "Small Arms and Light Weapons," *First Committee Monitor,* available at www.reachingcriticalwill.org.

49. Rebecca Peters, "Small Arms and Light Weapons: Making the UN Program of Action Work," *Disarmament Diplomacy* no. 82 (Spring 2006), available at www.acronym.org.uk/dd/dd82/82rp.htm.

50. UN Department of Public Information, "Security Council Affirms Determination to Strengthen Cooperation Aimed at Countering Nuclear, Chemical and Biological Weapons Proliferation: Presidential Statement Follows Day-Long Debate on Ways to Enhance Implementation of Resolution 1540 (2004)," SC 8964 (23 February 2007).

51. Peter Crail, "Implementing UN Security Council Resolution 1540: A Risk Based Approach," *The Nonproliferation Review* 13, no. 1 (2006): 356.

52. Wade Boese, "Progress on UN WMD Measure Mixed," *Arms Control Today* (May 2007), available at www.armscontrol.org/act/2007_05/UNwmd.asp ?print.

53. John Bergenas, "The Role of Regional and Sub-Regional Organizations in Implementing UN Security Council Resolution 1540: A Preliminary Assessment of the African Continent," paper prepared as part of a project conducted by the UN Institute for Disarmament Research and the Monterey Institute of International Studies, Center for Nonproliferation Studies, available at www.cns.miis.edu/stories /pdfs/070508.pdf.

54. Bristol et al., *A New Urgency for Nonproliferation,* p. 2.

55. Crail, "Implementing UN Security Council Resolution 1540," p. 378.

56. Many countries in the Arabian peninsula had not submitted their reports, including Dubai, which had been a major transshipment point for the A. Q. Khan network. Crail, "Implementing UN Security Council Resolution 1540," p. 373.

57. Quoted in Bergenas, "The Role of Regional and Sub-regional Organizations," p. 7.

58. "Meeting the Challenges of Reviewing the Biological and Toxin Weapons Convention—A Summary Report," Geneva: The Geneva Forum, June 2006. Available at www.geneva-forum.org/Reports/20060309-10.pdf.

Suggested Readings

"Arms Control in the Middle East," special issue, *Disarmament Forum* no. 2 (2008).

Borrie, John, and V. Martin Randin, eds., *Thinking Outside the Box in Multilateral Disarmament and Arms Control Negotiations* (Geneva: UN Institute for Disarmament Research, 2006).

Crail, Peter, "Implementing UN Security Council Resolution 1540: A Risk-Based Approach," *The Nonproliferation Review* 13, no. 2 (2006): 355–388.

Croft, Stuart, "South Asia's Arms Control Process: Cricket Diplomacy and the Composite Dialogue," *International Affairs* 81, no. 5 (2005): 1039–1060.

Durch, William J., *Constructing Regional Security: The Role of Arms Transfers, Arms Control, and Reassurance* (New York: Palgrave for the Century Foundation, 2000).

Kaye, Dalia Dassa, *Talking to the Enemy: Track Two Diplomacy in the Middle East and South Asia* (Santa Monica, CA: RAND, 2007).

Landau, Emily B., *Arms Control in the Middle East: Cooperative Security Dialogue and Regional Constraints*, (Brighton, UK: Sussex Academic Press; Tel Aviv: Jaffee Center for Strategic Studies at Tel Aviv University, 2006).

Parker, Sarah, and Sylvia Cattaneo, "Implementing the UN Program of Action on Small Arms and Light Weapons" (Geneva: UN Institute for Disarmament Research, July 2008).

8

The Role of Cooperative Security

Lewis A. Dunn

By the closing years of the Cold War, treaty-based arms control negotiations between the United States and the Soviet Union were increasingly used not only to regulate, but also to transform, the military competition between the two hostile Cold War camps. Over time, the substance, complexity, and scope of the resulting agreements had steadily expanded—limits on nuclear testing, strategic nuclear forces, missile defense, biological weapons (BW), intermediate- and shorter-range nuclear forces, conventional forces, and chemical weapons (CW) were all issues covered by East-West arms control treaties. Beginning with the 1963 Limited Test Ban Treaty (LTBT), the arms control negotiating process between Washington and Moscow also served political purposes. Ongoing negotiations reassured friends, allies, and onlookers; provided a channel for enhanced strategic predictability and understanding between the two superpowers; and signaled the two main protagonists' mutual interest in ensuring that the Cold War confrontation stopped short of a globe-destroying nuclear conflict. In practice, and for many in theory, the resultant process of treaty-based arms control negotiations came to define cooperative efforts to manage global strategic challenges.

Nonetheless, throughout the Cold War, skeptics periodically criticized the treaty-based arms control process. Their arguments focused on the substantive limitations of specific agreements, the difficulties of verifying other parties' compliance, and the lack of an effective response to such noncompliance. Some observers criticized the arms control process itself. For its critics, treaty-based negotiated arms control took too long, resulted in agreements that were too complicated and complex, limited US freedom of action in undesirable ways, and was seen as inherently too confrontational.[1]

With the election of President George W. Bush in 2000, this skeptical assessment of treaty-based arms control negotiations came to define official US policy. For senior Bush administration officials, moreover, a belief that pursuing treaty-based arms control would make it more difficult for Moscow and Washington to build a new nonadversarial political-strategic relationship to replace their Cold War confrontation reinforced the long-standing litany of criticisms. In their eyes, treaty-based arms control negotiations were inherently confrontational, resulting in the pursuit of national advantage rather than the building of partnerships.[2] Thus, after reluctantly agreeing to Moscow's demand to formalize both sides' commitment to reduce their deployed nuclear weapons via the 2002 Strategic Offensive Reductions Treaty (SORT, also called the Moscow Treaty), the new administration gave top priority to pursuit of a growing set of ad hoc cooperative initiatives to meet global strategic challenges. The Proliferation Security Initiative (PSI), the Container Security Initiative, and the Global Initiative to Combat Nuclear Terrorism are but a few examples. While the administration put forward in the UN Conference on Disarmament (CD) a treaty to ban the production of fissile material for nuclear weapons, its proposed treaty did not include any of the verification provisions that had come to characterize more traditional Cold War arms control negotiations. Still other US efforts at strategic dialogue with both Russia and China were pursued at best with little follow-through within the overall bureaucracy, and at worst with little commitment.

For their part, supporters of more traditional treaty-based arms control negotiations have been persistent critics of the George W. Bush administration's virtual rejection of that approach. Officials and experts around the globe also have been strong critics, particularly in the context of the ongoing five-yearly process of reviewing the implementation of the Nuclear Nonproliferation Treaty (NPT). The calls in 2007 and 2008 by the group of former secretary of defense William Perry, former secretaries of state Henry Kissinger and George Shultz, and former senator Sam Nunn for a US commitment to the abolition of nuclear weapons—along with pursuit of a range of arms control negotiations—have added new momentum to this ongoing debate.

Against that backdrop, this chapter explores the concept of cooperative security activities as an approach to meet the global strategic challenges of the early twenty-first century. It suggests that the dichotomy between Cold War treaty-based arms control negotiations and more ad hoc initiatives among coalitions of the willing as the preferred means to meet those challenges is too simplistic. To the contrary, the toolkit of potential cooperative security activities that officials in the United States, Russia, China, and other partnering nations can draw on to help meet today's strategic challenges is far richer.

To explore these ideas, the first section briefly defines the concept of cooperative security activity and describes the different potential "baskets" of cooperative activities. The discussion then illustrates the potential contribution of cooperative initiatives in meeting today's strategic challenges—from transforming the US-Russia strategic relationship through managing the US-China strategic relationship to avoiding runaway nuclear proliferation. By way of conclusion, this chapter sets out some overarching "strategic" considerations to guide future use of cooperative security activities.

Cooperative Security Activities: Setting Out the Concept

To meet today's global strategic challenges, US officials have recourse to many different strategies. Depending on the specific challenge, some mix of diplomacy, strategic communications, alliance and regime building, cooperative security activities, deterrence and defenses (including homeland security), and military operations might be considered. Within this overall context, cooperative security activities encompass many different, but interrelated, cooperative approaches to enhance countries' mutual security. Two aspects of this overall strategy warrant discussion: (1) the emphasis on cooperative pursuit of mutual security; and (2) the broad spectrum of specific activities, means, or tools that are encompassed by the concept of cooperative security activities.

The Underlying Principle of Cooperative Security

The concept of cooperative security activities reflects the effort to strengthen a shared commitment among partnering countries to manage their security choices to enhance their mutual security. It also emphasizes a readiness to acknowledge the security interests and perspectives of partners to find a mutual accommodation of interests. The concept recognizes that there sometimes will be differences of interests and perspectives between countries, and on occasion these differences can be quite pronounced. In those instances, pursuit of cooperative security activities would call for partners' readiness to manage areas of disagreement to reduce their scope and contain their spillover effects on areas of mutual interest.

This principle of cooperative pursuit of mutual security is consistent with a long-standing body of thought within the strategic affairs community. During the intellectual ferment of the late 1950s that led to traditional arms control, for example, one school of thought held that arms control's goal should be the cooperative management by Washington and Moscow of their national security decisions.[3] This view, however, gave way to the more formulistic definition of arms control's goals as reducing the risk of war, reducing the consequences of war, and reducing the costs of defense preparations.[4] More recently, experts in the United States and in Russia have proposed variants on cooperative security as an overarching concept for regulating the US-Russia strategic relationships and other competitive international settings.[5] The 1990s Nunn-Lugar Cooperative Threat Reduction (CTR) program, with its commitment to US-Russian cooperation to contain the nuclear risks that followed the collapse of the Soviet Union, perhaps best typifies a commitment to mutual security.

The Cooperative Security Activities Toolkit

The cooperative security toolkit comprises six baskets of cooperative activities: (1) strategic dialogue and the exchange of information and data; (2) visits, personnel exchanges, and more formal defense or military liaison arrangements; (3) joint studies, experiments, initiatives, and activities; (4) unilateral political-military actions, including reciprocal unilateral actions; (5) more traditional negotiated arms control agreements; and (6) joint programs, systems, and centers.

Strategic dialogue and the exchange of information and data. Strategic dialogue, combined with the exchange of information and data, comprises one set of cooperative security activities. Strategic dialogue can be a valuable means to enhance understanding of how other partners perceive potential opportunities and threats, to lessen the risk of miscalculation, and to help identify potential responses and initiatives. Strategic dialogue also can build professional relationships between the officials of participating countries, which can facilitate agreement on courses of action. To be most effective, however, strategic dialogue often requires either a formal mechanism to foster follow-through within national bureaucracies, continuing attention from senior officials, or both. The effectiveness of cooperation on nonproliferation between the United States and the Soviet Union during the Cold War, for instance, stemmed from a process of strategic dialogue coupled with high-level interest. By contrast, despite a formal commitment to strategic dialogue between Moscow and Washington after the 2002 Moscow Treaty agreement, this dialogue proved of modest utility in avoiding the growth of mutual uncertainties, in large part due to the lack of bureaucratic follow-through or senior-level attention.

Exchanges of information and data also are part of this first basket of cooperative security activities. Information exchanges are built into most recent arms control agreements. Declarations have covered, for example, the location, number, and status of baseline capabilities; plans for and execution of the elimination of capabilities under given agreements; plans for the replacement of systems and their deployment; and many other dimensions of day-to-day military postures. Exchanges of information and data, however, need not be directly linked to a specific treaty or arms control agreement. Non-treaty-related information also could be exchanged across a wide range of defense activities to provide partners with a window into each other's thinking, programs, planning, deployments, concepts, doctrine, and overall strategic decisionmaking.

Visits, personnel exchanges, and liaison arrangements. Visits, personnel exchanges, and liaison arrangements can help meet today's strategic challenges by building confidence and by providing windows into the thinking and activities of partnering countries.

Visits of many different types have become an established means of strategic confidence-building among countries. In some instances, such visits are ad hoc; in other cases, they are grounded in some type of prior arms control treaty or other facilitating legal agreement. One example would be visits of senior civilian and military officials to military bases and command locations. Mid-level officials and military personnel can also undertake site visits to familiarize each other with specific military operations, bases, locations, and activities under a given arms control agreement. Visits of technical experts from respective nuclear weapon laboratories to comparable sites in partner countries also have been undertaken since the end of the Cold War. Past experience suggests that reciprocity is likely to be a key issue in creating a process of visits and exchanges. To the extent that such visits can become a matter of routine, however, issues of reciprocity may become less important.

Personnel exchanges are more often used between allies or friendly countries. Perhaps the best example is exchanges of personnel to study at each other's defense colleges and senior-level military training courses. Such exchanges now have become a relatively common practice, including, for example, study by individuals from the former Soviet bloc countries at US defense institutions. Other personnel exchanges include reciprocal presence at technical institutions and laboratories, think tanks, and nongovernmental organizations involved in strategic analysis. In principle, such exchanges need not be limited only to allied or friendly countries. The temporary presence of Russian military personnel at the North American Aerospace Defense Command (NORAD), Cheyenne Mountain, Colorado, prior to the Year 2000 problem (Y2K) rollover is a precedent for the presence of foreign officers and officials at sensitive facilities and locations.

More formal military-to-military liaison arrangements also fall into this basket of tools. They provide yet another means to share information, allow discussions of strategic issues to help clarify positions, avoid miscalculation, create a basis for common action, build personal ties, and generally to provide windows into each partner's thinking. The presence of Russian military personnel at the North Atlantic Treaty Organization (NATO) Headquarters in Brussels as part of the NATO-Russia Partnership is a good example of this kind of exchange. Liaison arrangements involving senior military personnel serving at each other's military commands (e.g., the US Strategic Command [STRATCOM]) is an example of one that is more restricted in its usage. More formal joint commands also are conceivable, exemplified by the creation during World War II—and continued formal existence—of a US-UK joint command arrangement.[6]

Joint studies, experiments, initiatives, and activities. Joint studies may have many payoffs: building up a shared appreciation and understanding of a problem; helping partners to understand their differences better; identifying potential responses and areas for cooperation in meeting a given challenge; generating bureaucratic support and interest; and, sometimes, simply keeping a problem on the table until political conditions are ripe to deal with it. Joint experiments have many of the same payoffs, though sometimes with a more hands-on technical dimension of laying the foundation for later actions. Both studies and experiments can pave the way for additional cooperative activities. A good example is the Joint Verification Experiment of the late 1980s. During this experiment, US and Soviet technical experts from their respective nuclear weapon laboratories and test sites explored technical measures, including the carrying out of monitored nuclear tests at each other's nuclear test sites, that paved the way for creating a new Verification Protocol to the Threshold Test Ban Treaty (TTBT) and for that treaty's eventual entry into force.

Joint initiatives and activities are a long-standing approach for international cooperation to meet global strategic challenges. Both formal and less formal actions are conceivable. In the nonproliferation field, for instance, the Nuclear Suppliers Group, the Australia Group, and the Missile Technology Control Regime (MTCR) all stand out as means to foster cooperation to make it more difficult for countries to acquire technologies and materials for use in nuclear, chemical, biological, or missile programs. Most recently, pursuit of joint initiatives among so-called coalitions of the willing have been at the core of US proliferation prevention and counterterrorist efforts. Both the PSI and the Global Initiative to Combat Nuclear Terrorism typify such initiatives—with many dozens of partners, animated by agreement on shared principles, and reflecting an emphasis on practical cooperation. Such joint initiatives are an effective means to create personal and professional relationships among officials and to identify ways to strengthen national domestic authorities for cooperation.

Unilateral actions. Unilateral actions as a means to pursue shared strategic interests are often considered synonymous with the 1991 Presidential Nuclear Initiatives (PNI), whereby US President George H. W. Bush and Soviet President Mikhail Gorbachev committed their governments to remove from deployment and eliminate ground-launched and sea-launched tactical nuclear weapons. Precedents for unilateral action as a means of mutual security, however, go far back into the Cold War. The spectrum of unilateral action as a cooperative security effort is far broader, more varied, and richer than suggested by the PNI. These actions also vary in terms of whether reciprocal action by partners is anticipated or not.

Modest efforts—unilateral national statements, releases of information, and other transparency measures—are both readily conceivable and easily executed. Their purpose may simply be to enhance predictability and lessen the risk of misunderstanding. This is the goal, for instance, behind continuing releases of information concerning the US missile defense program. Or the purpose of releasing information, at the same time as encouraging reciprocating unilateral action by another country, may be to shape that country's choices to enhance mutual stability and security. This was the case in the early 1960s when the John F. Kennedy administration made highly publicized statements on US thinking about nuclear doctrine, nuclear command and control, and nuclear warfighting restraint and used informal channels to encourage Soviet officials to take those statements seriously.[7] More significant unilateral actions may include restraints on the production, numbers, testing, deployment, and operations of given military systems. Unilateral actions, as with the 1991 PNI, also can be a means of mutual reductions of capabilities between or among partners.

Unilateral actions can be taken as a means of reassurance and confidence-building without regard to whether such actions are reciprocated by partners or potential adversaries. Or there may be a hope or expectation of reciprocal action. Parallel or reciprocated unilateral actions also may follow from negotiations between partners on specific steps that both countries will be prepared to take cooperatively, but unilaterally.

Experience suggests that negotiated parallel and reciprocated unilateral actions often are a more rapid means of action than traditional treaty-based arms control. Progress can be made more quickly by the decision to set aside efforts to negotiate the details and specific modalities of how unilateral changes of defense posture will occur, or how any reduced capabilities will be eliminated. Relying on unilateral measures instead of cooperative means to verify all actions taken also can help move events along quickly. An urgent need for action to deal with an imminent challenge provides a justification for streamlined procedures (e.g., as was the case with the PNI whose driving consideration on the US side was concern about the security of tactical nuclear weapons in the midst of the breakup of the former Soviet Union).

Negotiated agreements. Negotiated agreements were at the center of US-Soviet efforts first to regulate and eventually to roll back the Cold War strategic competition. For many observers in the United States and overseas, negotiated agreements—in particular, legally binding treaties—remain the archetype of cooperative activities to meet today's strategic challenges.

The purposes of these agreements ranged widely and remain germane today. The first formal treaty, the 1963 Limited Test Ban Treaty (LTBT), regulated the US-Soviet competition by requiring that nuclear tests be conducted underground. Perhaps equally important, their agreement to the LTBT provided a means for the two Cold War adversaries to signal their mutual commitment to restrain the risks of a nuclear war in the wake of near disaster in the Cuban missile crisis six months previously. In some instances, limited agreements sought to contain potentially dangerous activities that could have escalated to a US-Soviet military confrontation (e.g., the 1972 Incidents at Sea Agreement aimed at reversing a trend toward peacetime naval confrontation). Somewhat differently, the first major US-Soviet strategic arms control treaties—the 1972 Strategic Arms Limitation Interim Agreement and the Anti-Ballistic Missile Treaty (ABM Treaty)—regulated offense-defense relationships and provided increased predictability.

By the closing years of the Cold War, more complex and detailed arms control agreements began the process of rolling back strategic competition between Washington and Moscow. The 1987 Intermediate-Range Nuclear Forces Treaty (INF Treaty), the 1991 Strategic Arms Reduction Treaty (START), and the Conventional Forces in Europe Treaty (CFE Treaty) all stand out. In parallel, the end of the Cold War also saw the negotiation of the 1992 multilateral Chemical Weapons Convention (CWC) banning chemical weapons as well as the 1996 Comprehensive Test Ban Treaty (CTBT) banning testing of nuclear weapons.

With isolated exceptions, these traditional negotiated arms control agreements took many years to negotiate. They also included detailed provisions for the elimination of systems reduced by these treaties to make reductions irreversible. Detailed verification provisions, including on-site inspections, also were negotiated to monitor parties' compliance. Most of these negotiated agreements were legally binding; although, in principle, politically binding agreements also fall within this basket of cooperative security activities.

Joint programs, centers, and systems. Precedents again exist for joint programs, centers, and systems from the US-Russian Nuclear Risk Reduction Centers in both countries' capitals (that were created during the 1970s) to the 1999 agreement to create a US-Russian Joint Data Exchange Center on warning in Moscow (yet to begin operations). Beyond such formal centers, joint military programs and systems also are conceivable. On a number of occasions over the past fifteen years, for example, there have been periodic proposals that the United States and Russia jointly develop and deploy ballistic missile defense (BMD) to counter missile threats from countries of proliferation concern. The purpose of such joint programs, centers, and systems can vary widely from building confidence, to providing an alternative to potentially destabilizing national programs, to facilitating implementation of other agreements.

Cooperative Security Activities and Early Twenty-first-Century Strategic Challenges

The United States confronts a mix of strategic challenges in the early twenty-first century, and cooperative security activities can help meet those challenges. There are a variety of ways that the concept of cooperative security activities can be applied to meet specific strategic challenges. To evaluate which measures are most important and stand the greatest chance of success, it is best to estimate the potential payoffs and likely feasibility of different cooperative activities in addressing specific threats.

Early Twenty-first-Century Strategic Challenges, Writ Large

The early twenty-first century combines both opportunities and dangers for the United States—often as reverse sides of the same strategic challenge. Both Russia and China are in the midst of fundamental and still uncertain political, economic, social, and military transitions. For US policymakers, one key strategic challenge is managing the strategic interaction between the United States and Russia and China, respectively, to reduce mutual uncertainties and to build habits of cooperation. In both cases, it also is important to contain pressures that could lead toward renewed or new strategic arms races—even if not on the scale of US-Russian competition during the Cold War. Along with these two core bilateral relationships, the United States also is a direct or indirect partner in a series of other political-military interactions in different regions of the globe. Managing these emerging strategic interactions (e.g., among the United States, Japan, and China; the United States, China, and Russia; Pakistan, India, China, and the United States) presents still other strategic challenges today. Building cooperation among the Permanent Five (P-5) of the UN Security Council—the United States, Russia, the United Kingdom, France, and China—also stands out as one of today's strategic challenges.

An additional set of less country-specific, but more cross-cutting, strategic challenges confronts the United States and other countries in the early twenty-first century. Preventing acquisition or use of chemical, biological, radiological, or nuclear weapons (often termed weapons of mass destruction [WMD]) by a terrorist group or nonstate actor stands out as a key challenge facing policymakers. Efforts to build habits of global cooperation, to support national efforts to strengthen controls against nonstate access to WMD, and to influence terrorists' calculations are more specific dimensions of this challenge. Preventing runaway nuclear proliferation—as many states around the globe acquire increasingly sophisticated commercial nuclear industries—is another cross-cutting global strategic challenge. This particularly calls for influencing countries' capabilities and motivations to acquire nuclear weapons so that they forgo transforming latent capabilities into real nuclear arsenals. The proliferation risks produced by the increasingly widespread use of nuclear power to help meet twenty-first-century energy needs are still not fully understood by the international community.

Five Examples of Cooperative Security Activities in Action

To illustrate the concept of cooperative security activities, the following discussion focuses on five examples: (1) reducing US-Russian mutual strategic uncertainties, (2) building habits of cooperation between the United States and China, (3) strengthening habits of international cooperation to prevent terrorist acquisition or use of WMD, (4) strengthening the legitimacy and effectiveness of existing nonproliferation institutions, and (5) avoiding an India-Pakistan nuclear crisis and conflict. These examples not only make clear the potential contributions, but also the limitations, of utilizing these types of cooperative security activities to shape the future global strategic order.

Managing the US-Russia strategic relationship: Reducing mutual strategic uncertainties. In both the United States and Russia, mutual uncertainties about each other's intentions, objectives, and longer-term political-military directions increasingly provide the backdrop for their overall security relationship. Within the United States, there is widespread uneasiness about rising Russian domestic authoritarianism. Although they are still quite modest in scope and pace, Russian decisions to deploy modernized strategic nuclear systems are nonetheless seen by some observers to augur a renewed Russian military competition with the United States. Perceptions that Russian officials are not particularly concerned about the proliferation threat—certainly less than they are about the threat of terrorism—also heighten US uncertainties, sometimes even leading to questions about whether Russian strategists would welcome more proliferation as a means of tying down an American Gulliver.

By contrast, there is a strong and widespread belief among the Russian political and military elite that the United States is seeking a position of absolute security vis-à-vis Russia and globally.[8] They fear that the US pursuit of limited missile defenses ultimately will expand incrementally until some combination of US strategic offensive and defensive nuclear and conventional forces—combined with a decline in Russian strategic capabilities as old Cold War systems age or are not replaced—will result in a US threat to eliminate Russia's nuclear deterrent. The US decision in 2007 to pursue deployment of a third missile defense site in the Czech Republic and Poland served to catalyze these concerns. Russian uncertainties also have been reinforced by over two decades of relative US political neglect, seen by Russians both as malign (e.g., rejection of Russian concerns leading up to NATO intervention in Bosnia in 1999 as well as NATO's expansion ever eastward) and as benign (e.g., the US focus on many issues other than Russia throughout most of the 1990s and early 2000s).

These mutual uncertainties are costly. They make it more difficult for Russia and the United States to work together to meet shared challenges, which require cooperative action. Over time, such uncertainties may yet contribute to competitive military procurements. Russian uncertainties about US intentions also reinforce today's authoritarian-nationalist trends in Moscow and among the Russian public.

Assuming a desire on both sides to take steps to reduce mutual uncertainties, there is a rich menu of potential cooperative security means to pursue that goal. One place to start would be a joint presidential-level decision by presidents Barack Obama and Dmitri Medvedev to reaffirm the goal of a nonadversarial political relationship and to pursue a strategic partnership. That reaffirmation could also give a needed high-level political push for a sustained, serious strategic dialogue to address the underlying issues that have led to such mutual uncertainties. Experience with US-Russian dialogue over the past decade and a half suggests that it will be important to establish an institutional mechanism for this dialogue to create momentum for bureaucratic follow-through (e.g., periodic reports to senior oversight officials in both countries). If possible, it would be desirable to achieve a "quick success" from this renewed commitment to strategic partnership and sustained dialogue. One possibility would be to bring into force the aforementioned US-Russian agreement to create a Joint Data Exchange Center for warning in Moscow. By providing information about the status of missile launches to Russia, the center also could lessen Russian concerns about the erosion of its nuclear deterrent.

With the end of the START I looming in late 2009, both Washington and Moscow acknowledge the need to negotiate a legally binding replacement. Streamlined to reflect the end of the Cold War, a new post-START agreement would provide mutual transparency and predictability for strategic deployments and decisions in a period of uncertainty. There is little doubt that reducing Russian uncertainties about US strategic intentions will require a readiness on the part of the United States to address Russian concerns about its pursuit of missile defenses. Several different, but mutually reinforcing, cooperative security activities warrant consideration. For instance, some combination could be pursued of a joint nuclear missile threat assessment, unilateral US efforts to continue providing information on its missile defense plans and programs, and a negotiated agreement on the modalities of US missile defense deployments (whether legally or politically binding). A commitment on the part of both the United States and Russia to explore a joint missile defense program—perhaps one that links together existing US and Russian missile defense capabilities to counter Iran's current missile threat to nearby countries—could also be pursued.[9] Readiness by the United States to share its missile defense capabilities would provide a critical incentive for Russia to participate in a renewed attempt to move to a nonadversarial relationship; and, from the US perspective, for heightened Russian cooperation in dealing with proliferation challenges.

Looking further ahead, a sustained strategic dialogue and such near-term agreements could give way to other cooperative security activities aimed at lessening the growth of mutual uncertainties between Washington and Moscow. Visits, personnel exchanges, and even liaison arrangements could be one means to provide valuable windows into the thinking of each side. Russian and US military officers could attend each other's military service academies. The Russian military presence at NATO in Brussels could be expanded to include a liaison presence at NORAD or even at the US Strategic Command. Additionally, a more formal, continuous set of flag rank military-to-military command discussions could be set up in both countries' capitals. Joint studies and experiments, linked to the ongoing strategic dialogue, could be used over time to enhance mutual understanding of each side's perspectives, interests, and approaches to specific problems. Precedents exist for such joint studies and experiments; future initiatives could range from an assessment of proliferation threats in 2025 through the elements of a transparency regime for conventional longer-range ballistic missiles to the technical-political conditions of abolishing nuclear weapons. Summaries of these discussions rather than actual reports might be the product, thereby helping to avoid a least common denominator outcome. Today's ongoing US-Russian joint initiatives, typified by the Global Initiative to Combat Nuclear Terrorism, also can build habits of cooperation to help lessen mutual uncertainties.

Many cooperative security means also would contribute to efforts to strengthen habits of cooperation between Washington and Moscow and roll back the Cold War nuclear legacy—the two other more specific dimensions of managing US-Russia strategic interaction. Indeed, what stands out across the US-Russia strategic relationship is the rich menu of potential cooperative initiatives that have a high potential payoff and are in principle quite feasible. This situation reflects the great changes that have occurred in the US-Russia political-military relationship since the height of Cold War competition as well as both countries' long experience in seeking to regulate that competition with arms control and other means.

Managing the US-China strategic relationship: Building habits of cooperation. Building habits of cooperation between the United States and China is part of the overall challenge of managing the US-China strategic relationship in the early twenty-first century. Those habits of cooperation facilitate reducing mutual uncertainties, lessening the risk of a military confrontation arising out of mutual miscalculation, and avoiding strategic arms competition. Building habits of cooperation between Washington and Beijing can contribute to global efforts to meet other cross-cutting strategic challenges such as preventing terrorist access or use of WMD, heading off runaway proliferation, and containing the proliferation risks of commercial nuclear energy.

Unlike the case of the United States and Russia, however, the potential menu of feasible cooperative security activities is not as extensive. Pursuit of many types of cooperative activities is impeded by differences of interest between the United States and China and by their different cultures, historic experiences, and ways of thinking about political and security issues. By way of example, China's strategic culture emphasizes secrecy, not transparency. Further, contrasted with the US-Russia relationship after the end of Cold War confrontation, there are possible flash points for a military confrontation between China and the United States, specifically over the status of Taiwan. This risk of conflict makes it both harder and more important to explore those opportunities that exist for applying the concept of cooperative security activities as one means to manage the relationship between Washington and Beijing.[10]

As in the case of Russia, strategic dialogue appears to be the necessary starting point of efforts to build habits of US-Chinese cooperation. Semiofficial Track Two exchanges involving US and Chinese academics, retired officials, and military personnel already are under way. They have proved a valuable way to understand each country's respective positions, interests, and thinking. With regard to a more official (or Track One) political-military dialogue with the United States, however, China's senior leaders have tended to turn on and off China's readiness to engage, depending on other US actions (e.g., arms sales to Taiwan or a visit by the Dalai Lama to Washington). Given China's strategic culture, a top-down approach to strategic dialogue could have greater chances for longer-term success. In fact, such an approach might help the two countries' presidents to reach initial agreement on initial principles and broad goals for the US-China relationship and then empower their senior political-military officials to pursue a strategic dialogue within the mandate set by those goals.[11]

Building habits of US-China strategic cooperation could also be facilitated by possible joint studies, experiments, and initiatives. Once more, top-down endorsement would help to facilitate such an activity but, again, the possibilities appear more limited than in the case of the United States and Russia. China's active participation in the Six-Party Talks aimed at the denuclearization of North Korea is a precedent. Similarly, China's 2007 decision to participate in the Global Initiative to Combat Nuclear Terrorism could offer other opportunities to build cooperation. China also might be encouraged to cooperate with the United States and other countries to provide needed assistance to third parties to accelerate implementation of UN Security Council Resolution 1540 (which obligates all countries to put in place controls against nonstate actors gaining access to WMD). Drawing on its own experience in establishing enhanced legal and regulatory controls over chemical-, biological-, and nuclear-related items, China's government could assist third parties with whom it has close ties. Joint assessments of emerging and future proliferation and terrorism threats also could pay off in building cooperation and providing insights into each side's thinking.

Unilateral actions by both the United States and China may have a potential role in helping to create a better context for building habits of cooperation. Such actions could contribute to reducing mutual uncertainties and avoiding strategic miscalculation as well as reducing the possibility of strategic arms competition. A readiness on the part of the United States to restrain the scope of its deployments of missile defenses—and statements to that effect—would be one important, if controversial, example of a unilateral initiative. Unilateral reassurance to China that the United States is not seeking a decapitating nuclear-conventional first strike against China's strategic forces would be another, but again controversial, step in helping to head off an arms race before it begins. In both cases, senior US officials would first need to answer the still unresolved question of whether the United States is prepared to accept some degree of nuclear vulnerability to China. For China, a unilateral statement aimed at increasing the transparency of its strategic thinking, capabilities, and decisionmaking could be a parallel, and possibly equally controversial, step. In turn, statements by the Chinese leadership that China would not use military force unilaterally to reunite Taiwan and China could positively impact US thinking.

By contrast, the other baskets of cooperative security activities do not appear ripe for joint pursuit, either because of Chinese or US interests and perspectives. Specifically as of 2009, it is difficult to envisage a significant role for routine ongoing exchanges of military personnel, let alone for a more formal military liaison arrangement, for the use of negotiated agreements to regulate aspects of each side's deployments of military capabilities, or for joint systems or programs in building habits of cooperation.

Even some of the more modest cooperative security activities posited above could prove to be a step too far for senior Chinese officials and leaders at the present. As a result, any US strategy toward China needs to include some thinking about how to increase the readiness of those leaders to become a partner in cooperative security activities. Beginning with small actions to set some precedents of mutually valuable successes would be part of that strategy. It also might be possible to use China's greater readiness to cooperate through the P-5 and the Six-Party Talks as means to build Chinese habits of cooperation with the United States as well as with the other P-5 states. The goal again would be to create precedents of successful cooperation. Areas for such cooperation could include joint studies; exploration of transparency measures that might be adopted unilaterally or by the P-5 overall; joint proliferation prevention activities; and possibly even agreement on guidelines for nuclear safety, control, and restraint that all of the P-5 would commit to follow.

Preventing WMD terrorism: Building global habits of cooperation. Strengthening global habits of cooperation is critical to meeting the challenge of WMD terrorism. Global cooperation is needed to limit access to dangerous materials, components, know-how, or weaponry, and for detection and interdiction of attempts to smuggle a stolen or diverted nuclear weapon into a country. Cooperative actions can influence assessment by terrorist leaders of whether escalation to chemical, biological, or nuclear violence would serve the goals of their groups. Cooperation can send a signal to potential individual criminals, crime syndicates, or state aiders and abettors of a terrorist WMD attack that the risks of using these weapons outweigh any conceivable reasons for doing so. Cooperation can also facilitate the response to a terrorist attack involving WMD to minimize the immediate consequences of loss of life and destruction while using the shock of an attack to put in place new policy initiatives. Across many of these areas, bilateral and multilateral cooperation already is under way. But the time also is ripe for other cooperative activities.

Joint studies and initiatives could be a starting point. Policymakers could pursue a joint P-5 initiative to put in place needed standby technical, organizational, and personnel capabilities to assist a non–nuclear weapon state (NNWS) in dealing with a terrorist nuclear incident. Procedures could be created to determine whether a terrorist nuclear threat is a hoax or real or to help in rendering safe an intercepted improvised or full-up nuclear device as well as in disposing of a device. In the worst case, cooperation could help a beleaguered government manage the consequences of an attack involving CW, BW, or nuclear weapons. A joint P-5 or G8 assessment—including possible gaming—of political-military responses to a terrorist attack involving WMD would be another way to strengthen global habits of cooperation.

Unilateral actions and negotiated agreements also have a potential contribution to make. On the one hand, unilateral—but coordinated—statements could be made by all of the P-5 that they would cooperate to hold accountable the leaders of states that support acquisition or use of WMD by terrorist groups. Such statements would send a signal aimed at deterring that support. Sufficient flexibility could be retained to allow the specific response to be tailored to the particular case. On the other hand, the P-5 could seek to reach agreement among themselves on guidelines that they would follow for nuclear surety, safety, and security. Other nuclear powers could be kept apprised of these discussions and eventually be given the opportunity to associate themselves unilaterally with any guidelines that emerge.

A joint P-5 or G8 program to assist countries around the world in implementing enhanced controls against acquisition of WMD-related materials, equipment, components, or know-how by nonstate actors—as required by Security Council Resolution 1540—would be a positive initiative. Without technical, financial, and organizational aid many countries will lack the capacity to meet their Resolution 1540 obligations. In turn, such a joint program would go far to strengthen national controls, itself one dimension of the overall WMD terrorism strategic challenge.

Preventing runaway nuclear proliferation: Strengthening the legitimacy of nonproliferation institutions and norms. Preventing runaway proliferation depends heavily on success in dealing with the proliferation problem countries, especially rolling back North Korea's nuclear weapon program and heading off Iran's acquisition of a nuclear arsenal. But strengthening international nonproliferation institutions and norms comprises an important dimension of this particular strategic challenge in its own right. There are many reasons to be concerned about the possible erosion of those nonproliferation institutions and norms, including possible failures in dealing with North Korea, Iran, and other emerging proliferation problem countries. The corrosive impact should not be underestimated of widespread perceptions that the nuclear weapon states (NWS) recognized by the NPT have not lived up to their commitments to move toward the abolition of nuclear weapons under Article VI of the treaty. Those perceptions reflect a deeper clash of cultures within the NPT and the global nonproliferation community about the importance of nuclear disarmament. Addressing that clash of cultures will play a critical role in strengthening global nonproliferation institutions and norms.

Cooperative security activities involving the United States, Russia, and the other NPT nuclear-weapon states offer many different means to address this issue. At a minimum, the NWS could either through coordinated unilateral statements or a joint statement reaffirm their commitment to the goal of abolishing nuclear weapons. Coordinated exchanges of data among the P-5 about their nuclear programs, plans, deployments, and drawdowns would be beneficial. Information exchanges also would be constructive within the context of the ongoing NPT review process between the P-5 and the broader NPT community. Such exchanges would be a means to meet repeated calls from the NNWS for so-called reporting by the NWS on their activities. Joint studies also could be launched and publicized as a means to show support for the progress toward the goal of nuclear elimination (e.g., ranging from a P-5 assessment of the technical, political, and other conditions of nuclear elimination to a bilateral US-Russian assessment of nuclear requirements in 2030).

The greatest payoff for demonstrating support for Article VI of the NPT and enhancing the perceived legitimacy of nonproliferation institutions and norms is to be found in the basket of negotiated nuclear arms control agreements. As mentioned before, US-Russian agreement to put in place an updated and streamlined transparency regime after START I ends in 2009 is one case in point. A US-Russian commitment to negotiate an agreement to continue the 2002 Moscow Treaty reductions after their instant of operation in 2012 is another—as would be the related commitment to further Moscow Treaty reductions after 2012. These agreements could be either politically or legally binding, although it is clear that the international payoffs would be enhanced if they were legally binding on the parties involved. Perhaps most controversial, a US readiness to ratify the 1996 CTBT would help bridge the two cultures embodied in the NPT and strengthen the NPT's legitimacy. Negotiation of a CTBT was part of the 1995 grand bargain, which resulted in the indefinite extension of the NPT. For the United States, ratification of the CTBT would be a difficult choice. Nevertheless, the United States has the worst of both worlds: it is extremely unlikely that it will resume US nuclear testing, but it enjoys none of the formal benefits provided by a treaty-based ban on testing while pursuing such negotiated, formal agreements. However, the potential contribution of unilateral measures to buttress nonproliferation institutions should not be dismissed. Assuming a US-Russian transparency agreement, the other P-5 NWS could be encouraged to associate themselves unilaterally with its obligations. This would be relatively straightforward for France and the United Kingdom. It would constitute a more significant policy shift for China. Still other unilateral actions that might be explored could include changes of nuclear doctrine and posture aimed at moving nuclear weapons as far into the background as possible in the defense postures of the P-5. Here, the greatest obstacles could well be Russia's increased reliance on nuclear weapons to compensate for conventional military weakness and the official US skepticism about proposals for de-alerting and for no first use of nuclear weapons. Even so, a possible interim step could be for the P-5 to undertake a joint assessment of possible options—and conditions—for moving toward reduced reliance on nuclear weapons as part of their defense strategies and by further relaxing their nuclear alert postures.

Managing emerging strategic interactions: Avoiding an India-Pakistan nuclear crisis or conflict. The strategic relationship between India and Pakistan stands out as one of the flash points of the early twenty-first century. At least twice in the past decade, there has been a serious risk of major conflict between these two countries. That risk includes a conflict that might be triggered by Islamic extremists with linkages to Al-Qaida. This is not a hypothetical threat: an attack by such extremists on the Indian parliament in 2002 nearly led to a wider India-Pakistan conflict. In the past, the risk of escalation to nuclear conflict was contained in lower-level crises and clashes involving these two countries. This could be so once again. Alternatively, a process of unintended escalation to nuclear use could be driven by some combination of mutual uncertainties and miscalculation, excessive optimism about managing risks joined to a reluctance on the part of both countries' leaders to back down, technical imperatives related to nuclear postures, and an overreliance on outsiders' readiness to impose restraint as a last resort.

In principle, a wide array of cooperative security activities could be pursued by India and Pakistan—and sometimes with outsiders' involvement—to help avoid nuclear escalation of a terrorist incident or a conventional conflict. Continued Track 2 strategic dialogue could be supplemented with more official exchanges or assessments to explore escalation risks. It is difficult to envisage, however, a joint India-Pakistan official study of the risks of miscalculation in South Asia. By contrast, it could be more feasible to pursue a generic assessment of the risks of nuclear miscalculation and escalation in the early twenty-first century. This sort of assessment might be carried out either semiofficially or preferably officially by experts or officials not only from India and Pakistan, but also the United States, Russia, China, the United Kingdom, and France. Or the United States and Russia could jointly prepare their own assessment of the lessons to be derived from managing their Cold War nuclear relationship and make that study available to other interested nuclear countries. Conceivably, it could be the subject for a wider discussion among experts and officials of India, Pakistan, China, the United States, and Russia. An important goal of these studies or exchanges would be to contribute to each country's understanding of the other side's redlines, points of tension, and overall thinking.

Reciprocal unilateral actions also could have a role in avoiding escalation of an India-Pakistan nuclear crisis or conventional conflict. A continuation of both countries' reported current practice of not mating nuclear warheads to their delivery vehicles, for example, would help to lessen "lose it or use it" pressures for precipitous action in a crisis. Or as suggested above, both countries could unilaterally associate themselves with and implement any P-5 nuclear surety, safety, and guidelines, thereby lessening the risk of nuclear loss of control and unintended nuclear war. In turn, Indian and

Pakistani participation in negotiation of a multilateral treaty limiting production of fissile material for nuclear weapons would serve as a signal of both sides' interest in mutual restraint.

In practice, nonetheless, the time may not be ripe for many India-Pakistan cooperative security measures. In the past, both countries agreed to various confidence-building measures (CBMs), but have not followed through in implementing them. Rather, it may be possible to continue a more semiofficial set of exchanges among experts and retired officials to lay the groundwork for more far-reaching activities later. Here, the best model may be that of the US-Russian negotiation of the LTBT in June 1963. At that time, six months after the Cuban missile crisis, both Washington and Moscow were looking for a way to signal their mutual desire for nuclear restraint and to signal that they both knew they had approached too close to the nuclear brink in October 1962. Drawing on several years' prior discussion of nuclear testing restraints, the two sides were then able to negotiate and sign the LTBT in a matter of weeks. A future, even more serious India-Pakistan nuclear crisis that stops short of a nuclear conflict could well energize comparable efforts by New Delhi and Islamabad to draw on the spectrum of cooperative security means to address this strategic challenge.

Concluding Thoughts

The concept of cooperative security activities comprises a principle, a set of means, and a process for meeting the strategic challenges of the early twenty-first century. The principle stresses cooperation to serve the mutual security of partnering countries. The means range widely across the specific baskets of activities, from strategic dialogue to joint programs and from unilateral actions to negotiated agreements. The process entails use of many different means tailored to the challenge and blended with other appropriate approaches from diplomacy to military operations. Sometimes it will be necessary to acknowledge that the time may not be ripe for use of certain initiatives in addressing a given challenge, even though those initiatives may appear promising. In such situations, the task will be to lay the groundwork for action when the time is right.

What stands out most in this discussion of cooperative security activities is the very breadth of initiatives from which officials in the United States and elsewhere can undertake to manage the strategic challenges of the early twenty-first century. To return to the starting point of this chapter, their choice is far broader, more complex, and more nuanced than simply a diametric choice between unilateral, ad hoc initiatives and formal arms control. All initiatives should be on the table when policymakers consider their options to reduce threats and build confidence. The ultimate task of government officials will be to bring to bear the right mix of cooperative security activities, traditional diplomacy, and military operations to shape the future global strategic order.

Notes

1. See, for example, Kenneth Adelman, "Arms Control Without Agreements," *Foreign Affairs* (Winter 1984–1985).

2. The nearly 1,000-page Verification Annex of the 1991 START agreement both reflected—and, in some sense, validated—this perception of treaty-based negotiations as inherently a process of confrontation.

3. See Donald G. Brennan, *Arms Control, Disarmament, and National Security* (New York: George Braziller, 1961).

4. See Thomas Schelling and Morton H. Halperin, *Strategy and Arms Control* (Washington, DC: Pergamon-Brassey's, 1985). (Orig. pub. 1961.)

5. Examples include former secretary of defense William Perry, writing with Ashton Carter, Belfer Center, Harvard University; Michael Krepon, Henry L. Stimson Center, Washington, DC; and Sergei Rogov, director, USA and Canada Institute, Moscow.

6. The existence of this US-UK joint command was pointed out to me by Maj. Gen. (ret.) William Burns, former director, US Arms Control and Disarmament Agency.

7. Perhaps the most prominent example is the commencement speech given by secretary of defense Robert McNamara at the University of Michigan, Ann Arbor, in 1962.

8. The following draws on my conversations with Russian experts and former officials as well as with US experts following Russian thinking.

9. This possibility of missile defense cooperation to protect against an Iranian missile threat was suggested to me by Sergei Rogov, director, USA and Canada Institute, Moscow.

10. More so than in the case of Russia, nuclear deterrence continues to form the backdrop of the US-China strategic relationship, not least to help avoid a conflict over Taiwan. Over time, however, it would be preferable to move beyond deterrence as a key regulating element of the US-China relationship and to put in place the same type of nonadversarial relationship being sought with Russia after the Cold War.

11. The importance of agreement first by the top leaders, to be followed by a more continuing strategic dialogue within the framework set by those leaders, was pointed out to me by Brad Roberts, Institute for Defense Analyses, Alexandria, Virginia.

Suggested Readings

Carter, Ashton B., William J. Perry, and John D. Steinbruner, *A New Concept of Cooperative Security* (Washington, DC: Brookings Institution Press, 1993).

Dunn, Lewis A., and Victor Alessi, "Arms Control by Other Means," *Survival* 42, no. 4 (2000): 223–238.

Krepon, Michael, *Cooperative Threat Reduction, Missile Defense, and the Nuclear Future* (New York: Palgrave Macmillan, 2003).

9

Beyond Arms Control: New Initiatives to Meet New Threats

Guy B. Roberts

For much of the past century, US defense has relied on the Cold War doctrines of deterrence and containment. A crucial part of those doctrines was the process and practice of arms control. Some have argued that arms control was key to reducing the risk of war[1] while others have opined that arms control actually made the United States less secure.[2] Nevertheless, the purpose of arms control, whose objectives were articulated by Thomas Schelling and Morton Halperin in the early 1960s (reducing the costs of preparing for war, the chances of war, and the damage that would result from any war if it should occur), was clear and compelling.[3] It is less clear that all of those objectives were achieved during the more than forty years of superpower rivalry. Nevertheless, there is a consensus that arms control helped stabilize superpower competition and contributed to a peaceful end to the Cold War.

Today, the United States and its allies face a threat posed by states and terrorist groups actively seeking weapons of mass destruction (WMD) and their means of delivery.[4] These threats require new thinking and new approaches. This emerging security environment is considerably more complicated, diffuse, rapidly changing, multifaceted, and threatening than the Cold War nuclear confrontation. Today's diverse and unpredictable threats are shaped by those who, by definition, flout their international obligations, violate treaties, and ignore widely accepted international norms in the pursuit of WMD.

Rogue states pursue these weapons even though they may be party to treaties that specifically prohibit such acquisition. Rogue regimes apparently assume that a lack of effective enforcement measures and an absence of political will to monitor compliance with agreements makes cheating an attractive option; thus, they have little to fear and possibly much to gain in acquiring their own WMD capabilities. Nations that clandestinely seek WMD also are the same countries that support terrorist groups.

Of particular concern are those state-sponsored or well-funded (through criminal or illegitimate activities) terror groups that have neither geography, infrastructure, nor population that can be threatened, which itself presents difficult if not problematic challenges to crafting an effective deterrent. The evidence is overwhelming that Al-Qaida and other terrorist groups are actively pursuing WMD and there is little doubt that, if they do acquire such a capability, they will readily use it.[5]

Although arms control practice and process had an important—at times critical—role in keeping the US-Soviet confrontation "cold," it is unlikely that future arms control proposals (if ever agreed to and implemented) would be as helpful or relevant in facing the new challenge of WMD proliferation. Typically, such agreements take years to negotiate, and the prohibitions or restrictions that they create are likely to be ignored or circumvented by those we fear most as proliferators or active supporters of WMD terrorism.

In fact, modern-day arms control treaties may be worse than no treaties at all.[6] These agreements can promote complacency, lulling the West into a false sense of security while other nations busy themselves by surreptitiously acquiring and deploying nuclear, biological, and chemical (NBC) weapons and ballistic missiles. Samuel Huntington has suggested that the West naively "promotes nonproliferation as a universal norm and nonproliferation treaties and inspections as means of realizing that norm" while some non-Western nations "assert their right to acquire and to deploy whatever weapons they think necessary for their security," seeing WMD "as the potential equalizer of superior Western conventional power."[7]

This chapter explores emerging proliferation challenges and how the international community has responded to meet these changing threats. It first addresses one of the greatest challenges to effective arms control by exploring potential international responses to growing noncompliance with existing international arms control agreements. Second, it addresses the historical basis for using force in self-defense to prevent proliferation as well as the criteria by which leaders make judgments about the legality and validity of preventive or preemptive uses of force. Third, it explores how new cooperative initiatives are emerging to combat proliferation, and how the international community has come to devise new barriers to trade in WMD and associated materials. These new cooperative initiatives are better attuned to today's challenges than traditional arms control agreements.

The Conundrum of Noncompliance

The difficulty in achieving an international consensus on how to deal with noncompliance by states that are party to nonproliferation agreements has been one of the biggest challenges to international security since the inception of modern arms control. In his classic 1961 article "After Detection—What?" Fred Iklé wrote:

> Yet detecting violations is not enough. What counts are the political and military consequences of a violation once it has been detected, since these alone determine whether or not the violator stands to gain in the end. In entering into an arms-control agreement, we must know not only that we are technically capable of detecting a violation but also that we or the rest of the world will be politically, legally and militarily in a position to react effectively if a violation is discovered.[8]

As the history of arms control has demonstrated, treaty-abiding nations have constantly had to confront the problem of noncompliance (noteworthy treaty violators include the Soviet Union, Iran, North Korea, and Iraq). The inability to exact costs for noncompliance, however, has not lessened the importance or relevance of the arms control agreements currently in place. But it has—at least partly—resulted in recognition that the diffuse and inchoate nature of the threat is not susceptible to an "arms control" solution. Instead, more proactive and rapidly adaptable activities or initiatives are required to curb the new types of threat posed by WMD.

These new initiatives do not fall within traditional arms control partly because legally binding treaties or agreements take too long and can quickly become outdated, and partly because proliferators and terrorists would unlikely be deterred even if they were asked and willing to sign such agreements. A further complicating factor has been the discovery of the nuclear weapon trafficking network run by Abdul Qadeer Khan (the A. Q. Khan network). Stopping international criminal organizations from trafficking in WMD-related materials, outside of and relatively immune to WMD export control regimes, is also beyond the scope of traditional arms control treaties, which are primarily directed toward state actors. Further, as a result of globalization and growing indigenous capabilities, we face and must take into account the growing cooperation among proliferant states and unscrupulous traders—the so-called secondary proliferation market. Consequently, new and nontraditional international mechanisms will be required to stop or eliminate proliferation, especially the possibility that WMD will fall into the hands of terrorists.

Some have argued that the definition of arms control should be expanded to include all activities that diminish the possibility or costs of future conflict or the costs of preparing for it, to include all economic, political, and military actions.[9] Yet responding to WMD terrorism and proliferation requires a more expansive approach than "arms control," one that goes far beyond the definitions normally associated with or limited by arms control practice and process. It is an approach that posits a holistic, multifaceted, and in most cases a multilateral approach, including activities or initiatives of which the term *arms control* could not adequately or comprehensively describe.[10]

Rather than arms control, the terms *international security negotiations* or *international security initiatives* more accurately describe the new expansive approach to the problem of WMD spreading to both state and nonstate actors. These new initiatives include nontraditional activities beyond the realm of arms control, which could potentially involve partnerships with governmental agencies not normally associated with international security, initiatives by intergovernmental organizations (IGOs), and cooperative partnerships on a wide and diverse variety of training, prevention, and interdiction efforts. These new international security initiatives are limited only by the imagination of governmental policymakers and nongovernmental actors willing and determined to challenge and stop WMD proliferation.

Although the traditional approach to arms control may have outlived its utility, the creation and implementation of nonproliferation agreements, which enjoy near-universal compliance and adherence, have established a normative legal basis for nations to enforce universal compliance and undertake more robust and proactive initiatives. This is an important observation when it comes to new types of international security initiatives, including legally supportable, but politically controversial, preemptive and preventive uses of force. It is important because the debate on the legitimacy of these and other counterproliferation activities is often centered on their international legal basis and the factual predicates for the use of force.

The Legal and Normative Basis for Counterproliferation Activities: *Jus Cogens* and Treaty-Imposed Nonproliferation Norms

One of the primary benefits of multilateral arms control agreements is that they enjoy almost universal adherence, which produces a legal and normative barrier to the further proliferation of WMD. With 189 states being party to the Nuclear Nonproliferation Treaty (NPT), and 163 (plus thirteen signatories) and 186 (plus four signatories) to the Biological Weapons Convention (BWC) and Chemical Weapons Convention (CWC), respectively, there is a compelling case to be made that these three "cornerstones" of nonproliferation are both a normative and legal barrier to the further proliferation of WMD. Why is this important? Under international law if a practice within the community of nations is longstanding, widely accepted, and generally adhered to, it then becomes a legally enforceable obligation on all nations. This is referred to as *jus cogens;* that is: "a peremptory norm of general international law . . . accepted and recognized by the international community of states as a whole as a norm from which no derogation is permitted and which can be modified only by a subsequent norm of general international law having the same character."[11]

Since the negotiation of the UN Charter, multilateral conventions with a large majority of states parties have been cited as the basis for establishing *jus cogens*. If states make known their objections and disavow any obligation to comply, however, then the "norm" cannot become legally obligatory with respect to those states. For example, a large majority of states (154) are party to the Ottawa Convention on Landmines, which bans antipersonnel landmines (APLs). Yet because the major producers of landmines (China, Russia, and India) and the United States have rejected an outright ban on all landmines, it cannot be argued that at this point such a ban is *jus cogens*.[12]

There is a danger, however, in the creation of *jus cogens* because of the absence of clearly defined procedures for recognizing the emergence of norms. States and international nongovernmental organizations (NGOs) are pressing for rapid reforms in the existing international legal order. In attempting to establish "instant customary international law," they have relied on the concept of *jus cogens* to achieve fundamental change in the existing international law. Further complicating matters is the fact that some states and well-funded NGOs have tried to reshape international relations by a process of "lawfare."[13] That is, many NGOs have argued that they represent the "global civil society," even though they are neither elected nor accountable to any body politic. They espouse or advocate changes in customary law and then use these "new" norms to limit or restrict the ability of nations to pursue legitimate strategic aims. Sometimes they use the violation of these new, dubious norms to bring indictments before international tribunals.

One should be aware of the difficulty and dangers of establishing *jus cogens*. Nevertheless, there remains a compelling argument to be made that the three treaties that form the cornerstones of nonproliferation have indeed established worldwide legal norms prohibiting the further proliferation of WMD.

The NPT, with its legally binding obligation not to acquire nuclear weapons as well as its provisions for international inspections and export controls, represents an almost universal commitment by the international community to stop and condemn as illegal the further proliferation of nuclear weapons. Only Israel, Pakistan, and India are nonsignatories of the treaty, and North Korea has withdrawn, presenting a serious compliance challenge to the international community. Pakistan and India have rejected the universal applicability of the NPT and have argued that it does not establish a peremptory norm prohibiting their possession of nuclear weapons. By contrast, several international initiatives have been undertaken in support of the NPT. A number of nuclear-weapon-free zones (NWFZs) have been established. The Treaty of Tlatelolco, for example, created an NWFZ in Latin America in 1967.[14] Since then, one other NWFZ (South Pacific) has been created,[15] another has been agreed to in Africa,[16] and several others are proposed.[17] These initiatives have further strengthened and validated the nuclear nonproliferation norm. The issue of noncompliance, however, continues to challenge the political will and imagination of the international community.

The BWC established the norm—along with the 1925 Geneva Protocol (prohibiting the use of biological weapons)—banning the possession and use of biological weapons (BW) by prohibiting the "development, production, stockpiling, acquisition or retention" of biological weaponry for offensive purposes.[18] The CWC prohibits the development, production, and use of chemical weapons (CW) for any purpose and obligates the parties to destroy all existing stocks. Although the CWC only came into force in 1997, it enjoys almost universal adherence, and arguably establishes an antiproliferation norm because no nation, including those not party to either of these treaties, has claimed a right to have or use CW or BW. Consequently, there is strong evidence that these two treaties reflect a legally enforceable normative barrier to CW or BW proliferation.

As early as 1974, like-minded nations also established export control groups to limit traffic in nuclear materials, equipment, and technology. These include the NPT Exporters Committee (also called the Zangger Committee), which created so-called trigger lists of controlled exports that could support a clandestine nuclear weapon program, and the Nuclear Suppliers Group, whose goal is to obtain the agreement of all suppliers (including nations not members of the regime) to control nuclear and nuclear-related exports. A similar consortium, the Australia Group, with its forty participants, was established in 1986 to control items and equipment related to BW and CW. The Wassenaar Arrangement, created after the end of the Cold War, currently has forty partners and is intended to prevent the transfer of dual-use technologies and goods so that they do not contribute to clandestine WMD programs.

These nonproliferation treaties and voluntary restraint regimes have been the primary engines for creating and sustaining the current nonproliferation norms that serve as political, moral, and legal barriers to WMD programs. They define acceptable behavior within the community of nations. In many ways, the establishment of these norms has been effective in reversing WMD programs or facilitating the decision not to acquire such weapons. Many nations that have the wherewithal to develop or acquire these weapons have chosen not to do so or have abandoned nascent programs based on their commitment to these norms.

Voluntary restraint arrangements are not legally binding, but as politically binding agreements, they do confer on all parties the right to expect commitment to mutually agreed obligations and are further evidence of normative nonproliferation behavior. There can be distinct advantages to accepting a nonbinding agreement over a legally binding one. Nonbinding agreements provide states with the flexibility to accept commitments they can later renounce without legal costs. Legal commitments also may be politically impractical and states are more willing to carry cooperative efforts further under these types of nonbinding arrangements. Moreover, while a nonbinding agreement avoids formal legal obligations, it may still establish political and moral expectations that could give rise to allegations of bad faith and involve political risks in the event of noncompliance. Nonbinding arrangements can become legally obligatory through national implementing legislation and regulations and through mutual compliance. Politically binding agreements have been the primary vehicle for creating the new international security initiatives.

The nonproliferation norms established by these agreements and export control arrangements received significant reinforcement with the passage in April 2004 of UN Security Council Resolution 1540.[19] This was the first resolution passed by the Security Council that legally obligated all nations to criminalize the proliferation of WMD and to establish effective domestic controls over the export and use of materials that could be used for illicit WMD programs. It strongly reinforces the nonproliferation norms established by the three cornerstone treaties by imposing legal obligations on those who are not parties to these treaties. It also provides a further legal basis for requiring financial, security and accountability, physical protection, border, and additional export control measures by member states. This is a significant barrier against WMD proliferation and will serve as a useful basis for prodding nations to cooperate to ensure that the legal means are in place to stop trafficking in WMD-related materials.

Despite the passage of Security Council Resolution 1540, there continues to be a lack of will to respond effectively to violations of nonproliferation norms. Even with the creation of international nonproliferation norms and legally binding treaty commitments as well as the creation and active pursuit of a multitude of interdiction, export controls, and detection and law enforcement initiatives, a minority of states continue to pursue these weapons and aid terrorist groups trying to acquire an NBC arsenal. If the mechanisms for stopping or rolling back proliferation fail, then states must face the prospect of using military force. To do so can have profound moral and political consequences. Nevertheless, there exists a strong legal basis for enforcing compliance through force when a state or terrorist group attempts to acquire or employ WMD.

When Norms Are Violated and Diplomacy Fails: The Customary International Law of Self-Help

The legal restraint on the use of force was enshrined in Article 2(4) of the UN Charter, which obliges nations to "refrain" from the use of force in their relations with each other.[20] The only exception is under Article 51:

the inherent right of individual and collective self-defense "if an armed attack occurs." This commitment is balanced, however, by the Charter's equally fundamental promise to provide an effective system of collective security measures to protect states from breaches of or threats to the peace. Unfortunately, the plan to replace state self-help with collective security failed because it was based, according to Thomas Franck, on "two wrong assumptions: first, that the Security Council could be expected to make speedy and objective decisions as to when collective measures were necessary; and second, that states would enter into the arrangements necessary to give the council an effective policing capability."[21] As a result of these flawed assumptions, the prevailing patterns of statecraft created a radically different world from the one originally contemplated by the founders of the UN. Additionally, a new juridical paradigm emerged because the old juridical paradigm of restraint as codified in the original Charter no longer worked.[22] It simply was no longer responsive to the threat facing nations.

The new legal paradigm reflects the emerging security environment in which national survival, regional security, and world peace, particularly in the face of the WMD proliferation threat, potentially necessitate the "preventive" or "preemptive" use of force to deter acquisition plans and programs or destroy illicit WMD sites at any stage in the proliferator's acquisition efforts.[23] This is fully consistent with the purposes of the UN Charter because illicit WMD programs are a threat to international peace and security.[24]

Thus, Article 51 is now interpreted to mean that a state might use military force when it "regards itself as intolerably threatened by the activities of another."[25] As one prominent jurist has stated: "It would be a travesty of the purposes of the Charter to compel a defending state to allow its assailant to deliver the first, and perhaps fatal, blow. . . . To read Article 51 otherwise is to protect the aggressor's right to the first strike."[26]

The United States also has consistently taken the view that the right of self-defense authorizes a state which, being a target of activities by another state, reasonably decides that such activities imminently require it to use military force to protect its territory, citizens, and vital interests.[27] As then-secretary of state Madeleine Albright stated, "When threats arise to us or to others, we will choose the course of action that best serves our interests. We may act through the UN, we may act through NATO, we may act through a coalition, we may sometimes mix these tools or we may act alone. But we will do whatever is necessary to defend the vital interests of the United States."[28] The threat posed by WMD, especially in the hands of terrorist organizations, has caused US policymakers to reassess the need to take prompt military action to defeat potential threats before they become a grim reality.

Preemptive and Preventive Military Action as a Noncompliance Response: Should We Wait for the Smoking Gun?

There is a clear distinction between preemptive and preventive uses of force. *Preemptive military actions* (also referred to as anticipatory self-defense) are defined as the use of force directed towards a palpable, imminent threat easily discernable through national technical means, diplomatic channels, or media reporting. *Preventive military actions* do not presuppose the imminence of an armed attack, but are premised on clear and convincing evidence that a state or nonstate adversary is attempting to acquire a threatening capability. Preemptive actions are generally accepted as more legitimate than preventive actions, but it can often be difficult to distinguish between these two circumstances involving the use of force. The distinction can be important because the issue of what constitutes preemption and prevention bears on what is perhaps the most vital question facing those arguing about the propriety (i.e., undertaken in self-defense) or impropriety (i.e., undertaken as an act of aggression) of using force.[29]

Preemption has long been recognized as legally justifiable. Hugo Grotius, the father of international law, in *The Law of War and Peace,*[30] recognized that a nation could legitimately respond to "present danger." Self-defense is permitted not only after an attack, but also in anticipation of such an attack or, in his words: "It be lawful to kill him who is preparing to kill."[31] Grotius' position has been endorsed by later legal scholars such as Emmerich de Vattel, who posited in 1758 that: "The safest plan is to prevent evil, where that is possible. A Nation has the right to resist the injury another seeks to inflict upon it, and to use force . . . against the aggressor. It may even anticipate the other's design, being careful, however, not to act upon vague and doubtful suspicions, lest it should run the risk of becoming itself the aggressor."[32] Secretary of State Daniel Webster, in the *Caroline* case of 1842,[33] also argued that preemption is legally supportable where the necessity "is instant, overwhelming, and leaving no choice of means, and no moment for deliberation."[34]

Eminent nineteenth-century strategist Karl Clausewitz also discussed the concept of preemptive war in his seminal *On War*. Clausewitz observed that the aggressor is often peaceloving, and it is his or her resistant victim who causes war to erupt: "A conqueror is always a lover of peace (as Bonaparte always asserted of himself); he would like to make his entry into our state unopposed; in order to prevent this, we must choose war."[35]

In its modern form, the idea of preemptive war caught the public's eye with President George W. Bush's 2002 West Point speech: "We cannot put our faith in the word of tyrants, who solemnly sign nonproliferation treaties, and then systemically break them. If we wait for threats to fully materialize, we will have waited too long. . . . [O]ur security will require all Americans to be forward-looking and resolute, to be ready for preemptive action when necessary to defend our liberty and to defend our lives."[36] This was further articulated and later affirmed in the 2002 National Security Strategy: "The United States has long maintained the option of preemptive actions to counter a sufficient threat to our national security. The greater the threat, the greater is the risk of inaction—and the more compelling the case for taking anticipatory action to defend ourselves. . . . To forestall or prevent such hostile acts by our adversaries, the United States will, if necessary, act preemptively."[37] The 2006 National Security Strategy is even more explicit:

> To forestall or prevent . . . hostile acts by our adversaries, the United States will, if necessary, act preemptively in exercising our inherent right of self-defense. . . . [U]nder long-standing principles of self defense, we do not rule out the use of force before attacks occur, even if uncertainty remains as to the time and place of the enemy's attack. When the consequences of an attack with WMD are potentially so devastating, we cannot afford to stand idly by as grave dangers materialize. This is the principle and logic of preemption. The place of preemption in our national security strategy remains the same.[38]

The right of preemptive and preventive use of force also was endorsed by the 2004 report of the Secretary-General's High-Level Panel on Threats, Challenges and Change.[39] The High-Level Panel, however, drew an important distinction: preventive use of force could be undertaken only with the approval of the Security Council. This was viewed as a way to ensure the legitimacy and general acceptability of such actions while also leaving time for other measures to be undertaken by the international community to stop or roll back threatening activities.[40]

The preventive use of force to stop a WMD program is more controversial than preemption, particularly if undertaken unilaterally, because the threat is not an immediate one and it is usually difficult to provide enough information to the world community to make a compelling case that military force is the only option available to ward off the threat. In any event, there are six criteria that can be used to judge whether a preventive attack on an illicit WMD activity is legally justifiable.

The first criterion is notice; that is, a declaratory statement by the UN, a regional security organization, or an individual state that WMD acquisition programs or the possession of such weapons is a violation of international nonproliferation norms. This declaratory statement also often identifies how proliferation constitutes a threat to the vital national security interests of the state, regional security, and international peace and security. The United States has declared a number of times that proliferation is a threat to its vital national security interests, and the UN has declared in Security Council Resolution 1540 that WMD proliferation poses a threat to international peace and security.

Second, the threat must be concrete and persuasive rather than speculative. Objective evidence reflects the existence of reasonable evidence that can support a conclusion that an illicit WMD program exists, and that past behavior or declaratory statements indicate that acquired WMD will be used against a state's vital national security interests or regional peace and security.

Third, there must be a force imperative. That is, there must demonstrably be (1) a manifest intent to injure; (2) a degree of active preparation that makes that intent a positive danger; and (3) a general situation in which waiting, or doing anything other than fighting, greatly magnifies that risk.[41]

Fourth, the response to the threat must be discriminate in that it must be focused on eliminating weapons and infrastructure related to the imminent threat. The use of force to eliminate the threat also should be proportional. That is, the least amount of force should be applied to eliminate the threat and care should be taken to avoid collateral damage.

Fifth, there should be a reasonable chance that the proposed use of force will result in a positive outcome. That is, it should eliminate the WMD program or site, or significantly degrade the ability of the proliferator to resurrect the illicit program.

Sixth, the use of force should be undertaken only as a last resort. The potential victim state should continuously seek to resolve the threat by peaceful means until further diplomatic efforts are judged to be futile, based on the negative behavior of the party attempting to acquire WMD.

The threat of preventive military action also has proven to be a useful adjunct to other proliferation prevention initiatives. An implicit threat of recourse to military force could back up political and diplomatic initiatives. During the Gulf War, for example, the threat of severe retaliation by the United States deterred Iraq from using CW.[42] Despite the extraordinary threat these weapons present, an indiscriminate use of force could have a devastating impact on the international norms that the United States is interested in defending and enforcing, thereby weakening rather than strengthening them. That is why both preemptive and preventive military action will remain controversial even though both are well grounded in customary international law.

To avoid the prospect of using military action to enforce compliance and stop proliferation, the United States aggressively embarked on another path that has launched a diverse group of new international security initiatives. The United States was quickly joined in these initiatives by other nations and international organizations.

The Ascendancy of Cooperative International Security Initiatives

Early in the Clinton administration, it became apparent that, even if US nonproliferation efforts worked reasonably well, they would only slow the spread of weapons of mass destruction. US policymakers began to prepare to react to the slowly unfolding failure of diplomacy, arms control, and export controls by devising policy options that included more than threats of retaliation.[43] Recognizing that, despite US nonproliferation efforts and institutional and legal norm building, determined states and terrorist groups would continue to pursue these deadly weapons, the United States in 1993 declared a new counterproliferation initiative. It would involve a multifaceted approach, consisting of nonproliferation efforts to prevent the spread of WMD and of Cooperative Threat Reduction (CTR) initiatives with the former Soviet Union. The United States, however, would also begin other counterproliferation efforts to deter, prevent, or, if those efforts failed, defend against the use of WMD.

The CTR initiatives had their genesis in the 1991 Nunn-Lugar Cooperative Threat Reduction Program, which provided funds to assist the former Soviet Union in dismantling and destroying old NBC weapons and to help protect and safeguard weapon-grade nuclear (fissile) materials. CTR initiatives became an integral part of the counterproliferation initiative, and have resulted in the destruction of thousands of weapons and delivery vehicles.[44] The CTR program has been so successful that, in 2003, Congress expanded the program worldwide to assist any nation in destroying these weapons or safeguarding WMD-related materials.

A key element of this new counterproliferation initiative was to maintain a capability to find and destroy weapon delivery forces and their supporting infrastructure elements with minimal collateral damage and to interdict WMD capabilities.[45] This counterproliferation initiative, after the terrorist attacks of 9/11 and the anthrax attacks in fall 2001, was expanded substantially by the George W. Bush administration. The 2002 National Strategy to Combat Weapons of Mass Destruction contemplates a strong conventional and nuclear deterrence capability "reinforced by effective intelligence, surveillance, interdiction, and domestic law enforcement capabilities. Such combined capabilities enhance deterrence both by devaluing an adversary's WMD and missiles, and by posing the prospect of an overwhelming response to any use of such weapons."[46] The 2002 strategy document also noted that the ability to eliminate a source of WMD would "have a powerful deterrent effect upon other adversaries that possess or seek WMD or missiles."[47]

Subsequent international security initiatives have been wide ranging. They also encompass a variety of agencies and organizations not normally associated with arms control or arms in general. Except for their focus on international security and stopping WMD proliferation, their membership and areas of concern are equally wide ranging and diverse.[48] When compared to an international agreement or treaty, these initiatives (which might also be called an activity, measure, program, joint action, or action plan) are far more flexible, allowing states to approve and implement them quickly and easily, or reject them if they become unworkable or outlive their usefulness. These initiatives allow states to deal with rapidly evolving threats by quickly implementing appropriate response mechanisms.

The principal structural feature of these initiatives is their diversity. Initiatives related to nonproliferation and security concerns extend into almost every area. They may be unilateral, bilateral, or multilateral and can address either global or regional objectives. Initiatives usually involve three types of obligations. Some are *active obligations*. These initiatives are used to coordinate the activities and participation in a given action. There are *passive obligations* in which participants merely accede to an agreement, perhaps publicly proclaiming their support, but they are not generally required to perform any specific function. There also are *support obligations,* in which members agree to provide support such as funding, information, training, or equipment.

Initiatives also include political-military cooperation, import and export control, nuclear and biological security, crisis management, health, legal issues, law enforcement, and intelligence. Some are led by IGOs. Some are led by traditional governmental security agencies (defense or foreign affairs ministries) while others are led by law enforcement, health, trade, or industry agencies. Some are exclusively government-to-government while others involve industry and NGOs. For example, Interpol provides assistance in criminal cases involving bioforensics; International Health Regulations established by the World Health Organization (WHO) help to measure, prevent, and respond to deliberate outbreaks of disease; the International Atomic Energy Agency (IAEA) works on nuclear security and has established an office to address nuclear terrorism; the North Atlantic Treaty Organization (NATO) has created the Weapons of Mass Destruction Centre to coordinate alliance efforts against proliferation; and regional organizations, such as the European Union, have developed a variety of nonproliferation cooperative initiatives. This dramatic growth and diversity of international security initiatives received an additional legal underpinning with the passage of UN Security Council Resolution 1540, which made it an obligation for all states to have effective export controls and to cooperate with other states in stopping terrorist groups and individuals from acquiring such weapons and related materials. As a result of Resolution 1540, there has been an increase in cooperative efforts by states to implement their legal obligations under the nonproliferation norms.

These new initiatives are open to and applicable to all states, are easy to apply in a collaborative way, and are creating actionable, proactive, and novel new forms of nonproliferation collaboration between state agencies, private industry, and NGOs. In May 2003, for instance, President George W. Bush announced the creation of the Proliferation Security Initiative (PSI). The PSI began with eleven countries and now includes over ninety supporting states that are committed to help each other with intercepting illegal transports of weapons and associated equipment at sea, in the air, and on land. Although PSI participants have agreed that North Korea and Iran are of particular concern, PSI efforts are not aimed at any one country but instead are intended to halt worldwide trafficking in proliferation-related items. PSI participants have committed to acting consistently with national legal authorities and relevant international law. The focus is on coordinating action by like-minded countries, not building bureaucratic structures. The PSI is information driven and, based on an analysis of shared information, discrete operations are undertaken against individual shipments rather than random checks against general trafficking flows. Nations participate only if needed as part of the execution of a specific operation.

Some PSI partners have entered into boarding agreements with flags of convenience nations that allow commercial shippers to use their flags for transit to expand the legal authority for inspections of seagoing vessels. PSI participants also have developed cooperative working relationships with the container shipping industry to increase monitoring and tracking capabilities of suspicious shipments. After one PSI-related interdiction of nuclear weapon related equipment bound for Libya, Libya renounced all of its clandestine WMD programs. As a result of these successes, partners are considering expansion of the PSI to include disrupting the efforts of individuals involved in supporting proliferation activities (e.g., suppliers, middlemen, financiers).

A related international security initiative is the Container Security Initiative (CSI). It involves sharing intelligence to identify and target containers that pose a risk, developing prescreening procedures for containers at ports of departure, the collaborative development of WMD material detection technology, and the deployment of "smarter" tamper-evident containers that are locatable with the Global Positioning System (GPS). Almost every major port in the world has signed on to the CSI and, as with the PSI, a strong working relationship is being developed between governments and private industry to monitor international traffic in shipping containers.

Other similar international security initiatives include the Dangerous Materials Initiative, a project based on international assistance to help criminalize proliferation and remove or secure dangerous materials. The Illicit Activities and Regional Maritime Security Initiatives compose a program whereby nations collaborate to stop illicit trafficking of all dangerous goods in the Asia Pacific region. The Caspian Guard Initiative was developed to assist Caspian littoral states in establishing effective border control regimes to stop WMD and other illicit material smuggling. The Asia-Pacific Economic Cooperation (APEC) Health Security Initiative is intended to improve disease monitoring and response, increase security of biological pathogens, strengthen controls on dual-use biological materials and equipment, and establish strict codes of ethical and operational conduct for bioscientists.

IGOs have an increasingly prominent role to play in ensuring compliance with nonproliferation norms. Subject matter–specific organizations, such as WHO, the International Maritime Organization (IMO), and the World Customs Organization (WCO), focus on taking measures to effect legal nonproliferation obligations. For example, WHO recently approved a new version of the International Health Regulations, which requires nations to report suspicious outbreaks of disease and to cooperate in the event of a deliberate attack. The IMO recently approved a Protocol to the Suppression of Unlawful Acts at Sea Convention, which requires nations to pass laws mandating prosecution for merchant ships transporting terrorists or WMD materials. The WCO also has an active program to detect the transportation across borders of radioactive materials and other materials that could be used for WMD.

These ad hoc international security initiatives will increase in number and scope. New efforts to interdict the illegal flow of controlled technology and materials will emerge. New initiatives to cooperate in aggressive international prosecution of companies and individuals involved in proliferation also probably will be adopted by several leading states. Furthermore, it is increasingly likely that coordination with IGOs to monitor compliance with proliferation agreements will become commonplace, and expanded partnerships with commercial entities could be a new front in the effort to stop the flow of contraband.

Conclusion: Creating a Web of Proliferation Denial

In view of the increasingly complex and diverse international security environment, it is unlikely that traditional arms control will ever again have the prominence or relevance it had during the Cold War. Countering today's threats simply cannot be accomplished by more international conventions. We cannot assume that our deterrence strategies are credible or will work in the face of complex threats posed by nascent nuclear powers and nonstate actors.[49]

Instead of traditional arms control, policymakers must be prepared to respond quickly to meet and defeat the capabilities and objectives of today's adversaries. Past arms control and nonproliferation agreements, particularly the NPT, BWC, and CWC, remain important as a reflection of the will of the community of nations to establish enforceable norms against proliferation. But if these nonproliferation norms are to survive, a comprehensive and multifaceted approach to emerging proliferation threats is necessary.

In sum, there is no single or simple solution to the threats created by CW, BW, or nuclear weapons in the hands of terrorists. Instead, policymakers must adopt a multidimensional approach to security. In the face of noncompliance, nations must be prepared to respond to states that ignore nonproliferation norms and treaties. States will need to work together not only with other states, but with IGOs, NGOs, and industry to create a web of initiatives that will ensure our best chance for denying these weapons to terrorists and rogues. If our "web of denial" should fail, in the face of proliferation and noncompliance with legal norms, we nevertheless will have the legal tools readily available to stop or eliminate the proliferation threat.

Notes

1. See Emanual Adler, "Arms Control, Disarmament, and National Security: A Thirty Year Retrospective and a New Set of Anticipations," *Daedalus: Journal of the American Academy of Arts and Sciences* (Winter 1991): 1; Albert Carnesale and Richard N. Haass, eds., *Superpower Arms Control* (Cambridge, MA: Ballinger, 1987).

2. Malcolm Wallop and Angelo Codevilla, *The Arms Control Delusion* (ICS Press: San Francisco, 1987).

3. Thomas C. Schelling and Morton C. Halperin, *Strategy and Arms Control* (New York: Pergamon-Brassey's, 1985), p. 2.

4. There is no consistent use of this term. For the purposes of this chapter, the term *weapons of mass destruction* refers to chemical, biological, radiological, and nuclear (CBRN) weapons and their means of delivery. It will be abbreviated as WMD. See Seth W. Carus, "Defining 'Weapons of Mass Destruction,'" Weapons of Mass Destruction Center Occasional Paper No. 4 (National Defense University, January 2006), available at www.ndu.edu/WMDCenter/docUploaded//OP4Carus.pdf (accessed 15 August 2007).

5. See James Phillips and James Carafano, *Terrorists in Their Own Words* (Washington, DC: Heritage Foundation, 2007), available at www.heritage.org/Research/National Security/bg2057.cfm (accessed 15 August 2007); Lewis A. Dunn, "Can al Qaeda Be Deterred from Using Nuclear Weapons?" Occasional Paper No. 3 (Washington, DC: National Defense University, Center for the Study of Weapons of Mass Destruction, July 2005).

6. Samuel P. Huntington, "The Clash of Civilizations?" *Foreign Affairs* 72 (Summer 1993): 22.

7. Ibid., at p. 45.

8. Fred Iklé, "After Detection—What?" *Foreign Affairs* 39 (January 1961): 208.

9. John A. Nagl, "Defending Against New Dangers: Arms Control of Weapons of Mass Destruction in a Globalized World," *World Affairs* (Spring 2000).

See also Jeffrey A. Larsen, "National Security and Neo-arms Control in the Bush Administration," *Disarmament Diplomacy* no. 80, (Autumn 2005), available at www.acronym.org.uk/dd/dd80/80jal.htm#en12#en12. Larsen proposed defining *arms control* as "a process involving specific, declared steps by a state to enhance security through cooperation with other states. These steps can be unilateral, bilateral, or multilateral. Cooperation can be implicit as well as explicit."

10. The US State Department, recognizing the need for a broader approach than traditional arms control, announced in 2005 a reorganization of its arms control and nonproliferation bureaus into a single Bureau of International Security and Nonproliferation. The intent was to change the focus of effort away from arms control. More specifically, it would "feature a new office to focus on the nexus between WMD and terrorism, the preeminent threat we face as a nation." US State Department Fact Sheet, *Rice Announces Reorganization of Arms Control, International Security Bureaus* (Washington, DC: US State Department, 29 July 2005), available at http://usinfo.state.gov/is/Archive/2005/Jul/29-576547.html (accessed 22 August 2007).

11. Art. 53, The Vienna Convention on the Law of Treaties (1969), 1155 U.N.T.S. 331. See also Art. 64. For a fuller explanation of the concept, see Verdross, "*Jus Dispositivum* and *Jus Cogens* in International Law," *American Journal of International Law* 60 (1966): 55.

12. The text of the Ottawa Convention on Landmines is available at www.icbl.org/treaty (accessed 23 August 2007).

13. Jeremy Rabkin, "Lawfare," *Wall Street Journal*, 17 July 2004, available at www.opinionjournal.com/forms/printthis?id=110005366 (accessed 23 August 2007).

14. Treaty for the Prohibition of Nuclear Weapons in Latin America, 14 February 1967, 6 I.L.M. 521 (1967).

15. See "United States, France, and the United Kingdom to Sign Protocols of the South Pacific Nuclear-free Zone Treaty [Treaty of Raratonga]," US State Department, *Dispatch* 7, no. 15 (8 April 1996) (White House statement of 22 March 1996).

16. "Fact Sheet: African Nuclear Weapons-Free Zone Treaty," US Department of State, *Dispatch* 7, no. 16 (15 April 1996); African Nuclear-Weapon-Free Zone Treaty [Pelindaba Text], 35 I.L.M. 698 (1996).

17. There already exist agreements prohibiting nuclear weapons in Antarctica, in outer space and on the seabed. Proposals for nuclear-weapon-free zones (NWFZs) exist in every region of the world.

18. There is also a norm-creating 1925 Geneva Protocol banning the use of poisonous gases and biological weapons (BW) in war. Although signed and ratified by few parties (the United States ratified 22 January 1975), it does arguably create a legal norm against the first use of BW in wartime.

19. The full impact of UN Security Council Resolution 1540 is discussed in detail in Olivia Bosch and Peter van Ham, eds., *Global Non-Proliferation and Counter-Terrorism* (London: Royal Institute of International Affairs, 2007).

20. Art. 2(4) states that "all members shall refrain in their international relations from the threat or use of force against the territorial integrity or political independence of any state, or in any other manner inconsistent with the purposes of the United Nations."

21. Thomas Franck, "The Charter Law Pertaining to States' Autonomous Use of Force," *Washington University Journal of Law and Policy* 5 (2001): 52.

22. The following discussion is based in large part on Tony Arend and Robert Beck, *International Law and the Use of Force: Beyond the UN Charter Paradigm* (London: Routledge, 1993); Guy B. Roberts, "The Counterproliferation Self-Help

Paradigm: A Legal Regime for Enforcing the Norm Prohibiting the Proliferation of Weapons of Mass Destruction," *Denver Journal of International Law and Policy* 27 (Summer 1999): 483.

23. Thomas Kuhn in *The Structure of Scientific Revolutions,* 2nd ed. (Chicago: University of Chicago Press, 1970) first coined the term *paradigm.* A paradigm denotes "one sort of element in [a constellation of beliefs], the concrete puzzle-solutions which, employed as models or examples, can replace explicit rules as a basis for the solution of the remaining puzzles of normal science." Ibid., at p. 175. The use of paradigm is appropriate because what is discussed is the embodiment of a distinct and coherent explanation of a new legal norm for using force that explains and validates the use of that force and should guide future practitioners in responding to the extraordinary threat posed by WMD proliferation.

24. That fundamental purpose is maintenance of international peace and security. UN Charter, Art. 1, para. 1.

25. *Proceedings of the American Society of International Law at Its Fifty-Seventh Annual Meeting,* April 25–27 (Washington, DC: American Society of International Law, 1963), p. 165.

26. Sir Claude Humphrey Meredith Waldock, "The Regulation of the Use of Force by Individual States in International Law," *Hague Recueil* 81, no. 45 (1952): 498.

27. See Myers McDougal, "The Soviet-Cuban Quarantine and Self-Defense," *American Journal of International Law* 57 (1963): 597–598.

28. Warren Christopher, "A New Consensus of the Americas," US State Department, *Dispatch* 5, no. 20 (1994).

29. Anthony F. Lang Jr., "Evaluating the Preemptive Use of Force," *Ethics and International Affairs* 17, no. 1 (2003): 1. This volume has a number of useful articles on the issues associated with preventive and preemptive military actions. For example, see Richard K. Betts, "Striking First: A History of Thankfully Lost Opportunities," *supra,* at pp. 17–24. See also Michael Byers, "Preemptive Self-Defense: Hegemony, Equality, and Strategies of Legal Change," *Journal of Political Philosophy* 11, no. 2 (2003), 171–190.

30. H. Grotius, *On the Law of War and Peace* (1625), in Francis Kelsey, ed. and trans., *Classics of International Law,* vol. 3 (Washington, DC: Carnegie Endowment for International Peace, 1925).

31. Ibid., at chap. 1. Elsewhere H. Grotius wrote that "the first just cause of war . . . is an injury, which even though not actually committed, threatens our persons or our property," book 2, chap. 1, sec. 2.

32. E. de Vattel, *The Law of Nations* 4 (1758). in Charles Fenwick, trans., *Classics of International Law,* vol. 3 (Washington, DC: Carnegie Endowment for International Peace, 1916), p. 130.

33. The *Caroline* was an American steamboat that was accused of running arms to Canadian rebels. A Canadian military force crossed over into the United States and set the ship ablaze, killing an American citizen in the process. A Canadian was arrested in New York for the murder, and the British government protested. Although never admitting culpability, the British apologized to the United States for the incident. See Jennings, "The Caroline and McLeod Cases," *American Journal of International Law* 32 (1938): 82, 85, 89; J. Moore, *Digest of International Law* 2 (1906): 409–414.

34. See also D. P. O'Connell, *International Law* (Dobbs Ferry, NY: Oceana, 1965), p. 343.

35. Clausewitz, *On War,* trans. Michael Howard and Peter Paret (Princeton: Princeton University Press, 1976), p. 370.

36. "President Bush Delivers Graduation Speech at West Point," White House press statement (1 June 2002), available at www.whitehouse.gov/news/releases/2002/06/20020601-3.html (accessed on 22 August 2007).

37. "The National Security Strategy of the United States of America," p. 15, available at www.whitehouse.gov/nsc/nss.pdf (accessed 20 August 2007).

38. "The National Security Strategy of the United States of America" (2006), available at www.whitehouse.gov/nsc/nss/2006/sectionV.html (accessed 20 August 2007).

39. Available at www.un.org/secureworld (accessed 22 August 2007).

40. *Report of the Secretary-General's High-Level Panel on Threats, Challenges and Change*, 2004, *Part 3: Collective Security and Use of Force*, p. 59, available at www.un.org/secureworld/report3.pdf (accessed 22 August 2007).

41. Michael Walzer, *Just and Unjust Wars*, 2nd ed. (New York: Basic Books, 1992), p. 81.

42. During the Gulf War, President George H. W. Bush informed Saddam Hussein that "the United States will not tolerate the use of chemical or biological weapons. . . . The American people would demand the strongest possible response. You and your country will pay a terrible price if you order unconscionable acts of this sort." Quoted in Terry N. Mayer, "The Biological Weapon: A Poor Nation's Weapon of Mass Destruction," *Air War College, Studies in National Security* 3 (September 1995): 206.

43. *The Proliferation Primer, a Majority Report of the Sub-Committee on International Security, Proliferation and Federal Services*, US Senate, January 1998, Summary. Available at www.senate.gov/~gov_affairs/prolifbk.pdf (accessed 15 August 2007).

44. See Michael Krepon, *Cooperative Threat Reduction, Missile Defense, and the Nuclear Future* (New York: Palgrave, 2003).

45. Department of Defense, Counterproliferation Program Review Committee, *Report on Activities and Programs for Countering Proliferation and NBC Terrorism* (Washington, DC: US Government Printing Office, May 1998), pp. 1–3.

46. National Security Presidential Directives, *NSPD-17/HSPD 4*, "National Strategy to Combat Weapons of Mass Destruction," (December 2002), available at www.fas.org/irp/offdocs/nspd/nspd-17.html (accessed 22 August 2007).

47. Ibid.

48. See the Appendix in this volume for a partial list of current international security initiatives.

49. There is no one best way to assure deterrence through credibility or uncertainty. What deters regional adversaries is complex and what works in one case may not work in another. See John J. Mearscheimer, *Conventional Deterrence* (Ithaca: Cornell University Press, 1983); John Arme, "Deterrence Failures: A Second Look." *International Security* (Spring 1987): 96–124.

Suggested Readings

Albright, David, and Corey Hinderstein, *Uncovering the Nuclear Black Market: Working Toward Closing Gaps in the International Nonproliferation Regime* (Institute for Science and International Security, Washington, DC, 2 July 2004.

Arend, Tony, and Robert Beck, *International Law and the Use of Force: Beyond the UN Charter Paradigm* (London: Routledge, 1993).

Bernstein, Paul, *International Partnerships to Combat Weapons of Mass*

Destruction, Occasional Paper 6 (Washington, DC: National Defense University Press, May 2008).

Bosch, Olivia, and Peter van Ham, eds., *Global Non-Proliferation and Counter-Terrorism: The Impact of UNSCR 1540* (Washington, DC: Brookings Institution Press, 2007).

Ellis, Jason D., "The Best Defense: Counterproliferation and US National Security Policy," *Washington Quarterly* 26, no. 2 (2003): 115–133.

Gray, Christine, *International Law and the Use of Force* (Oxford: Oxford University Press, 2000).

Harbaugh, Erin E., "The Proliferation Security Initiative: Counterproliferation at the Crossroads," *Strategic Insights* 3, no. 7 (July 2004).

Roberts, Guy B., "The Counterproliferation Self-Help Paradigm: A Legal Regime for Enforcing the Norm Prohibiting the Proliferation of Weapons of Mass Destruction," *Denver Journal of International Law and Policy* 27 (Summer 1999): 483.

10

Arms Control, Universality, and International Norms

Rebecca E. Johnson

The arguments for universality in arms control derive from the view that global security requires the informed and active participation of as many of the world's nations and peoples as possible.[1] This in itself is a recent recognition. Arms control developed during the Cold War to manage relations between the major powers and to mitigate the worst excesses of the nuclear arms race. Though arms control still has a role to play, traditional approaches are proving too limited to deal with the twenty-first century's mass destructive threats, which are capable of killing millions and threatening the environment on which human civilization depends. In response, civil society and many governments are moving from state-centered concepts of national security and arms control toward global security regimes in which a norm-based, universalized concept of human security forms the basis for limiting the acquisition, accumulation, and use of arms.

As the Cold War divide crumbled, the resulting strategic shifts not only have changed threat perceptions, but also have brought broader security interests and actors to the fore. China, India, and the European Union, for example, are emerging as major regional and international powers. But though they undoubtedly will have different economic and security interests, it would be a mistake to assume that they will emulate the US hegemonic model or reproduce twentieth-century-style military rivalries. By contrast, Vladimir Putin's Russia may now be attempting to counter US hegemony and reinvent itself as a superpower by rebuilding its military-industrial strength and restocking its arsenals with new generations of conventional and nuclear weapons.

Since the 9/11 attacks on the United States, there is greater global awareness of the security threats to cities and institutions posed by networks of transstate terrorists. Assessments of the terrorist threat are compounded by the possibility that attacks will become ever more destructive, and that some terrorists will seek to acquire and use chemical, biological, radiological, or nuclear (CBRN) weapons. Instead of being the purview of a few dominant countries, security is increasingly seen as the responsibility (and right) of everyone. This is as applicable to controls on weapons of mass destruction (WMD) and weapon-usable materials as to landmines or cluster bombs. Though no one should yet write off the role of nation-states in the international system, security threats and security solutions will be determined by partnerships between state, nonstate, and transstate actors and networks. This is the new security paradigm and arms control, like most of security policy, still needs to catch up with both new threat assessments and new ways to overcome these challenges.

To explore this new security paradigm, this chapter considers how the principle of universality has increasingly come to be applied to arms control and the construction of international legal regimes to deal with certain kinds of weapons. It then examines the implications of these developments on the use of arms control to foster security, the credibility of international norms and institutions, and the verification and enforcement of arms control objectives and obligations.

Collective Security, Responsibility, and International Law

International law and arms control have played an important role in building collective security by embedding norms and rules to limit the production, deployment, and use of certain types of weapons. International conventions, arms control treaties, and agreements help to reduce the circulation of armaments and weapon-usable materials, stigmatize uses and practices deemed especially inhumane, promote international cooperation in monitoring and eliminating certain kinds of armed threats, facilitate the demilitarization and settlement of conflicts, and provide a medium for communication and cooperative security. Though no multilateral arms control instruments have yet achieved full universality in terms of signatures and ratifications, they add to the body of international humanitarian law. Their provisions come to be generally accepted as customary law—applicable to all—when the principles and norms have been accepted by a significant majority of the "international community."[2]

For most of the twentieth century, the United States participated in efforts to establish a non-Communist version of international community with the League of Nations, the UN, and Eleanor Roosevelt's Universal Declaration of Human Rights. All of these efforts sought to embed humanitarian, nonproliferation, and human rights norms and standards in international relations. After 2001, the George W. Bush administration has caused consternation around the world by appearing to repudiate international laws and norms, acting as though it regarded the United States to be above (or outside) international law. This neoconservative assertion of US exceptionalism not only flew in the face of developments in US and international law, it also proved counterproductive for US national security objectives and undermined Washington's ability to exercise international leadership.

In addition to deciding that the Geneva Convention and Protocols and International Criminal Court would not be recognized as applying to the United States and its military personnel and practices, the George W. Bush administration cherry-picked among international arms control treaties. It unilaterally withdrew from the Anti-Ballistic Missile Treaty (ABM Treaty); publicly opposed the multilaterally negotiated Comprehensive Test Ban Treaty (CTBT), which the United States had pushed for in 1993 and signed in 1996; and refused to sign the 1997 Ottawa Convention on Landmines, although veterans of the Vietnam War had played a significant role in bringing this multilateral treaty to fruition. At the same time, however, the United States (together with the United Kingdom and others) made use of the UN Security Council to universalize states' responsibilities with regard to terrorist activities and acquisition of technologies or materials that could be used for WMD.[3]

These countervailing approaches toward the importance of universalizing arms control mirror some of the contradictions at the heart of international law. A trade-off between the perceived interests of powerful states and the building of universal standards and norms to govern relations between nations, international law gives institutional weight to the values of the dominant culture(s) while also limiting the exercise of power and arms by the dominant states and protecting the interests of the less powerful. Russia and China have periodically criticized arms control as a mechanism for the United States to maintain its military dominance, but few were prepared for the unapologetic obviousness of the George W. Bush administration's strategies to universalize international laws that control others' options and behavior while refusing to accept legal restraints on US choices. These challenges to multilateral arms control have highlighted the necessity to resolve questions about the role of law in national and international security, in terms of state sovereignty, national self-defense, universal jurisdiction, and whether international law can be applied in national courts against individuals or governments.

In addition, the doctrine of "responsibility to protect" has sparked discussions about the use of force in humanitarian intervention, including the conditions under which it would be lawful. This doctrine, embraced during the 1990s by the United States, the UK, and many others, implies acceptance that universal norms (regarding genocide, terrorism, and WMD, for example) take precedence over state sovereignty when brutal governments or savage civil wars threaten the lives or human rights of their peoples. The diverse examples of Bosnia (1991–1995), Rwanda (1994), Kosovo (1999),

Afghanistan (2001), and Iraq (2003), however, raise questions about who determines whether armed humanitarian intervention is necessary and lawful, and who should stand accountable for the consequences of international inaction or inappropriate military action by governments.

What conditions ought to be met before military intervention or the use of certain weapons can be considered lawful? Is agreement by the UN Security Council required? Must intervention be a collective endeavor (as implied in the doctrine of international community that Tony Blair and others enthusiastically endorsed) with responsibility to protect?[4] Or in the absence of UN agreement or broad international participation, what are the legal and security implications if the United States, acting as sole superpower, acts on its own or with a coalition of the willing? Is it enough that much of the rest of the world expects the United States to shoulder these burdens, and that it is not merely behaving as a self-appointed police force and law enforcer? We may assume that the interveners see themselves as taking military action with the best of intentions—to save lives, prevent massacres and human rights abuses, root out WMD or terrorists, or spread freedom and democracy. But what actually are the grounds for legitimacy and authority? If such actions are not in accordance with international law, then they risk returning the world to the law of the jungle, where all choose for themselves what is morally or politically justified or expedient and the most powerful get to impose their choices on the rest. Indeed, this is the very definition of *hegemony:* "though it is partial and subjective, it claims to be universal and objective."[5] These questions matter, not only because disarmament and arms control agreements may be regarded as a subset of international humanitarian law, but because the United States—and some other states—have at times asserted "exceptional" rights or needs to justify their exemption from international controls or prohibitions on weapons or weapon uses that are legally binding on everyone else. The International Court of Justice, however, has generally given short shrift to claims based on exceptionalism or arguments that some governments are exempt from the requirements of international law.

Universality does not necessarily mean that there has to be universal participation in arms control negotiations or that there must be uniform application of all provisions. With 188 states parties, the 1970 Nuclear Nonproliferation Treaty (NPT) comes closer to universality than other treaties, yet it was based on a text agreed first between the US and Soviet governments, and it contained two categories of parties and obligations. The NPT imposed disarmament and nontransfer obligations on the five states that had already conducted nuclear weapon tests by a specified date while all other countries were invited to sign the treaty as non–nuclear weapon states (NNWS), obliging themselves not to acquire nuclear weapons and to conclude safeguards agreements with the International Atomic Energy Agency (IAEA).

Dissimilar obligations, restrictions, or incentives in treaties may reflect geostrategic differences, technological developments or constraints, or some other acknowledged fact on the ground. These variations in specific treaties do not necessarily conflict with the principle of universality, but differential obligations may affect the credibility and sustainability of a treaty regime. Though it is nearly universal, the NPT is perceived as eroding, due in part to its lack of autonomous institutional and enforcement powers. A factor contributing to its weakness is that it is widely perceived—in the eyes of some states parties and at least two nonsignatories, India and Pakistan—as perpetuating an institutional discrimination in favor of the states that already had nuclear weapons when the NPT was concluded.

Arms Control: From Strategic Management to Human Security

The Geneva Conventions, the UN Charter, and various principles developed through human rights and humanitarian law provide a bedrock of principles, norms, rules, and institutions that now underpin international humanitarian law. Arms control treaties tend to be more specific, but they contribute to security by banning certain practices, for example, nuclear testing, the use of certain conventional weapons deemed to be excessively injurious or to have indiscriminate effects, or other types or classes of weapons (such as chemical and biological weapons [CBW] and antipersonnel landmines [APLs]).

During the Cold War, arms control became first and foremost a mechanism for avoiding nuclear war and managing the strategic relationship between the United States and the Soviet Union. The major powers decided the terms and were the custodians (depositaries), not only of their own bilateral agreements, but also of many multilateral arms treaties. Even multilateral instruments, such as the 1963 Partial Test Ban Treaty (PTBT) and the NPT that arose out of public antinuclear pressure, were concluded only after the major nuclear powers had come to their own agreements on the key provisions.

Before the UN came to be identified as the depositary for international treaties, the United States and the Soviet Union (often with the UK) acted jointly as depositaries, with responsibility for monitoring compliance, implementation, reviews (where appropriate), and determining action in the event of noncompliance or other problems. Because it was assumed that the two superpowers would verify the treaties using their national technical means and other resources, several multilateral treaties, such as the 1972 Biological Weapons Convention (BWC), entered into force without any formal or multilateral verification provisions. It was assumed that, on the basis of evidence gathered through national monitoring of other states' capabilities and actions, the United States and the Soviet Union would oversee compliance and implementation. In some treaties, including the BWC, any notice of withdrawal would have to be given not just to the depositaries, but also to the other states parties and to the UN Security Council. The BWC also was one of the first multilateral arms control treaties to give the Security Council responsibility for investigating allegations of noncompliance.

By the early 1990s, the UN Secretary-General rather than any specific state had come to be identified as the depositary for international treaties. In addition, the UN Security Council and General Assembly are increasingly specified in treaty provisions relating to compliance and sanctions. Any powers ceded to the Security Council effectively extend the special role of China, France, the United States, Russia, and the UK and their power to veto assessments they do not like as the Permanent Five (P-5) members of the Council.

The processes and functions of arms control began to change at the end of the Cold War, in response to the shifts in power, diversity of significant weapon holders, and the multiplicity of interests that sought to be represented at the negotiating table. The multilateral arms control treaties of the 1990s incorporated sophisticated and negotiated verification systems, with states sharing responsibility for implementation by means of their participation in treaty-specific organizations. The Security Council came to be the formally identified and generally accepted final arbitrator and authority for collective action if serious noncompliance was proved.

The 1993 Chemical Weapons Convention (CWC), the CTBT, and the Ottawa Convention on Landmines are examples of the initial post–Cold War enthusiasm for multilateral arms control. The first two treaties had been long on the international agenda, but were completed when the George H. W. Bush and Bill Clinton administrations respectively decided to exercise international leadership. The Ottawa Convention on Landmines was achieved by a driving coalition of developing and middle-power nations and civil society that pursued negotiations outside the traditional fora in which powerful states could exercise a veto, thereby bypassing opposition from a handful of states, including the United States, China, and Russia.

The CWC and Ottawa Convention on Landmines managed to enter into force before the end of the 1990s and have wide, but not universal, adherence. Though some significant states remain outside each agreement, these treaties are now perceived to have entered the canons of international law. The norms against chemical weapons (CW) and landmines are having a positive influence on all governments, even if they are not legally binding on those states that have not yet acceded to the formal treaties.

The CTBT became the first treaty to fall victim to the neoconservative trend growing in the Republican Party, which rejected international constraints on US freedom of action. The neoconservative approach derived in part from a hegemonic perception of the United States as having special responsibilities for the diffusion of its values and for its particular brand of freedom and democracy. It overturned previous decades of bipartisan internationalism, which included a US-led drive toward creating universal norms and laws as well as the early post–Cold War assumption that universality was a desirable and achievable objective in arms control.

The George W. Bush administration also moved the United States away from norm-based nonproliferation to counterproliferation, involving selected coalitions of willing (or politically pressured) allies backed up by the threat or use of force. Using the terror attacks of 9/11 as a springboard to transform US foreign policy, Bush's team pursued counterproliferation on several fronts, most notably in the Iraq war and the creation of the Proliferation Security Initiative (PSI). Where possible, UN Security Council resolutions were harnessed to this project to give specific measures greater international legitimacy. For example, Security Council Resolution 1373 on "threats to international peace and security caused by terrorist acts," enacted in the immediate aftermath of the 9/11 attacks, drew on the text of the recently concluded treaty for the suppression of the financing of terrorism. It reinforced that treaty's objectives while bypassing the lengthy ratification processes that such treaties normally undergo before they enter into force. Resolution 1373 was used to create binding international law and require active state cooperation "to prevent and suppress terrorist acts," requiring "increased cooperation and full implementation of the relevant international conventions relating to terrorism." In effect, Resolution 1373, passed by the fifteen-member Security Council, made all 192 governments represented in the UN responsible for preventing terrorism and prosecuting people residing within their borders who may be funding, planning, or carrying out terrorist acts anywhere in the world. Resolution 1373 also set up a committee of the Security Council to take forward the implementation of this resolution.

Security Council Resolution 1373 was not an instrument of arms control per se, but it paved the way for Resolution 1540 on WMD, adopted three years later. Resolution 1540 was driven through the Security Council by the United States and UK to give the imprimatur and legitimacy of enforceable international law and the UN to their efforts undertaken as part of the "war on terror." Resolution 1540 followed from the Proliferation Security Initiative, established in 2003 to coordinate the actions of a "partnership" of countries to "halt shipments of dangerous technologies to and from states and nonstate actors of proliferation concern—at sea, in the air, and on land."[6] The PSI had attracted criticism from Russia, China, and others on grounds that it lacked international legal authority and would enable a cartel of states to act outside the institutions established to oversee and implement the WMD regimes. Fears were expressed that the PSI gave authority to coercive actions without accountability under law, and that it would be used to impede legitimate trading or technology transfers among the West's economic rivals and developing states.

To bring critics of US unilateralism and the Iraq war on board, Security Council Resolution 1540 went beyond the PSI and derived its authority from existing multilateral treaties. Adopted in April 2004, Resolution 1540 evoked enforcement powers under Chapter VII of the UN Charter.[7] It required states to enact domestic controls and national legislation to prevent the acquisition and use of CW, biological weapons (BW), and nuclear weapons and materials by nonstate actors for terrorist purposes.[8] In the post-9/11 threat environment, this plugged an increasingly problematic gap in traditional arms control. It also extended to all UN member states the obligations contained in disarmament and nonproliferation agreements relating to CW, BW, and nuclear weapons whether or not those states had formally signed or ratified such agreements. Resolution 1540 epitomized a new approach to universalizing arms control obligations through the Security Council.

This development, however, was not without its critics. Some complained that it was inappropriate and unacceptable for the Security Council to arrogate to itself a legislative role. In response, supporters argued that the Council was not really making law through resolutions such as 1540 and 1373 because these resolutions had existing multilateral treaties as their basis. Hence, the Council was only carrying out its enforcement powers by requiring states to adopt domestic measures, accepting that these would vary in accordance with national legislative rules and practice. Despite such concerns, these resolutions are now widely supported and many states participate in the committees established by the Security Council to oversee their implementation. It is perhaps ironic that the Security Council route to backdoor universalization had been spearheaded by a US administration noted for its skepticism about the UN and legally binding arms control treaties and its reluctance to accept international legal constraints and accountability.

However it is accomplished, whether through laboriously negotiated treaties or Security Council resolutions, arms control is no longer just the purview of dominant states for managing their relationships and controlling potential rivals or troublemakers. As the twenty-first century progresses, governments and military leaders are beginning to catch up with their peoples in understanding that "national security" has been superseded by "human security" and that the imperatives of human security require more diverse approaches, based on cooperative security arrangements.

Establishing Norms and Building Security Regimes

When a particular arms control or disarmament treaty is adopted, it adds to the "networks of treaties, agreements and organizations" that constitute security regimes.[9] Defined by Stephen Krasner as "sets of implicit or explicit principles, norms, rules, and decisionmaking procedures around which actors' expectations converge,"[10] the concept of regimes was largely associated with neorealist and neoliberal attempts to understand and explain collective action in international relations. The role of security regimes, however, needs to be reexamined in light of the changing threat environment.

Policymakers who saw themselves as realists dominated arms control during the Cold War. According to the realist worldview, states will seek cooperation with others to aggrandize their power or avoid the greater insecurity of a free-for-all in the Hobbesian bear pit. The primary drive is for national autonomy and self-interest, but "there are times when rational self-interested calculation leads actors to abandon independent decisionmaking in favor of joint decisionmaking."[11] Regimes could be developed to deal with questions of common interest (to achieve relative gains) or, as is the case with arms control, to resolve dilemmas of common aversion (such as insecurity due to the proliferation of nuclear weapons).[12]

International security is interdependent, but governments enter multilateral arms control with different needs, expectations, and objectives. Some governments will possess greater military or economic powers than others. Some will be in possession of sophisticated weapon technologies, others may be ambitious to acquire them, while still others may have abjured such weapons and want to see them eliminated altogether. They will therefore perceive their national and security interests and the role of arms control and international law differently. Assuming cooperation is shaped by the relative power and interests of asymmetric actors, realists expect multilateral negotiations to be both a tool and a reflection of the interests of dominant states. The distribution of power among states determines the context of interaction and negotiating agendas and thus determines the prospects of multilateral negotiations. The processes and products of multilateral arms control are expected to yield differential benefits, with the more powerful states ensuring that their significant interests are met. Realists have tended to dismiss the normative element in multilateralism, except where it serves a public relations function to persuade others to go along with what the dominant states prefer.[13]

Neoliberal analysts are more comfortable than realists with complex interdependence and norm-based regimes, although they share many of realism's theoretical assumptions, notably regarding states as unitary, rational actors pursuing their interests in an anarchic international system.[14] Neoliberals view multilateral negotiations as primarily taking place among states, but they also recognize that transnational corporations, nongovernmental organizations, and interest groups play a constitutive role in shaping states' interests and influencing the conditions for cooperation. Furthermore, neoliberals believe that the institutions of arms control and nonproliferation play a dynamic role in sustaining security regimes, embedding and giving legitimacy to particular norms and practices. As they become universalized and constituted in particular institutions and in the institution of multilateralism itself, these norms and practices feed back into and shape the interests of states. This feedback loop helps sustain cooperation even when strategic relations, relative power, and the interests of states fluctuate or shift.[15]

Another approach now gaining importance in the diplomatic arena conceives of multilateralism as a tool and institution for promoting the normative goals of global governance and international law. This approach, which may be characterized as "neoglobalism,"[16] is developing in response to transboundary security challenges such as poverty, pollution, climate change, terrorism, drugs, crime, and violence. Neoglobalism, like global governance theories, is critical of state-centered politics and emphasizes the multiplicity of actors: not just governments and intergovernmental institutions, but transnational corporations, nongovernmental organizations, and, most importantly, civil society actors and networks and citizens' movements.[17] Neoglobalism perceives a different security environment, identifies threats in terms of human security rather than national security, and encompasses nongovernmental, intergovernmental, and transgovernmental actors and relations. It is embedded, according to Robert Cox, with the normative "commitment to greater social equity, greater diffusion of power among countries and social groups, protection of the biosphere, moderation and nonviolence in dealing with conflict, and mutual recognition of the values of different civilizations."[18] Neoglobalism also challenges the rationalist view of states, seeing them as conditional entities[19] and representative institutions subject to "capture and recapture, construction and reconstruction," by social and political actors through elections, coups, or other forms of governmental change.[20]

In sum, neorealists emphasize states and view multilateral arms control as a mechanism for conflicting powers to coordinate their actions to increase their relative power or mitigate security threats; neoliberals emphasize interstate cooperation for mutual benefits, and regard international regimes and institutions as being themselves instrumental in stabilizing and sustaining cooperation and security; and neoglobalists emphasize universality and participatory decisionmaking by states and civil society to promote the norms and objectives of collective security, global governance, and international law. One way to understand the increasing importance of universality and reciprocal commitments and compliance is to view the handover from the late twentieth to the twenty-first century as a transition from the Cold War realist paradigm to postcolonialist interdependent globalism.

Universality in Arms Control: Desirable, Feasible, or Unnecessary?

In 1978, the first UN Special Session on Disarmament stated:

> All the peoples of the world have a vital interest in the success of disarmament negotiations. Consequently, all States have the duty to contribute to efforts in the field on disarmament negotiations. All States have the right to participate in disarmament negotiations. They have the right to participate on an equal footing in those multilateral disarmament negotiations which have a direct bearing on their national security.[21]

Although this proclamation was ahead of its time, it is now widely accepted that, from landmines to nuclear weapons, disarmament negotiations have a direct bearing on the security of all peoples, not least through the diffusion of values about what constitutes inhumane warfare. States that have renounced certain weapons have an even greater interest in ensuring the universal implementation of controls and prohibitions than states that have retained possession of regulated weapons.

In the process of emerging from centuries of colonialism, and under the shadow of the Cold War balance of terror and alliances based on East-West spheres of influence, many states may have been willing to accept lesser roles in determining their own security. In the modern world, it is widely recognized that security and human rights are universal needs, and that the rights and needs of less powerful peoples and nations are as valid as those of more powerful states. Therefore, weaker states are less likely to accept indefinitely arms control arrangements that allow some states to retain, develop, and rely on certain weapons—notably, the most powerful, nuclear weapons—while they remain forever prohibited for the rest of the world.

International law has been characterized as "obligatory, but not compulsory" because it must accommodate many different traditions of domestic law, and because its mechanisms for enforcement are still under construction and are by no means universally accepted. US law, for example, has long recognized a "universal principle" for certain offenses that are so widely condemned that any state may prosecute an offender on behalf of the world community.[22] Two decades before UN Security Council Resolution 1540, US domestic law recognized that certain heinous actions addressed in international conventions or treaties could be "identified as a universal crime over which all states should exercise jurisdiction."[23] This concept of universal jurisdiction was enshrined in US law in 1987, and understood to be available regardless of who committed the act and where it occurred. Moreover, it was understood to be applicable whether or not a particular country had acceded directly to the international conventions or treaties concerned.

In keeping with the general principles of customary international law, a convention or treaty that is widely adhered to may be regarded as legally binding even on states that have not actually signed or ratified the treaty. In this way, universal jurisdiction is achieved without full universality. Even if 100 percent universal adherence is not achieved, the principle of universality in arms control and regime building matters for security. The problems besetting the NPT regime are in part due to frustration by the NNWS that the treaty's discriminatory arrangements—viewed as temporary in 1968—have been extended indefinitely.

Although it is recognized that the drawing of distinctions between parties may be necessary for a treaty such as the NPT to be negotiated in the first place, difficulties may arise if there is little movement toward a nondiscriminatory baseline. The NPT's problems are exacerbated when some of the nuclear powers behave as if they regard the disarmament obligation (Article VI) as less binding and important than the obligations on NNWS parties. Such attitudes might have been accepted in the Cold War, but they are not as acceptable now.[24] In addition to concerns about "vertical proliferation" and the continued possession and renewal of nuclear weapons in the arsenals of the P-5, the NPT's credibility takes a battering when the NNWS perceive that countries that remained outside the treaty and developed nuclear weapons (such as India, Israel, and Pakistan) have received preferential treatment. One example that has provoked worldwide consternation is the ill-starred US-India nuclear deal announced by President George W. Bush and India's prime minister Manmohan Singh in 2005.

Verification and Practical Compliance

Although nondiscriminatory provisions are not a condition of universality, equal obligation treaties tend to carry more weight and are easier to implement. Verification is technically and politically more straightforward for agreements that are comprehensive and universal rather than partial. For example, if a prohibition is universal and comprehensive, any detection of a banned technology, material, or facility can be taken as a clear indication of violation. Although dual-use nuclear and pharmaceutical technologies require close monitoring of certain materials and processes to ensure they are not diverted toward weapon production, the task is made much more complicated if the arms control is partial or some states are exempted. This then requires not only detection, but also forensic analysis and political judgment to determine if the activity indicates a violation of law.

These are not only technical questions. In verification, intrusion such as on-site inspections is often the most politically sensitive component of a multilateral verification regime. Intrusion, interdictions, and other potentially coercive approaches are more likely to be accepted in an arms control regime based on universality and nondiscrimination. By fostering participation in negotiations, collective responsibility, and "ownership," multilateral processes help to maximize genuine consent. The more collective ownership governments and peoples feel toward an international law or treaty, the more likely they are to take compliance seriously.

There are, however, limits to this rosy picture. Even though India's leaders had for decades been at the forefront of calls for a comprehensive test ban treaty and India's diplomats participated fully in the Conference on Disarmament (CD) negotiations on the CTBT, India balked in the final months. Declaring that "India will never sign this unequal treaty, not now, nor later," India's ambassador to the UN condemned the treaty's entry into force provision as coercive and predicted that, because of it, the treaty would never enter into force.[25] Two years later, in May 1998, India conducted a series of nuclear explosive tests and declared itself a nuclear weapon state (NWS). It was closely followed by Pakistan.

India's defection from the CTBT contains lessons for multilateral diplomacy, requiring careful thought about how the processes of participation and consent can contribute to ensure greater levels of accession, legitimacy, and compliance. China's gradual transition from nuclear testing to nuclear test ban bears out this argument. Like India, China was equivocal about the CTBT when it entered the negotiations, and actually conducted several nuclear weapon tests while the talks were taking place. As negotiations proceeded, however, China increasingly came to see that its interests lay in acceding to the multilateral regime. Once it decided to accept the test ban, China dropped or modified some of its most contentious positions and fought hard for key practical provisions, particularly relating to verification and inspections.

In keeping with traditional concepts of the primacy of nation-states, most current treaties contain a provision for withdrawal on the grounds of "supreme national interest." Long assumed to be a state's sovereign right to put its perceived national interests above those of the international community, the right of withdrawal from disarmament and nonproliferation treaties has come under scrutiny because of North Korea's decision in 2003 to cite this and withdraw from the NPT. North Korea then saw itself as free to reject controls on its nuclear program and to develop nuclear weapons, thereby posing a potentially serious threat to regional and international security. Although the other NPT states parties appeared unable to prevent North Korea's withdrawal from the NPT, the UN Security Council imposed sanctions, and diplomacy through the Six-Party Talks was intensified, especially after the nuclear test of 9 October 2006. There are now calls to revise states' rights to withdraw from disarmament treaties that have a universal objective.

Conclusion

As the twenty-first century progresses, the primary human security threats arise less from interstate conflict among similarly armed nation-states than from global challenges like climate change, nuclear proliferation, and natural or induced pandemics. Almost all other significant state and nonstate security challenges are created or fed by multinational and transboundary actors and traffickers. These include terrorism, particularly if combined with CW, BW, or nuclear weapon acquisition. Gang crimes and trafficking in arms, drugs, and refugees (particularly women) also create profound security challenges in failed states and failing cities (which are prevalent in developed as well as developing countries). There is mounting evidence that such criminal activities are also associated with increased threats from terrorism or WMD. In short, the security of one nation is interdependent with the security of others. National security is impossible to sustain in conditions of international insecurity.

Although these nontraditional threats have a military dimension, hard power and arms are practically irrelevant to their prevention or mitigation. Similarly, in an age characterized by a few technologically dominant militaries, asymmetric warfare is a growing challenge, and mass destruction may be inflicted on the economically and militarily powerful by transnational or domestic actors. These transstate, substate, and nonstate actors may be disaffected individuals or armed groups. Their objectives may be to terrorize, disrupt, or destroy specific targets for ideological, religious, or political purposes; private gain; or adrenaline kicks. They may participate in networks or act in concert with dispersed populations who share a particular ideology rather than inhabiting shared national territory.

Traditional arms control has been failing to deliver, suggesting that, in order to gain security benefits commensurate with the objectives pursued through arms control during the Cold War, the approach and practices need to be rescued from their Cold War structure and connotations. In particular, just as certain nonstate entities are recognized as greater problems (and more unpredictable and undeterrable threats than traditional state actors) in the post-9/11 world, so also regime formation, norm promulgation, and compliance monitoring in the modern era are increasingly recognized as needing the participation and engagement of civil society for the most effective operations of disarmament, arms control, and nonproliferation.

From a security perspective, the traditional concept of arms control is giving way to a more universal practice of regime building. The progressive establishment of humanitarian norms and laws is directed toward restricting not only the hardware, but also the use of particular weapons. Although there are moral and legal dimensions to these disarmament developments, the changes are driven by security considerations. However powerful or militarily resourced an individual nation, it cannot hope to protect itself from transboundary threats without the help of others. Promoting a universal sense of collective responsibility for interdependent and international security therefore becomes a national security as well as ethical imperative.

Disarmament and universal prohibitions are much more likely to work in twenty-first-century international relations than attempts to impose the privileges of the old, discriminatory arms control systems whereby some remained outside the full obligations undertaken by others. A destabilizing consequence of a lack of universality is that further governments often feel compelled to opt out or at least hedge their bets when a geostrategic or regional rival remains outside an arms control regime. Hence, though limited arms control approaches may work in the short term, they are essentially unsustainable over time. By contrast, universalizing prohibitions and controls helps to embed the norms and practices, leading to a more sustainable and secure approach based on voluntary mutual consent rather than coercive policing.

Notes

1. For the purposes of this chapter, I am interpreting the term *arms control* to include disarmament and nonproliferation; that is, to encompass both the regimes that control, limit, and reduce armaments, and those intended to prohibit and eliminate types or uses of particular weapons.

2. This concept is not without its own ambiguities. As Martti Koskenniemi noted, "when somebody today claims to be acting on behalf of the 'international community' we immediately recognize the hegemonic tendency at work." Koskenniemi, "What Is International Law For?" in Malcolm D. Evans, ed., *International Law,* 2nd ed. (Oxford: Oxford University Press, 2006), p. 76.

3. UN Security Council Resolution 1373 (2001) and Resolution 1540 (2004), discussed below.

4. See, for example, Tony Blair, "Prime Minister's Speech on Doctrine of the International Community, Delivered at the Economic Club, Chicago," 24 April 1999, available at www.number10.gov.uk/page1297.

5. Koskenniemi, "What Is International Law For?" p. 72.

6. "Principles for the Proliferation Security Initiative" (Washington, DC: White House, Office of the Press Secretary, 4 September 2003), available at www.whitehouse.gov.

7. UN Charter, Chap. VII: Action with Respect to Threats to the Peace, Breaches of the Peace, and Acts of Aggression.

8. International lawyer Merav Datan noted that "the first three operative paragraphs of UNSC 1540 use the language 'all states shall,' thereby creating enforceable legally binding obligations on states. The remaining elements of the resolution carry politically binding implications in that they advocate principles and establish mechanisms for cooperative implementation." See Datan, "Security Council Resolution 1540: WMD and Non-state Trafficking," *Disarmament Diplomacy,* no. 79 (April/May 2005): 47–55.

9. See, for example, Joseph Cirincione, "Historical Overview and

Introduction," in Joseph Cirincione, ed., *Repairing the Regime* (New York: Routledge, 2000), p. 3.

10. Stephen D. Krasner, ed., *International Regimes* (Ithaca: Cornell University Press, 1983). Krasner defined his terms thus (page 2): "Norms are standards of behaviour defined in terms of rights and obligations. Rules are specific prescriptions or proscriptions for action. Decisionmaking procedures are prevailing practices for making and implementing collective choice." See especially "Structural Causes and Regime Consequences: Regimes as Intervening Variables" in the same volume.

11. Arthur Stein, "Coordination and Collaboration: Regimes in an Anarchic World," ibid., at p. 132.

12. Ibid., at pp. 115–140.

13. Martin Wight, *Power Politics,* 2nd ed. (Leicester, UK: Leicester University Press, 1978). (Orig. pub. 1946.); Hedley Bull, *The Anarchical Society: A Study of Order in World Politics* (London: Macmillan, 1977).

14. Robert O. Keohane and Joseph S. Nye, eds., *Transnational Relations and World Politics* (Cambridge: Harvard University Press, 1972); Robert O. Keohane and Joseph S. Nye, *Power and Interdependence,* 3rd ed. (New York: Longman 2001). (Orig. pub. 1977.)

15. Robert O. Keohane, *After Hegemony: Cooperation and Discord in the World Political Economy* (Princeton: Princeton University Press, 1984), especially chaps. 5 and 6.

16. This is a better descriptive term than *new multilateralism,* which was the term coined by some of its early analysts during discussions in the Multilateralism and the United Nations System (MUNS) program under the auspices of Robert Cox during the late 1990s.

17. See James N. Rosenau, "Governance, Order, and Change in World Politics," in James N. Rosenau and Ernst-Otto Czempiel, eds., *Governance Without Government: Order and Change in World Politics* (Cambridge: Cambridge University Press, 1992), p. 4; and the essays in Michael G. Schechter, ed., *Future Multilateralism: The Political and Social Framework* (Basingstoke, UK: Macmillan/United Nations University Press, 1999).

18. The quotation, attributed to a paper presented by Robert Cox at the United Nations University, 17 August 1993, is from "Preface," in Michael G. Schechter, ed., *Innovation in Multilateralism* (Basingstoke, UK: Macmillan/United Nations University Press, 1999), p. ix; it also appears in Jonas Zoninsein, "Global Civil Society and Theories of International Political Economy," in Michael G. Schechter, ed., *The Revival of Civil Society: Global and Comparative Perspectives* (Basingstoke, UK: Macmillan Press, 1999), p. 50.

19. Paul Taylor, "The United Nations and International Order," in John Baylis and Steve Smith, ed., *The Globalization of World Politics,* 2nd ed. (Oxford: Oxford University Press, 2001), p. 338.

20. Andrew Moravcsik, "Taking Preferences Seriously: A Liberal Theory of International Politics," in Paul R. Viotti and Mark V. Kauppi, *International Relations Theory,* 3rd ed. (Boston: Allyn & Bacon, 1987), p. 250.

21. Para. 28, Final Document, Special Session of the General Assembly on Disarmament, 1 July 1978 (New York: United Nations, May 1988 reprint), p. 13.

22. *United States v. Yunis,* 681 F. Supp. 896 (1988), US District Court, District of Columbia, quoted in Robert McCorquodale and Martin Dixon, *Cases and Materials on International Law,* 4th ed. (Oxford: Oxford University Press, 2003), p. 288.

23. *Restatement (Third) Foreign Relations Law of the United States (1987),* discussed in McCorquodale and Dixon, *Cases and Materials,* pp. 288–290.

24. By comparison with the Nuclear Nonproliferation Treaty (NPT), which had differentiated the obligations of those already possessing nuclear arsenals from those that were to undertake never to acquire such weapons, the universal approach taken by the Chemical Weapons Convention (CWC) in 1996 was considered revolutionary.

25. Arundhati Ghose, Indian ambassador to the UN, United Nations General Assembly, 10 September 1996, available at www.indianembassy.org/policy/CTBT/ctbtunseptember1096.html.

Suggested Readings

Borrie, John, and Vanessa Martin Randin, eds., *Thinking Outside the Box in Multilateral Disarmament and Arms Control Negotiations* (Geneva: United Nations, 2006).

Florini, Ann, ed., *The Third Force: The Rise of Transnational Civil Society* (Washington, DC: Carnegie Endowment for International Peace, 2000).

Krasner, Stephen D., ed., *International Regimes* (Ithaca: Cornell University Press, 1983).

Rosenau, James N., and Ernst-Otto Czempiel, eds., *Governance Without Government: Order and Change in World Politics* (Cambridge: Cambridge University Press, 1992).

Sands, Philippe, *Lawless World: Making and Breaking Global Rules* (London: Penguin Books, 2006).

Schechter, Michael G., ed., *Future Multilateralism: The Political and Social Framework* (Basingstoke, UK: Macmillan/United Nations University Press, 1999).

11

The New Cooperative Security Paradigm

James J. Wirtz

Arms control and cooperative security measures have been part of the foreign and defense policies of the United States and other nations for nearly fifty years. Nevertheless, they remain a controversial subject among scholars and policy analysts who continue to debate the role and importance of existing and proposed treaties and initiatives. Many national security analysts, including the contributors to this volume, agree that we are unlikely to see renewed interest in negotiating formal arms control treaties, an endeavor that had reached its zenith in the years surrounding the end of the Cold War. Instead, they anticipate new types of cooperative security initiatives designed to cope with the externalities created by globalization and the horizontal and vertical proliferation of dangerous technologies. Our contributors outline a future where new types of formal and informal multilateral initiatives emerge to deal with common threats that transcend international boundaries and bilateral relationships. They also anticipate a shift from agreements that limit state action to initiatives that commit states to take specific actions to secure the common good.

Kerry M. Kartchner called this shift in practice a "new paradigm for arms control." Our other contributors agree with Kartchner: they have described how new cooperative security initiatives are emerging across several issue areas, helping to shape the future of arms control. The contributors are optimistic about the way this new paradigm is helping to shape international initiatives to defeat emerging threats. Nontraditional arms control and cooperative security initiatives are viewed as an effective way to cope with transnational threats that escape direct national control. There is a spirit of innovation and urgency behind the new effort to devise effective international measures to control and combat the trafficking and use of dangerous materials, weapons, and associated delivery systems.

What strategic and technological changes prompted this paradigm shift? How might arms control and cooperative security initiatives evolve in the future to meet new challenges and opportunities? This conclusion highlights the changes that have placed cooperative security initiatives on the international agenda, setting these developments in the broader context of our ongoing study of arms control.[1] Officials and theorists have responded to a changing strategic environment by searching for new cooperative measures to mitigate threats.

The Changing Strategic Context

Arms control was traditionally viewed as a state enterprise because war itself was largely conducted by states. What better way to limit the costs, consequences, and likelihood of war than to constrain the behavior of national governments? This idea, combined with the notion that even adversaries shared an interest in avoiding certain technologies or activities, were the principles that shaped the well-known arms control initiatives undertaken during the Cold War.[2]

Arms control negotiations continued after the collapse of the Soviet empire but, following a flurry of arms control activity in the early 1990s, the urgency behind these efforts began to wane. In the absence of acute political hostility, Washington and Moscow seemed content to rely on their Cold War "surplus" nuclear arsenals. US and Russian nuclear modernization programs were largely suspended by the mid-1990s. As obsolescence and shrinking budgets began to result in "natural" arms reductions, it became clear that arms control was slowly becoming simply a way to codify what was inevitable. It thus is not surprising that strategic nuclear arms control seems to have culminated, at least for the time being, with the 2002 Strategic Offensive Reductions Treaty (SORT, also called the Moscow Treaty). This simple and brief accord was the latest in a series of strategic arms control treaties that codified an 80 percent reduction from Cold War levels in the number of nuclear warheads deployed by the United States and Russia, a remarkable achievement that would have been nearly impossible to envision just a few decades ago. Nevertheless, some observers complained that this agreement created a floor, not a ceiling, in terms of force reductions, while others suggested that the Moscow Treaty might have been the last in a long line of strategic arms accords between the superpowers. For many observers, it made no sense to conduct arms control negotiations between states that lacked political hostilities and whose arsenals were already shrinking. Under these circumstances, arms control agreements might be easily negotiated, but supply limited benefits.[3]

The George W. Bush administration energized this debate over the future of arms control when it decided in 2001 to withdraw from the 1972 Anti-Ballistic Missile Treaty (ABM Treaty). Critics charged that US withdrawal from the treaty would mark the end of the Cold War arms control regime. The Bush administration responded that the treaty was obsolete because it prevented the United States from responding to emerging ballistic missile threats while erroneously suggesting to Americans and Russians alike that US-Russia strategic relations were destined to remain hostile. Administration officials wanted to put an end to traditional arms control because they saw it as a vestige of what was once an implacably hostile relationship. They believed that, as an instrument designed for relations among adversaries, arms control was the wrong tool to use among friends or at least among states that had no significant grievances.[4] Critics suggested that the administration's decision opened Pandora's box, again creating the opportunity for an offense-defense strategic nuclear arms race. So far at least, this worst-case scenario has failed to materialize. The relatively limited missile defenses being deployed and developed by the United States have sparked little more than a rhetorical reaction on the part of other nuclear weapon states.

The 9/11 terror attacks on the World Trade Center and the Pentagon, however, redirected the debate about the future of arms control. At first, arms control and cooperative security activities seemed to have little to offer when it came to the threat posed by transnational terrorist networks. Arms control was intended to cope with foreign enemies. It never was intended to deal with networks that operated across national borders. Arms control was largely directed at national military forces under direct government control. By contrast, Al-Qaida and other criminal and terrorist syndicates used the organizational, transportation, and communication capabilities created by globalization and the information revolution to undertake international operations. These civilian systems had largely been left unregulated by international arms control agreements. Like many of the Cold War–era policies of the US defense, intelligence, and law enforcement establishments, arms control seemed ill suited to addressing the new threat posed by nonstate actors.

Another troubling development was the emergence of spontaneous cells or individuals who had access to materials directly prohibited by arms control agreements. In the wake of the Al-Qaida attacks, it now appears that a scientist at the US Army Medical Research Institute of Infectious Diseases sent anthrax through the US mail, killing five individuals and exposing hundreds of people to the deadly spores.[5] As a signatory of the Biological Weapons Convention, however, the US government is charged with taking "any necessary measure to prohibit and prevent the development, production, stockpiling, acquisition, or retention of the agents, toxins and weapons . . . within the territory . . . under its jurisdiction."[6] Although no states parties to the treaty protested, the United States actually has an obligation under the convention not to allow the possession or use of anthrax as a weapon on its territory—by anyone. The fact that the anthrax was placed in the mail without the authorization or knowledge of the US government does not relieve Washington of its responsibility to police its territory. Arms control compliance, as many observers recognized at the time, was increasingly becoming a domestic matter that demanded the immediate attention of the law enforcement community.[7] Arms control was no longer just a matter of ensuring that foreign governments complied with agreements. It was becoming a matter of guaranteeing that a nation's own government, commercial enterprises, citizens, and even visitors were not violating treaty provisions within its own territory.

The Changing Technical Setting

The response to the 2001 anthrax attacks was muted. Because the attacks involved a biological agent, occurred largely in a domestic setting, and were undertaken by an individual whose motives remain unclear, there was a tendency to hope for the best and to treat the event as an isolated incident.[8] Moreover, because the 2001 anthrax attacks and several additional events, including the Las Vegas ricin incident in February 2008 and a series of white-powder hoaxes, seemed to be undertaken by mentally unbalanced or emotionally disturbed individuals, it was difficult to generate a sustained political response to the private use of biological agents and toxins. There was more sustained concern about the possibility that Al-Qaida or other terrorist organizations might acquire chemical weapons, biological weapons, or nuclear weapons, but scholars and policymakers alike came to believe that continued military, economic, and political pressure against these organizations was the best way to head off this threat. Some scholars also suggested that Al-Qaida might be deterred from using weapons of mass destruction (WMD).[9]

The international community, however, could not ignore revelations about the activities of Abdul Qadeer Khan, a Pakistani scientist who was involved in Pakistan's nuclear program. Khan established an international syndicate (the A. Q. Khan network) that supplied nuclear-related technology and know-how, including working nuclear bomb designs, to clients around the word. These activities demonstrated that nuclear weapon related technology was becoming dangerously accessible and was escaping state control, although doubts linger about the role of other Pakistani officials in facilitating the network's activities. Khan, who is often portrayed as "the father of the Pakistani nuclear bomb," eventually will come to be better known for another achievement: he was the first person to commercialize nuclear weapon technologies and scientific know-how.[10]

Khan's activities shook the nuclear nonproliferation regime to its foundations because it demonstrated that significant nuclear technologies were escaping regulation by the regime and by states themselves. The fact that working equipment, weapon designs, and technical advice were trafficked in clandestine networks was a development that simply was intolerable for most of the international community. Actions had to be taken to stop this trafficking in materials and technologies related to nuclear, chemical, and biological weapons, but the necessary transnational instruments to stop this trade were not readily available. For example, when a Spanish warship stopped a North Korean vessel en route to Yemen to deliver ballistic missiles in December 2002, US officials were forced to concede that, under international law, the United States and its allies did not have the right to interdict the shipment.[11] The Scuds were allowed to proceed to Yemen, but the incident clarified the need to find a way to interdict clandestine weapon traffic.

A New Mission for Arms Control and Cooperative Security

Globalization has created a new venue for proliferation to emerge, one that did not exist in a significant way until recently. New actors, operating in what amounts to relatively permissive domestic environments, seem beyond the reach of the nonproliferation regime, which was never really intended to stop individuals or collective actors from trafficking in prohibited weapons or materials. Individuals are now manufacturing, handling, and employing deadly BW and toxins for personal reasons, which fundamentally eliminates the possibility that the demand side of the proliferation problem can be addressed. If individuals or syndicates fail to advance political, economic, or social grievances that can be addressed by government action, there is no way to end the demand for these weapons. Individuals or groups continue to seek WMD for personal or highly idiosyncratic reasons, making it difficult to anticipate threats. This suggests that activities to stop the demand side of the emerging proliferation vectors are unlikely to be successful. Governments everywhere need to take greater efforts to control access and trafficking in these weapons and dangerous materials.

The paradox thus emerges that a national government, or a group of national governments, could be highly compliant with existing nonproliferation and arms control agreements, yet still face a serious threat of attack from their own citizens or the citizens of other states. The battle against proliferation has changed. Governments today not only have to monitor their own programs and institutions in terms of compliance with international agreements, but nonproliferation increasingly involves monitoring the activities of individuals or collective actors in a domestic setting. The threat is no longer confined to states and the realm of international relations. The effects of globalization on proliferation are evidenced by the fact that proliferation is no longer best viewed as an external problem involving other states. The borders of a state are porous and the proliferation problem can now manifest as a domestic issue. As individuals, spontaneous terror cells, and international terrorist syndicates are empowered by globalization and the information revolution, and as technology continues to trickle down, the nature of the threat posed by chemical, biological, and nuclear weapons is changing.

Our contributors have recognized this changing nature of the proliferation challenge. They—and the international community that they write about—are responding to the emerging milieu by suggesting that the time has arrived to delegitimize, criminalize, and police both domestic and international realms when it comes to the possession, transport, and use of WMD and related technologies. The best way to undertake these initiatives is in a cooperative setting: if states take actions to secure their territories, borders, and the transportation networks that run through them, it will become increasingly difficult for individuals and groups to obtain and traffic in dangerous materials.

Placed in the broader perspective of our ongoing study of arms control, these new initiatives are encouraging. By the turn of the century, the euphoria and surge in arms control activity that followed the end of the Cold War had waned, leaving scholars and officials alike to doubt the continued relevance of traditional arms control. There was a recognition that new ideas and approaches were needed if arms control and cooperative security were to remain relevant, but the so-called arms control community seemed mired in the past, attempting to replicate activities and agreements that were slowly being overtaken by events. One can only hope that the change from a Republican to a Democratic administration in Washington will not rekindle the Cold War arms control debate, and that President Barack Obama and members of his administration will integrate existing cooperative security initiatives into their arms control policies. New cooperative security activities that transcend national boundaries are beginning to close the loopholes and ungoverned spaces that can be exploited by individuals and groups bent on nefarious activity. The need to monitor commercial, scientific, and transportation enterprises and networks is now clear. Individuals and groups can exploit these resources to obtain dangerous materials and know-how that once were possessed only by governments and national defense establishments.

Future arms control and cooperative security initiatives thus will differ from previous efforts in several significant ways. First, arms control and cooperative security might increasingly be seen as effective tools among allies and like-minded states, providing both formal and informal ways to achieve shared objectives. Increasingly, cooperation is seen as a way both to prevent local problems from producing global consequences and to stop transnational actors from launching domestic operations. Second, new initiatives are more likely to require states to take actions, not simply forgo weapon deployments or cut existing arsenals. Traditional arms control agreements might be negotiated among enduring rivals, but most governments seem more interested in devising ways to coordinate activities than to take national action to meet common threats. Third, initiatives are likely to be ad hoc and informal, allowing states to respond to what amounts to an unpredictable and evolving threat. Because globalization and the information revolution generate a changing array of local, regional, and global benefits and externalities, officials and scholars recognize that even the most effective collective programs could quickly be rendered obsolete by social and technical change.

Arms control is based on the idea that even adversaries share common interests and can cooperate to achieve those interests. Today, the international community is increasingly recognizing that only a collective effort can contain or eliminate several of the threats created by globalization and the information revolution. What is needed now is creativity and imagination in devising ever more effective cooperative security initiatives that can achieve these objectives.

Notes

1. Some products of this fifteen-year effort include Jeffrey A. Larsen and Gregory J. Rattray, eds., *Arms Control Toward the 21st Century* (Boulder: Lynne Rienner, 1996); Jeffrey A. Larsen, ed., *Arms Control: Cooperative Security in a Changing Environment* (Boulder: Lynne Rienner, 2002).

2. These ideas were advanced in Thomas C. Schelling and Morton H. Halperin, *Strategy and Arms Control* (Washington, DC: Pergamon-Brassey's, 1985), p. 3. (Orig. pub. 1961.)

3. Colin S. Gray, *House of Cards: Why Arms Control Must Fail* (Ithaca: Cornell University Press, 1992).

4. James J. Wirtz and Jeffrey A. Larsen, eds., *Nuclear Transformation: The New US Nuclear Doctrine* (New York: Palgrave Macmillan, 2005).

5. Sarah Abruzzese and Eric Lipton, "Anthrax Suspect Made Threats, Witnesses Say," *International Herald Tribune,* 2 August 2008, available at www.iht.com/articles/2008/08/02/america/ivins.php; D. B. Jernigan, P. L. Raghunthan, B. P. Bell, R. Brechner, E. A. Bresnitz, and J. C. Butler, "Investigation of Bioterrorism-related Anthrax, United States, 2001," available at www.cdc.gov/ncidod/EID/vol18no10/02-053.htm.

6. "Convention on the Prohibition of the Development, Production, and Stockpiling of Bacteriological (Biological) and Toxin Weapons and on Their Destruction," available at www.opbw.org.

7. Eric Croddy, "Biological and Toxin Weapons Convention (BTWC)," in Eric Croddy, James J. Wirtz, and Jeffrey A. Larsen, eds., *Weapons of Mass*

Destruction: An Encyclopedia of World Wide Policy, Technology and History (Santa Barbara, CA: ABC-CLIO, 2005), p. 46.

8. Fear of copycat attacks might also have encouraged authorities to minimize the 2001 anthrax incidents. White powder hoaxes were already common prior to 2001. See John Sullivan and James J. Wirtz, "Terrorism Early Warning and Counter-terrorism Intelligence," *International Journal of Intelligence and Counterintelligence* 21, no. 1 (2008).

9. Lewis A. Dunn, "Can al Qaeda Be Deterred from Using Nuclear Weapons?" Occasional Paper No. 3 (Washington, DC: National Defense University, Center for the Study of Weapons of Mass Destruction, July 2005).

10. Jeremy Bernstein, *Nuclear Weapons: What You Need to Know* (New York: Cambridge University Press, 2008).

11. Brian Knowlton, "Ship Allowed to Take North Korea SCUDs on to Yemeni Port: US Frees Freighter Carrying Missiles," *International Herald Tribune,* 12 December 2002, available at www.iht.com/articles/2002/12/12/scuds_ed3_.php.

Appendix: Treaties, Agreements, and Organizations of Particular Interest

Jeffrey A. Larsen, Maeghin Escarcida, and Guy B. Roberts

The Agreed Framework with North Korea

The Agreed Framework with North Korea was signed in October 1994, ending a crisis that had been building for several years. This measure shored up stability on the Korean Peninsula at a time when North Korea was dangerously flaunting its responsibilities under the International Atomic Energy Agency (IAEA) rules, and was running the risk of war with the United States in so doing. It offered proliferation-resistant nuclear reactors, food, and oil to North Korea in exchange for the exposure, deconstruction, and monitoring of its nuclear weapon infrastructure—particularly its plutonium reactors and reprocessing facilities. Although not a traditional arms control agreement per se, the Agreed Framework reduced a threatening military capability at reasonable political and economic cost. The Agreed Framework established a new international organization, the Korean Peninsula Energy Development Agency, to finance and construct the new nuclear power plants. There were thirteen members of this organization as of mid-2001, with Japan and South Korea providing most of the funding.

In 2002, it was revealed that North Korea had initiated a second concealed nuclear weapon program under which they were successfully enriching uranium. It has been estimated that, under this clandestine program, North Korea produced enough fissile material for five to twelve nuclear weapons. After this revelation, North Korea declared its withdrawal from the Nuclear Nonproliferation Treaty (NPT). In August 2003, North Korea announced that it would participate in the Six-Party Talks with the United States, China, Russia, South Korea, and Japan in an attempt to resolve this international issue. In September 2005, North Korea agreed to terminate its nuclear programs, return to the NPT, and accept IAEA safeguards in exchange for security guarantees from the United States.

But on 9 October 2006, North Korea detonated its first nuclear device, with only moderate success. Immediately following this detonation, Pyongyang declared itself a nuclear state. International outrage led the North Koreans to agree to return to the Six-Party Talks in December 2006.

In February 2007, North Korea agreed to suspend its nuclear programs within sixty days and to allow inspectors back into the country in exchange for 50,000 tons of heavy fuel. The North Koreans signaled a willingness to continue with the denuclearization process and announced they would shut down their reactors in Yongbyon. But North Korea reversed course once again in 2008, threatening in September that it was going to reactivate its nuclear reactor and asking the IAEA to remove all nuclear seals and cameras observing its reprocessing facility.

The Antarctic Treaty

The Antarctic Treaty came into force on 23 June 1961 after ratification by the twelve states active at the time in Antarctic science. The treaty covers the area south of 60° south latitude. Its objectives are simple: to demilitarize Antarctica, to establish it as a zone free of nuclear tests and the disposal of radioactive waste, to ensure that it is used for peaceful purposes only, and to promote international scientific cooperation in Antarctica.

The treaty remains in force indefinitely. Since its entry into force, forty-six states, comprising around 80 percent of the world's population, have acceded to it. Consultative (voting) status is open to all states who have demonstrated their commitment to the Antarctic by conducting significant research.

Article I states that Antarctica shall be used for peaceful purposes only. It specifically prohibits any military activities of any kind, to include the establishment of military bases and the testing of any kind of weapon. Article V establishes Antarctica as a nuclear-weapon-free zone (NWFZ) by prohibiting any nuclear explosions in Antarctica or the disposal of radioactive waste material.

The Anti-Ballistic Missile Treaty

Signed on 20 May 1972, the Treaty Between the United States of America and the Union of Soviet Socialist Republics on the Limitation of Anti-Ballistic Missile Systems (referred to throughout this volume as the Anti-Ballistic Missile Treaty [ABM Treaty]) was one result of the Strategic Arms Limitation (SALT I) negotiations. The ABM Treaty prohibited the deployment of an antiballistic missile (ABM) system for "the defense of the territory" or the provision of "a base for such a defense." The former prohibition included a nationwide defense, whether on land, sea, air, or space; the latter encompassed items such as powerful, large phased-array radars, which are the long-lead-time items of a deployed land-based ABM system. An *ABM system* was defined as a system "to counter strategic ballistic missiles or their elements in flight trajectory" and consisted of three components: launchers, interceptor missiles, and radars. The ABM Treaty encompassed all ABM systems, whether based on current or future technology. It prohibited the testing in an ABM mode of non-ABM systems such as surface-to-air missile systems. The ban covered development and testing as well as deployment, but no restraints were placed on research that precedes field testing.

The ABM Treaty limited each side to two ABM deployment sites (later reduced to one site by a 1974 protocol). The United States chose to locate its site at the Grand Forks, North Dakota, intercontinental ballistic missile (ICBM) fields (later dismantled) while the Soviet Union chose to defend Moscow. (The Moscow system is still in existence and upgraded.) The treaty imposed a ceiling of 100 ABM launchers and 100 ABM missiles at launch sites in the ABM deployment area.

Provisions of the ABM Treaty were to be verified solely by national technical means (NTM); each party agreed not to interfere with the other's NTM and not to use deliberate concealment measures that would impede verification by NTM.

The treaty was of unlimited duration, with Review Conferences every five years. A party could withdraw from the treaty with six months' notice. The Standing Consultative Commission in Geneva was the forum for addressing compliance issues.

The United States and Russia signed a series of agreements on 27 September 1997 regarding demarcation between theater and national ballistic missile defenses, and to allow Belarus, Kazakhstan, Russia, and Ukraine to succeed the Soviet Union as state parties to the treaty.

The ABM Treaty came under increasing scrutiny and reconsideration in the late 1990s as the United States began to seriously consider the deployment of a national missile defense system. The William J. Clinton administration hoped that Russia would be willing to renegotiate or modify the treaty to allow for modest defenses against rogue states, theater protection, and accidental launch, but Russia (indeed, most of the world community) opposed this idea. Many arms control advocates called the ABM Treaty "the cornerstone of strategic stability" in the international system. In May 2001, President George W. Bush announced that the United States would not be constrained by an outdated treaty that did not reflect the political realities of a world with new threats posed by rogue states armed with weapons of mass destruction (WMD) and the means to deliver them against US territory. In December 2001, the United States announced that it would withdraw from the treaty in six months in order to develop a missile defense system.

The United States formally withdrew from the ABM Treaty on 13 June 2002.

The Australia Group

The Australia Group was formed in June 1985 to control the export of materials used in the manufacture of chemical and biological weapons (CBW). It created a control list of dual-use chemicals, facilities, equipment, and related technology that could have both commercial and military application. The group of forty industrialized nations (and the European Commission) meets annually to exchange data and coordinate actions.

In June 2002, the member states of the Australia Group adopted a set of formal guidelines specifying certain criteria for evaluating export requests. These guidelines were an effort to improve intelligence sharing regarding CBW proliferation. The guidelines explicitly state that a member cannot approve a particular export to a specific country if that export had been previously denied. Under these circumstances, the approving member would have to first consult with other members of the Australia Group. These guidelines also state that member states have to halt the transfer of any suspicious export if the item is capable of being used in a chemical weapons (CW) or biological weapons (BW) program.

The Biological Weapons Convention

Building on the Geneva Protocol of 1925, which bans the use of CBW in war, the Convention on the Prohibition of the Development, Production, and Stockpiling of Bacteriological (Biological) and Toxin Weapons and on Their Destruction (referred to throughout this volume as the Biological Weapons Convention [BWC]) bans the development, production, stockpiling, and acquisition of biological weapons. It was opened for signature on 10 April 1972 and entered into force on 26 March 1975. As of December 2008, there were 163 states parties to the convention. Twenty states have neither signed nor acceded to the BWC, the most significant of those being Israel.

The BWC states parties met for their Fifth Review Conference in November 2002. During this conference, the member states came to an agreement on a work program meant to help strengthen the convention. This work program consists of annual meetings between technical experts and representatives of the states parties to discuss and work on collateral measures aimed at reinforcing the convention.

The Chemical Weapons Convention

The Convention on the Prohibition of the Development, Production, Stockpiling, and Use of Chemical Weapons and on Their Destruction (referred to throughout this volume as the Chemical Weapons Convention [CWC]) bans the development, production, stockpiling, transfer, acquisition, and both retaliatory and first use of chemical weapons (CW). It prohibits a state from aiding any other state, even if not a party to the convention, in the pursuit of treaty-banned activities. Parties are required to declare all chemical weapons and facilities and to destroy all CW within ten years of entry into force. The convention requires declarations on the production of precursor and dual-purpose chemicals.

The convention entered into force on 29 April 1997, and currently has 185 signatories (of which, as of December 2008, 181 had also ratified the convention). Six states have yet to sign the CWC. Its duration is unlimited.

The verification regime includes routine, intrusive on-site inspections of declared government CW facilities as well as civilian facilities that use certain chemicals that could be used or converted to make weapons. When necessary, it also allows for short notice inspections. The CWC is implemented by the Organisation for the Prohibition of Chemical Weapons (OPCW) in The Hague, the Netherlands.

In December 2006, the OPCW granted deadline extensions to China and Japan (until 2012, for destruction of CW abandoned by Japan in China during World War II), India (until 2009), South Korea (until 2008), Libya (until 2010), Russia (until 2012), and the United States (until 2012).

As of 16 March 2007, 100 percent of confirmed CW production facilities were inactivated with 90 percent of these facilities destroyed or converted for peaceful purposes. The CWC has verified that 30 percent of the world's chemical munitions and containers have been destroyed, and almost 25 percent of the world's declared stockpile of chemical agents has also been removed.

States parties with the largest remaining CW stockpiles are the United States and Russia, and most experts feel that neither state will meet the 2012 deadline for complete destruction of their CW arsenals. The destruction process has proved more difficult, time consuming, and costly than originally anticipated.

The Comprehensive Test Ban Treaty

The concept of a comprehensive test ban can be found in the Preamble to the Limited Test Ban Treaty (LTBT), signed in 1963. Negotiations on a comprehensive ban between the United States, the United Kingdom, and the Soviet Union from 1977 to 1980 ended without result. Nonetheless, all five nuclear powers have enacted unilateral testing moratoriums. The US moratorium was initiated by Congress on 4 September 1992 and was extended through 2001 by President Clinton. President George W. Bush also urged all states to continue the existing testing moratoria.

After initial consultation between the five nuclear powers, on 19 November 1993 the First Committee of the UN General Assembly approved a resolution by consensus that advocated a global treaty to ban all nuclear weapon tests. As urged by the UN resolution, the Conference on Disarmament (CD) created the Nuclear Test Ban Ad Hoc Committee of the CD, which held several negotiating rounds beginning in 1994. The result was the Comprehensive Test Ban Treaty (CTBT), opened for signature on 24 September 1996. Although 180 states have signed the treaty, it cannot enter into force without 44 states having ratified it, including 13 key states. As of mid-2008, only thirty-five of those states had done so. The group of states that must still ratify the treaty includes the United States and China, as well as India, Pakistan, Israel, and North Korea, who have yet to sign it. The United States was the first state to sign the CTBT; however, citing concerns with verifiability, the US Senate voted against ratification on 13 October 1999.

Although it has yet to enter into force, the CTBT verification regime has moved forward with concrete steps. It now includes a global network of hydroacoustic and seismic stations and infrared and radionuclide sensors as well as the right to conduct on-site inspections. The treaty established a new international organization in Vienna, the Comprehensive Test Ban Treaty Organization (CTBTO), to implement the treaty and oversee compliance.

As of the end of 2008, the CTBT had achieved 148 ratifications. Although the detonation of a nuclear test by North Korea in October 2006 had been viewed as a setback and the North Koreans have yet to indicate a willingness to sign the treaty, the test helped to validate the importance of the CTBT with the states that had not yet signed or ratified. Six of the ten remaining states who had yet to ratify the treaty finally did so following the North Korean tests: China, Colombia, Egypt, Indonesia, Iran, and Israel.

The Conference on Disarmament

The Conference on Disarmament (CD) is the independent negotiating body of the UN for arms control treaties. It is one of three international disarmament fora (with the UN Disarmament Commission and the First Committee of the UN General Assembly), but the only body that negotiates treaties. The conference consists of sixty-six members, including all five nuclear weapon states

(NWS). Additional states are allowed to participate as nonmembers. Although they maintain an open agenda, participants normally discuss WMD, conventional weapons, reduction of military budgets and armed forces, and confidence-building measures (CBMs). Most of the work on these topics is accomplished in ad hoc committees. The CD is located in Geneva.

During the September 2007 session of the CD, speakers expressed frustration that, after ten years, they remain at an impasse on achieving the goal of consensus on a program of work. The 2007 CD discussed the following topics: ending the nuclear arms race, nuclear disarmament, prevention of a nuclear war, deterrence of arms in outer space, new types of WMD, radiological weapons, and a detailed program for disarmament. The 2007 annual report of the CD indicated the desire of all members to regain focus on the original purpose of the Conference on Disarmament: eliminating nuclear weapons.

Confidence- and Security-building Measures

Confidence- and security-building measures (CSBMs) are intended to foster transparency and trust through purposely designed cooperative measures. They help clarify states' military intentions, reduce uncertainties about potentially threatening military activities, and constrain opportunities for surprise attack or coercion. As one example of a CSBM in the European context, the Conference on Security and Cooperation in Europe (CSCE, the forerunner of the OSCE) established a series of agreements and procedures designed to increase the security of members through increased military transparency and cooperation. The Helsinki Final Act, signed in 1975, was the first of these measures.

A CSCE subcommittee, the Conference on Disarmament in Europe (CDE), met from 1984 to 1986. One of the results of this conference was the Stockholm Document, which entered into force in January 1987, expanding the requirements for notification and providing for observation of military activities. Members of the CSCE met in 1989 and 1990 to strengthen existing CSBMs. The result was the Vienna Document 1990, which entered into force on 1 January 1991. Vienna Document 1992 supplemented these measures and entered into force on 1 May 1992. Vienna Document 1994 was signed 28 November 1994. Vienna Document 1999 entered into force 1 January 2000. Each of the Vienna Documents updated and expanded the previous constraints on the fifty-four OSCE participants, including restrictions on the size and notification procedures for large-scale military activities in Europe. Vienna Document 1999 also provides for the evaluation and inspection of OSCE members' military facilities.

There are two issues of current emphasis in the OSCE region. In May 2006, over 20,000 tons of deteriorating rocket fuel, known as mélange, was stored in aging containers across the former Soviet Union. This threatened both the security and the environment in much of the OSCE region. In April 2007, the OSCE helped Georgia dispose of obsolete munitions that the Soviets had left behind when they withdrew from Georgia in the early 1990s. The OSCE has completed recycling this fuel in Georgia, and is now working with Armenia, Azerbaijan, Kazakhstan, and Ukraine. OSCE officials hope to complete this project by 2010.

The Conventional Forces in Europe Treaty

The Treaty on Conventional Armed Forces in Europe (referred to throughout this volume as the Conventional Forces in Europe Treaty [CFE Treaty]) was signed by the sixteen members of the North Atlantic Treaty Organization (NATO) and the eight former Warsaw Pact states on 19 November 1990. There are now thirty states parties to the treaty. The area of application for the CFE Treaty is commonly referred to as the Atlantic to the Urals (ATTU). For those states that either do not fall within this area (such as the United States and Canada), or those that have territory extending outside of the area (such as Russia, Turkey, and Kazakhstan), the treaty's limits apply only to forces stationed in the ATTU zone.

The treaty divides Europe into two groups: (1) the North Atlantic Treaty Organization and (2) the members of the former Warsaw Pact, limiting conventional arms equally in both. Each group's holdings are limited in five major categories: tanks, artillery, armored combat vehicles, combat aircraft, and attack helicopters.

Four nested zones were created with specific limits on the ground equipment allowed in each zone. These limits allow for free movement away from, but not toward, the center of Europe, thus decreasing the threat of a surprise attack. Limits were placed on the number of forces that could be stationed in the so-called flank zone. This was done to prevent the Soviet Union (or Russia) from repositioning its forces previously located in Central Europe to the borders of Turkey and Norway, forcing them instead to be moved deep within Russia.

Although each group decides on the equipment levels allotted to each country, limits on the amount a single country can possess are stated in the treaty. These single-party limits stress the importance that no one nation can dominate the continent. Additionally, restrictions were placed on the amount of equipment that one state could station on the territory of another. Personnel limits were addressed in the Concluding Act of the Negotiation on Personnel Strength of Conventional Armed Forces in Europe (CFE 1A Treaty), signed in Vienna in June 1992. Each state sets its own manpower limits, which are open to discussion but not negotiation.

The CFE Treaty allows for several methods of ensuring compliance, including national or multinational technical means, information exchanges, and on-site inspections, all of which are supervised by the Joint Consultative Group in Vienna.

In May 1992 the members of the Commonwealth of Independent States that had territory within the area of application met in Tashkent to divide the former Soviet Union's allotment of equipment.

At the 1 December 1996 Organization for Security and Cooperation in Europe (OSCE) Heads of State summit in Lisbon, states parties to the CFE Treaty agreed to revise it. On 24 July 1997, a plan was devised to set national maximum force levels for each signatory rather than keeping collective limits on the original groups of states. A document revising the treaty in this manner was signed at the OSCE summit in Istanbul in November 1999. Entry into force for a "new" CFE Treaty will take place following ratification by all thirty states parties.

At the Second Review Conference of the CFE Treaty in 2001, states parties noted that over 50,000 items of treaty-limited equipment (TLE) had been eliminated. Also in May 2001, Russia and Georgia agreed that Russia would withdraw its bases in Georgia in 2008.

As of 2007, only Russia, Ukraine, Belarus, and Kazakhstan had ratified the adapted version of the treaty. President Vladimir Putin announced that Russia would begin a moratorium on Russian compliance with the CFE Treaty. The reasons for this decision by Putin were due in part to proposed US missile defense deployment in Poland and the Czech Republic, and new basing arrangements between the United States and Poland, Bulgaria, and Romania. Putin viewed these arrangements as unacceptable and a threat to Russia's security.

On 14 July 2007, Putin announced the intention of the Russian Federation to suspend all compliance with the CFE Treaty.

The Convention on Certain Conventional Weapons

The Convention on Prohibitions or Restrictions on Use of Certain Conventional Weapons Which May Be Deemed to Be Excessively Injurious or to Have Indiscriminate Effects (known as the Inhumane Weapons Convention or, as referred to throughout this volume, the Convention on Certain Conventional Weapons [CCWC]) was opened for signature in 1981 and entered into force on 2 December 1983. The convention's purpose is to regulate conventional weapons that risk indiscriminate damage and injury to civilians or can cause unnecessary suffering. As of February 2008, there were 106 states parties who had agreed to one or more of the four protocols involving restrictions on the manufacture, stockpiling, or use of certain conventional weapons. The first three protocols cover nondetectable fragmentation weapons; mines, booby traps, and other devices; and incendiary weapons. During the 1995–1996 Review Conference, a fourth protocol was added regarding blinding laser weapons. At the December 2001 Review Conference, states parties considered other weapons of war, and also discussed the possibility of expanding the convention to internal conflicts rather than its current focus on international conflicts. They also examined inspection, compliance, and enforcement measures.

In November 2003, states parties approved Protocol V (Explosive Remnants of War) under the CCWC. This protocol entered into force 12 November 2006. It covers unexploded munitions, grenades, gravity bombs, and other explosive devices that fail to explode on impact and are intact, abandoned, or uncontrolled.

The CCWC states parties are struggling with the controversial issue of whether or not to restrict the use of cluster munitions, and also whether or not to limit the use of antivehicle mines. The United States originally opposed negotiations on cluster munitions, but changed its stance in June 2007 stating that, as a stipulation for its support, the CCWC must not include a total ban of cluster munitions. In 2007 several CCWC states parties, led by Norway, increased their efforts to ban all cluster munitions.

On 28 May 2008, a large number of states reached an agreement to ban cluster bombs. The United States refused to join the ban, stating that cluster munitions were vital weapons in the US military arsenal. Although the United States, Russia, China, Israel, India, and Pakistan did not participate in this sanction, 111 other nations agreed to ban their use of cluster munition–type weapons. After a year of negotiations, separate from the CCWC process, 107 nations adopted the Cluster Munitions Convention in May 2008, and 94 nations signed the convention in December 2008.

The Cooperative Threat Reduction Program

In fall 1991, conditions in the disintegrating Soviet Union created a global threat to nuclear safety and stability. The US Congress, recognizing a window of opportunity to materially reduce the threat from nuclear weapons in the former Soviet Union and the proliferation potential they represented, enacted the Soviet Nuclear Threat Reduction Act—also called the Nunn-Lugar legislation. Subsequently, the Cooperative Threat Reduction (CTR) program has expanded to include all weapons of mass destruction, assistance for defense conversion, and military-to-military contacts.

The CTR program provides assistance to reduce or eliminate the threat posed by the thousands of existing WMD and associated infrastructure remaining in the former Soviet Union. Through the program, Kazakhstan, Ukraine, and Belarus are now nuclear-weapon free. In Russia, primary program objectives include accelerating WMD dismantlement and destruction while ensuring a strong chain of custody for fissile material transport and storage. These objectives also foster compliance with the Strategic Arms Reduction Treaty (START I), the Lisbon Protocol, the NPT, the CWC, and the 1994 Biological Weapons Trilateral Statement. As of 2008, the United States had spent some $17 billion on threat reduction programs, including the CTR program managed by the Department of Defense (DoD). Other programs in this category include the Materials Protection, Control, and Accounting efforts of the Department of Energy (DoE) and various smaller Department of State programs.

As of 30 June 2008, the CTR program had eliminated 7,292 strategic nuclear warheads, 698 intercontinental ballistic missiles (ICBMs), 496 ICBM silos, 131 ICBM mobile launchers, 631 submarine-launched ballistic missiles (SLBMs), 456 SLBM launchers, 30 nuclear submarines capable of launching ballistic missiles, 155 bombers, 906 nuclear air-to-surface missiles, and 194 nuclear test tunnels. Other accomplishments include securing 388 nuclear weapon transport train shipments, upgrading security at sixteen nuclear weapon storage sites, and building and equipping fifteen biological monitoring stations. Ukraine, Belarus, and Kazakhstan (formerly the third, fourth, and eighth largest nuclear weapons states in the world) are nuclear-weapons free as a result of cooperative efforts under the program.

The Environmental Modification Convention

On 18 May 1977, thirty-four states signed the Convention on the Prohibition of Military or Any Other Hostile Use of Environmental Modification Techniques (also called the Environmental Modification Convention) in Geneva. It entered into force on 5 October 1978. Although the use of environmental modification techniques was not considered likely in military planning when the convention was signed, this treaty reflected an attempt to preempt the consideration of such techniques in the future. The convention includes a prohibition against the deliberate manipulation of natural processes of the earth, the atmosphere, or outer space, including changes in the weather, the ozone layer, or the ionosphere, or upsetting the ecological balance of a region. As of 2008, some ninety-two states had signed the convention, seventy-five of whom had ratified it.

The Fissile Material Cutoff Treaty

The idea of a fissile material production cutoff gained prominence from 1956 through 1969. Limited success was realized in 1964 when the United States, the UK, and the Soviet Union announced reductions in the production of weapon-grade fissionable material. The success of superpower arms control initiatives, a US halt in production of fissile material, and President Clinton's speech to the UN in September 1993 all provided renewed impetus for a cutoff convention.

The Conference on Disarmament began preliminary discussions on a fissile material cutoff convention during its 1994 session. In tandem with these negotiations, technical discussions were held in Vienna, with assistance from the IAEA, to address technical and verification issues. Among the more prominent obstacles to serious negotiations were differing views on whether the talks would cover only future production or also encompass existing stocks of weapon-grade nuclear material. The CD reached consensus on a negotiating mandate in 1998. Today, however, some delegations want the Fissile Material Cutoff Treaty (FMCT) to be negotiated only in parallel with other discussions on nuclear disarmament and preventing the weaponization of outer space. Such perspectives have prevented the development of a consensus on the treaty within the CD.

In July 2004, the George W. Bush administration announced that the United States still supported a legally binding treaty banning production of nuclear materials for weapons; however, it no longer supported verification measures in the FMCT. Verification is extremely costly and requires a broad inspection regime; there is the chance of compromising key signatories' national security interests.

The Forum for Security Cooperation

At the July 1992 Helsinki summit of the CSCE, a decision was made to form the fifty-four-nation Forum for Security Cooperation (FSC). This organization, which meets weekly in Vienna, is tasked with carrying out follow-on negotiations to the CFE and CFE 1A Treaties and the CSBMs included in the Vienna Documents. Additionally, this body oversees implementation, implementation assessment, discussion, and clarification of existing CSBMs.

The purpose of the FSC is to implement a work program to address concerns regarding arms control, disarmament, and CSBMs; enhance regular consultation and cooperation among participating states relating to security matters; and further the process of reducing the risk of conflict.

Geneva Protocol

The Protocol for the Prohibition of the Use in War of Asphyxiating, Poisonous or Other Gases, and of Bacteriological Methods of Warfare was an attempt by the victorious powers of World War I to ensure that chemical weapons were never again used on the field of battle. The restrictions imposed on Germany, Austria, Bulgaria, and Hungary in their peace treaties, including the Versailles Treaty, were codified in the Washington Naval Treaty of 1922 and, three years later, in the Geneva Protocol against chemical and bacteriological warfare. The protocol was signed on 17 June 1925, and entered into force on 8 February 1928. The protocol was honored by most parties during World War II, but violations by Iran and Iraq in the 1980s led to an international conference in Paris in 1989 that resulted in the Chemical Weapons Convention. The United States did not ratify the protocol until 22 January 1975. The protocol has subsequently been signed by 184 nations.

The Hague Conventions

The Hague Conventions were adopted in the Netherlands at the turn of the twentieth century and represented one of the earliest multinational attempts at regulating war. The Hague Convention II (1899) limited sieges and bombardments, and pronounced that the right of belligerents to adopt means of injuring the enemy is not unlimited. Specifically, the convention restricted the use of poisoned arms, to kill or wound "treacherously," to kill or wound soldiers who are surrendering, to declare that no quarter will be given, to employ weapons that cause superfluous injury, to misuse a flag of truce or the uniform of an enemy, to wantonly destroy property, to attack an undefended city, to attack without warning, or to pillage a city. Before sieges or bombardments all opportunities should be taken to warn the besieged authorities, and to protect cultural and scientific sites and hospitals.

The Helsinki Agreements

Presidents Bill Clinton and Boris Yeltsin agreed on a Joint Statement on Parameters on Future Reductions in Nuclear Forces at their meeting in Helsinki, Finland, in March 1997. This statement underscored the requirement for ratification of START II by both the United States and Russia, and an agreement to begin negotiations on START III once START II entered into force. The goal of START III negotiations was to delimit a ceiling of 2,000 to 2,500 strategic warheads by 31 December 2007. This date was also the extended deadline for START II eliminations. In order to ensure the irreversibility of these reductions, the new treaty would include inventory transparency provisions and call for the destruction of nuclear warheads. The two sides also agreed to discuss nonstrategic nuclear weapons (tactical weapons and sea-launched cruise missiles) in a separate but parallel forum, and they agreed to the goal of making all START treaties unlimited in duration. The March agreement was codified in memorandums of understanding signed in New York on 26 September 1997. But the agreements never entered into force; the 2002 Moscow Treaty made START III irrelevant, and START II was allowed to lapse.

The Helsinki Final Act

Signed in 1975, the Helsinki Final Act was the first of a series of agreements and procedures designed to increase the security of the members of the Conference on Security and Cooperation in Europe (later the Organization for Security and Cooperation in Europe). It was signed by the United States, Canada, and all European nations except Albania. In addition to recognizing existing borders and the need for economic cooperation, the act required advance notification of military maneuvers involving more than 25,000 troops. This agreement set the foundations for the complicated and increasingly intrusive measures that followed in the realm of CSBMs.

The Hotline Agreements

In order to minimize the chances of miscommunication leading to miscalculation during times of emergency, the first of three agreements between Washington and Moscow was signed in Geneva on 20 June 1963. Both sides agreed to a direct communications link between their capitals using telegraph-teleprinter terminals, duplex wire telegraph circuits, and radiotelegraph circuits, and procedures for sending nearly instantaneous messages in both languages. In a revised treaty, signed in Washington on 30 September 1971, the United States and the Soviet Union agreed to a direct communications link encompassing satellite communications systems and teleprinter terminals. Another memorandum of understanding was signed by both parties on 17 July 1984 in Washington, in which they agreed to improve direct communications by establishing links employing Intelsat satellites and modems, facsimile machines, and computers. This agreement was subsequently updated by an exchange of diplomatic notes in Washington, DC, on 24 June 1988.

The Incidents at Sea Agreement

The Agreement Between the Government of the United States of America and the Government of the Union of Soviet Socialist Republics on the

Prevention of Incidents On and Over the High Seas (referred to throughout this volume as the Incidents at Sea Agreement) was signed in Moscow on 25 May 1972. The agreement was a confidence-building measure designed to reduce the frequency and severity of incidents of ships and aircraft interfering with one another at sea, thereby increasing stability and reducing the possibility of conflict by accident, miscalculation, or the failure of communication. It established steps to avoid collision, to remain safe distances from the other sides' formations, to use standard international signals when maneuvering near one another, and similar measures.

The Intermediate-Range Nuclear Forces Treaty

The Treaty Between the United States of America and the Union of Soviet Socialist Republics on the Elimination of Their Intermediate-Range and Shorter-Range Missiles (referred to throughout this volume as the Intermediate-Range Nuclear Forces Treaty [INF Treaty]) provided for the complete elimination of all US and Soviet intermediate-range (1,000 to 5,500 kilometers) and shorter-range (500 to 1,000 kilometers) ground-launched ballistic and cruise missiles. The INF Treaty was signed on 8 December 1987, and entered into force on 1 June 1988. The treaty is of unlimited duration; the inspection regime lasted thirteen years, ending on 31 December 2001. The INF Treaty was marked by an unprecedented use of intrusive inspections.

Despite the fact that the final elimination of missiles was completed by 1 June 1991, the on-site inspection regime continued until 2001 to ensure compliance with the treaty. This included continuous monitoring of the ground-launched cruise missile final assembly facility at Magna, Utah, and the SS-20 missile facility at Votkinsk, Russia. Additionally, on-site inspections of former missile operating bases and missile support facilities were allowed until 31 May 2001. Some of these facilities were located in successor states other than the Russian Federation. The Special Verification Commission was the body tasked with overseeing verification and compliance; it was based in Geneva.

On 31 May 2002, Bulgaria signed an agreement with the United States to destroy all of its missiles that were relevant to the INF Treaty. Bulgaria completed the destruction within five months with the help of US funding.

Recently, Russia has raised the possibility of withdrawing from the INF Treaty. Moscow asserts that the treaty unfairly prevents it from possessing weapons that its neighbors, such as China, are developing. On 10 February 2007, President Putin declared that the INF Treaty no longer serves Russia's interests, yet the ultimate purpose of that statement has yet to be determined.

The Limited Test Ban Treaty

The Treaty Banning Nuclear Weapon Tests in Atmosphere, in Outer Space, and Under Water (known as the Partial Test Ban Treaty or, as referred to most commonly throughout this volume, the Limited Test Ban Treaty [LTBT]) was signed on 5 August 1963 by the United States, the UK, and the Soviet Union and entered into force on 10 October 1963. The signatories agreed not to carry out any nuclear weapon test explosion in the atmosphere, in outer space, underwater, or in any other environment that would cause radioactive debris to spread outside the territorial limits of the state that conducted the test. There are currently 123 states parties to the treaty, as well as ten others that have signed but not ratified.

The Missile Technology Control Regime

In April 1987, the United States, Canada, France, West Germany, Italy, Japan, and the UK created the Missile Technology Control Regime (MTCR) to restrict the proliferation of missiles and missile technology. The MTCR is the only multilateral missile nonproliferation regime. It is a voluntary arrangement, not an international agreement or a treaty, among states with an interest in stopping the proliferation of missile technology. The regime develops export guidelines that are applied to a list of controlled items, and implemented according to each state's procedures. In January 1993, the MTCR Guidelines were expanded to restrict the spread of missiles and unmanned air vehicles with a range of at least 300 kilometers capable of delivering a 500-kilogram payload or a weapon of mass destruction. They are designed not to impede a state's space program as long as it does not contribute to the delivery of WMD. Membership in the MTCR is open to any state that commits to the principles of nonproliferation and has a record of effective export controls. The MTCR regime currently has thirty-four partners.

In November 2002, the MTCR partners pushed forth an initiative, the International Code of Conduct against Ballistic Missile Proliferation, which called on all states to show greater restraint in their own development of ballistic missiles and to reduce their existing missile arsenals. The aim of the initiative was to establish a norm against missiles capable of carrying chemical, biological, or nuclear warheads. As part of the initiative, participating states were required to annually exchange information on their ballistic missile and space launch vehicle programs. Under the initiative, the participating states were also required to provide advance notice of any launches of ballistic missiles or space launch vehicles. More than 100 states, including all of the MTCR's partners (except Brazil), have pledged to participate.

The Nuclear Nonproliferation Treaty

The Treaty on the Non-Proliferation of Nuclear Weapons (referred to throughout this volume as the Nuclear Nonproliferation Treaty [NPT]) obligates nuclear weapon states (NWS) parties to the treaty—the United States, Russia, the UK, France, and China—to three main principles: not to transfer nuclear weapons or control over such weapons to any recipient, directly or indirectly; not to assist, encourage, or induce any non–nuclear weapon state (NNWS) to manufacture or otherwise acquire such weapons, or seek control over them; and to actively work toward nuclear disarmament as well as general and complete disarmament. Additionally, the NWS are required to assist the NNWS in the use of nuclear energy for peaceful purposes, including the benefits of peaceful nuclear explosions.

Non–nuclear weapon states may not receive the transfer of nuclear weapons, nor have control over them. These states are also prohibited from manufacturing, seeking help in manufacturing, or otherwise obtaining nuclear weapons. Although known to have or suspected of having nuclear weapons, India, Pakistan, and Israel are officially NNWS, according to the treaty, because they did not openly possess a nuclear weapon on 1 July 1968.

All states must accept safeguards negotiated with the IAEA to prevent the diversion of nuclear energy from peaceful purposes to nuclear weapons. The IAEA is the treaty's implementation and compliance body; it meets in Vienna. The NPT is also reinforced by two multilateral nuclear export control organizations: the NPT Exporters Committee (also called the Zangger Committee) and the Nuclear Suppliers Group (NSG).

The NPT was signed on 1 July 1968, and entered into force on 5 March 1970. The original duration called for a review after twenty-five years. At the 1995 Review Conference, the states parties agreed to an indefinite extension of the regime. They also agreed to a set of Principles and Objectives for Nuclear Nonproliferation and Disarmament, including the goal of achieving a comprehensive nuclear test ban. The conference called on the states in the Middle East to agree to the creation of a region-wide zone free of WMD. Review Conferences will continue to take place every five years.

At the 2000 Review Conference in New York, the NWS made a political commitment to unequivocally seek "the total elimination of their nuclear arsenals, leading to nuclear disarmament," but no time line for doing so was agreed on.

The Nuclear Suppliers Group

The NPT Nuclear Suppliers Group (NSG) was formed in 1976 to help implement the export control restrictions of the NPT. Like the Zangger

Committee, it has adopted a so-called trigger list of items related to nuclear weapon production. The forty-five members of the NSG have agreed to restrict exports of sensitive technology, including uranium enrichment and reprocessing equipment. In 1992, the group adopted the rule that members would make nuclear exports to NNWS only if the recipient had accepted IAEA inspections on all of its nuclear facilities—a situation known as full-scope safeguards. This rule has banned exports to Israel, India, and Pakistan. China is a member of the NSG.

The NSG held an Extraordinary Plenary Meeting in Vienna in December 2002. There, members agreed to several comprehensive amendments to strengthen their existing guidelines, intended to prevent and counter the threat of nuclear exports and nuclear terrorism. The Extraordinary Plenary Meeting stressed that effective export controls are an extremely important tool to combat the threats of nuclear terrorism. Further, at a May 2004 meeting, NSG members adopted a new catchall mechanism authorizing members to block any export suspected to be destined to a nuclear weapon program even if the export does not appear on one of the control lists.

Nuclear-Weapon-Free Zones

There have been several efforts by both international and regional organizations to ban or limit the use of nuclear materials in specific regions of the world. In addition, three separate treaties, which have been signed by almost all the nations of the world, prohibit nuclear materials from being stored or tested in outer space, on the seabed floor, and in Antarctica.

Five other regional NWFZs have been established through treaties. The South Pacific Nuclear Free Zone, created on 6 August 1985 with the signing of the Treaty of Rarotonga, entered into force on 11 December 1986. It is a multilateral treaty that bans the stationing, manufacturing, testing, and dumping of nuclear weapons or nuclear waste within the zone. The issue of ship and aircraft traffic is left up to individual countries. There are eleven parties to the treaty, including Australia and New Zealand. The Latin American Nuclear Free Zone was formalized in the Treaty of Tlatelolco, signed on 14 February 1967 with entry into force on 25 April 1968. The treaty bans the storage and testing of nuclear weapons within the signatory countries, but does allow for the peaceful use of nuclear material. All Latin American states have ratified the treaty. Cuba was the final state in the region to ratify the treaty, in October 2002. The Treaty of Pelindaba was signed on 11 April 1996 in Cairo, to create the African Nuclear Weapon Free Zone. Entry into force awaits ratification by twenty-eight African states. The Treaty of Bangkok, signed 15 December 1995, established a Southeast Asian Nuclear-Weapon-Free Zone. Seven of the ten regional states had to ratify the treaty before entry into force, which occurred on 28 March 1997. Its provisions cover foreign ships and aircraft transiting the region, but the United States has not recognized this treaty. The Central Asian Nuclear-Weapon-Free Zone Treaty opened for signature on 8 September 2006, and entered into force on 21 March 2009 following Kazakhstan's ratification of the treaty. This treaty established the first NWFZ in the northern hemisphere, and the first in a region that formerly contained nuclear weapons.

Efforts are currently under way to establish additional NWFZs in the Middle East, South Asia, and the South Atlantic.

The Open Skies Treaty

The Treaty on Open Skies (also referred to as the Open Skies Treaty) was signed in Helsinki on 24 March 1992 by members of NATO and the former Warsaw Pact. The United States ratified it on 3 November 1993. Each participating state has the right to conduct, and the obligation to receive, overhead flights by unarmed fixed-wing observation aircraft. The aircraft can carry a variety of sensors. Normally, the inspecting party will provide the aircraft used in the overflight; however, the host nation may require that one of its aircraft be used. The number of flights each state can conduct and must receive is limited to negotiated annual quotas. Any state may acquire the data from any overflight.

On 2 November 2001, Russia and Belarus deposited their instruments of ratification. The treaty entered into force on 1 January 2002. It is of unlimited duration with an initial review after three years and at five-year intervals thereafter.

With entry into force of the Open Skies Treaty, states parties began formal observation flights in August 2002. During the first year of the treaty, they conducted sixty-seven observation flights. They conducted seventy-four missions in 2004 and 110 missions in 2005.

On 14 July 2008, a commemorative event took place in Vienna to recognize the 500 observation flights carried out under the Open Skies Treaty since it entered into force.

The Ottawa Convention on Landmines

The Convention on the Prohibition of the Use, Stockpiling, Production and Transfer of Anti-Personnel Mines and on Their Destruction (referred to throughout this book as the Ottawa Convention on Landmines, also known as the Mine Ban Treaty) was opened for signature on 3 December 1997, and entered into force on 1 March 1999 following ratification by forty states. The negotiations for this convention took place in Ottawa, Ontario, and were led by a group of nongovernmental organizations, supported by several states. This convention hoped to achieve a global ban on landmines by the year 2000. The United States resisted the treaty due to, among other things, its perceived need for mines to defend the border of South Korea. Other key states refused to participate in the process.

In 1992, the United States announced a moratorium on exports of antipersonnel landmines (APLs) and in 1996 unilaterally ended its use of non-self-destructing APLs except in marked and monitored areas on the Korean Peninsula. In May 1998, the Clinton administration announced the US intention to sign the Ottawa Convention on Landmines in 2006 if appropriate substitutes to landmines could be developed by that time. (As of early 2009, however, the United States had not yet signed the convention.) The United States has sought to pursue landmine agreements through the CCW and the CD.

The Outer Space Treaty

The Treaty on the Principles Governing the Activities of States in the Exploration and Use of Outer Space, Including the Moon and Other Celestial Bodies (also called the Outer Space Treaty) was negotiated primarily between the United States and the Soviet Union. As of January 2007, ninety-eight states were party to the treaty. An additional twenty-seven states had signed but not ratified the treaty, which serves to limit the militarization of outer space. Signed on 27 January 1967, the treaty prohibits any state from placing weapons of mass destruction in outer space or deploying WMD on celestial bodies. In addition, all celestial bodies are to be used solely for peaceful purposes and may not be used for military bases, military fortifications, or weapon testing of any kind.

In February 2008, China and Russia submitted a draft treaty text to the CD in Geneva to further negotiations of a treaty that would prevent an arms race in outer space. These states (and others) support outer space agreements in addition to the Outer Space Treaty. The additional treaties would allay the fears of some states about US missile defense plans and space policy. The United States has stated that additional treaties are not necessary because there is currently no arms race in outer space.

The Peaceful Nuclear Explosions Treaty

The Treaty Between the United States of America and the Union of Soviet Socialist Republics on Underground Nuclear Explosions for Peaceful

Purposes (referred to throughout this volume as the Peaceful Nuclear Explosions Treaty [PNET]) was signed on 28 May 1976, but its protocol on the verification of compliance was not completed until 1 June 1990. It allows peaceful nuclear explosions outside declared testing sites, but prohibits any individual explosion exceeding a yield of 150 kilotons. Group explosions are limited to a yield of 1.5 megatons, provided that each individual explosion's yield can be verified and does not exceed 150 kilotons. The PNET's protocol requires notification of explosions and allows for on-site inspections and other methods of measuring the yield of the detonation.

China is not a member of the PNET. Although China has never conducted a peaceful nuclear explosion, during negotiations for the Comprehensive Test Ban Treaty, its delegates adamantly stated that peaceful nuclear explosions must be allowed under the CTBT during that treaty's negotiations. However, China finally dropped its insistence in June 1996 after stating that the ban on peaceful nuclear explosions should be temporary and should be reviewed after ten years.

The Presidential Nuclear Initiatives

Between September 1991 and January 1992, a series of initiatives by the presidents of the United States and Russia (known as the Presidential Nuclear Initiatives [PNI]) significantly affected the nuclear force structure. Some measures simply accelerated measures mandated by START I while others were incorporated into START II. In addition, there were binding actions not addressed in either treaty. In late 2001, presidents George W. Bush and Vladimir Putin agreed to additional unilateral, but reciprocated, reductions.

On 27 September 1991, President George H. W. Bush announced that the United States would remove all its strategic bombers and 450 Minuteman II ICBMs from day-to-day alert; remove all tactical nuclear weapons on surface ships, attack submarines, and land-based naval aircraft; and cancel plans to develop a nuclear short-range attack missile, the Peacekeeper rail garrison ICBM, and the mobile portion of the Small ICBM. He also proposed eliminating all multiple independently targetable reentry vehicle (MIRVed) US and Soviet ICBMs.

On 5 October 1991, President Mikhail Gorbachev responded by declaring similar reductions. He also suggested reducing each side's nuclear arsenal to 5,000 warheads (below the START I limit of 6,000) and reducing strategic offensive arms by approximately one-half. He suggested discussions on non-nuclear ABM systems and a one-year moratorium on nuclear testing.

In his State of the Union Address to the US Congress on 28 January 1992, President George H. W. Bush announced further reductions in the US strategic force to include limiting B-2 bomber production to twenty planes, limiting advanced cruise missile production to 640, and canceling the Small ICBM and Peacekeeper missiles and the W-88 warhead for Trident missiles. Additionally he stated that, if Russia were to eliminate all MIRVed ICBMs, the United States would take the following actions to cut strategic nuclear warheads to approximately 4,700: eliminate Peacekeeper missiles, reduce Minuteman III missiles to one warhead per missile, reduce the number of Trident submarine warheads by one-third, and convert a large number of strategic bombers to conventional use.

Russian president Boris Yeltsin responded on 29 January 1992 by stating Russia's intention to abide by all arms control agreements signed by the Soviet Union as well as his support for the NPT, MTCR, CTBT, and FMCT. He made public additional reductions in Russian strategic offensive forces, and proposed several new US-Russia reciprocal actions.

In January 1994, presidents Clinton and Yeltsin agreed at the Moscow summit that strategic forces under their control would be detargeted (no longer aimed at each other) by 30 May of that year. The UK took a similar initiative.

In November 2001, President Putin met with President George W. Bush in both Washington, DC, and Crawford, Texas, to agree to further reductions in each side's nuclear arsenal. Attempting to overcome the stalemate in strategic negotiations, the two leaders established a goal of 1,700 to 2,200 long-range warheads on each side. Putin expressed Russia's desire to eventually have the deal formalized in a treaty, which was accomplished in the Moscow Treaty of June 2002.

In June 2005, Russia proposed that additional talks regarding tactical nuclear weapons could take place based on the US withdrawal of its remaining nuclear weapons in Europe. The United States responded that its weapons in Europe are deployed as part of NATO policy and that making the decision to withdraw them would require the consensus of all twenty-six alliance members. Government officials in Belgium and Germany called for the withdrawal of these US weapons, but this has not been officially discussed by NATO. In 2005, Congress passed legislation asking the Bush administration to investigate measures to assist Russia in accounting for and securing its tactical arms and assessing whether tactical nuclear reductions with Russia should be pursued.

As of March 2006, the United States possessed nearly 1,100 tactical nuclear warheads while Russia maintained an estimated 3,000 to 6,000 non-strategic weapons. Under the PNI, the United States and Russia have been unable to agree on additional measures through which to share information or limit their tactical nuclear weapons. Russia has refused to confirm that the reductions proposed under the PNI have been implemented, and subsequent statements regarding employment of tactical nuclear weapons (e.g., nuclear artillery shells) indicate that Russia has rejected following the example of the United States.

The Proliferation Security Initiative

The Proliferation Security Initiative (PSI) is an informal, cooperative effort initiated by the United States in 2003 to interdict shipments of weapons of mass destruction, ballistic missiles, and related materials to states and non-state actors of proliferation concern. In May 2003, the initiative was launched with eleven original members (Australia, France, Germany, Italy, Japan, the Netherlands, Poland, Portugal, Spain, and the United States). Canada, Norway, and Singapore joined in February 2004, and today over ninety nations have endorsed the initiative's objectives and participate on an ad hoc basis.

In September 2003, members adopted politically binding principles committing them to take measures to interdict transfers to states and non-state actors of items of proliferation concern, including WMD, missiles, and related materials; to streamline related intelligence sharing; to strengthen relevant national and international law; and to take other specified steps to facilitate interdiction of proliferation-related cargo.

The Seabed Treaty

The Treaty on the Prohibition of the Emplacement of Nuclear Weapons and Other Weapons of Mass Destruction on the Seabed and the Ocean Floor and in the Subsoil Thereof (also called the Seabed Treaty) was signed by the United States and the Soviet Union on 11 February 1971, and entered into force on 18 May 1982. Like the Antarctic Treaty, the Outer Space Treaty, and the various nuclear-weapon-free zones, the Seabed Treaty seeks to prevent the introduction of international conflict and nuclear weapons into an area previously free of them. Negotiations over the treaty, however, took several years, as interest in the seabed grew with advances in the science of oceanography. The treaty outlaws a party from placing WMD on or in the seabed beyond a twelve-nautical-mile coastal zone.

Review Conferences on the Seabed Treaty were held in 1977, 1983, and 1989. In 1992, the CD considered further measures regarding the treaty and decided against the need for an additional Review Conference.

The Strategic Arms Limitation Treaty (SALT I)

Both the ABM Treaty and the Interim Agreement Between the United States of America and the Union of Soviet Socialist Republics on Certain Measures with Respect to the Limitation of Strategic Offensive Arms were included in what was referred to throughout this volume as the Strategic Arms Limitation Treaty (SALT I). Both were signed on 26 May 1972 and were the result of the first series of Strategic Arms Limitation Talks, which had begun in November 1969. The Interim Agreement froze the number of strategic ballistic missile launchers at existing levels (1,054 US and 1,618 Soviet) and prohibited the conversion of older launchers to accommodate modern heavy ICBMs. An increase in SLBMs was allowed on condition that an equal number of land-based launchers were destroyed. The United States was authorized up to 710 SLBMs and the Soviet Union 950. Mobile ICBMs were not covered by the agreement.

SALT I was perceived as a holding action and its duration was limited to five years in the hope that a more comprehensive agreement would be reached. The US Congress passed a joint resolution supporting SALT I, and it entered into force on 3 October 1972.

The Strategic Arms Limitation Treaty (SALT II)

The Treaty Between the United States of America and the Union of Soviet Socialist Republics on the Limitation of Strategic Offensive Arms (referred to throughout this volume as the Strategic Arms Limitation Treaty [SALT II]) resulted from talks lasting from November 1972 until 18 June 1979, when the treaty was signed in Vienna. The treaty placed limits on ballistic missiles and their launchers, but did not require the reduction of such items. Each state was limited to 2,250 launchers, with a sublimit of 1,320 launchers for missiles with MIRVs. MIRVed ballistic missiles were limited to 1,200, of which only 820 could be ICBMs. In addition, new ICBMs were limited to ten warheads while SLBMs were allowed to carry up to fourteen warheads. The treaty prohibited spaced-based nuclear weapons, fractional orbital missiles, and rapid reload missile launchers.

A protocol to the treaty was signed at the same time and was to remain in effect until 31 December 1981. The protocol prohibited the deployment of ground-launched cruise missiles (GLCMs) and sea-launched cruise missiles (SLCMs) with a range of over 600 kilometers as well as mobile ICBMs. Additionally, MIRVs, GLCMs, and SLCMs with a range over 600 kilometers could not be tested.

President Jimmy Carter submitted the treaty to the Senate immediately following the signing but, due to political considerations and the Soviet invasion of Afghanistan, he was forced to remove it from congressional review in January 1980. Because the treaty was never ratified, it became a politically, not legally, binding agreement. On 27 May 1986, President Ronald Reagan, citing Soviet violations, declared that the United States would no longer abide by the limits of SALT I and II, and the United States exceeded those limits on 28 November 1986.

The Strategic Arms Reduction Treaty (START I)

The Treaty Between the United States and the Union of Soviet Socialist Republics on the Reduction and Limitation of Strategic Offensive Arms (referred to throughout this volume as the Strategic Arms Reduction Treaty [START I]) was signed on 31 July 1991. START I reduced US and former Soviet strategic offensive arms (ICBMs, SLBMs, and heavy bombers) to 1,600 and attributed warheads (an agreed upon number of warheads that are associated with each weapon system) to 6,000. There were additional sublimits for attributed warheads: 4,900 warheads on deployed ballistic missiles and 1,100 warheads on deployed mobile ICBMs. The former Soviet Union was also limited to 154 deployed heavy ICBMs (down from 308 before the treaty), each carrying ten warheads.

Warheads carried by heavy bombers, including those in long-range, nuclear-armed air-launched cruise missiles were counted at a discount rate. Especially significant was the discount rate for penetrating bombers, which counted as only one warhead regardless of how many missiles they were capable of carrying. Politically binding side agreements also limited the number of deployed nuclear SLCMs and Soviet Backfire bombers.

An extensive series of on-site inspections and an exchange of geographical and technical data for all systems, with regular updates, complemented each party's national technical means to monitor compliance with the treaty. The two sides agreed to exchange telemetric information from all test flights of ICBMs and SLBMs. The Joint Compliance and Inspection Commission (JCIC) is tasked with monitoring compliance with the treaty and has been meeting in Geneva since 1991.

On 23 May 1992, a protocol was signed in Lisbon that made START I a five-nation, multiparty treaty. The protocol and appended presidential letters obligated Belarus, Kazakhstan, and Ukraine to become non-nuclear state parties to the NPT. On 14 January 1994 in Moscow, the presidents of Ukraine, Russia, and the United States signed a trilateral agreement that promised Ukraine financial and security assistance as a means of persuading Kiev to ratify START I and the NPT. On 5 December 1994, Ukraine deposited its instruments of ratification for the NPT, allowing START I to enter into force. Its duration was fifteen years, with an option to extend at five-year intervals. Treaty limits were officially reached by 5 December 2001. START I will remain in force through December 2009, at which point it may be extended by five-year intervals if all states parties to the treaty are in agreement. Negotiations on whether to pursue an extension or a follow-on treaty began between the United States and Russia in 2008.

The Strategic Arms Reduction Treaty (START II)

The 1991–1992 Presidential Nuclear Initiatives set the foundation for the signing of a joint understanding at the June 1992 summit between presidents George H. W. Bush and Boris Yeltsin in Washington, DC. The joint understanding called for the elimination of all MIRVed ICBMs and deep cuts in SLBMs, forming the basis of the Treaty Between the United States of America and the Russian Federation on Further Reduction and Limitation of Strategic Offensive Arms (referred to throughout this volume as the Strategic Arms Reduction Treaty [START II]). This treaty was signed at the 3 January 1993 Moscow summit by presidents Bush and Yeltsin. It relied heavily on START I for definitions, procedures, and verification. The US Senate ratified START II on 26 January 1996, and the Russian Duma did so on 14 April 2000, but with a condition that the United States continue to abide by the 1972 ABM Treaty.

The eliminations were to take place in a two-phase process. Within seven years of entry into force, each side was required to reduce its deployed strategic forces to 3,800 to 4,250 attributed warheads, within which the following sublimits applied: 1,200 warheads for MIRVed ICBMs, 650 warheads for heavy ICBMs, and 2,160 warheads for SLBMs. Phase II limits were to be reached by the year 2003. At that time, each party was to have reduced its deployed strategic forces to 3,000 to 3,500 attributed warheads, within which the following sublimits would apply: zero warheads for MIRVed ICBMs, 1,700 to 1,750 total warheads for SLBMs, and elimination of all heavy ICBMs. At the March 1997 Helsinki summit, presidents Clinton and Yeltsin agreed to extend the time for START II implementation and reductions to 31 December 2007. Systems to be eliminated under this treaty had to be deactivated, however, by removing their warheads by December 2003. Because the treaty did not enter into force until April 2000, both phases were to be completed simultaneously.

In order to reach the lower warhead ceilings, Russia was allowed to download 105 SS-19 ICBMs by five warheads, leaving only one warhead per missile. Additionally, any missile that was previously equipped with six warheads or more, except the SS-19s, must have been destroyed while those equipped with five or less could be retained, provided they were downloaded to only one warhead.

The treaty also had several provisions regarding bombers. The B-2 was to be exhibited and inspectable. A one-time reorientation of up to 100 nuclear heavy bombers to a conventional role was allowed without adhering to the START I conversion procedures as long as they were never accountable as long-range nuclear heavy bombers. The United States chose this option for its B-1 fleet. Additionally, conventional and nuclear bombers were to be based separately and crews separately trained, and have differences observable by national technical means and visible during inspection. START II provided the right to change the number of nuclear warheads attributed to a bomber if there was a visible change in the plane's configuration. Approximately 1,300 warheads could be attributed to bombers in the United States and in Russia, depending on the number of ICBMs and SLBMs retained by each party.

Although this treaty built on START I, some additional verification measures were included. START II significantly increased the number of on-site inspections, mostly relating to the retention of converted Russian heavy ICBM (SS-18) silos and the conversion of heavy bombers. Compliance was to be governed by the Bilateral Implementation Commission in Geneva.

In the end, both sides chose to allow START II to lapse. On 14 June 2002, the day after the United States withdrew from the ABM Treaty, Moscow announced that it would no longer be bound by the provisions of START II. The Moscow Treaty, signed in May 2002, also effectively meant that START II was no longer necessary.

The Strategic Offensive Reductions Treaty

The Strategic Offensive Reductions Treaty ([SORT]; referred to throughout this volume as the Moscow Treaty) was the latest in the series of offensive strategic nuclear weapon treaties between the United States and the Soviet Union (Russia). It effectively served as a surrogate for a START III treaty, and was signed in Moscow on 24 May 2002. It was the shortest bilateral arms control treaty ever signed, at two pages in length. Its brevity was meant to reflect the changed relationship between the United States and Russia since the end of the Cold War; the two were now considered strategic partners rather than adversaries. The principle elements of the treaty had been agreed by presidents George W. Bush and Vladimir Putin at the Crawford, Texas, summit the previous December. Both parties committed to continuing their reductions of operationally deployed strategic nuclear weapons, with a target of 1,700 to 2,200 deployed warheads on 31 December 2012. There are no provisions for verification, compliance, or inspections, relying instead on START I provisions in these areas. Nor does the treaty require the parties to destroy or even account for the weapons that they remove from deployed status.

The Threshold Test Ban Treaty

The Treaty Between the United States of America and the Union of Soviet Socialist Republics on the Limitation of Underground Nuclear Weapons Tests (referred to throughout this volume as the Threshold Test Ban Treaty [TTBT]) was signed by the United States and the Soviet Union on 3 July 1974. It prohibits parties from the underground testing of nuclear weapons with a yield greater than 150 kilotons at declared testing sites. A subsequent protocol requires notification of explosions and provides various options for measuring the yield of the explosions, including on-site inspection for tests with a planned yield above 35 kilotons.

The United States has only one declared testing site, located in Nevada. The former Soviet Union maintains two testing sites, one within the Russian Federation and the other in Kazakhstan.

The TTBT entered into force on 11 December 1990. China is not a signatory to the treaty; however, it has remained in compliance with the treaty since its last underground test on 21 May 1992.

The UN Register of Conventional Arms

The UN Register of Conventional Arms entered into effect following the signing of UN General Assembly Resolution 46/36L, Transparency in Armaments, on 9 December 1991. To date, a total of 172 states have reported to the register one or more times.

The technical procedures for the register were developed by a panel of experts that were appointed by the Secretary-General in 1992 and endorsed by the General Assembly. There have been periodic reviews of the register by the Secretary-General in 1994, 1997, and 2000. The register covers weapons and materials in the five categories of weaponry found in the CFE Treaty (tanks, armored combat vehicles, artillery pieces, attack helicopters, and combat aircraft) as well as warships, missiles, and missile launchers. The register includes no verification provisions; it was hoped that increased transparency would encourage restraint by both buyers and sellers, and lead to public pressure on those states that supported irresponsible or destabilizing arms transfers.

In 2002, seventeen of fifty-three African member states; thirty of fifty-three Asian member states; twenty-one of twenty-two Eastern European member states; twenty-six of thirty-three Latin American and Caribbean member states; and all twenty-nine Western European and other member states had submitted information to the register.

The Wassenaar Arrangement

On 18 December 1995, the delegates of twenty-eight nations meeting in Wassenaar, the Netherlands, agreed to set up an export control organization. The Wassenaar Arrangement on Export Controls for Conventional Arms and Dual-Use Goods and Technologies (referred to throughout this volume as the Wassenaar Arrangement) calls on participating states to exchange data, notify other participants of violations of the controlled items list, and coordinate export licenses. Participation is voluntary. There is no enforcement mechanism, but a secretariat is located in Vienna and a Plenary Session is held at least annually.

The participating states agree to implement controls on a two-part list of technologies and conventional weapon systems, known as the List of Dual-Use Goods and Technologies and the Munitions List. The latest updates to this list were approved at the Plenary Session held on 1 December 2000. As of January 2002, there were forty-four participating states.

In 2007, the Plenary Session conducted the first dialogue between the Wassenaar Arrangement Experts Group and its counterpart from the MTCR. The purpose of this dialogue was to develop a common understanding of terminology and technical parameters on controls of certain navigation equipment. The Plenary Session agreed to update the 2002 Best Practices for Exports of Small Arms and Light Weapons with the common language agreed on by the UN in 2005 on marking and tracking small arms and light weapons.

The Zangger Committee

The Zangger Committee was formed in 1974 to establish guidelines for implementing the export control provisions of the Nuclear Nonproliferation Treaty. Its official name is the NPT Exporters Committee. The committee developed a trigger list of materials and equipment that triggers safeguards by the IAEA. It includes items that might otherwise be used to develop a nuclear explosive such as plutonium, highly enriched uranium (HEU), reactors, reprocessing and enrichment facilities, and associated equipment and supplies. The list is updated regularly. There are thirty-seven members of the Zangger Committee, all of whom are also members of the Nuclear Suppliers Group.

Sources: Jeffrey A. Larsen and Gregory J. Rattray, *Arms Control Toward the 21st Century* (Boulder: Lynne Rienner, 1996), pp. 296–328; Jeffrey A. Larsen, *Arms Control: Cooperative Security in a Changing Environment* (Boulder: Lynne Rienner, 2002), pp. 371–392); Jeffrey A. Larsen and James M. Smith, *Historical Dictionary of Arms Control and Disarmament* (Lanham, MD: Scarecrow, 2002); *The Arms Control Reporter* (Cambridge, MA: Institute for Defense and Disarmament Studies, annual); Richard Dean Burns, *Encyclopedia of Arms Control and Disarmament* (New York: Charles Scribner's Sons, 1993); websites of the US State Department (www.state.gov/t/ac/trty/index.cfm), the Federation of American Scientists (www.fas.org), and the US Air Force National Security Policy Division (www .sunman1.saic.com:8002/xon/xonpu/armsctrl/profile_summary/index.shtml).

Acronyms

AAAS	American Academy of Arts and Sciences
ABM	antiballistic missile
ABM Treaty	Anti-Ballistic Missile Treaty
ACDA	Arms Control and Disarmament Agency
ACRS	Arms Control and Regional Security Working Group (also ACRS Working Group)
APEC	Asia-Pacific Economic Cooperation
APL	antipersonnel landmine
ASEAN	Association of Southeast Asian Nations
ASTOP	Asian Senior-Level Talks on Nonproliferation
ATTU	Atlantic to the Urals
BMD	ballistic missile defense
BW	biological weapons
BWC	Biological Weapons Convention
CARICOM	Carribean Community and Common Market
CBM	confidence-building measure
CBRN	chemical, biological, radiological, or nuclear
CBW	chemical and biological weapons
CCWC	Convention on Certain Conventional Weapons
CD	Conference on Disarmament (UN)
CDE	Conference on Disarmament in Europe (CSCE)
CFE Treaty	Conventional Forces in Europe Treaty
CFE 1A Treaty	Concluding Act of the Negotiation on Personnel Strength of Conventional Armed Forces in Europe
CPPNM	Convention on the Physical Protection of Nuclear Materials
CSBM	confidence- and security-building measures
CSCE	Conference on Security and Cooperation in Europe
CSI	Container Security Initiative

CTBT	Comprehensive Test Ban Treaty
CTBTO	Comprehensive Test Ban Treaty Organization
CTR	Cooperative Threat Reduction
CW	chemical weapons
CWC	Chemical Weapons Convention
DoD	Department of Defense
DoE	Department of Energy
ECOWAS	Economic Community of West African States
EU	European Union
FBI	Federal Bureau of Investigation
FMCT	Fissile Material Cutoff Treaty
FSC	Forum for Security Cooperation
GLCM	ground-launched cruise missile
GPS	Global Positioning System
HEU	highly enriched uranium
IAEA	International Atomic Energy Agency
ICBL	International Campaign to Ban Landmines
ICBM	intercontinental ballistic missile
IGO	intergovernmental organization
IMO	International Maritime Organization
IMS	International Monitoring System
INF Treaty	Intermediate-Range Nuclear Forces Treaty
ISM	Inter-sessional Meeting
ISTC	International Science and Technology Center
IW	information warfare
JCIC	Joint Compliance and Inspection Commission
JCS	Joint Chiefs of Staff
LEU	low-enriched uranium
LTBT	Limited Test Ban Treaty
MAD	mutual assured destruction
MIRV	multiple independently targetable reentry vehicle (also MIRVed)
MTCR	Missile Technology Control Regime
NAM	Non-Aligned Movement
NATO	North Atlantic Treaty Organization
NBC	nuclear, biological, and chemical
NGO	nongovernmental organization
NIS	newly independent states
NNWS	non–nuclear weapon state(s)
NORAD	North American Aerospace Defense Command
NPT	Nuclear Nonproliferation Treaty
NSG	Nuclear Suppliers Group
NTM	national technical means

NWFZ	nuclear-weapon-free zone
NWS	nuclear weapon state(s)
OPCW	Organisation for the Prohibition of Chemical Weapons
OSCE	Organization for Security and Cooperation in Europe
P-5	Permanent Five (of UN Security Council)
PNET	Peaceful Nuclear Explosions Treaty
PNI	Presidential Nuclear Initiative(s)
POA	Program of Action (UN)
PSI	Proliferation Security Initiative
PTBT	Partial Test Ban Treaty
SADC	Southern African Development Community
SALT	Strategic Arms Limitation Talks *or* Treaty
SALW	small arms and light weapons
SDI	Strategic Defense Initiative
SLBM	submarine-launched ballistic missile
SLCM	sea-launched cruise missile
SORT	Strategic Offensive Reductions Treaty (Moscow Treaty)
START	Strategic Arms Reduction Treaty
STRATCOM	US Strategic Command
SVC	Special Verification Commission
TLE	treaty-limited equipment
TTBT	Threshold Test Ban Treaty
UAV	unmanned aerial vehicle
UNAEC	UN Atomic Energy Commission
UNSCOM	UN Special Commission (Iraq)
USEC	United States Enrichment Corporation
WCO	World Customs Organization
WHO	World Health Organization
WMD	weapon(s) of mass destruction
Y2K	Year 2000 problem

The Contributors

Lewis A. Dunn is a senior vice president of Science Applications International Corporation. He currently serves as an expert adviser on the Congressional Commission on the US Strategic Posture. He served as assistant director of the US Arms Control and Disarmament Agency from 1983 to 1987, as ambassador to the 1985 Nuclear Nonproliferation Treaty review conference, and ambassador to the 1987 United Nations Peaceful Uses of Nuclear Energy conference. He has a Ph.D. in political science from the University of Chicago.

Maeghin Escarcida is a national security analyst with Science Applications International Corporation in Albuquerque, New Mexico, where she supports the Defense Nuclear Weapons School. She earned her masters degree in international security and homeland defense from the University of Denver.

Rebecca E. Johnson is executive director of the Acronym Institute for Disarmament Diplomacy, London, and publishes the international policy journal *Disarmament Diplomacy*. A former senior adviser to the International WMD Commission and UN consultant, she holds a Ph.D. from the London School of Economics and has authored numerous reports and articles on nonproliferation, international security, and peace activism.

Kerry M. Kartchner is senior adviser for strategic planning in the Bureau of International Security and Nonproliferation, US Department of State. He has previously served as chief of the Division of Strategy and Policy Studies of the Advanced Systems and Concepts Office at the Defense Threat Reduction Agency. He is the author of *Negotiating START: The Quest for Strategic Stability* (1992) as well as other edited volumes, journal articles, and book chapters. His masters degree and Ph.D. in international relations are from the University of Southern California.

Jeffrey A. Larsen is president of Larsen Consulting Group and a senior policy analyst with Science Applications International Corporation in Colorado Springs, Colorado. He also serves as an adjunct professor of international relations in the graduate programs of the University of Denver and Northwestern University, and as president of the International Security and Arms Control section of the American Political Science Association. He is the author or editor of multiple books and articles on arms control, nuclear weapons policy, and international security. He was NATO's 2005–2006 Manfred Wörner Fellow, and holds a Ph.D. in politics from Princeton University.

Michael Moodie is an independent consultant on international security affairs, specializing in issues at the intersection of security, science, technology, and politics. He held the position of president of the Chemical and Biological Arms Control Institute for twelve years. He has served as assistant director for multilateral affairs at the US Arms Control and Disarmament Agency and special assistant to the ambassador at the US Mission to NATO. He is currently editor-in-chief of *WMD Insights* and director of nonproliferation of the Long-Range Analysis Unit of the National Intelligence Council.

Guy B. Roberts is the deputy assistant secretary general for weapons of mass destruction policy at NATO headquarters in Brussels, Belgium. Prior to that he served as the principal director for arms control and nonproliferation policy in the Office of the Secretary of Defense. He has written extensively on arms control, nonproliferation, and international law. He received his Juris Doctor degree from the University of Denver, and is licensed to practice law in Arizona, California, and Colorado.

Jennifer E. Sims is visiting professor in the Security Studies Program and director of intelligence studies at Georgetown University. She has taught as a professorial lecturer at Johns Hopkins University School of Advanced International Studies, and served as senior intelligence adviser to the undersecretary for management at the Department of State. She earned her Ph.D. from Johns Hopkins University School of Advanced International Studies.

James M. Smith is director of the Air Force Institute for National Security Studies located at the US Air Force Academy, where he is also professor of military strategic studies. He is on the adjunct faculties of the University of Denver's Graduate School of International Studies and The Bush School of

Government and Public Service, Texas A&M University. He earned his Ph.D. from the University of Alabama.

Leonard S. Spector is deputy director of the Monterey Institute of International Studies' James Martin Center for Nonproliferation Studies, and leads the center's Washington, D.C., office. From 1997 to 2001, he served as assistant deputy administrator for arms control and nonproliferation at the National Nuclear Security Administration of the US Department of Energy (DoE). Before joining DoE, he led the Nuclear Nonproliferation Project of the Carnegie Endowment for International Peace, where he authored a series of books on nonproliferation trends and established the Program on Post-Soviet Nuclear Affairs at the Carnegie Moscow Center. He holds a Juris Doctor degree from Yale Law School.

Forrest E. Waller Jr. is a senior research fellow at National Defense University's Center for the Study of Weapons of Mass Destruction. From 1992 through 2006, he was a corporate officer and chief scientist at a large US corporation providing management services to the national security community. Prior to that, he was an officer in the US Air Force assigned to positions in the White House, the State Department, the Agency for International Development, and the Office of the Secretary of Defense. He holds a masters degree in International Affairs from Princeton University.

James J. Wirtz is dean of the School of International Graduate Studies and a professor of national security affairs at the Naval Postgraduate School, Monterey, California. He has published extensively in the fields of strategic studies, intelligence, deterrence theory, international relations, and US defense policy. He holds a Ph.D. in political science from Columbia University.

Index

About the Book

Reflecting the current debate about the value of traditional arms control in today's security environment, *Arms Control and Cooperative Security* thoroughly covers this complex topic.

The authors critically review the historical record, highlight recent changes in the security arena, and consider the likelihood of new arms control agreements. Throughout, the discussion is presented in the context of current events in international relations. The result is a comprehensive assessment of the present state and likely future of arms control and cooperative security—especially relevant as many of the treaties crafted during the Cold War are nearing their expiration dates.

Jeffrey A. Larsen is senior policy analyst with the Science Applications International Corporation (SAIC) and president of Larsen Consulting Group in Colorado Springs, Colorado. **James J. Wirtz** is dean of the School of International Graduate Studies and professor of national security affairs at the Naval Postgraduate School, Monterey, California.